Feminist Family Therapy

Empowerment in Social Context

PSYCHOLOGY OF WOMEN BOOK SERIES

Cheryl Brown Travis, Series Editor

Bringing Cultural Diversity to Feminist Psychology: Theory, Research, and Practice
    Hope Landrine, Editor

The New Civil War: The Psychology, Culture, and Politics of Abortion
    Linda J. Beckman and S. Marie Harvey, Editors

Shaping the Future of Feminist Psychology: Education, Research, and Practice
    Judith Worell and Norine G. Johnson, Editors

Sexuality, Society, and Feminism
    Cheryl Brown Travis and Jacquelyn W. White, Editors

Practicing Feminist Ethics in Psychology
    Mary M. Brabeck, Editor

Relationships Among Asian American Women
    Jean Lau Chin, Editor

Feminist Family Therapy: Empowerment in Social Context
    Louise B. Silverstein and Thelma Jean Goodrich, Editors

Feminist Family Therapy

Empowerment in Social Context

Edited by

Louise B. Silverstein and
Thelma Jean Goodrich

American Psychological Association • Washington, DC

Second Printing January 2005

Published by
American Psychological Association
750 First Street, NE
Washington, DC 20002
www.apa.org

To order
APA Order Department
P.O. Box 92984
Washington, DC 20090-2984
Tel: (800) 374-2721
Direct: (202) 336-5510
Fax: (202) 336-5502
TDD/TTY: (202) 336-6123
Online: www.apa.org/books/
Email: order@apa.org

In the U.K., Europe, Africa, and the
Middle East, copies may be ordered from
American Psychological Association
3 Henrietta Street
Covent Garden, London
WC2E 8LU England

Typeset in Goudy by World Composition Services, Inc., Sterling, VA

Printer: Sheridan Books, Ann Arbor, MI
Cover Designer: Naylor Design, Washington, DC
Technical/Production Editor: Jennifer L. Zale

The opinions and statements published are the responsibility of the authors, and such opinions and statements do not necessarily represent the policies of the American Psychological Association.

Library of Congress Cataloging-in-Publication Data
Feminist family therapy : empowerment in social context / edited by
Louise B. Silverstein and Thelma Jean Goodrich.—1st ed.
    p. cm.—(Psychology of women book series)
  Includes bibliographical references and index.
  ISBN 1-59147-021-8 (alk. paper)
  1. Family psychotherapy. 2. Feminist therapy. I. Silverstein, Louise
B. II. Goodrich, Thelma Jean, 1940- III. Series.

  RC488.5.F453 2003
  616.89'156—dc21   2003005349

British Library Cataloguing-in-Publication Data
A CIP record is available from the British Library.

Printed in the United States of America
First Edition

To our beloved children,
Eva and Jesse and
Dolly, Davey, Kelly, and Mila

one hesitates to bring a child into this world without fixing it up a little. paint a special room. stop sexism. learn how to love. vow to do it better than it was done when you were a baby. vow to make, if necessary, *new* mistakes. vow to be awake for the birth. to believe in joy even in the midst of unbearable pain.

—Alta, "I Would Be a Fool to Want More Children," from *Shameless Hussy: Selected Prose and Poetry*

CONTENTS

Contributors .... *xi*

Foreword .... *xiii*
Rachel T. Hare-Mustin

Preface .... *xv*

Acknowledgments .... *xix*

I.   CONSIDERING THE HISTORICAL CONTEXT
     OF FEMINISM IN FAMILY THERAPY 1

Chapter 1.   A Feminist Family Therapist's Work Is Never Done 3
             Thelma Jean Goodrich

Chapter 2.   Classic Texts and Early Critiques 17
             Louise B. Silverstein

II. REFRAMING LIFE-CYCLE ISSUES 37

Chapter 3.   Over the Rainbow: The Lesbian Family 39
             Kris Halstead

Chapter 4.   "I Can't Go Back": Divorce as
             Adaptive Resistance 51
             Joy K. Rice

Chapter 5.   Repairing the World: An Adolescent and
             Her Parents 65
             Kaethe Weingarten

Chapter 6.   Loyalty to Family of Origin 79
             Roberta L. Nutt

Chapter 7.   Gender in Stepfamilies: Daughters and Fathers 91
              Anne C. Bernstein

III. CONTEXTUALIZING RACIAL AND ETHNIC
      IDENTITIES IN FAMILIES 105

Chapter 8.   Contemporary African American Families 107
              Ruth L. Hall and Beverly Greene

Chapter 9.   Relationships Between Women in Families:
              Voices of Chivalry 121
              Leslye King Mize

Chapter 10.   Confucian Past, Conflicted Present:
              Working With Asian American Families 135
              Liang Tien and Kari Olson

Chapter 11.   The Black Madonna: The Psychospiritual
              Feminism of Guadalupe, Kali, and Monserrat 147
              Lillian Comas-Díaz

IV.   RECOGNIZING POWER IN FAMILIES 161

Chapter 12.   Helping Men Embrace Equality 163
              Gary R. Brooks

Chapter 13.   Treating Male Alexithymia 177
              Ronald F. Levant

Chapter 14.   Women's Secrets in Therapy 189
              Evan Imber-Black

Chapter 15.   Gendered Constraints to Intimacy
              in Heterosexual Couples 199
              Cheryl Rampage

Chapter 16.   Gender, Marriage, and Depression 211
              Peggy Papp

Chapter 17.   Bringing Power From the Margins to the Center 225
              Lynn Parker

V.   ANALYZING SERVICE DELIVERY SYSTEMS 239

Chapter 18.   Incarcerated African American Women 241
              Janet Brice-Baker

Chapter 19.   A Venn Diagram: Feminism, Family Therapy,
              and Family Medicine 253
              Lucy M. Candib

Chapter 20.   Gender, Couples, and Illness: A Feminist
              Analysis of Medical Family Therapy 267
              Susan H. McDaniel and Kathleen Cole-Kelly

Chapter 21.   The Women's Center: Feminism in the
              Treatment of AIDS 281
              Anitra Pivnick

VI.   ADDRESSING SOCIOPOLITICAL FORCES 291

Chapter 22.   Creating Collectives of Liberation 293
              Rhea V. Almeida

Chapter 23.   Biracial Lesbian-Led Adoptive Families 307
              Natalie S. Eldridge and Susan E. Barrett

Chapter 24.   Assessment of Domestic Violence 319
              Michele Harway

Chapter 25.   Class, Culture, and Gender in
              Immigrant Families 333
              Jaime Inclán

VII. EXAMINING SUPERVISION IN FEMINIST
      FAMILY THERAPY 349

Chapter 26.   The Gender Metaframework 351
              Betty Mac Kune-Karrer and Catherine Weigel Foy

Chapter 27.   Naming Injustice, Engendering Hope: Tensions
              in Feminist Family Therapy Training 365
              Jean Turner and Judith Myers Avis

Author Index 379

Subject Index 385

About the Editors 393

CONTRIBUTORS

Rhea V. Almeida, PhD, Institute for Family Services, Piscataway, NJ

Judith Myers Avis, PhD, University of Guelph, Ontario, Canada

Susan E. Barrett, PhD, private practice, Atlanta, GA

Anne C. Bernstein, PhD, The Wright Institute and the University of California, Berkeley

Janet Brice-Baker, PhD, Ferkauf Graduate School of Psychology, Yeshiva University, New York

Gary R. Brooks, PhD, Baylor University, Waco, TX

Lucy M. Candib, MD, University of Massachusetts Medical School, Worcester

Kathleen Cole-Kelly, MS, MSW, Case Western Reserve University, Cleveland, OH

Lillian Comas-Díaz, PhD, Transcultural Mental Health Institute, Washington, DC

Natalie S. Eldridge, PhD, Boston University Mental Health Clinic, Boston

Catherine Weigel Foy, MSW, The Family Institute at Northwestern University, Evanston, IL

Thelma Jean Goodrich, PhD, University of Texas Medical School at Houston

Beverly Greene, PhD, St. John's University, New York

Ruth L. Hall, PhD, The College of New Jersey, Trenton

Kris Halstead, LCSW, private practice, Bethesda, MD

Rachel T. Hare-Mustin, PhD, The Common, Amherst, MA

Michele Harway, PhD, Antioch University, Santa Barbara, CA

Evan Imber-Black, PhD, The Ackerman Institute for the Family, New York

Jaime Inclán, PhD, Roberto Clemente Family Guidance Center and
New York University School of Medicine, New York

Ronald F. Levant, EdD, Nova Southeastern University,
Fort Lauderdale, FL

Betty Mac Kune-Karrer, MA, LMFT, The Family Institute at
Northwestern University, Evanston, IL

Susan H. McDaniel, PhD, University of Rochester School of Medicine
and Dentistry, Rochester, NY

Leslye King Mize, PhD, University of Houston—Clear Lake,
Houston, TX

Roberta L. Nutt, PhD, Texas Woman's University, Dallas

Kari Olson, PhD candidate, University of Iowa, Iowa City

Peggy Papp, MSW, The Ackerman Institute for the Family, New York

Lynn Parker, MSW, PhD, Graduate School of Social Work, University
of Denver, Denver, CO

Anitra Pivnick, PhD, The Women's Center, Montefiore Medical Center
and Albert Einstein College of Medicine, New York

Cheryl Rampage, PhD, The Family Institute at Northwestern
University, Evanston, IL

Joy K. Rice, PhD, University of Wisconsin Medical School,
Madison

Louise B. Silverstein, PhD, Ferkauf Graduate School of Psychology,
Yeshiva University, New York

Liang Tien, PsyD, Antioch University Seattle, Seattle, WA

Jean Turner, PhD, University of Guelph, Ontario, Canada

Kaethe Weingarten, PhD, The Family Institute of Cambridge,
Cambridge, MA

FOREWORD

RACHEL T. HARE-MUSTIN

I would have liked to say more about this exceptional book than space permits here. What these diverse and insightful essays uncover and then address in turn are the fundamental issues of therapy's place in society.

Therapy is a cultural activity of modern European-related society, a social practice that has unwittingly reproduced the oppressive practices of society. Whether conducted in private practice or in state-funded institutions, therapy has inflicted on patients the same dominant discourses by which they have previously been harmed. The efforts of most therapists represent the prevailing moral standards and unquestioned values of the culture, such as "maintain the family," "avoid divorce," "keep the children in school." Moreover, all therapy is political, either supporting the status quo or challenging the status quo. Therapists may claim neutrality, but neutrality always supports the status quo. Claiming neutrality regarding gender is an insidious form of sexism that covers up differences in power and privilege.

When we look at our world we see power inequities, resource inequities, and life choice inequities. We see a frequent crushing of the spirit that starts with our domination of the environment and of other animals. If there is an ethical impulse in family therapy worth preserving, I think it is the impulse toward social justice. These chapters point out that justice means not only helping people adapt to social norms but also examining and challenging those norms. It involves questioning the traditional meanings enshrined in our therapies.

The question in therapy is always about the choice of question. What are we failing to see? What has been left unsaid? What has been pushed to the margins? What biases of ours affect our seeing and hearing? What does our social location cause us to know and not know? What ends does a particular view serve? Who benefits? Who loses?

The chapter authors in this book wrestle with such questions, and in the process, they provide an extensive and eye-opening overview of the ways that feminists address a range of family constellations and problems. The book is clear, inclusive, well written, and well edited, achieving its purpose of integrating the latest developments in theory with research and specific approaches to practice. The fact that so many notable and busy therapists have contributed to the volume attests to the importance with which those in the field have viewed the project. To have so many experts represented in one volume makes this an exceptional contribution. I believe that this book is destined to become a classic in both family psychology and family therapy.

PREFACE

A book about women must start with a creation story, so we offer ours. It is a story about support and cooperation among women. The original impetus for this book came from Norine G. Johnson in 1995, during her tenure as president of the American Psychological Association's Division 35 (Society for the Psychology of Women). Norine was well aware that, although psychologists have been at the forefront of developing most areas of feminist theory, research, and practice, only a few psychologists have been involved in feminist *family* therapy and theory.

Psychological theory in general has been so focused on the development of the individual that most psychologists receive little, if any, training in family systems theory and practice. Norine felt strongly that feminist family theory and practice should be integrated into the feminist psychological community. She requested that Louise B. Silverstein chair a task force, organize a symposium, and ultimately produce an edited book to introduce psychologists to the latest developments in feminist family therapy.

As part of the process of integrating feminist family therapy into feminist psychology, Silverstein invited Thelma Jean Goodrich to collaborate on this project. Goodrich is an integral member of the feminist family therapy "pioneers," women who began the feminist revision of family therapy in the 1970s. Thus our collaboration in itself brings together the two worlds of feminist psychology and feminist family therapy.

Goodrich's interest in joining this project was not only to promote family therapy in a sister discipline but also to encourage a renewed focus on feminism within family therapy. Much of the recent theorizing within family therapy, even by feminists, has focused on other areas. One prominent area of theorizing has been in terms of cultural diversity. However, many diversity theorists have not maintained a strong feminist focus. Inviting feminist family therapists to write about their current work with specific attention both to feminism and to social location seemed a felicitous way to achieve the dual goals of promoting family therapy within psychology and feminist theory within family therapy.

GOALS FOR THE BOOK

Our goal was to produce a book that includes both theory and practical applications. We hope to interest young practitioners in becoming trained in feminist family therapy and also to inspire seasoned professionals to increase the complexity of their thinking about the relevance of a feminist stance in all forms of therapy. Recent books in the field have presented an exposition of specific issues that are important to consider when working with women. However, these books lack an explicit emphasis on psychotherapy. Other books include a discussion of gender-sensitive, rather than feminist, therapy (see glossary in chapter 2, Appendix A, for definitions of terms). This book examines the implications of the gendered differential of power in families and larger systems. In addition, it is focused on how these power differentials can be addressed in family therapy.

We believe that simply presenting theory would leave psychologists with little idea of how to use theoretical concepts in the presence of an actual family. Similarly, because most psychologists are so unfamiliar with family systems theory in general, we believe that giving examples of therapeutic interventions without a strong theoretical base would not be useful.

We have also struggled with the goal of synthesizing the variables of gender and ethnorace. White feminists have been correctly criticized for focusing primarily on the interior of the family in a way that makes White power and privilege invisible. As two White, middle-class women, we take seriously our responsibility to reflect accurately the lived experiences of less privileged women, that is, women of color, poor women, immigrant women, and differently abled women. We have tried to avoid conceptualizing gender as primary and then "adding on" diversity, as mainstream family therapy originally tried to "add women and stir." We would like to acknowledge our mentors in this effort: Beverly Greene, Janet Brice-Baker, Lillian Comas-Díaz, and Karen Wyche. These sisters of color have given good advice, have answered stupid questions with patience and tact, and continue to remain good friends.

In an effort to give gender and ethnorace equal weight, the original title of the book was *Gender and Diversity in Family Therapy*. In its first incarnation, Silverstein had conceptualized the book as having various sections: classic feminist family therapy texts, ethnic and cultural issues, lesbian couples and families, women with disabilities, and so on. However, as our collaboration evolved, we came to the conclusion that many books contain a discussion of "issues." What is really lacking in the field is a book that focuses on how those issues should be addressed in the clinical practice of feminist family therapy. We also felt that separating aspects of women's lives into "sections" did not accurately represent women's lived experience.

We have struggled long and hard to find a way to express the intertwined and layered ways in which gender, ethnicity, race, class, and other variables (e.g., immigration) construct women's lives. Our best attempt to reflect this reality so far is to conceptualize the multifaceted aspects of women's lives as similar to a crystal. Some parts of a woman's lived experience might be encountered through the prism of race. In a different context, the facet of class might be primary in structuring her experience. Still another experience might be lived simultaneously through the intersecting facets of race and gender. Thus, we think of these variables as acting both independently and interactively, depending on context. Our second title was *Feminist Family Therapy: Empowerment and Social Location* because, in our view, feminist practice can only empower women (as well as men) by attending to all of the multifaceted parts of their lives. However, the term *social location* was not as well-known in the United States as it is in Europe. Because we wanted the book to be inviting, rather than off-putting, we finally settled on the current title, *Feminist Family Therapy: Empowerment in Social Context*, which continues to emphasize the importance of power.

In our choice of contributors, our first criterion was that the author used a family systems theoretical perspective. Our second criterion was that the author focused on feminist issues in family therapy. Because of this *family* focus, many important theorists writing about both feminism and diversity have not been included in the book. Similarly, because we have a *clinical* focus, many important family theorists and researchers are not represented. Our goal has been to reflect feminist family therapy as a distinct genre of clinical practice.

We begin with the early critiques of family therapy to give the reader a historical overview. Our criterion for defining the "classics" was to choose family therapists who most influenced the development of feminist family therapy. We had originally hoped to reprint many of the classic texts. Because of space considerations, we have been unable to do so. Rather, we have provided a summary of these early critiques. However, we encourage the reader to return to these early texts as important source materials.

In addition to listing these classic texts and providing a summary of their content, we have invited the authors of these classics to comment on their earlier work and also to write about their current interests. Some of the authors were not able to contribute to this book because of prior work commitments. Many of the authors who have contributed chose not to comment on their earlier work, or to comment briefly, and then to discuss issues that are of current interest to them.

We have also included a large number of contemporary family therapists who are working within a feminist framework. Some important content areas have been left out of the book. For example, a feminist perspective on working with differently abled women in a relationship context is not included because none of the contributors chose to write about that population of women.

Although we have tried to provide a diverse sample of authors, we cannot claim that the book is either exhaustive or necessarily representative of all approaches to feminist family therapy. In an effort to decrease our ethnocentrism and heterocentrism, we have consulted with some of our lesbian sisters and sisters of color. Nevertheless, we have probably missed some important aspects of women's experiences. We look forward to the responses to this book so that we can continue to expand our understanding of the complexity and diversity of women's lives.

The 1980s saw an explosion of writing about feminist issues in family therapy. The 1990s brought an explosion of writing about multicultural issues in family therapy. We believe that the 21st century is the right time for blending these two scholarly discourses. We hope to illustrate the power of feminist family therapy to improve the lives of real women in the context of their families. Our goal is to inspire psychologists who have been working within an individual psychotherapy paradigm to pursue training in feminist family therapy as well. We also hope that this book will inspire a new eruption of culturally sensitive feminist theorizing about family therapy.

ACKNOWLEDGMENTS

We thank several members of the American Psychological Association's Society for the Psychology of Women: Norine G. Johnson, who had the original vision for the book; Cheryl Brown Travis, who gave generously of her time and wisdom throughout the three years of the project; and Sue Rosenberg Zalk, who stepped in to help and then was too soon taken from us.

In addition, we give thanks for the blessing that is the Society for the Psychology of Women, which has been a haven of feminist mentoring and support for countless women over the years.

We are grateful for the support of our department chairs, Carlos A. Moreno at the University of Texas Medical School at Houston and Abraham Givner and Larry Siegel at Ferkauf Graduate School of Psychology, Yeshiva University.

Finally, we express our gratitude to the contributing authors for the generous gift of their time and wisdom. We are especially grateful to Rachel Hare-Mustin, the mother of feminist family therapy, for her encouragement and guidance throughout the development of this volume.

I

CONSIDERING THE HISTORICAL CONTEXT OF FEMINISM IN FAMILY THERAPY

1

A FEMINIST FAMILY THERAPIST'S WORK IS NEVER DONE

THELMA JEAN GOODRICH

In 1999, ten Foreign Ministers gathered for dinner at the Museum of Modern Art in New York City. After 3 hours, they emerged with a letter to United Nations Secretary General Kofi Annan asking him to take to the U.N. General Assembly their concern about "the repulsive trafficking in human beings, predominantly women and children." The Foreign Ministers—all women—and their host, Secretary of State Madeleine K. Albright, aimed to put women's issues at the center of foreign affairs. "We all had the feeling that . . . unless you make [women's issues] central to your foreign policy, then they get kind of shunted aside," noted Ms. Albright. Ms. Halonen, the Finnish Foreign Minister, added that there were "unexpectedly strong emotions" during dinner. She said that women are always initially "very brave" and say that they have no special gender problems—until they start really talking with one another and tell their unhappy stories (Crossette, 1999).

This book reflects our belief that unless therapy makes women's issues central, then they are at risk of getting "shunted aside." In a way, this book offers us a forum for sharing unhappy stories. In chapter after chapter, we read about the many and varied consequences that befall women living in male-centered, male-dominated society. The shape of these consequences varies by race and class—and racism and classism bring their own consequences—but no woman escapes. Even privileged women are not free.

We also read here about courage, survival, triumph—testimony to the resilience of spirit, but not of spirit in isolation. Rather, the accounts testify to the significance of intimate alliances in supporting resilience and causing it to thrive. These are accounts of women seeking to form and reform familial connections with sisters, mothers, fathers, daughters, sons, friends, lesbian partners, and husbands. Therapists have the opportunity to be one of those connections.

This chapter forecasts the themes of the later chapters by addressing three topics. First, feminists know that complicated entanglement of the personal and the political brings someone to therapy, and so our work cannot be confined to our offices. We are invested in feminism's work in the world. Second, the importance families hold for women, and women hold for families, requires us to have a clear-eyed understanding of families in our therapy with women. Third, family therapy has certain features that make it an important modality of treatment for women.

INVESTMENT IN FEMINISM'S WORK

This Just In: Women Still Oppressed

Phrases like *postfeminist era* notwithstanding, discrimination against women is still pervasive. Statistics demonstrate women's continued disadvantage in employment, wages, housework, child care, violence, the courts, medical care, welfare, prisons, caregiving, health care, and positions of power in government and media and corporations. Here are a few highlights:

- A full-time working woman receives only 73 cents to every dollar received by a man (U.S. Census Bureau, 2001).
- Women are paid less than men in every occupational classification (U.S. Census Bureau, 2001).
- Woman hold only 12% of the board seats in the Fortune 500 and only 8.9% of the board seats in the Fortune 501–1000 (Catalyst, 2001).
- Women make up 46.5% of the U.S. labor force, hold 49.5% of managerial and specialty positions, and are 12.5% of the corporate officers and 4.1% of the top earners in the Fortune 500 (Catalyst, 2000).
- Over 60% of poor adults are women (U.S. Census Bureau, 2002).
- Women make up only 13% of the Senate and 14% of the House.
- From January 1, 2000 to June 30, 2001, women represented only 11% of all guest appearances on the Sunday political talk shows (The White House Project, 2002).
- Women make up 13% and 14% of radio and television general managers, 20% of news executives in Fortune 1000 news companies, 12% of corporate board members in media/entertainment companies, and 26% of local television news directors (studies cited in Annenberg Public Policy Center, 2001).

The gains women have made may be significant in some areas, but the hoopla with which these are greeted seems chiefly designed to distract us from reaching total equality with White men.

If we turn from statistics to attitudes, we find that attitudes support and reflect the statistics. Misogyny continues unabated. Marilyn French (1992) described the sticky web of disparagements that still entrap women. Women are condemned for not having children, or for having children and being employed and using professional day care, or for having children and being employed and not using professional day care. Women are blamed for needing welfare to help support their children, for getting a divorce, for being beaten and not fighting back, for fighting back, for leaving or not leaving their abusers. Women are scolded for being sexually free, for being sexually constrained, for being attached to their virginity, for having extra-marital affairs, for being raped. Women are castigated for being assertive, or for being meek; for not devoting themselves solely to husband and children, or for sacrificing themselves to husband and children. Women are denounced for being ambitious, or for lacking ambition; for being rich, or for being poor; for being fat, or for being thin; for having a career, or for not having a career. French wrote, "In all patriarchal cultures, woman-hatred is common currency, the small change lying in every man's (and many women's) pocket, easy to pull out to pay for—justify—any action" (1992, p. 25).

The effects of misogyny are small, personal, individual as well as large, sweeping, systematic. Indeed, each level shapes the other. Slights that a woman would not mention for fear of seeming too sensitive actually add up to enormous consequences. Virginia Valian (1998) described a computer simulation showing what happens in an organization with eight levels of hierarchy when it is initially staffed with equal numbers of men and women. Allot the men only a tiny advantage in the promotion process, 1%. Run the simulation until there has been a complete staff turnover at this fictitious organization. The top level now has 65% men, 35% women.

Patriarchy infects all relationships, not only those between men and women. Women in higher positions in various hierarchies—race, class, employment—may oppress women below them. Nelson's (1990) study of women who run day-care centers in their homes and Rollins's (1985) work on Black domestics and their White employers demonstrated the multiple oppressions of gender, race, and class. In a system so well entrenched and multilayered, personal intentions hold no relevance. What is in place will wield its destructive effects regardless of personal intentions.

Women's Relation to Their Oppression

Despite statistics and experience, women in the main indicate in surveys that they do not think of themselves as oppressed. For example, only 25% of women say that they are very concerned about women's status (The Roper Center, 1990). Only 7% of women belong to any organization dedicated to advancing women's position (Harris Associates, 1995). Rhode (1997) explained the gap between facts and perception as denial that takes several forms. Women tend to see individual incidents, not collective pictures and trends over time. Too often, women think, "If it's not happening to me, it's not happening," or "I managed, why can't you?" Rhode argued that most women prefer to believe in a just world, so they blame themselves or other women: "Women don't work hard enough" or "Women suffer from fear of success." Many women think they can make things different on their own and for themselves and by themselves. They can make their own marriage different. They can make their own job different. They can raise their own children to be different. They can spot the batterer, avoid the harasser, and fight off the rapist. They can personally decide not to be oppressed.

Denial refuses to see a large picture, an oppressive social order. So denial has it that low pay has nothing to do with having to do all the housework, and that having to do all the housework has nothing to do with how much progress can be made at work. Denial has it that neither amount of pay nor amount of housework has any connection to male privilege.

A different way of assessing women's relation to oppression comes from a study by Landrine and Klonoff (1997). They surveyed women from all ages and classes and races to find how many reported certain events, such as being discriminated against by their employer (64%), having unwelcome sexual advances and sexist jokes (95%), and suffering sexist intimidation (62%). Landrine and Klonoff then investigated what effect such stressful events have on women. They found that sexist events contribute to the occurrence of a variety of symptoms of physical and mental ill health and are a stronger predictor of those symptoms than are ordinary generic stressors. In addition, they found that sexist events contributed even more to the symptoms of women of color than of White women and more to the symptoms of nonfeminists than of feminists. Finally, they found that the presence and frequency of sexist events—rather than women's personal, subjective evaluations of those acts—predicted women's symptoms. In other words, whether women found sexist acts to be upsetting or dismissed them as inconsequential made little difference. Sexist acts contributed to their symptoms in any case.

Discouraging as are these reports from the public world, perhaps the least recognized—certainly least mentioned—*lack* of progress for women is in their intimate relationships with men, especially in marriage and in motherhood. Feminist calls to break down the gendered division of labor in the home as well as in the office, factory, and university aim at a primary source of male power. The effort to block such change gives clear evidence of that fact.

WOMEN AND FAMILIES

The word *family* evokes romantic pictures of safety and well-being that survive evidence to the contrary, survive feminists' rude challenges. Safety for whom? Well-being bought by whose service?

Even though demographics show that there are many family patterns with none in the majority, the romance enshrines only one pattern: man, woman, married with children. Because of its status as paradigmatic and because many people spend some time in it, how things work in it or are said to work in it wields strong influence over other family patterns. In particular, the power relations there cast a long shadow, for they continue to reproduce the gendered schemas that direct by class and race how to certify as a man or a woman. These gendered schemas also direct how men and women should relate to one another; that is, women should be attuned to men's needs and adapt to them to a degree not reciprocated by men.

The paradigmatic heterosexual nuclear family is focused on here because its power relations not only reproduce gendered schemas for men and women in general but also shape the politics in other family structures. For example, gay partners compete not to have the "wife" position—not to be the one who holds primary responsibility for housekeeping, not to always be in a subordinate position in sex (Blumstein & Schwartz, 1983). Lesbian partners are vigilant about sharing in areas such as money and housework, typical sites of disadvantage and inequality for women in heterosexual marriage (Peplau & Gordon, 1991). Single mothers are considered handicapped without the valued male, whereas men who parent as single fathers are seen as heroes (Lorber, 1994). In poor families, men often leave their families altogether when they cannot make sufficient income to be The Provider to buttress an expectation of Head of Household.

Heterosexual Marriage

Layers of structure, process, and ideology accomplish the oppression of women, not just individual men exercising control over individual women. Yet, the primary site where the basic principles of this vast system are taught, by precept and example, is the family—most particularly, the family formed by heterosexual marriage. Paradoxically, women appear to reign in that arena. Women are told that they reign in that arena. In fact, however, most women have power only in the areas of family life where men have no interest in having power. Even in those, even in the areas of detergent and cooking oil, if the husband takes it into his head to have Brand X instead of Y, many shelves will host the new brand by the morrow.

Although there are differences by race and class concerning how often and over what, there is no race or class in which wife is not expected finally to defer to husband. Who routinely continues to change whose surname acts as symbol and substance of the joint enrollment in acknowledging his greater status. When wife has circumstances that create a transgression of the expected hierarchy—for example, when wife is employed and husband is out of work—she typically must look for ways to put the order right. She may do all the housework even though he is free by day. She may look to him for all decisions concerning money even though she earns it. When such strategies do not work, there is often high cost ranging from shame and resentment in both parties to his violence against her "to show her who's boss." The strength of the rule against wife having more power than husband is shown dramatically in the scorn behind the (error-filled) description of Black women as dominating matriarchs.

The process of domination in many couples may be unintended, disavowed, difficult to decipher, but it nevertheless results in men benefiting from women's services. The very way power works in marriage helps keep the romance of family in place (Komter, 1989). Power can hide itself, sometimes behind a big display. Bullying, for example, distracts family members—and therapists—from covert operations. If there is no bullying, family members—and therapists—may assume there are no gender politics at all, and again miss covert operations. When the wife chooses battles carefully, anticipates and aligns with the desires of her husband, becomes resigned to things as they are, these represent results of covert power as the wife works to "keep in line" so as not to jeopardize her safety or her marriage. Even more difficult to spot is the action of power derived from the cultural valuation of men over women and of men's characteristics and activities over women's. This invisible power is like the wind: unseen, and known only by its results.

Invisible power produces three characteristic results:

1. *Predictable gender differences in self-esteem and in the respect given to each other.* As a reflection of a higher cultural valuation of men over women, the typical arrangement shows wife deferring more to husband than husband to wife, and giving him more respect, valuing his opinion more, monitoring his needs more, thinking his needs matter more, taking him more seriously. This situation is replicated in the standing of son versus daughter.

2. *The perception of daily life.* Sociologists find that husbands regularly underestimate their wives' share in child care and housework and overestimate their own (Hochschild, 1989). Both husband and wife are trained into social norms holding that his time, his leisure, his work, and his tasks are more significant than hers, and so both, without awareness, exaggerate what he takes away from "his life" to give to the family's and exaggerate the

8   *THELMA JEAN GOODRICH*

significance of his contribution. Similar perceptions occur regarding sons and daughters.

3. *Apparent consensus*. The majority of husbands and wives seem to agree that the inequality between them is acceptable. Both spouses tend to use cultural themes about masculinity and femininity to create stories that mask the lopsided power and privilege held by men in the family. These feel-good stories work because, in the main, neither men nor women want to believe that they are subject to the effects of sexism. Most men want to believe that they get what they get because they deserve it and because women want to give it. Most women want to believe that they give what they give out of free choice, "given how men are." For example, to justify why her husband has fewer household chores or more freedom to come and go at will, a wife rarely refers to power or privilege. Instead, most women call on such constructions as "(fragile) male ego," "a man's sense of independence," or "his important work." To explain women's lesser privilege and lesser power, there are the cultural myths of "the feminine giving nature," "personal preference to do all the housework," "not having a head for money." Sons and daughters are busy watching and listening, learning what to expect.

The point is not that most women are totally powerless in marriage. The point is that most women do not have power equal to their husbands or, even more forbidden, do not have more power than their husbands. This ordering is institutionalized in marriage and embedded in gender roles. Furthermore, women are generally charged with enforcing and instilling gender inequality in their children, along with an understanding of the social consequences of noncompliance. These gender roles, with their embedded hierarchy, affect the experience of self and family in single-mother families, single-father families, gay and lesbian families. When the expected hierarchy is disrupted, there are real penalties.

Efforts to build egalitarian heterosexual marital partnerships appear to have some recent success under certain circumstances, most particularly certain financial circumstances (Schwartz, 1995). But the gendered selves created in nonegalitarian households and coerced in traditional enclaves of nonegalitarian culture continue to create enormous barriers to true peer partnerships. Peer relationships require a man to believe he is no more valuable than a woman, no more important than a woman. In a patriarchal world, that is a tall order. Peer relationships require a woman to believe that she is not less valuable than a man, not less important. In a woman-hating culture, that also is a tall order.

As Betty Carter (personal communication, March 1998) has taught us, the new man supports the *idea* of equal partnership but still expects to have a veto on money decisions and to focus on his own career. The new man supports the *idea* of equal involvement in child rearing but expects the woman to oversee it and be the primary parent. The new woman supports the *idea* of the involved father who shares housework, as she shares in providing money, but in reality she still thinks she needs to be the primary parent in order to be a good mother. She still expects him to support her financially if she needs to cut back, for she still believes that juggling work and family is basically *her* problem.

Motherhood

A second major unreconstructed area of women's family life is motherhood. As with the discussion of family in general, romance colors the discussion of motherhood, painting it as inherently rewarding, instinctive, and natural to women. The picture has no sign of the immeasurable time spent doing the thankless labor that most men find intolerable for half an hour. In general, men do not seem to be under the spell of the romance. The 1990's extension of the romance about marriage may have men and women subscribing to the *idea* of equal partnership in rearing children. However, it is still the mother whose meal is interrupted by cutting up the child's food, her work that is postponed by a child's sudden stomach virus, and her dwelling that contains the children in the event of a divorce.

Contradiction is a primary feature of women's relation to motherhood (Baber & Allen, 1992). Most women are charged with ultimate responsibility without having ultimate power to perform it, given their subordinate position in the family, the culture—and in the universe for that matter. So many uncontrollable elements affect the trajectory of a child's life. Moreover, the societal and even family environments too often work against rearing a child that is well nourished and well nurtured. Television drivel and violence, community drugs and violence, family troubles and violence overwhelm parental good intentions. So also do poverty and discrimination. But when children do not "turn out," most often mothers get blamed. Little or no blame assails the father, who either helps or does not, is there or is not. Only rarely do social commentators blame patriarchy or economic conditions or racism or a culture of male violence. Just mothers.

Contradictory too is women's relation to the lopsided setup of mothering. Women are trapped in it but also cooperate in it. Many mothers entreat men to take more responsibility for their children but then excuse them from doing so (Goode, 1982), often because the women are reluctant to entrust men with their children's care (Stacey, 1990). Many women find great satisfaction in mothering—this very aspect of their life that oppresses them. They gain a sense of power and influence not matched anywhere else in their life, as long as fathers find child care too uninteresting to challenge them.

Excusing father from equal responsibility while bemoaning his failure to take it is a contradiction that happens inside the mainstream romance narrative, for the romance only holds for mothering under male control (DiLapi, 1989). In the context of the heterosexual, married narrative, opprobrium attaches to single mothers and lesbian mothers because they are mothering outside this aegis. Their struggles for legitimacy in a hostile surround can create a view of themselves as inferior, mothering on their own. They may then lay their troubles, not to economic circumstances or to the prejudice against them, but rather to failure to supply a "male role model." This message straight from the male-centered culture is, on the one hand, understandable given its consonance with other messages from the culture. On the other hand, it astounds, for its form reduces what might have been described as a rich contribution from the other parent to merely the male principle. The implicit presumption of the concept of the male role model is that a "model" is not only necessary but also sufficient.

Still other contradictions derive from the notion that good mothering comes naturally to women. In truth, what even counts as good mothering is ideological, not innate; prescribed, not natural; culturally specific, not international; tied to the times, not to the ages. The arguments holding that a mother (but not father) who works outside the home thereby damages the child is an argument meant to support a model of mothering that is a recent one. It is not even available for many mothers. Most families cannot get along without two incomes, and many mothers have no income-producing partner. Further, exclusive devotion to children even when married with sufficient income makes for a dangerous choice with divorce rates at 50%, small likelihood of getting alimony, and child support irregularly paid and insufficient in any case.

The work of mothering varies by race and class. For many women of color, the work of mothering has had to focus on the economic survival and physical safety of their children. Yet this struggle is either ignored altogether or counted inferior to the "sensitive mothering" idealized in the White middle class and in the professional as well as popular literature (O'Reilly, 1996). Mothers in hard times are finding the struggle worsening. Inner cities are marked by the collapse of schools, the flight of jobs, the breakdown of community associations, the damage wrought by drug use and drug trafficking, and the daily assault of poverty. These conditions erode the kin and nonkin networks that traditionally buffer low-income families (Roschelle, 1997). At the same time, the government has curtailed assistance programs. This kind of piling-on disproportionately affects ethnoracial families, the mothers of whom get blamed for the state of their family.

Finally, a major contradiction for mothers mothering in patriarchy is that they must teach their daughters how to be subordinates or how to survive the punishments if they refuse. They must give their sons what it takes to be a member of the dominant gender—and thus higher than the identity they themselves have—and how to survive the punishments if they refuse to belong. Some mothers want to believe that they can outwit the system if they teach their daughters assertive speech and teach their sons to be thoughtful and polite. These are, however, purely matters of style with no relation to the distribution of power and privilege.

Women are held responsible for family life, and generally take responsibility for family life. Understanding the strengths and tensions of this key context of our clients' lives helps clients and therapists alike. Beyond the personal instance of treatment, because family is the mediator and reproducer of the patriarchal culture around it, we have important business there as feminists.

FEMINIST FAMILY THERAPY

As a modality of treatment, feminist family therapy offers several advantages for women. First, seeing a client in the company of family has a benefit similar to what we derive from seeing a friend in the company of family: We observe behavior we would likely not observe outside that setting. We learn anew. In the case with clients, we gain not only in knowledge but also in the possible points of impact. Helping family members talk with one another, understand one another, change routes of communication, specify triumphs, buttress resilience, create room for individuality, find new ways to connect, link up with supports—these interventions can create movement in relational patterns that otherwise hinder a client's progress.

However much help such interventions give, from a feminist point of view they do not go to the heart of the matter. As described earlier, relational patterns inside families derive from patriarchy just as do relational patterns outside families. Men in the family generally follow the patriarchal model to dominate with their greater power rather than nurture with it. Women as well may follow that model and use what power they are allotted in the family to dominate the members who have even less power rather than to nurture them. Deprived for so long of a significant role in public life, women in the home may fight with one another over the scarce territory and resources assigned to them.

Therapy must address not only the position of women in the culture but also how the family reproduces this positioning within its own ranks whether or not there is an adult male in the family. Women, in fact, often hold subordinate status to their own sons. Even when no man is physically present at all, the institution of patriarchy acts as a stand-in, requiring women of any age and relation to learn their "place," thus affecting how women view themselves and each other. Without steady and articulated awareness of this fact, therapy may become the handmaid of patriarchy and help squeeze the family into its mold by working toward adjustment.

Family therapy can offer families opportunities for discussion of significant areas that may have found no other arena. For instance, a family may never have put into words how racism has affected its course as a family. Such reflections may feel uniting to the family in the injustice suffered and in the resilience identified. A similar talk about sexism may entail much more conflict than a talk about racism because members are implicated in their behavior toward one another. Those latter discussions are important nevertheless to clarify that the source of the problematic patterning began before and outside of this particular family.

A majority of clients are women, and a majority of women have subordinate status in their family. Seeing a woman only within an individual therapy paradigm means that she leaves a therapy session with her plans for change, only to enter a primary context of influence that limits her. Family therapy gives the therapist an important way to strengthen and support a woman in her efforts toward her goals.

There is a question that often arises: How does feminist family therapy benefit men? The answer depends on whose point of view is considered. Women involved in partnerships with men, for example, might answer that with a lessening of differentials in power and privilege in the family, true intimacy becomes possible, an outcome that is its own reward. They might say that taking care of children and domestic life will afford men a kind of personal growth and gratification not available elsewhere. Men in some versions of the men's movement say that men will gain authenticity, being able to posture less and experience and express their feelings more.

The problem with this surmising is that the coin of the realm in mainstream America continues to be power in its hierarchical and dominating form with men valued over women. The family remains both a reflection of and contributor to this arrangement. Under these conditions, men who are asked to give up power and form egalitarian partnerships in families may look askance at the potential gains. In the first place, these gains represent values identified with women, not men. Values would have to change before these benefits would look like benefits to many men. In the second place, people in power—men versus women, White people versus people of color, upper classes versus lower classes—experience even small inroads into their privilege and status as great and painful losses (Goode, 1982). The pluses for keeping power and the minuses for giving it up may create a stronger valence for the status quo than for the promised benefits.

One other thought regarding the question of benefits for men. This question arises routinely when women are the initiators and beneficiaries of some activity. The corresponding question of what benefits might accrue for women rarely arises for men as they plan their activities. How different things would be if the standard for any action became the one proposed by Wendell Berry (1975, p. 17):

> So long as women do not go cheap
> for power, please women more than men.
> Ask yourself: Will this satisfy
> a woman satisfied to bear a child?
> Will this disturb the sleep
> of a woman near to giving birth?

REFERENCES

Annenberg Public Policy Center of the University of Pennsylvania. (2001). *Progress or no room at the top? The role of women in telecommunications, broadcast, cable and e-companies.* Retrieved from www.appcpenn.org.

Baber, K. M., & Allen, K. R. (1992). *Women and families: Feminist reconstructions.* New York: Guilford Press.

Berry, W. (1975). Manifesto: The mad farmer liberation front. *The Country of Marriage.* (pp. 16–17). New York: Harcourt Brace Jovanovich.

Blumstein, P., & Schwartz, P. (1983). *American couples.* New York: William Morrow.

Catalyst. (2000). *2000 Catalyst census of women corporate officers and top earners.* Retrieved from www.catalystwomen.org

Catalyst. (2001). *2001 Catalyst census of women board directors of the Fortune 1000.* Retrieved from www.catalystwomen.org

Crossette, B. (1999, November 26). Albright gathers top women to address women's issues. *The New York Times,* p. 27.

DiLapi, E. M. (1989). Lesbian mothers and the motherhood hierarchy. In F. W. Bozett (Ed.), *Homosexuality and the family* (pp. 101–121). Binghamton, NY: Harrington Park.

French, M. (1992). *The war against women.* New York: Summit Books.

Goode, W. J. (1982). Why men resist. In B. Thorne & M. Yalom (Eds.), *Rethinking the family: Some feminist questions* (pp. 131–150). New York: Longman.

Harris Associates. (1995). *Women's equality poll.* New York: Feminist Majority Foundation.

Hochschild, A. with Machung, A. (1989). *The second shift: Working parents and the revolution at home.* New York: Viking.

Komter, A. (1989). Hidden power in marriage. *Gender & Society, 3,* 187–216.

Landrine, H., & Klonoff, E. A. (1997). *Discrimination against women: Prevalence, consequences, remedies.* Thousand Oaks, CA: Sage.

Lorber, J. (1994). *Paradoxes of gender.* New Haven, CT: Yale University Press.

Nelson, M. K. (1990). Mothering others' children: The experiences of family day care providers. *Signs, 15,* 586–605.

O'Reilly, A. (1996). "Ain't that love?" Antiracism and racial constructions of motherhood. In M. T. Reddy (Ed.), *Everyday acts against racism* (pp. 88–98). Seattle, WA: Seal.

Peplau, L., & Gordon, S. L. (1991). The intimate relationships of lesbians and gay men. In J. N. Edwards & D. H. Demo (Eds.), *Marriage and family in transition* (pp. 479–496). Boston: Allyn & Bacon.

Rhode, D. L. (1997). *Speaking of sex: The denial of gender inequality*. Cambridge, MA: Harvard University Press.

Rollins, J. (1985). *Between women: Domestics and their employers*. Philadelphia: Temple University Press.

The Roper Center. (1990). *The 1990 Virginia Slims opinion poll*. Storrs, CT: Roper Public Opinion Research Center.

Roschelle, A. R. (1997). *No more kin: Exploring race, class, and gender in family networks*. Thousand Oaks, CA: Sage.

Schwartz, P. (1995). *Love between equals: How peer marriage really works*. New York: Free Press.

Stacey, J. (1990). *Brave new families: Stories of domestic upheaval in late twentieth century America*. New York: Basic Books.

U.S. Census Bureau. (2001). *Current population reports P60–213: Money income in the United States 2000*. Washington, DC: Author.

U.S. Census Bureau. (2002). *Annual Demographic Survey, March Supplement*. Retrieved from http://ferret.bls.census.gov.

Valian, V. (1998). *Why so slow? The advancement of women*. Cambridge, MA: MIT Press.

The White House Project. (2002). Who's talking? An analysis of Sunday morning talk shows [cited by the National Organization for Women]. Retrieved from www.now.org/nnt/spring-2002

2

CLASSIC TEXTS AND EARLY CRITIQUES

LOUISE B. SILVERSTEIN

It seems incomprehensible now, after more than 20 years of feminist theorizing, that gender was invisible to the early family therapy theorists. However, as Deborah Luepnitz (1988) has pointed out, family therapy emerged during the 1950s, a politically conservative phase of U.S. history. Men had just returned from the Second World War, and women had to be convinced to leave the workplace and return home. Social scientists such as Parsons and Bales (1955) provided the rationale for this return by asserting that the gendered division of labor between public and private spheres was "natural." Luepnitz speculated that the early family therapists did not challenge this public/private split in the "normal" family because they were already so embattled fighting traditional psychiatry's exclusive emphasis on individual pathology. They may not have felt that they could challenge the normal family as well.

Another factor contributing to the absence of gender issues in family therapy may have been that, except for Virginia Satir, all of the prominent family therapy theorists of the 1960s and early 1970s were White, middle-class men (e.g., Nathan Ackerman, Gregory Bateson, Murray Bowen, Jay Haley, and Salvador Minuchin). Becoming aware of one's own power and privilege is a difficult task for everyone (see, for instance, the critique of White feminists by women of color, e.g., hooks, 1984). Janet Helms (1990) has pointed out that most White people, because they have not experienced discrimination based on race, do not think of themselves as having a racial identity. Similarly, the early family therapists had not faced discrimination based on gender. Thus, gender was not a salient variable for them.

Interestingly, although Virginia Satir did experience discrimination based on gender, she did not openly critique family therapy in terms of gender. Luepnitz (1988) reported that the majority of therapists responding to a 1970 survey named Satir as the theorist who had most influenced their work. Yet, Satir was omitted from the *Handbook of Family Therapy* (Gurman & Kniskern, 1981). Despite this omission and a general lack of recognition of her accomplishments, Satir did not write explicitly about gender. Videotapes of her work do indicate that she urged people to go beyond traditional gender socialization, for example, by encouraging women to work and men to express emotion. She also identified mother blaming as endemic to the field. However, she refused to label herself a feminist, preferring instead to call herself a humanist who did not see a need to focus on women's issues as a separate field of study.

Rachel Hare-Mustin was the first to publish a feminist challenge to family therapy. She accused the field of reinforcing stereotyped gender roles by refusing to address gender issues within the family. In an early article, Hare-Mustin (1978) introduced many of the issues that the field would spend the next decade addressing. These included the importance of the larger societal context in constructing gender roles, the unequal distribution of power between husbands and wives, and the need to work with men in therapy from a feminist perspective.

This chapter describes the emergence and evolution of the feminist critique of family therapy. At the end of the chapter, we have included two Appendices: a glossary of terms (Appendix A) commonly used in family therapy that nonfamily therapists might not be familiar with, and a list of selected classic texts (Appendix B) organized into subject categories as suggestions for further reading. These selections are not exhaustive of the important early texts but have inevitably been influenced by those texts that had a major impact on our own development. We have tried to give the reader a flavor of the early critique, hoping that she or he will be inspired to read more extensively.

MAKING GENDER VISIBLE

Traditional family therapy theory of the 1960s conceptualized the family as a "natural" organism within which men and women had complementary, but equal roles. Ackerman (1966), for example, viewed attempts to reverse the "normal," that is, gendered division of labor, as the root of most child psychopathology.

Most of the families referred for psychotherapy in the 1960s and 1970s were conceptualized as having an "overinvolved" or "enmeshed" mother and a "disengaged" father. The typical intervention, called *unbalancing*, involved moving the father closer to the children and moving the mother out of the arena of discipline. The need for this restructuring was usually explained as caused by the mother's unwillingness to "allow" the father to become more involved with the children (Minuchin & Fishman, 1981). The solution was to devalue the mother as "inadequate" and to idealize the father as he was brought in to manage the acting-out child.

Early feminists have written how this acceptance of traditional gender roles structured their own thinking. Michele Bograd (1986) acknowledged that, as she began to rethink her own practice, she realized that many of her interventions were unconsciously gender-biased, for example, asking the mother, rather than the father, about a child's developmental history; asking the father, not the mother, about finances.

The first task then for the feminist pioneers was to elevate gender to an equivalent status with generation, as the two organizing principles of family life. After Hare-Mustin had broken the silence, several feminist family therapy articles, books, and workshops emerged in the early 1980s. However, most women were working in isolation, feeling unsupported, and at times embattled by the field at large. In response to this isolation, Monica Mc-Goldrick, Carol Anderson, and Froma Walsh organized 50 prominent women in family therapy to meet at Stonehenge, Connecticut, in 1984. This meeting established a network for women to support each other and to discuss the issues of women in family therapy (McGoldrick, Anderson, & Walsh, 1989a). The sense of solidarity that emerged from that meeting contributed to an explosion of feminist critiques of family therapy.

The Women's Project in family therapy, organized by Marianne Walters, Betty Carter, Peggy Papp, and Olga Silverstein (1988), was part of that feminist explosion. This was the first public venue where concern about women's issues in family therapy, both in terms of women as clients and women as therapists, could be discussed from a scholarly perspective. The Project conducted training workshops throughout the United States and England over several years, and eventually authored a book (Walters et al., 1988). The authors analyzed traditional family therapy concepts such as circularity and reciprocity from a gendered (i.e., feminist) perspective (see Appendix A: Glossary for definition). They devised feminist guidelines for family therapists that completely transformed the way that family therapy was practiced. These guidelines suggested that therapists relinquish their neutral stance and assume a feminist one by identifying how gender socialization constructs behavior, recognizing that women have limited access to financial resources, challenging the internalized sexism that inhibits many women, and acknowledging that no intervention is gender-neutral.

The Women's Project was also important because it was the first example of women collaborating in leadership roles within family therapy. In our view, the nature of the collaboration was also important. These four senior therapists agreed to try to achieve consensus about women's issues while preserving their individual clinical approaches to working with families. Forming a community and at the same time maintaining respect for individuality was a model that inspired other women to work together toward feminist goals.

McGoldrick, Anderson, and Walsh (1989b) established a similar collaboration. They asserted that women's voices had been ignored in family therapy. They assembled 22 prominent family therapists to "restory" family therapy in a way that made women's experiences central. They also argued for the importance of a "sisterhood" (p. 5) of feminist colleagues to provide ongoing support for the continued deconstruction of family therapy. Like the Women's Project, they described their own collaboration as providing intellectual and emotional bonding while respecting differences.

Thelma Jean Goodrich, Cheryl Rampage, Barbara Ellman, and Kris Halstead established such a sisterhood. They founded The Women's Institute for Life Studies to offer feminist programs, and authored a book together (1988). Rather than dividing their book and each writing a section, they decided to struggle together to produce theory through collective analysis. Their theoretical analysis posited that family therapy had ignored the oppression of women within patriarchal culture and thereby had created a system of theory, practice, and training that perpetuated this oppression. They provided specific suggestions for reforming the field. They also provided case examples of "archetypal" families, for example, the corporate marriage, the lesbian couple, the abusive relationship, and they illustrated how feminist principles could inform and transform family therapy with these types of families.

Lois Braverman (1988a), echoing the concern that women's voices had been silenced in the field, put together a volume dealing with a wide range of issues, for instance, disclosure in the context of lesbian mothers and lesbian daughters (Krestan, 1988) and women and abuse (Cotroneo, 1988). In her own chapter, Braverman (1988b) pointed out that the invisibility of gender had structured what were considered to be "normal" family processes and "significant" life-cycle events and had ignored other developmental issues, often those that were most salient for women. For example, family therapy literature had overlooked the importance of menarche in restructuring family relationships. In 1988, Lois Braverman became the founding editor of the *Journal of Feminist Family Therapy*, thereby establishing a permanent publishing outpost supportive of feminist work.

The emergence of these anthologies broadened the base of feminist family therapy, adding lesbians, women of color, and men to the critique. However, Hare-Mustin (1986) called for a total feminist revision of the field. She pointed out that mainstream culture was characterized by two forms of gender bias: alpha bias that *over*emphasized biological or "natural" gender differences (e.g., defining women as "relational" and men as "instrumental"), and beta bias that *under*stated societal gender differences in access to resources and power (e.g., assuming that men and women have equal opportunities to advance professionally). Hare-Mustin argued that both of these cultural biases permeated all aspects of family therapy practice.

Marianne Ault-Riché (1986) and Deborah Luepnitz (1988) took up the gauntlet of revising the entire field by directly challenging the male therapists who had defined family therapy. Luepnitz began with a feminist critique of Bateson's (1972) theory that had formed the epistemological basis of the entire field of family therapy theory. She then proceeded to analyze the videotapes of the "Master (i.e., male) Therapists" (e.g., Nathan Ackerman (1966), Salvador Minuchin (Minuchin & Fishman, 1981)). She pointed out the explicit sexism and misogyny in the behavior of these men. For example, in Minuchin's famous tape, "Taming Monsters," she pointed out how disrespectful Minuchin was to the mother. He told the child, "Your mother has been telling you a pack of lies" (about the father's potential for violence). At the end of the session, Minuchin threw his shoe against the wall, paralleling the father's violent behavior, and in that way legitimizing it. Minuchin concluded the session by telling the mother that she had to change. However, he did not explore the father's violent behavior, nor did he suggest that the father also needed to change.

The feminist critique pointed out that the pattern of overinvolved mother and disengaged father was not a personal characteristic of a specific family but rather the political construction of patriarchal society. Feminist family therapists noted that men were socialized to overfunction in the public world of work, whereas women were socialized to overfunction within the private world of the family. Thus the enmeshed mother and peripheral father were actually cultural roles created by gender socialization within patriarchy, rather than an expression of the natural family. The feminist critique that linked these parental behaviors to patriarchal gender roles illuminated this intervention as a blatant example of mother blaming rather than a neutral rebalancing of the family system.

Similarly, Ault-Riché (1986) began her critique with a series of questions addressed to each traditional family therapy approach developed by the "master therapists": Is the nuclear family idealized? Is the interplay between family life and the larger society acknowledged? Are the unequal power relations between husbands and wives recognized? Does the traditional model reflect the fact that what may be good for the family may not be good for the individual? On the basis of answers to these questions, she outlined how traditional approaches were compatible with or conflicted with feminist principles. These two texts provided depth to the feminist critique by addressing the misogyny embedded in traditional family theory and practice.

In addition to making gender salient in family therapy, the issue of power (i.e., the gendered distribution of power) in families had to be made visible. Within traditional family therapy theory, the only differences in power that were acknowledged in the family were those based on age. As Virginia Goldner (1988) pointed out, this hierarchical organization distinguished the power discrepancy between parents and children and obscured the fact that the two parents operated from very different power positions, both within the family and beyond it. As long as age was the only variable acknowledged as conferring differences in status and power among family members, differences in status and power between men and women could remain invisible.

Another factor contributing to the invisibility of power was that family systems theory was derived from natural systems theory. Natural systems are those that occur in nature, such as the solar system or an ant colony. Family systems theory assumed that the human family was a natural system, organized by natural laws that are rooted in evolutionary processes. Although there are power differences within the social systems of many animals (especially other primates), we do not ordinarily associate institutionalized power relationships with natural processes. Thus, family systems theory originally developed as if power were not a meaningful variable within the organization of families. The theoretical concepts that form the basis of family systems were conceptualized as neutral in terms of power.

From the perspective of natural systems theory, the emotional functioning of individual family members was considered so interdependent that it was the family, rather than the individual, that was conceptualized as the emotional unit. For example, the theory proposed that, if one family member generally acted very competently, another tended to behave in an incompetent or inadequate fashion. In an overfunctioning/underfunctioning dyad, each family member's behavior was tied inexorably to the behavior of the other. This interdependence between family members became translated in family systems theory as the concept of reciprocity.

According to family systems theory, if either member of the dyad was to change their behavior, the behavior of the other person would automatically change as well. A common intervention in family therapy was to encourage the overfunctioning partner to stop overfunctioning. This intervention usually involved telling the mother to stop being overinvolved with the children. Interestingly, we are not aware of a family in which the husband was encouraged to work less and earn less, or the wife was advised to stop doing the laundry or cooking dinner. Because power was invisible, family systems theory did not acknowledge that women's economic dependence on men made it unlikely that a wife would have the same freedom as her husband to choose to stop over (or under)-functioning.

Harriet Lerner (1988) challenged the absence of power in the theoretical framework of Murray Bowen (1978) by pointing out that families exist within a particular sociocultural context. She argued that simply challenging rules *within* a given family is not sufficient to change dysfunctional relationship patterns. Lerner (and others, e.g., Goldner, 1985; Hare-Mustin, 1978) pointed out that intrafamily rules are constructed and maintained by the gendered power relations in the sociocultural context of patriarchy. Thus, the rigid rules of the larger society also had to be confronted. Neither families nor therapists could be conceptualized as neutral. The feminist critique thus moved the locus of therapy from an exclusive focus on the interior of the family to include the need to change external social structures as well.

Making the issue of power a legitimate subject for therapy has proved to be more difficult than making gender salient. Men, like most dominant groups, are reluctant to give up power voluntarily. Many women, socialized to believe that their only access to power is through men, are reluctant to challenge male authority. This reluctance on the part of women is appropriate because being with a man does in reality give most women access to more power and resources than they could have on their own. Married women typically have less power than their husbands, both because women continue to earn significantly less money than men and also because women have been socialized to avoid power. Men, in contrast, have been socialized to embrace it. Thus, empowering women continues to be a challenge for feminist family therapy.

Thelma Jean Goodrich (1991a) organized a collection of papers dedicated to addressing discrepancies in power within the family. This book challenged the field to acknowledge the pervasiveness of women's oppression and to recognize that the family is the context within which this oppression is enacted and perpetuated. In the essay that opens the book, Goodrich (1991b) outlined the connections between power, marriage, and sex. She raised the question as to whether "consensual" sex can be a meaningful concept, even within the confines of marriage, because sex occurs between people who are physically and economically unequal. Unless family therapists openly explore the distribution of power within families, she argued that we too are contributing to and legitimizing women's oppression.

In addition to examining how power constructs sexual relations, Goodrich's (1991a) book confronted many other controversial issues, such as redistributing assets so that wives have as much money as their husbands (Carter, 1991) and raising the question of whether male therapists can empower women (Doherty, 1991). Many of the issues raised in this volume continue to be controversial among family therapists.

These challenges to examine and reconfigure the power relations within families led some feminist family therapists to propose that men be recruited as consumers of feminist family therapy. Goodrich (1991b) raised the issue of how to work with men to empower women. Michele Bograd (1991) edited a collection of chapters that articulated the goal of translating feminist practice into caring, effective clinical practice with men. For the first time within the family therapy field, masculinity was examined as something that might be pathogenic to *men* as well as to women. Excessive emphases on achievement, competition, sexuality, and stoicism were identified as the negative effects for men of masculine gender role socialization. Ganley (1991) proposed that feminist family therapy should include the resocialization of both men and women.

Almeida and Bograd (1991) presented an innovative model for working with men's violence against women in the family. These authors pointed out that, just as domestic violence has traditionally been considered a "private" matter because it occurred within the privacy of a man's family, psychotherapy represents a private solution to what is really a widespread social problem. Further, dealing with domestic violence through psychotherapy requires that women assume primary responsibility for this problem, that is, the mostly female mental health profession or the female members of the family. These authors called for men to assume responsibility for other men's violence against their wives through a community mentoring program. This model of intervention described a way that feminist practice can work toward changing the societal context of women's oppression in addition to the internal dynamics of family life.

The Gender and Violence Project at the Ackerman Institute for the Family (Goldner, Penn, Sheinberg, & Walker, 1990) also focused on innovative methods for working with violent couples. The four women constituting the collaborative team in this project struggled to develop a treatment that went beyond the either/or victim/perpetrator approach to domestic violence. They wrote about the challenge of working within the paradoxical world of violent couples. For example, the team confronted the fact that gender constructed inequalities in these couples; that is, the husband was physically and economically more powerful than his wife. At the same time, they acknowledged that some aspects of the couple's interactions were reciprocal; that is, the wife was sometimes involved in initiating the cycle of violence, and she had chosen not to leave the relationship. The both/and perspective goes to the very heart of the compatibility of feminism with family systems theory. The authors maintained both that feminism was correct in its deconstruction of battering as an enactment of male power and privilege and, at the same time, that family systems theory was accurate in its identification of the wife's participation in the cycle of violence.

Marsha Mirkin (1990) has similarly argued for the integration of a traditional family therapy approach with feminist therapy in the treatment of women with anorexia and bulimia. Mirkin argued that structural family therapy overlooked the link between the larger cultural context and anorexia and could be experienced as pathologizing and blaming (especially of mother). She speculated that adolescent girls were reacting to the unrealistic expectations that our culture has for women, that is, to be a traditional woman—beautiful, fragile, and dependent on men; and also to be more like a man—independent, assertive, and focused on work. Anorexia represents overconformity to the cultural expectations of being both beautiful and fragile, and more like a man.

Mirkin also proposed that these girls were reacting to the devaluation of intimate relationships within patriarchal culture. Mirkin argued that girls who develop anorexia believe that growing out of childhood will lead to isolation from supporting relationships. Anorexia allows girls to remain in a dependent, childlike relationship with their parents, thereby avoiding the danger of an isolated adulthood.

Mirkin combined structural interventions, like putting clearer boundaries around the parental couple, with a narrative that explicitly valued feminine socialization. For example, structural family therapy might explain encouraging the parents to spend more time together as a way of proving to the adolescent that the parents can survive without her. A feminist revision of that intervention would emphasize demonstrating the possibility of developing rewarding relationships as an adult. Similarly, encouraging a mother to devote more energy to her own life would be interpreted as another example of the possibility for women to make a positive adjustment to cultural expectations. Mirkin argued that anorexia does not reflect a need to separate, as traditional structural therapy has suggested, but rather a need to achieve a more satisfying intimacy within the context of relationships.

Joan Laird and Ann Hartman (1988) used feminist theory to achieve a deeper understanding of how rituals, a traditional tool in family therapy, could be mobilized to enhance a positive sense of self and change women's lives. They reviewed how most rituals for women focus on preparing them for serving others in domestic life—marriage, childbirth, and ritual purification of their bodies. In contrast, Laird and Hartmann recommended helping women develop self-affirming rituals, such as celebrating menarche as a new phase in a young girl's life when she can experience the power of being able to create new life.

Laird and Hartman also illustrated how a woman could decide to change a ritual as a first step in beginning to change the power relations in her life. They described helping a woman redefine a more limited role for herself in creating a holiday dinner as the beginning of restructuring a more equitable sharing of household responsibilities. These authors also cautioned family therapists against enacting domestic roles in professional rituals. They noted that women in the helping professions have often accepted lesser roles in national organizations and tolerated the presence of only a token woman on important symposia. They warned that until feminist family therapists enact their own self-affirming rituals, they might be less than successful in helping women clients harness the power of ritual in their lives.

Kaethe Weingarten (1992) examined the possibility of combining feminist principles and family systems techniques in an effort to deepen our understanding of the therapist–client relationship. By using a feminist approach to narrative therapy (Anderson & Goolishian, 1988), she explored the interplay of gender and power on the potential for intimacy between therapist and client. Narrative therapy is an approach that assumes that an individual constructs a self through telling stories that give meaning to their lived experiences. Like feminist therapy, narrative therapy assumes that the therapist is an active collaborator rather than an objective observer, such that therapist and client collaborate in the cocreation of meaning. With case examples of intimate and nonintimate (at times abusive) therapeutic encounters, Weingarten challenged feminist family therapists to acknowledge how much their own feelings, opinions, and values influence therapy. She raised many difficult questions about how much and when to disclose these experiences to clients. Weingarten's exploration of intimacy between therapist and client contrasts sharply with the distant, expert stance typical of more traditional paradigms in family therapy.

Another step in the institutionalization of gender in family therapy theory was to ensure that feminist theory was integrated into the curriculum for training family therapists. Judith Myers Avis (1989) was one of the first to write about the need to revolutionize the curriculum. She noted that in a 1980 survey of 25 directors for graduate training in marriage and family therapy and 20 supervisors approved by the Association of Marriage and Family Therapists, gender was mentioned in only 1 of 63 core content areas (Winkle, Piercy, & Hovestadt, 1981). A later survey of 285 training programs asking how gender was integrated into their curriculum yielded only 55 responses (Coleman, Avis, & Turin, 1990). Fewer than half of these responses indicated that gender was addressed at all.

Avis argued that omitting research about gender was the equivalent of training surgeons with outdated knowledge and skill. She discussed both the content for and process of developing a course on gender issues in family therapy. She raised many questions about training. These included whether to have a separate course on gender issues or to ensure that gender was integrated into all courses, how to address the political issues raised by faculty members in response to a proposal for a course on gender, and what emotional reactions to anticipate from male and female students within such a course.

GIVING LESBIANS STATUS IN FAMILY THERAPY

Early in the development of the feminist critique of family therapy, Jo-Ann Krestan and Claudia Bepko (1980) examined the complex interrelationships between the heterosexual community and lesbian couples. They challenged the idea, common in traditional family therapy, that aspects within the personality or relationship of lesbians make them more likely than heterosexual couples to have a fused relationship. These authors pointed out that within the larger social system, a lesbian relationship is considered either invisible or pathological. This invalidating context creates continual pressure to dissolve the relationship. In reaction to this pressure toward dissolution, some lesbian couples generate rigid boundaries around the relationship and intensify normal tendencies toward closeness into a more fused couple system. Krestan and Bepko defined the central therapeutic task in working with lesbian couples as acknowledging the unique pressures these couples face, while coaching them to deal with these issues without becoming fused.

Sallyann Roth (1985) described her clinical experience of working with 65 mostly White, middle-class lesbian couples and families in private practice. She delineated six major issues most often presented at the beginning of therapy. These included problems of closeness and distance, sexual expression, unequal access to resources, different stages in the process of coming out, choosing to have children, and how to end the relationship.

Roth pointed out that, except for the issue of coming out, these problems are all concerns of heterosexual couples as well. Roth outlined the impact of both the heterosexual and lesbian communities on the particular ways in which lesbian couples deal with these issues. For example, partners who are isolated from a larger lesbian community may have more difficulty negotiating a balance between closeness and distance than couples who have a network of lesbian friends. Similarly, the inability to express physical affection within heterosexual society may inhibit the warming-up stage, thereby contributing to difficulties with sexual expression. Like Krestan and Bepko, Roth argued for the necessity of addressing the reciprocal relations between the couple and the larger systems in which they are embedded.

The presence of only two early texts on working with lesbian couples in family therapy testifies to the intense homophobia endemic to the field from the 1960s to the 1990s.

RAISING THE ISSUES OF ETHNICITY AND COLOR

Beginning in the 1980s, the family therapy field began to explore the impact of ethnic, cultural, and racial differences on therapy (e.g., Falicov, 1982; Garcia-Preto, 1982). However, many authors did not integrate feminist principles into their recommendations for working with ethnic minority families (McGoldrick, Pearce, & Giordano, 1982). The earliest exception to that rule was Elaine Pinderhughes (1986), who identified ethnic minority women as the societal crossroads where discrimination based on both gender and ethnorace (see Appendix A: Glossary) come together.

Pinderhughes pointed out that ethnic minority women are often blamed for the oppression caused by the larger social system and must also pay the cost for that oppression. With the stereotype of African American women as matriarchs, she illustrated how these women are blamed for the high unemployment rate of African American men actually caused by institutionalized racism. When the men abandon their children because their chronic unemployment prevents them from providing economic stability to their families, the "overbearing" woman, rather than the racist system, is blamed. The women are then left to suffer the consequences of the system in that they are forced to raise children without the support of the children's father.

Pinderhughes expanded the idea of the African American woman as the nodal point in a system of multiple oppressions by pointing out that women often agree with the societal view and blame themselves for their husband's/partner's irresponsible or abusive behavior. Given the racism that African American men experience within society, women often feel disloyal if they attempt to hold their male partners accountable for their behavior.

Pinderhughes recommended that therapy be conceptualized as liberating minority women from entrapment in their nodal role. Rather than focusing exclusively on intrapsychic or intrafamily issues, effective treatment would include helping women get access to material resources (housing, tutoring), linking them to community support groups, and working from a strength perspective.

An additional important point was Pinderhughes's discussion of Murray Bowen's concept of the societal projection process (Bowen, 1978). Bowen hypothesized that the dominant group in society projects its own anxiety onto another group, identifying that group as impaired and needing "help." Rather than helping that group, however, this process actually helps the dominant group manage anxiety by feeling superior and benevolent. Pinderhughes challenged White therapists to give up the "benefactor" role and help minority women gain access to power so that they can help themselves.

After Pinderhughes's complex and challenging chapter was published in 1986, few authors continued to expand on the connection between gender and ethnorace in family therapy. Although the number of books and articles dealing with race, ethnicity, and culture in family therapy continued to proliferate (e.g., Boyd-Franklin, 1989; Saba, Karrer, & Hardy, 1991), it was not until the mid-1990s that the interlocking oppressions again became the subject of theorizing within family therapy. This disconnection between gender and ethnorace may have been caused by the fact that the culture of feminist family therapy, like the original culture of traditional family therapy, was made up of primarily White therapists. White feminist therapists were continuing to challenge the field on gender issues, and ethnic minority therapists were ensuring that race and ethnicity became salient variables in family therapy theory. Unfortunately, there was little overlap between these two groups.

We speculate that by 1994, a critical mass of articles and books about ethnorace had been published such that ethnic minority family theorists could now turn their attention to the complex interaction of gender with these issues. Because women are often the first members of a family to contact the mental health system, Nancy Boyd-Franklin and Nydia Garcia-Preto (1994) presented an extensive discussion of issues relevant to working with African American and Latina women in family therapy. In particular, these authors pointed out how racism constructed many aspects of gender socialization.

For example, because institutionalized racism has resulted in large numbers of African American men being incarcerated or killed at an early age, African American women have often had to raise children without the benefit of the children's father. Although boys as well as girls are given responsibility for child care within African American families, the likelihood that a girl will become a single mother has led to a tendency to socialize daughters to become overresponsible. Another stress on families is the fact that African American men have been more rigidly kept out of the economic system than have African American women. Thus, African American women often earn more than their husbands. Within the larger context of societal male dominance, this economic and power discrepancy often causes additional problems for couples and families.

Boyd-Franklin and Garcia-Preto (1994) pointed out that Latinas find themselves in similar cultural paradoxes. On the one hand, the cultural value of *marianismo* suggests that they are morally and spiritually superior to men. On the other hand, *machismo* dictates that women should submit to male authority. Like African American women, immigrant Latinas often have less difficulty obtaining employment than their husbands because their domestic skills are in demand. Thus, the circumstance of wives entering the workplace creates pressure on traditional Latina/Latino gender roles.

Lillian Comas-Díaz (1994) expanded on the complexity of the interplay between gender and ethnorace by looking at the impact of intrafamily racism on LatiNegras, Latinas with dark skin. These multiracial women defy the cultural value of *mejorar la raza*, that is, lightening the family by marrying √ light-skinned partners (p. 41). Therefore, although they may be taught how to deal with discrimination based on their ethnicity, they are often not given family support to help them cope with societal racism. Dark-skinned men and women both suffer from this lack of family support, but the lack is particularly difficult for women because of the centrality of family in their lives. Comas-Diaz introduced the idea of feminist family therapy with one person as a culturally congruent approach for dealing with the multiple oppressions of gender, race, and ethnicity.

All of these authors cautioned White feminist therapists to rethink the primacy of gender in the lives of Latinas and African American women, suggesting that racism, ethnicity, immigration status, and socioeconomic class all interact with gender issues in the lives of minority women. Just as the early feminist therapists had to rethink theoretical principles such as reciprocity and complementarity, these authors argued that feminist therapists had to rethink their attitudes toward such issues as generational boundaries and reliance on extended family members. Within ethnic minority families, relying on parental children or extended family members may reflect economic necessity rather than lack of boundary differentiation.

Greene and Hall (1994) addressed this need to rethink the primacy of gender within White feminist family therapy theory by challenging White therapists to become culturally competent. They proposed that feminist family therapists must recognize that African American (and by extension, all ethnic minority) men and women are bicultural, forced to live within both the dominant White culture and the subordinate minority culture. This biculturalism operates differently for men and women. Men are part of the dominant gender and the subordinate race, whereas women are members of two subordinate groups. These authors argued further that cultural competence requires not simply a theoretical understanding of racism but a personal awareness as well. They proposed that there is an ethical mandate for therapists to confront and understand their own racial identity and racism.

CONCLUSION

This brief summary of the feminist revision of family therapy brings us to the present. From our perspective, gender is now clearly visible within family therapy. However, the thornier issue of how to address power, intimacy, and cultural diversity simultaneously within family therapy remains a challenge to the field. We hope that this book will contribute to an expansion of feminist family theory and practice.

APPENDIX A: GLOSSARY

1. *Both/and perspective*: holding two apparently contradictory views as simultaneously correct, for example, holding that battering enacts male power and also that the less powerful woman plays a part in constructing the relationship in which she is battered.

2. *Circularity*: understanding behavior as interactional patterns that are instigated by people in reaction to one another and reinforced by all parties.

3. *Covert/overt hierarchy*: In general, a covert hierarchy is an unacknowledged ranking of elements into an order of value and power, whereas an overt hierarchy is an acknowledged ranking. In families, rankings by gender are covert in some cultures (e.g., the United States) and overt in others (e.g., many Muslim countries), whereas rankings by generation are overt.

4. *Ethnorace*: This term indicates how ethnicity and race interact to construct an individual's social location. For example, African Americans and African Caribbeans share the same race but different ethnicities. LatiNegra/LatiNegro refers to individuals from Latin countries who are also of African descent.

5. *Gendered power relations*: systematic ways of relating between men and women reflecting and recreating the sociocultural ordering of men as dominant over women as subordinate.

6. *Gender-sensitive*: a term that emerged in contrast to the term *feminist* as a way to signify that men also experience gender role strain. We eschew this term because it has been used to deny the fact that cultural gender ideology creates or reflects power inequalities between men and women.

7. *Nodal point*: the intersection of several actions, for example, a poor woman of color may be understood as a nodal point reflecting the multiple oppressions of sexism, racism, and classism.

8. *Overfunctioning/underfunctioning dyad*: two people create a stable, reciprocal pattern in which one person carries major responsibility for the relationship, whereas the other carries little. Although the overfunctioning person may appear to be more competent, both members of the dyad take turns lending and borrowing self. If the underfunctioning person begins to become more active, the overfunctioning person will begin to underfunction.

9. *Patriarchy*: the organization of society that elevates men along with their defining attributes and tasks as more important, more valued, and therefore more privileged and powerful than women.

10. *Postmodernism*: an intellectual movement that came to flower in the 1980s as a counterpoint to positivism. It challenges the positivist view that reality is objective and can be reliably observed and measured. Postmodernists hold that "reality" is socially constructed, that is, each social context operates as a community of meaning-makers.

11. *Reciprocity*: a description of a complex interactional behavioral chain in which each person's behavior in the family influences other people's behavior. For example, if one person acts helpless most of the time, another person will act more competent. Similarly, if one person changes the way that they are acting, for example, becomes less helpless and more assertive, other people in the family will also change their behavior.

12. *Social location*: the place in society inhabited by an individual that determines their access to resources, power, and status. For example, in the United States, race, class, gender, sexual orientation, and ethnicity construct social location.

13. *Unbalancing/rebalancing interventions*: therapeutic moves aimed at shifting focus, power, or direction of interactions away from the usual routine into a new routine.

14. *Mother blaming*: holding mothers responsible for all aspects of their children's lives.

APPENDIX B: CLASSIC TEXTS

Making Gender Visible

Ault-Riché, M. (Ed.). (1986). *Women and family therapy*. Rockville, MD: Aspen Systems.

Avis, J. M. (1989). Integrating gender into the family therapy curriculum. *Journal of Feminist Family Therapy, 1*, 3–26.

Bograd, M. (1986). A feminist examination of family therapy: What is women's place? *Women and Therapy, 5*, 95–106.

Bograd, M. (Ed.). (1991). *Feminist approaches for men in family therapy*. New York: Harrington Park Press.

Braverman, L. (Ed.). (1988a). *A guide to feminist family therapy*. New York: Harrington Park Press.

Goldner, V. (1985). Feminism and family therapy. *Family Process, 24*, 31–47.

Goldner, V. (1988). Generation and gender: Normative and covert hierarchies. *Family Process, 27*, 17–32.

Goldner, V., Penn, P., Sheinberg, M., & Walker, G. (1990). Love and violence: Gender paradoxes in volatile attachments. *Family Process, 29*, 343–364.

Goodrich, T. J. (Ed.). (1991a). *Women and power: Perspectives for family therapy*. New York: Norton.

Goodrich, T. J., Rampage, C., Ellman, B., & Halstead, K. (1988). *Feminist family therapy: A casebook*. New York: Norton.

Hare-Mustin, R. T. (1978). A feminist approach to family therapy. *Family Process, 17*, 181–194.

Hare-Mustin, R. T. (1986). Autonomy and gender: Some questions for therapists. *Psychotherapy, 23*, 205–212.

Laird, J., & Hartman, A. (1988). Women, rituals, and family therapy. In L. Braverman (Ed.), *A guide to feminist family therapy* (pp. 157–173). New York: Harrington Park Press.

Lerner, H. (1988). Is family systems theory really systemic? A feminist communication. In L. Braverman (Ed.), *A guide to feminist family therapy* (pp. 47–63). New York: Harrington Park Press.

Luepnitz, D. (1988). *The family interpreted: Psychoanalysis, feminism, and family therapy.* New York: Basic Books.

McGoldrick, M., Anderson, C., & Walsh, F. (Eds.). (1989a). *Women in families: A framework for family therapy.* New York: Norton.

Mirkin, M. P. (1990). Eating disorders: A feminist family therapy perspective. In M. P. Mirkin (Ed.), *The social and political contexts of family therapy* (pp. 89–119). Boston: Allyn & Bacon.

Walters, M., Carter, C., Papp, P., & Silverstein, L. (1988). *The invisible web: Gender patterns in family relationships.* New York: Guilford Press.

Weingarten, K. (1992). Intimate and non-intimate interactions in therapy. *Family Process, 31*, 45–59.

Giving Lesbians Status in Family Therapy

Krestan, J. A., & Bepko, C. S. (1980). The problem of fusion in the lesbian relationship. *Family Process, 19*, 277–389.

Roth, S. A. (1985). Psychotherapy with lesbian couples. Individual issues, female socialization, and the social context. *Journal of Marital and Family Therapy, 11*, 273–286.

Raising the Issues of Ethnicity and Color

Boyd-Franklin, N., & Garcia-Preto, N. (1994). Family therapy: A closer look at African American and Hispanic women. In B. Greene & L. Comas Diaz (Eds.), *Women of color: Integrating ethnic and gender identities in psychotherapy* (pp. 239–264). New York: Guilford Press.

Comas-Díaz, L. (1994). Latinegra: Mental health issues of African Latinas. *Journal of Feminist Family Therapy, 5*, 35–74.

Greene, B., & Hall, R. (1994). Cultural competence in feminist family therapy. *Journal of Feminist Family Therapy, 6*, 5–28.

McGoldrick, M., Pearce, J. K., & Giordano, J. (Eds.). (1982). *Ethnicity and family therapy.* New York: Guilford Press.

Pinderhughes, E. (1986). Minority women: A nodal position in the functioning of the social system. In M. Ault-Riché (Ed.), *Women and family therapy* (pp. 51–63). Rockville, MD: Aspen Systems.

Additional Chapter References

Ackerman, N. (1966). *Treating troubled families*. New York: Basic Books.

Almeida, R. V., & Bograd, M. (1991). Sponsorship: Holding men accountable for domestic violence. In M. Bograd (Ed.), *Feminist approaches for men in family therapy* (pp. 243–260). New York: Harrington Park Press.

Anderson, H., & Goolishian, H. A. (1988). Human systems as linguistic systems: Preliminary and evolving ideas about the implications for clinical theory. *Family Process, 27*, 371–393.

Bateson, G. (1972). *Steps to an ecology of mind*. New York: Ballantine.

Bowen, M. (1978). *Family therapy in clinical practice*. New York: Jason Aronson.

Boyd-Franklin, N. (1989). *Black families in therapy: A multisystems approach*. New York: Guilford Press.

Braverman, L. (1988b). Feminism and family therapy: Friends or foes. In L. Braverman (Ed.), *A guide to feminist family therapy* (pp. 5–14). New York: Harrington Park Press.

Carter, B. (1991). Everything I do is for the family. In T. J. Goodrich (Ed.), *Women and power: Perspectives for family therapy* (pp. 215–217). New York: Norton.

Coleman, S. B., Avis, J. M., & Turin, M. (1990). A study of the role of gender in family therapy training. *Family Process, 29*, 365–374.

Cotroneo, M. (1988). Women and abuse in the context of the family. In L. Braverman (Ed.), *A guide to feminist family therapy* (pp. 81–96). New York: Harrington Park Press.

Doherty, W. (1991). Can male therapists empower women in therapy? In T. J. Goodrich (Ed.), *Women and power: Perspectives for family therapy* (pp. 151–165). New York: Norton.

Falicov, C. (1982). Mexican families. In M. McGoldrick, J. K. Pearce, & J. Giordano (Eds.), *Ethnicity and family therapy* (pp. 134–163). New York: Guilford Press.

Ganley, A. (1991). Feminist therapy with male clients. In M. Bograd (Ed.), *Feminist approaches for men in family therapy* (pp. 1–23). New York: Harrington Park Press.

Garcia-Preto, N. (1982). Puerto Rican families. In M. McGoldrick, J. K. Pearce, & J. Giordano (Eds.), *Ethnicity and family therapy* (pp. 164–186). New York: Guilford Press.

Goodrich, T. J. (1991b). Women, power, and family therapy: What's wrong with this picture? In T. J. Goodrich (Ed.), *Perspectives for family therapy* (pp. 3–35). New York: Norton.

Gurman, A., & Kniskern, D. (Eds.). (1981). *Handbook of family therapy*. New York: Brunner/Mazel.

Helms, J. E. (1990). *Black and White racial identity: Theory, research, and practice*. New York: Guilford Press.

hooks, b. (1984). *Feminist theory: From margin to center*. Boston: South End Press.

Krestan, J. A. (1988). Lesbian daughters and lesbian mothers: The crisis of disclosure from a family systems perspective. In L. Braverman (Ed.), *A guide to feminist family therapy* (pp. 113–144). New York: Harrington Park Press.

McGoldrick, M., Anderson, C. M., & Walsh, F. (1989b). Women in families and family therapy. In M. McGoldrick, C. M. Anderson, & F. Walsh (Eds.), *Women in families: A framework for family therapy* (pp. 3–15). New York: Norton.

Minuchin, S., & Fishman, H. C. (1981). *Family therapy techniques*. Cambridge, MA: Harvard University Press.

Parsons, T., & Bales, R. F. (1955). *Family, socialization, and interaction process*. New York: Free Press.

Saba, G. W., Karrer, B. M., & Hardy, K. V. (Eds.). (1991). *Minorities and family therapy*. Binghamton, NY: Haworth Press.

Winkle, W. C., Piercy, F. P., & Hovestadt, A. J. (1981). A curriculum for graduate-level marriage and family therapy education. *Journal of Marital and Family Therapy, 7*, 201–210.

II

REFRAMING
LIFE-CYCLE ISSUES

3

OVER THE RAINBOW: THE LESBIAN FAMILY

KRIS HALSTEAD

The term *family* brings to mind and heart a number of thoughts, feelings, and even physical reactions for many people. We know a family to be a group of people usually connected by blood, sometimes living in the same house, with a mother, a father, some children, and maybe a dog and a cat. We think of *family* as the group of people we grew up with. As we grow up, we hope that some day we can "start" a family. The family should be a safe group of people who love us and nurture us. We use the term *family* in combination with reunions and photos, with history and money. Family traditions are powerful for many of us. Who among us is not aware of the concept of the dysfunctional family? The term *family* is used so often that we hardly take time to consider its political implications.

The family has traditionally functioned to maintain the power structure in any particular political system. In the "modern family"—the post-Industrial Revolution family—the role of mother, children, animals, and slaves has been to protect and guard the property of the father so that he can go to work. Although the emergence of feminism has radically transformed the notion of family, traditional beliefs and values still abound and still profoundly affect theories about families and how families should function.

> Feminists . . . are committed to countering the ideology of the "normal" family because of its inaccurate representation of actual families, its harmful prescription for women, its stigmatization of other arrangements, in short, because it is based on a single notion of class (middle), race (White), religion (Protestant), affectional preference (heterosexual), and gender privilege (male). (Goodrich, Rampage, Ellman, & Halstead, 1988, p. 8)

As a family therapist, I am aware on a daily basis of how traditional notions of family can cause pain for women, men, and children. I watch as children struggle to have a voice, as women attempt to earn equal pay for equal work, and as men continue to succumb to the stress of carrying the load. Although this is a gross simplification, it continues to be the basis for most of the conflict in families as they exist today.

In a culture as diverse as our universal culture, it is astounding to observe the power of heterosexual privilege in the formation of family values. In our world, rituals and traditions grow from the different needs people have because of factors such as race, size, climate, religion, natural resources, and language, to name a few influences. In the midst of this diversity, what remains constant in all cultures is the dominance of male authority and establishment of heterosexual arrangements as the norm. Outside of the "norm" are those who are considered different: single parents, gay and lesbian couples, persons who choose to live in intentional communities. Diverse family groupings challenge the norm and serve to call us to expand our definitions of "normal." Gays and lesbians, in particular, are choosing to live in committed same-sex partnerships, have and raise children together, and visibly celebrate these choices. The rainbow flag seen on the cars, homes, clothes, and jewelry of gay, lesbian, transgendered, and bisexual people is a visual symbol of this diversity and is the reason for the title of this chapter.

In this chapter, I explore the reciprocal effects that traditional family norms and gay "family" concepts have on one another. The term *family* in the gay community is a powerful renaming and reconstituting of a traditional arrangement that historically has been difficult, at best, and abusive, at worst, for gays, lesbians, bisexuals, and transgendered persons as well as for women and children.

LAURA AND TISHA

I received a call from Laura, who, with her partner, Tisha, has been a client of mine for a few years. I had not seen them for 6 months prior to Laura's call. Laura asked, "Can we come in for a few sessions to work on our decision to have a commitment ceremony?" She and Tisha felt committed in all ways and referred to each other as "family." Their work to keep communication open and honest resulted in their ability to create systemic arrangements that they felt were respectful of each other and of the relationship. Each was supportive of the other's choice of career, need for more or less contact with family of origin, patterns of managing money, sleeping, eating, beliefs about spirituality and politics, and styles of recreating. When disagreements about any of these occurred, they "hung in" with each other and talked, or scheduled a few sessions to resolve the conflict.

When Laura and Tisha came in for their "commitment session," they explained their concerns as relating to the following: their desire to proclaim their commitment publicly; their desire to have a child together; and cultural, racial, and class differences in their families of origin.

Laura and Tisha were continuing to grapple with coming out as individuals and as a couple. Their concerns cannot be worked out separately because these concerns hold hands and affect one another.

When Tisha and Laura met, they were very aware of their differences. Tisha is the daughter of two African American university professors of sociology who fought the racial crusade alongside people such as Eldridge Cleaver and Angela Davis. Laura is one of six children born to working-class Italian Catholic parents who still live in the neighborhood where they grew up in an industrial East Coast city. This is where their parents settled when they emigrated from Italy at the turn of the century.

When Tisha came out to her parents at the age of 15, they were supportive and very accepting. Their major concern was for Tisha and how vulnerable she could be as a Black lesbian in a world where prejudice is alive and well. Their fears were fed by memories of their own activism and also by the fact that Tisha's brother has embraced the lifestyle of a conservative corporate executive and has made no effort to understand or accept Tisha or his parents. Tisha's parents responded to her lesbianism from the perspective of educated, liberal activists whose own experiences informed their acceptance of differences in their children. As a result of my study of cultural differences, I was prepared to view Tisha's family according to the more typical descriptions of African American culture. Beverly Greene and Nancy Boyd-Franklin (1996) have reminded us of the "triple jeopardy" experienced by African American lesbians who are marginalized because of race, gender, and sexual orientation (p. 58).

However, the lesson for me as a therapist was *make no assumptions*. As soon as we learn the rule, we meet the exception. As feminist therapists, we can tend to take pride in our awareness of cultural norms, applying them indiscriminately. Another client told me one day, "If you don't live on my street, you won't know me until you come to visit." Coming to visit is about observing, listening, paying attention to what our clients tell us about where they live. Jackson and Greene (2000) have noted that it is important to know the client's degree of assimilation into the dominant cultural community and the client's family attitude about their assimilation.

Laura's family adopted a "don't ask, hope she doesn't tell" stance regarding Laura's lesbianism and her relationship with Tisha. According to them, the "girls are best friends," living together to save money. When Laura came out to her parents and sister just recently, her father stormed out of the room, her mother cried, and her sister became silent and has not spoken of Laura's sexuality to this day. When Laura and Tisha visit Laura's family, the whole family holds the pretense of friendship tightly. In contrast to this denial of their relationship, Tisha and Laura were about to invite both families and their many friends to a ceremony in which each would express to the other her desire to love and honor the relationship.

My initial reaction to Laura and Tisha's request for help was an enthusiastic feeling of anticipation. A commitment ceremony is usually where people go after they have "done their work," so these sessions will be fun! They will be about the icing on the wedding cake, so to speak. Could I have been idealizing the lesbian couple? Commitment ceremonies in the gay community challenge all of us to ask some important questions. As therapists, we must be clear about the issues that emerge when gays and lesbians decide to exchange promises publicly. The following are areas of discussion therapists must be ready to consider with clients:

1. Validity: What makes a relationship valid?
2. Stages of coming out: What is the nature of the process of moving from the closet all the way through to a public proclamation of a same-sex love? How typical are these stages, how universal?
3. Family traditions: What happens to these when they are challenged in a nontraditional manner?
4. Religious values: What happens to these when families organize around them as a way to maintain prejudice?

These are the questions that can pose dilemmas for the gay couple as well as for their families of origin and their families of choice. As we examine the questions, it is incumbent upon us as therapists to embrace values that will enhance our ability to understand, appreciate, and respect the differences between straight and gay cultures.

RELATIONSHIP VALIDITY

Men and women who develop and live in same-sex relationships face daily the heterosexist belief that their relationships are inferior to heterosexual arrangements, which are held up, in traditional theory, as normal and healthy. "Women who remove themselves from the ranks of the available are met with all the diagnostic, medical, legal, religious, and social power at the disposal of those who suffer their loss and resent their nerve" (Goodrich et al., 1988, p. 141).

As therapists, it behooves us to understand how relationship validity is measured in particular cultures. As I write this, family dinners in my history come to mind. I have vivid memories of those who got to sit at the main table and those who were relegated to the children's table. My single sister and her "boy" friend never quite made it to the adult table. A heterosexual marriage was the ticket.

As Tisha and Laura prepared their commitment ceremony, they struggled with images of heterosexual marriage ceremonies. Both grew up learning that someday they would marry a man, in a religious setting, with a legal document condoned by society. An alternative image came to them from their recent history in their lesbian community. They had been present at numerous commitment ceremonies planned by women for the purpose of having their union witnessed by their community. During the preparation, they asked questions like, "Is this union valid if we don't have a priest, break a glass, walk down an aisle, have Dad give me to a man?" These kinds of questions come from their own internalized heterosexism. This had to be articulated and explored in sessions.

As a therapist, my tendencies were to try to relieve Laura and Tisha of their worry about validity. A simple "Of course you are valid" coming from me was not enough. Tisha and Laura clearly did not need me as a cheerleader. They needed me as a witness. They needed me to be aware of their own deep-seated fears about validity and to provide a holding environment as they expressed and released their own biases.

STAGES OF COMING OUT

A commitment ceremony brings to awareness the many stages of coming out. Various writers have articulated these stages differently. One of these is Richard Niolon (2000, http://www.psychpage.com), who described the process as happening in this order:

> *Self-Recognition as Gay.* More than just an attraction to members of the opposite sex, it involves confusion, some attempts at denial, repression of feelings, anxiety, trying to 'pass,' counseling, and often religious commitment to 'overcome' sexuality. There may be some grief over . . . loss of a traditional heterosexual life.
>
> *Disclosure to Others.* Sharing one's sexual orientation with a close friend or family member; rejection may cause return to the Self-Recognition stage. . . . Usually disclosure is a slow process. As it progresses, a self-image of what it means to be gay develops, and the individual studies stereotypes, incorporates some information about gays while rejecting other information.
>
> *Socialization With Other Gays.* Provides the experience that the person is not alone in the world, but that there are other people like him or her. A positive sense of self, indeed pride, develops and is furthered in

this stage by acceptance, validation, support, and possibly contact with positive gay or lesbian role models.

Positive Self-Identification. Entails feeling good about one's self, seeking out positive relations with other gays or lesbians, and feeling satisfied and fulfilled.

Integration and Acceptance. Entails an openness and non-defensiveness about one's sexual orientation, or . . . being quietly open . . . available for support to others and not needing to hide . . .

When men and women decide to have a commitment ceremony, they may or may not have negotiated these first five stages. The public expression of promises can be considered one more stage in the coming-out process. When gays and lesbians have a public commitment ceremony, they are celebrating their sexuality, their sexual preference, and their right to have a long-term committed relationship. The assumption is that they have achieved a level of integration and acceptance of themselves to proclaim themselves publicly.

Both Tisha and Laura recognized and started to wonder about their feelings for girls at a young age. They were aware of attractions during their high school years. They struggled at that time of their lives with feelings of confusion and denial. For both of them, college was the time and place where they experimented with sexual encounters and relationships with other women and began to disclose and share their feelings with close friends. Tisha came out to her family at that time. Laura, however, withheld information about her sexuality from her family, knowing that it would be met with a negative reaction.

Both Tisha and Laura have described the relief and support they experienced as they began to socialize with other lesbians. As they became involved in gay and lesbian events, political work, and simple social gatherings, they began to develop more and more positive self-identification and more and more sense of self-fulfillment. They consider the onset of their relationship and their decision to have a commitment ceremony as a major step toward integration and acceptance.

If one or both members of the couple struggle with the decision to have a ceremony, the therapist might attempt to take them back to the previous stage of coming out. Therapists would do well to be ready to continually help gay clients with integration and acceptance of their sexuality. Heterosexist values seep in easily and we are all susceptible.

When gays and lesbians ask family and friends to celebrate with them and to serve as witnesses, the process becomes a coming out for families as well. As a therapist, I struggled with my own need to support my illusions that Laura's and Tisha's families would be present, supportive, happy, and goose-bump accepting. As our sessions progressed, these family voices became more audible in the office, and systemic issues abounded.

As an example, Tisha's and Laura's families were very concerned about the guest list for the event. There was a great deal of discussion in both households regarding which aunts, uncles, and cousins should be invited. Tisha and Laura struggled with whether they wanted their ceremony to be a gathering of supportive people or a forum for political change. They decided not to invite those who would be offended and found it difficult to determine who those might be. From a family systems perspective, preparation of a guest list turned out to be a powerful family intervention, especially in Laura's family. It stimulated a conversation that needed to happen, and it provided a forum for examination of homophobia in the system.

My tendency to view Tisha's sexuality as approved by the whole family was naïve at best. As she discussed her guest list, it became evident that her sexuality had been kept secret from her extended family. "Mental health clinicians should not view the apparent 'tolerance' of some families as if it constitutes approval or as if there are no African American families who . . . disown a lesbian family member" (Jackson & Greene, 2000, p. 89). As Tisha prepared her guest list, she and her parents began to reevaluate the extent and depth of homophobia in the family as a whole and in some members in particular. It was evident that certain family members would view a public ritual as "flaunting" or a public expression of "joining the enemy camp."

FAMILY TRADITIONS

Tisha and Laura discussed, in great detail, how they would express their promises to each other. They wondered aloud what, in fact, they wanted to say to each other. In most cultures, the words of a marriage ceremony are written in stone. They are very familiar and are invested with generations of tradition and, therefore, with tremendous power. Laura and Tisha did not want to be trapped by words that, to them, were meaningless, and they did not want to be trapped by their own reactivity to those words and concepts.

At one point, Laura and Tisha decided not to speak vows aloud as part of the ceremony. They wanted, instead, to show slides depicting many facets of their relationship. The reaction from their friends, their family of choice, was intense. They challenged Tisha and Laura with their belief that silence should not be part of the ceremony.

This reaction created in the two women a struggle with the question of whether they had the right to make a commitment without the use of words and how this would affect their responsibility to the lesbian community. Tisha, in particular, was affected by this struggle at her deepest core. In response to this challenge, she reacted with, "These are progressive people who themselves rejected other conventions. It was shocking to hear that one element of a ceremony was deemed critical."

Tisha used therapy sessions to examine her conviction that she and Laura were inviting people to a ceremony, not to witness the exchange of vows, but "to witness whatever it is that happens." Her work resulted in her strong statement that although she did not want to speak vows, she did want "the energy I am putting into the ceremony to be recognized as my *speaking.* . . . The work is not in justifying the wedding elements, but having a dialogue about its meaning to us . . . who dares to suggest it's not what we say it is?"

I struggled with my role as support, witness, one who empowers, and one who challenges. Yes, the personal is the political; however, as feminist therapists, we run the risk of turning every situation into a forum for social change. In this case, Tisha and Laura needed to be supported in their decision *not* to speak vows and empowered to request this same support from their lesbian family of choice.

DESIRE TO HAVE A CHILD

As Tisha and Laura discussed their commitment ceremony, they also announced their desire to have a child. The issues of lesbian parenting presents yet another challenge to everyone's image of how a family should look and function. Tisha's parents, upon hearing that their daughter wished to be the biological mother, went into their own parenting mode. Concern for Tisha's health was uppermost in their minds. Because of chronic back pain, Tisha could have difficulty with carrying a child. Laura's family expressed concerns. Unspoken, however, were other concerns that can emerge in all of us from internalized heterosexist bias:

1. How will a mixed-race child of two lesbians fare in this culture?
2. If Tisha cannot get pregnant, how easy or difficult will it be for a mixed-race lesbian couple to adopt?
3. Can lesbians really be good parents anyway?
4. Will there be enough community and family support to empower this couple?
5. If insemination is their choice, will there be a male parent successfully involved in this child's life?
6. If adoption is the choice, how will both women be equally involved, given that lesbians cannot legally adopt as couples?

Although these questions were not on the front burner during our sessions, they did come up and they played in the background of all of the ceremony planning. When lesbians discuss commitment and parenting with their families, it is inevitable that deeply held and deeply felt beliefs will get stirred in all concerned. For many family members, religious values are stored in the part of the self where prejudices also live. Even if not articulated, family members, and even lesbians themselves, struggle with questions regarding morality. Will "god" really bless this marriage, and is it really morally correct for lesbians to have a child?

As a feminist therapist, I found myself wanting to expound my belief that these women have the right to get married and have children. I had to remember that having a right does not automatically create a healthy environment for decision making. The issue of having a child was tabled for discussion at a later time even though I supported their right to add that into future plans. It was important to acknowledge the issues that having a baby can bring up for gay persons. Although we agreed to postpone the discussion, the issues were acknowledged.

Laura's sister continues to be the most adamant of all family members. She is explicitly opposed to the commitment ceremony, and she is horrified at the prospect of having a mixed-race child in the family who will be considered her niece or nephew. She holds tightly to her position, remains silent, and has not responded to her invitation. She therefore provides, for both families, an extreme position, which all others can reject.

Paradoxically, she offers other family members an opportunity to find their position of acceptance and to behave visibly different from her. In this context, Tisha describes her mother's acceptance in these terms: "My mother is very self-conscious and . . . it would look backwards to most folks for her not to be supportive, so her shunning me would be, ironically, more a negative commentary on her . . . than her having a gay child. For that I am grateful to history and my forerunners for having created an environment in which it is not politically correct or socially acceptable to discriminate against your child on the basis of sexual orientation."

CONCLUSION

At this point in time, Laura and Tisha have not yet had their ceremony. Their work in therapy serves to

1. Strengthen their resolve to find their own voices as they proclaim their commitment.
2. Clarify their beliefs about the politics of coming out as a couple.
3. Increase their ability to communicate with one another, their families of origin, and their families of choice regarding who they are in the world and what they need from supportive others.

4. Continue to examine and celebrate the differences between them.
5. Continue the journey toward enlarging their system by including a child.

The therapist's work is to

1. Validate a same-sex relationship by understanding the culture of the lesbian couple and the value of their struggle.
2. Understand that coming out is a profoundly personal, political, and spiritual process of knowing self in relation to other. The commitment ceremony makes this process public and, consequently, has an effect on family and friends. Be willing and able to include family and friends of the couple in therapy sessions.
3. Be ready to help clients examine their own internalized homophobia by bringing up the discussion of homophobia in sessions. Be willing to examine one's own homophobia and bring this up in peer consultation.
4. Be aware that a major source of homophobic thinking regarding a commitment ceremony is deeply held beliefs about good and evil, heaven and hell, punishment and salvation. Be ready and willing to examine these beliefs with clients.
5. Know that, among lesbians, there exists a multitude of different beliefs about the validity of public commitment ceremonies. Not all lesbians are heading off to Vermont to take advantage of the new laws regarding same-sex marriages. Help prepare clients for a variety of reactions that may come from their lesbian community, some of which may be positive, some of which may be negative. Be prepared to include some of the clients' important friends in therapy sessions.

Laura and Tisha have requested a session, or sessions, that will include some of the primary women in their family of choice. Their desire is to have an ongoing dialogue with these women to acknowledge their importance in Tisha's and Laura's lives, and to empower the connections. As a team, we will stay open to how the therapy process can be adjusted and recreated in the best interest of these women.

These two women have been a blessing to me as a therapist. I am learning from them about how difficult and how necessary it is to stay conscious and awake in relationship. I am learning, from observing myself in the process, how easy and harmful it is to fall asleep to my own internalized heterosexual bias and homophobia.

My work with Laura and Tisha underlines the following feminist therapy principles:

1. Diversity in systems is to be understood and respected.
2. *Culture* is the design, the tapestry portraying all of the ways a particular group of people has lived throughout their history. We must view our clients' cultures with reverence and intelligence.
3. *Heterosexism* is the belief that heterosexuality is the norm. *Homophobia* is a fear and mistrust of same-sex relationships. Living in our world has caused all of us to absorb both of these, and we must be able to identify these in our thinking and reacting.
4. In every system, there is a dynamic of power. It is vital that we are able to examine how power is attained, used, lost, and managed in every system.
5. Because of differences in culture, values, power arrangements, histories, and experiences, boundaries must be flexible and yet effective—boundaries between members of a couple, between persons and their families of origin, between couple and their families of choice, between therapist and all of the above. Boundaries must be continually examined and measured for effectiveness.
6. Our theories about these principles must be continuously examined for the presence of sexist beliefs. Sexism is insidious and is often embedded in what appear to be state-of-the-art psychotherapeutic theories. Feminist theory holds, as a value, a respectful and mutual arrangement of power in all systems, and we must be ready to examine every system, every theory, every interaction for the nature of all power arrangements.
7. Racism, sexism, and heterosexism form a powerful trio affecting psychodynamic theory and practice and affecting every therapist's feelings and reactions to every client. Not only must we continually examine our own internal biases about this interacting trio, but also we must continuously commit ourselves to the relational dialogue with our clients—the dialogues that change demands.

As therapist and client(s), we all participate in an evolving relationship in which everyone changes. Our hope for change, as therapists, resides in our ability to be authentic and respectful in our relationship with our clients. As I attend and participate in Laura and Tisha's ceremony, I will have the opportunity to celebrate their spirit and courage, and I will have the opportunity to remember that our work as clinicians extends far beyond the office.

REFERENCES

Goodrich, T. J., Rampage, C., Ellman, B., & Halstead, K. (1988). *Feminist family therapy: A casebook*. New York: Norton.

Greene, B., & Boyd-Franklin, N. (1996). African American lesbian couples: Ethnocultural considerations in psychotherapy. In M. Hill & R. Rothblum (Eds.), *Couples therapy: Feminist perspectives* (pp. 49–60). New York: Harrington Park Press.

Jackson, L. C., & Greene, B. (Eds.). (2000). *Psychotherapy with African American women: Innovations in psychodynamic perspectives and practice*. New York: Guilford Press.

Niolon, R. (2000). Coming out. *Gay and Lesbian Resources*. Retrieved from http://www.psychpage.com/learning/library/gay/comeout.html

4

"I CAN'T GO BACK": DIVORCE AS ADAPTIVE RESISTANCE

JOY K. RICE

Divorce has been blamed for everything from juvenile delinquency to social disintegration. Yet divorce, like any marker event or change, has the potential for development as well as regression; there can be tremendous growth and gain as well as intense pain and loss. Therapists working with women who have left oppressive and abusive marriages bear witness to the significant transformations that divorce can engender (Rice & Rice, 1986). In this chapter I outline several issues and strategies for the therapist working with women who are separated or divorced or in the process of divorce within a feminist and systemic therapeutic framework.

THE FICTIONAL FAMILY

Today nuclear families with employed fathers and stay-home mothers only represent about 3% of American households (Stacey, 1996). Traditional definitions of a "family," that is, White, intact, middle class, heterosexual with a male head of household and homemaker wife, have been critiqued by feminist family therapists as biased and inadequate. As feminist theory and practice has evolved, we have recognized that ethnic, cultural, racial, and sexual identity and historical time profoundly affect how we define our families and experience our place with our family. We have also observed that there are significant within-group differences among the families in any culture or society, and that people in the modern Western world continue to redefine family and kinship networks (Stacey, 1996). "Families" can be defined today as changing collectives in which close associates bond, come together, come apart, and reorganize across lifetimes (Baber & Allen, 1992).

Changes in family forms are directly related to the changes in marriage and divorce. Marriage is rapidly becoming "deinstitutionalized" because its primary elements—economic necessity, extended family bonds, and religious prohibitions—are being weakened by women's greater independence, fewer kin ties, and a generally more secular society. Marriage as a rite of passage to adulthood or as a predictable adult stage in the life cycle is losing importance as increasing numbers of young people never marry or choose to cohabitate indefinitely.

Nor is marriage today necessarily the prerequisite for parenthood. The increase in single-parent families headed by women has risen exponentially. Studies document portraits of unmarried, financially independent, adult women who are single mothers by choice, a social phenomenon that dramatically illustrates women's agency (Mannis, 1999). Marriage and parenthood are no longer a universal part of individual and family life cycle. Roughly 50% of marriages can be projected to end in divorce or permanent separation. Thus, divorce is becoming a more predictable part of the individual and family life cycle. Because women are twice as likely as men to initiate divorce, to experience more disillusionment with marriage, to parent alone, and to choose to live alone, divorce can be also seen as a feminist issue for the marriage and family therapist (Rice, 1994).

DIVORCE AS ADAPTIVE RESISTANCE

Divorce can be considered a form of resistance to women's oppression and inequality in the patriarchal family and a marker of societal and historical change and transformation (Rice, 1994). The traditional definition of patriarchy refers to the dominance of men and men's interests over women's interests, and the power of fathers over mothers and children in families. The contemporary phenomena of women choosing to live alone, to divorce, and to parent without a husband challenge the foundations of patriarchy— namely, the presence and authority of the father in the household. As women increasingly do not accept conditions of inequality, oppression, and abuse in their relationships and marriages, they are more likely to initiate divorce. It is easy to see how the phenomenon of divorce and women making it on their own threatens the established order, especially patriarchal marriage. With women no longer there to take care of the infrastructure, men, too, are forced to fend for themselves and to do more of "women's work."

A therapist can consider divorce in terms of ego and role loss, a catastrophic disruption in individual and family life cycle, and a societal disaster. Reframing divorce as a mode of adaptive resistance for women as well as a difficult and challenging opportunity for growth, differentiation, and development, however, changes our image of a female client from a passive victim to an active decision maker of her fate and life (Rice & Rice, 1986). An individual woman becomes an agent of personal change. Collectively, women become active agents of tremendous change within the culture who do have power to transform themselves and the society. The feminist therapist helps women experience this power.

DIVORCE IN SYSTEMS THEORY

A feminist view of divorce and its impact for women also has significant implications for how we consider and apply principles of psychotherapeutic practice. Some of the core elements of a family systems approach to therapy are the ideas of reciprocity, equilibrium, balance, and boundaries within families.

In systems theory, the central idea of *reciprocity* means that each person plays a part in the ongoing marital conflict by reinforcing the behavior of the other. Reciprocity has been used to explain the dynamics of a couple conflict, of the abusing husband and the victim wife who nags or hits him (Walters, 1988). Playing a part, however, does not mean that the part is equal. Nor is the power equal. The male abuser is likely to be stronger physically, and the husband more powerful economically. In a patriarchal society, a woman's power is largely covert and acquired through her relationship to a man, usually a husband. A feminist view of reciprocity recognizes the inequality of the situation, and how women may have to leave or divorce if they do not have the resources to fight back within the marriage or cannot equalize the power in the relationship.

In systems theory, all behaviors have an equalizing function designed to restore *equilibrium* in the self-contained family unit. However, this conceptualization of family organization is not value-free or necessarily egalitarian. A woman may have to completely disrupt the system, throwing it into disequilibrium with a separation and divorce, seeking to create a new life that is more independent, healthier, and freer. The feminist therapist recognizes, supports, and maximizes the possibilities for a woman who chooses to divorce and parent alone, but is also quite sensitive to the circumstances of other women who do not leave because they feel trapped by economic dependency and maternal responsibilities. Unequal access to economic resources and social support and unequal responsibility for children may lead a woman to stay in an oppressive marriage and even to engage in unhealthy behaviors to maintain the fragile equilibrium in the marriage. Destabilization of the system may be necessary and potentially very helpful long term, but problematic for such a woman.

The idea of a *balance* of forces is central to family systems theory. Bowen's (1971) study of families led him to define two counterbalancing life forces within relationships: a force toward individuality and a force toward togetherness. *Togetherness* is the need in everyone for approval from others, whereas *individuality* is the need in everyone to define a distinct self regardless of the approval of others. A balance between togetherness and individuality leads to positive self-differentiation as a person. Systems theory predicts that the higher the level of individual self-differentiation, the better a person will function in the midst of conflict, stress, and anxiety (Kerr, 1981). What is not explicated here is how gender roles and cultural norms permeate and influence these forces. Gender power relations in our society make it more difficult for women to act independently, and feminine role socialization emphasizes pleasing others at the expense of pleasing oneself. Furthermore, systems theory came out of Western culture, which strongly values the maintenance of appropriate boundaries and separation between family members and family generations. Individualism is touted in our American culture, but it is individualism for one gender, and it is often independence without attachment—hardly a choice most women would embrace.

A woman who divorces and becomes independent often finds herself feeling happy and liberated, yet worried about the effects of her decision on the people she loves, especially her children and parents. A therapeutic approach that is simultaneously systemic, feminist, and developmental helps her to carefully sort out her needs and rights without cutting off from her family. She becomes free to live her own life yet able to meet her children's needs and, if possible, to stay connected to her own family and to work with her ex-husband as a responsible coparent. An implicit, important goal of such an approach is to also help the woman understand her decision to marry and divorce in developmental terms, that is, in terms of delayed differentiation and delayed identity. The following two cases illustrate aspects of all these issues. Therapy involved both individual and family sessions with both biological and nonbiological members of newly created nontraditional "families" postdivorce, and the therapeutic paradigm presented does not depend on how many people are actually present in the session.

TWO CASE STUDIES

Elizabeth

Elizabeth was known as "Ellie" to her friends. A 52-year-old separated woman, she had grown up in the East and was a Midwest transplant, following her husband Gary as he got better jobs in academia and finally achieved tenure. A very bright woman herself, she married her husband because he was "brilliant and challenging." He was also subtly controlling and quite narcissistic, as she found out in the many years she spent supporting his career advances, raising their son and twin girls alone, and generally ignoring her own aspirations. Ellie initially came into therapy with me for symptoms of depression and anxiety. She was separated and had decided to divorce after 27 years of marriage.

Her husband was shocked by this decision because he felt he had been a good, stable husband and provider, albeit mostly absent. He wanted no part of couple therapy and refused treatment. Ellie strongly felt that even if he would make some superficial changes to increase the parity in the marriage, it would not matter, for she had slowly but irrevocably lost any feelings of intimacy for him. Furthermore, she was beginning to enjoy being alone and felt pleasure in her new independence and freedom. Ellie's parents were deceased, and she was on good terms with her only younger brother. Her father was killed in military action when she was very young, and her mother and grandfather raised her. As therapy progressed, she decided that in her marriage she had tried to reclaim a paternal love she never knew, and the love of a critical maternal grandfather she could never please.

Ellie: This is . . . really the first time in my life that I feel independent. I can't go back. And I feel like I'm finding out who I am. There was never any time for that, not that I would have made the time either. I just never questioned that they (husband and children) came first. It was just so easy not to question. Just to go along. He was doing so well, and I really admired him. Yet at the same time I grew to dislike him, and also I think myself. There was just no respect from him, no understanding of what it was like to hold the whole show together. Like the time I told you about going to the hospital with the twins and he didn't make it. I truly believe he loves Carrie and Cassie, but to this day he couldn't see what he did wrong, that he always ultimately puts his needs above theirs and mine. It's not that he ever physically abused me, but now I'd say what I lived through was emotional abuse.

Joy: And it was a slow process of unraveling your feelings about that neglect, abuse, because on the surface it looked good?

Ellie: Exactly. My friends, my brother, they think I'm nuts for leaving him, because our life, the trappings of it, it just looked so good. And for years I thought I was crazy, too. I'd question why I couldn't make him happy, what was the matter with me? It wasn't until my depression got so bad, you know at one point, like a zombie, going through the motions, so bad that I could finally face how much I had lost. How stifled I felt. But I can't just blame Gary. I was looking for a man like Gary, a man who would be all the things I couldn't be, like in that dream about my Grandpa Carl and wanting him to tell me I was good.

Joy: That's something it took some time to realize too, the deeper reasons why you got married and how you put your own identity on hold.

Ellie:	Yes, I wasn't very mature. I probably wanted a real father, but (laughs) instead I got another child. A very controlling child— do you know for years, he never told me what he made or that the genetic company was only in his name? Of course, I paid in spades for that ignorance. It's been hard financially, but I'm making it now. Even without any maintenance. The promotion will help. And did I tell you I have decided to go back to school?
Joy:	No, that's wonderful! You've really made some important changes in your life, on your own: by yourself.
Ellie:	I feel so much better, I hardly recognize who I was just two years ago. That spunky little person, you know the one who left the track? She's back and running!
Joy:	Ellie, she's not just back, she's transformed.
Ellie:	(silence) There was a lot of pain, but yes, I'm different. It's my turn.

Cases like Elizabeth illustrate how the exploding divorce rate is not only about exposing battering and abuse. Ellie spent years trying to maintain the fragile equilibrium in her marriage based on an inequitable division of power and a hierarchical system in which Gary's best interests and desires dominated while hers were subordinated. The subtle denigration, lack of praise and support, disrespect, and assumptions of one-sided accommodation and denial of these attitudes when confronted were her daily bread. She initially blamed herself, and the blame became internalized into self-denigration and depression. Getting a job and getting into therapy helped her recognize how she had married before she knew who she was, how she sought an emotional intimacy she had not experienced in her family of origin, and how her husband developmentally could not give that to her.

Divorce is frequently about women being tired of being the emotional caretakers of relationships, the managers of intimacy, single parents who are married. Women are seeking equality not only in the division of labor, money, and power but also in the responsibility for the emotional labor and management in the relationship. Indeed the divorce rate mirrors women's disillusionment with this quest. In therapy many women, like Ellie, come to realize how they must find their own voice and path, and how the painful and developmental process of divorce propels them into working out a much better balance between intimacy and identity (Rice & Rice, 1986).

Society's stereotype of the older divorced woman is a picture of loneliness and bitterness. Yet the great majority of older women who divorce report that they have grown stronger emotionally; are more adaptable, self-reliant, and happier; and have forged new identities. After an adjustment period that is often difficult, the divorce experience becomes a developmental spur to change in ways they had not thought possible (Hayes, Anderson, & Blau, 1993; Patterson, 2001).

One year after our initial course of therapy, Ellie returned to therapy to discuss her new situation and, in particular, her brother's rejection of her new partner, a woman. Ellie had also been helped by a divorce support group of women in which she learned from the life experiences of other women. In the process she became increasingly close to a long-time friend, Liz, who had never married. Ellie's new household and "family" consisted of herself, her oldest child, Jason (age 23, a college student), Liz, and Liz's elderly aunt. Ellie was not only reparenting herself and discovering herself, but she was also breaking new ground in forming a family of "creation" (Weston, 1992).

Another way in which women resist the patriarchy of marriage and dependency on a man is to choose to partner with a woman. In one study about 5% of older divorced women partnered with a woman for the first time after the demise of their marriage (Hayes et al., 1993). This, too, was Ellie's choice. After some family sessions that included her new partner, her children were fairly accepting of the divorce and her involvement with Liz. Liz was not a new person in their lives, but what was new was the open intimacy between the two women and the creation of a new household.

After an initial period of adjustment and conflict, her twin girls (age 25) expressed to Ellie that it was great to finally have an "aunt" and "grandma," but that they would never tolerate three mothers! Ellie maintained a distant friendship with Gary. She had worked through her anger and blame, had a much more realistic appreciation of their individual contributions to the demise of the marriage, and was ultimately more compassionate about her brother's difficulty in accepting her new situation.

After their divorce, Gary threw himself even more into his work. He rationalized that the divorce had more to do with Ellie's feelings for women than with his behavior. He was content to be a distant part of the family, and as is common, saw his grown children more than he ever had before the divorce. Not surprisingly, a large body of research has found that women make greater psychological gains after divorce than men in terms of happiness, self-esteem, and adjustment. Such effects have been found up to 10 years post-divorce (Diedrick, 1991). Divorce is about change and transformation, crisis and conflict, all precursors and motivators for development. Because the majority of women get on with their lives, or more aptly, reclaim their lives, there is no regret, little anger, and a fair amount of forgiveness and compassion for themselves, their ex-spouses, and their families (Hayes et al., 1993).

Deborah

Deb, age 32, was a divorced single mother with a 12-year-old daughter, Sarah. Deb was an adult survivor of incest. Her mother was deceased, and her father was a former alcoholic, elderly, and now retired. With the help of therapy, her family, and Al-Anon, Deb had confronted and made peace with her father. She no longer was afraid of and angry with him but saw him now as old and pathetic.

Deb had just gotten on her feet after the divorce. She conscientiously had maintained her job and household, worked through the prior sexual abuse, and had a cordial coparenting relationship with her ex-husband, when a bomb dropped. She discovered she was pregnant by an old boyfriend whom she actively disliked. All her old guilt over her situation came to the fore again with a vengeance. Her sister told her she should have an abortion. Her best friend encouraged her to give up the baby for adoption, saying she could never provide for it financially especially because the father was a "deadbeat." Deb agonized over being a single parent again, yet strongly resisted the pressure to marry a man she did not love or respect.

No wonder she felt such intense guilt, for with either alternative she failed as a "good mother." Moms who give up children or who have abortions are castigated, but so are women who have children outside of marriage, especially if they happen to be poor. Only the media romanticizes the fictional, exciting lives of young, beautiful, affluent single parents. In White, American, middle-class culture, motherhood is glorified most often in the context of a male–female relationship.

Nontraditional mothers are not as valued as traditional mothers. All mothers in our culture are penalized by the lack of institutional supports for child care and child welfare, but penalties are especially punitive for women who reproduce and parent apart from male control (DiLapi, 1989). With the help and support of therapy, Deb ultimately did decide to have the child, a healthy boy, Daniel. Her household changed dramatically when the baby arrived, and even more so when a new boyfriend, Ted, moved in with her. Her cooperative family mix of kin and nonkin now included her ex-husband, her daughter, her infant son, the son's father, her new partner, and her teenage niece, Sharon, who baby-sat Daniel in exchange for room and board.

The themes in working with Deb and her family in therapy revolved around her consuming feelings of guilt and inadequacy, particularly with regard to her children after the divorce. She often felt like she could not provide enough for them emotionally and financially, and she questioned her judgments as a single parent on issues of discipline, boundaries, and engagement. I saw a different picture. The family was inventive; the mother resilient, creative, and devoted.

Deb: Sometimes I feel like I'm a bad parent.
Joy: Why, Deb?
Deb: I always worry about whether they have enough, there's just not enough of me to go around. Sometimes I think I never should have divorced, then we could make it.

Joy:	But you are "making it."
Deb:	I had to tell Sarah today she couldn't have money for the video she wants, and she won't be able to go with her friend on vacation over break unless her father finds the money. I'm still in debt from Christmas. You know how I want them to have everything. I'd give them anything (cries).
Joy:	Deb, do you really think that Sarah will think you're a bad mom if you tell her there's only so much money, that she may have to baby-sit or earn some dollars to pay for her extras?
Deb:	Sometimes I think she's ashamed of me, like when I couldn't pay the rent. This morning she was really mad at me. We had a fight over the video money. But maybe I can talk to her tonight again, maybe explain that . . . (pause)
Joy:	That your love for her isn't going to be measured by how much money or things you can give her?
Deb:	Yeah. I know that's true, but it's so hard to explain it to a kid sometimes.
Joy:	You so much want them not to feel your pain, not to experience any fallout from the divorce or from your situation. You want to be a perfect mother. Do you think some of that has to do with feeling guilty, irrationally guilty over the divorce?
Deb:	I do feel guilty. I know I can't completely protect them or give them everything even though I try. And maybe that's not good either. Sometimes I worry that I'm "too much" mother for the kids.
Joy:	Deb, do you remember what you told me about how your parenting had changed after you divorced? How you thought it was better?
Deb:	It was better; it felt good to be able to make decisions independently. I felt like I had more control and Sarah and I were on the same beam. But there have been so many changes, Daniel, Daniel's father, Ted.
Joy:	And Sharon's living with you now, too. So maybe this isn't just about Sarah's trips or videos, it's about you and her and both of you negotiating a new relationship with a lot of new other people involved that significantly change things.
Deb:	It is complicated. And she probably is confused about where we stand now. But I know she knows I love her.
Joy:	So maybe you can have that talk with her tonight not just about the money, but about how the family has changed and where your relationship fits in, and how your bond with her is still strong.

The anxiety and guilt that single moms go through can be at times overwhelming. My goals in therapy with Deb were to help her understand that lack of material possessions was not a character defect or family failing, to remind her that she is a good and creative parent, and that since the divorce she has been able to feel more competent and independent. In a session with Sarah and Ted, I continued to reframe the conflict with her daughter as one related to her struggle to form a new family. This helped everyone understand that they were in the process of transforming their relationships in the midst of many other new relationships, and that was not bad. In fact, there was the potential for creating a healthier, more independent bond as Sarah approached adolescence. No matter how rebellious, angry, manipulative, or guilt-provoking her daughter might become, Deb's stronger sense of identity and competence could inoculate her against taking her children's feelings personally.

Therapists working from an individual therapy paradigm are more apt to look for intrapsychic causes and individual behavioral solutions to life problems. Thus single parents may be advised to analyze their own dysfunctional contributions to the conflicts, to grieve, and ultimately to adjust to the multiple losses entailed in divorce. All of the work of therapy would occur with the individual client. In family therapy with one person, in contrast, behavior is conceptualized as embedded in both the individual client, and also in a web of multiple reciprocal relationships. Thus the therapy might include multigenerational work with family-of-origin members, children, as well as current partners and ex-spouses. Even if other family members never enter the therapy office, the multigenerational emotional process is always the context of therapy. Family therapy is defined by a theoretical paradigm rather than by the number of people in the room.

Feminist family therapy applies a cultural interpretation to the conflicts and struggles that individuals face. This social constructivist stance helps divorced single mothers appreciate how the patriarchal family structure and social policy make it hard for mothers to succeed without a man in the picture. This understanding of how larger systems impact on their behavior also ameliorates irrational self-blame. For example, in Deb's case, Daniel's father refused to get a job. Yet, the courts awarded Deb a very small child support payment that he infrequently paid and stopped paying altogether when Daniel was 5 months. She was very angry with him. However, to her credit, she realized that depriving Daniel of contact with his father who, despite his job failures, was responsible in terms of visitation and child care, would not help her son.

Today we have many more joint custody arrangements, but mothers still bear the primary responsibility for child rearing. Yet these efforts fail to be compensated for, as only about half of child support payments are paid in full, another 25% of payments are not fully paid, and 25% are not paid at all (U.S. House of Representatives, 1996). The widespread failure of fathers to pay child support, even among those who can do so, can be also seen as backlash, a reaction against the mothers and wives who leave them.

Thus, my other goal was to help Deb see the child support problem as structural and systemic. She appreciated this new perspective and was able to complain that the system was more compassionate toward her baby's "deadbeat" father than toward herself. She pointed out how she had survived bankruptcy; struggled with two jobs; employed a live-in niece as babysitter; got clothes at Goodwill; sought out food stamps, coupons, and free household items whenever she could; and, despite everything, prudently banked a part of her ex-husband's child support in a savings account for Sarah's college education. Thus, with encouragement, Deb proactively researched her options and went to court. The court appointed a public defender for the father because he said he was under stress.

Deb: Stress! Can you believe it? I can't afford a lawyer, but they give him a public defender because he's under stress. Stress, sitting at the clubhouse all day watching TV! Stress, living at his mom's and getting a handout from her and having her buy diapers and formula. I can't believe it! But they do this to mothers, you know. We're supposed to have it together no matter what, to come up with the time, the money. It doesn't count that I'm under mega stress, and that I have another kid and two jobs.

Joy: You're absolutely right, Deb. Moms, even if they parent alone with no help or support, are unfairly expected to take the brunt of responsibility. And it is unjust. What are you going to do about it?

Deb was able to see that it was the system, not just her. That knowledge empowered her. She made up a special file in which she put all the papers and the notes from the calls to the court personnel and to Daniel's father. This relieved her guilt, blame, and frustration. Therapy "expanded the context," illustrated that her dilemma was not just her own, but the result of an inequitable system. And after doing all she could, Deb did come to peace, realizing that Daniel's father might go to jail if he continued in arrears. Unlike the old days, she did not blame herself.

Working with Deb and her ever-changing "family" reinforced my belief that the life-cycle narrative at times may be progressive, stable, or regressive but is never one-dimensional. An alternative to the traditional linear, one-dimensional biological portrayal of a woman's life course might instead view the family life cycle in terms of multiple and shifting attachments, separations and reattachments with family, children, friends, spouses, ex-spouses, and significant others. It becomes the therapist's task to appreciate the many meanings and layers of these attachments and separations for the client's development within and apart from kinship bonds.

The family life cycle as it has been traditionally defined in family therapy literature is largely mythological (Rice, 1994). It is more helpful to look at the family life cycle as a constructed narrative with the potential for new narratives to emerge in each culture, society, and historical era. Even our static ideas and "truth" about marker events based on biology and the ability to bear children have changed over time and continue to change. In some cultures now and throughout history, the child becomes an adult with a pregnancy at age 14 or earlier. In 21st-century Western culture, a woman is not defined as an adult by a pregnancy and may never have a child. More and more women never marry, and many more cohabitate like Deb rather than marry, even when they have a child. The "normal" developmental pathway for a woman has perhaps not so much changed as never existed except as a social construct for three decades of the 20th century (Coontz, 1992).

CONCLUSION

Divorce is generally considered a disruption in the family life cycle. However, I would suggest that therapists need to reframe it instead as a fairly predicable life stage with potential for positive growth and gain as well as disequilibrium and loss (Rice & Rice, 1986). When half of all marriages end in divorce, it cannot be considered a "paranormative" event in the family life cycle. For the feminist therapist, divorce can be seen as an opportunity for a woman's healthy identity redefinition and ego differentiation that has been delayed. Many women use separation and divorce, as well as the choice to live alone, as a way to resist the oppression, neglect, and abuse they may have experienced in former relationships. Other women fear reenacting the same scenario with another man or that they will replicate their parents' marriages and the abuse of their mothers. Women living and parenting alone today are also implicitly creating new family forms of kin and nonkin relationships.

The systemic concepts of reciprocity, equilibrium, balance, and boundaries come into question for the therapist who applies a gender and cultural context to the situation of the woman client choosing to divorce. The task of the therapist is to avoid pathologizing separation and singleness, to support the client's path in developing new arrangements and family forms, and to help each woman understand how the society and culture impose a deficit model on her efforts.

REFERENCES

Baber, K. M., & Allen, K. R. (1992). *Women and families: Feminist reconstructions*. New York: Guilford Press.

Bowen, M. (1971). Family therapy and family group therapy. In H. Kaplan & B. Sadock (Eds.), *Comprehensive group psychotherapy* (pp. 384–421). Baltimore: Williams & Wilkins.

Coontz, S. (1992). *The way we never were: American families and the nostalgia trap.* New York: Basic Books.

Diedrick, P. (1991). Gender differences in divorce adjustment. *Journal of Divorce and Remarriage, 14,* 33–45.

DiLapi, E. M. (1989). Lesbian mothers and the motherhood hierarchy. In F. W. Bozett (Ed.), *Homosexuality and the family* (pp. 101–121). New York: Harrington Park Press.

Hayes, C., Anderson, D., & Blau, M. (1993). *Our turn: The good news about women and divorce.* New York: Pocket Books.

Kerr, M. (1981). Family systems theory and therapy. In A. S. Gurman & H. P. Kniskern (Eds.), *Handbook of family therapy* (pp. 226–264). New York: Brunner/Mazel.

Mannis, V. J. (1999). Single mothers by choice. *Family Relations, 48,* 121–128.

Patterson, W. (2001). *The unbroken home: Single-parent mothers tell their stories.* New York: Haworth Press.

Rice, J. K. (1994). Reconsidering research on divorce, family life cycle, and the meaning of family. *Psychology of Women Quarterly, 18,* 559–584.

Rice, J. K., & Rice, D. G. (1986). *Living through divorce: A developmental approach to divorce therapy.* New York: Guilford Press.

Stacey, J. (1996). *In the name of the family: Rethinking family values.* Boston: Beacon.

U.S. House of Representatives, Ways and Means Committee. (1996). *Overview of entitlement programs: 1996 Green Book.* Washington, DC: U.S. General Accounting Office.

Walters, M. (1988). Toward a feminist perspective in family therapy. In M. Walters, B. Carter, P. Papp, & O. Silverstein (Eds.), *Gender patterns in family relationships* (pp. 15–30). New York: Guilford Press.

Weston, K. (1992). The politics of gay families. In B. Thorne & M. Yalom (Eds.), *Rethinking the family: Some feminist questions.* (pp. 119–139). Boston: Northeastern University Press.

5

REPAIRING THE WORLD: AN ADOLESCENT AND HER PARENTS

KAETHE WEINGARTEN

> The Jewish ideal is in some sense a political one: not the perfection of individual souls, but *tikkun olam*—the repairing of the world. We are bound to commit ourselves to creating a more just, more whole world. This can take place only through interactions between people and between communities . . . . (Strassfield & Strassfield, 1980, p. 47)

When Sharon called me about her 12-year-old daughter, Molly, I was listening to a National Public Radio account of the recent school shootings in Jonesboro, Arkansas, by 11- and 13-year-old boys. I sensed great urgency in her voice. I had worked with her family a few times briefly and knew that Sharon, her husband Mark, and their daughter Molly were devoted to each other despite the regular intrusion of cycles of anger and withdrawal.

Sharon informed me that she and Mark wanted the appointment for the family because there had been a great deal of tension the previous few weeks, capped by a note from Molly apologizing for her angry outbursts. Molly had written that she was so filled with anger and hatred that she could not contain herself. She warned them, "Don't have any guns or poison in the house." Sharon and Mark feared that she was potentially a danger to herself and to others, perhaps even to them.

I agreed to meet with the family and we scheduled an appointment a few days later. I did not suggest that I meet with the parents alone or with Molly alone, although many therapists would have. Much of my theoretical work has been devoted to challenging the cultural discourses that promote the values of autonomy and independence so relentlessly that interdependence between parents and children, particularly adolescents, is undermined. The traditional psychodynamic perspective on adolescence posits adolescence as the second phase of separation and describes the work of this phase as a painful and prolonged severance (Blos, 1962). The dominant cultural messages bombarding adolescents and their parents at every turn trivialize their relationship, valorize the adolescents' relationship with peers, and encourage silence not voice in relation to each other (for an alternative view, see Weingarten, 1997, 1998a). In the work that I do, I try to counter these dominant messages in favor of others that support parent–adolescent interaction and promote parents as resources for struggling adolescents. Congruent with a systemic approach, I view the idea of separation as a "restraint" that limits rather than enhances problem-solving in families with adolescents (Bateson, 1972; Dickerson & Zimmerman, 1992). I help families set aside a preoccupation with the "task" of separation to observe what their particular adolescent needs now.

Although labels are as good for chafing against as defining oneself, for good or ill, I call myself a postmodern narrative feminist family therapist (Weingarten, 1998b). Let me select out postmodern and narrative to elaborate. By *postmodern*, I am referring to a worldview that posits that "truth," knowledge, and power are negotiated by persons in relationship (Foucault, 1980; Freedman & Combs, 1996). This translates into working with families to understand what people mean in the context of their own lives, not in relation to a set of a priori normative criteria. By *narrative*, I mean that I see my task as the creation of a conversational space in which people can notice aspects of their experience that contradict restrictive views of themselves, others, and the problems that beset them. When this occurs, choices for the development of new stories about their lives become possible and preferable. Because the stories we tell about ourselves construct our experience rather than represent it (White, 1995), people who tell new stories about themselves are creating paths for new thinking, feeling, and action. Thus, a postmodern narrative therapist does not explain, advise, or intervene, but rather tries to generate possibilities for the client to develop alternative storylines.

It is also important to me to try to understand how some people's experiences become dominant and other people's experiences—often those of women, children, people of color, homosexuals, and people with different abilities—are pushed to the edge. I find discourse analysis helpful for this purpose, and I have written about this elsewhere (Weingarten, 1997, 1998b). I have been particularly interested in how North American culture trivializes and devalues the parent–adolescent relationship and emphasizes the mechanisms by which adolescents are "detached" from their parents. Certainly, one of these mechanisms is the ideological position that pervades standard mental health practice: "adolescents need privacy to work in therapy." By meeting with adolescents and their parents together, I am counterposing this idea with another: that a parent and adolescent can benefit from hearing each other's stories and that each may be a resource for change for the other. This way of working is consistent with a feminist ethic of collaboration. It is also consonant with the cultural values of many ethnic groups, including Jewish, Latino, African American, and Italian families. Therapists are turning to collaborative models to assist them in becoming "appreciative allies" in their clients' lives (Madsen, 1999). The spirit of this kind of clinical work fits feminist practice principles well.

CASE CONSULTATION

The description of the consultation that follows is taken from five pages of single-spaced notes that I wrote immediately after the session. It is a narrative reconstruction of the interview, based now on memory and the writerly desire to make the speech of each person sound believable. Sections in italics provide my reasons for my part in the conduct of the interview.

Hours before the interview, Sharon called to inform me that Molly was angry about coming to the appointment and angry that she had not been consulted. I thanked Sharon for the warning and told her I would deal with it in the session. The three arrived just after a downpour, looking weary, as we all were, after several days of unpredictable rains that had flooded streets and homes, taking a toll on everybody. Molly sat slumped on the couch, sticking her long legs out into the middle of the room. Her mother sat beside her; her father on a chair across from, but close to, her. Sharon was the first to speak.

Bridging Between Father and Daughter

Sharon: Molly doesn't want to be here. She's upset that I made this appointment without consulting her.

Kaethe: Well, let's talk for a bit. At least you and Mark can tell me why you wanted to come, and then we can see what happens. Molly, I think it's important that you find out why your parents wanted this appointment.

Both parents start to talk at the same time. Exchanging looks with Mark, Sharon begins by telling me about the fighting of recent weeks and then describing the note itself. Then Mark speaks.

Mark: I'm upset about the last few weeks, of course. But I'm particularly worried about the last line of the note. I am truly worried that Molly has so much hate and anger in her.

At first, as her parents are talking, Molly looks surprised, even taken aback. Then tears run down her cheeks, and she draws her legs up and curls into herself.

Kaethe:	You look really upset that your Dad is saying this. Is this the first time you've heard him say that he took that part of the note seriously?
Molly:	(Nodding. With sarcasm . . .) Cops have guns.
Mark:	What does that mean?

Molly is crying.

Kaethe: I can't know for sure what you are feeling, but I am wondering if you're upset because you feel your Dad has misunderstood you in some way?

Molly nods in agreement.

Kaethe:	Is your Dad a worrying sort in general?
Molly:	I don't know. (She is using her sleeve to wipe her tears.)
Kaethe:	Well, let's give his worry a number. If the most a person could worry is a 10, and that person is just a mess, worrying all the time, and the least a person could worry is a 1, and that person is always mellow, and nothing bothers him, what would you rank your Dad?
Molly:	A five.
Kaethe:	And your Mom?
Molly:	A five also.
Kaethe:	What about you?
Molly:	I don't know.
Kaethe:	Well that's interesting. I'm glad that I asked you these questions because I might have thought you were feeling misunderstood by your Dad's worry that you might hurt yourself or someone else because you think he is just a big worrier. But that doesn't seem to be how you think about your Dad. Are you aware of any events in the world or in your Dad's life that could account for his worry about your anger?
Molly:	No.

This was a remarkable response considering the publicity surrounding the school shootings in Jonesboro.

Mark:	I would rank myself much higher than Molly did. I do worry a lot.
Kaethe:	Do you think your worry might contribute to your alarm about Molly's note?
Mark:	Definitely.
Sharon:	I think Mark's inner world is a lot like Molly's and I think when he gets stressed he feels a lot of rage . . .
Mark:	No, sadness. Not rage.

Sharon:	Well, when you were younger, I think you did feel rage.
Mark:	True.
Kaethe:	Molly, did you know that when your Dad was younger he was the kind of person who felt rage?

I observe through the verbal and nonverbal interaction in this family that Molly is less comfortable with her father than her mother, a frequent by-product of patriarchal societal arrangements in the work/family matrix. I am asking questions that may promote more understanding between them, bridging the distance between father and daughter.

Molly:	No.
Kaethe:	What do you think about that?
Molly:	Well, I think all kids feel rage.

Situating Molly's Anger

Kaethe:	You do? Tell me about that. What are the kinds of things that young people feel rage about?
Molly:	Well, if they have a teacher who is bad and nobody does anything about the teacher. And if their parents force them to do things that they don't want to do and they don't believe they should have to do. And if they feel they deserve something better than what they've got. And if they put in a lot of effort in a subject, like art, and gotten a bad grade because they weren't good at art but they really tried.
Kaethe:	So, Molly, what I hear is that you think kids get angry when they think things aren't fair. Am I putting it accurately? That kids react to injustice?
Molly:	Yes.
Kaethe:	Is that something you do, protest unfairness and injustice?
Molly:	Protest is when workers don't like what their boss is doing and then they protest.
Kaethe:	Yes, workers might protest, like a strike or a demonstration. But I meant protest like get angry or upset *about* something. That kind of protest. Is that what you think you do?
Molly:	Yes, but it doesn't work.
Kaethe:	Hmm. What do you think about a young person who is against unfairness and injustice? Does that suit you? Do you think that is a good thing for you?
Molly:	A good thing.

An alternative story develops out of what is latent in the story being told but is not recognized as being present or, if recognized, is not seen as important. Given the opportunity to talk about why she was angry, Molly recounted a story of anger and distress about unfairness.

Kaethe:	OK. Let me ask your parents for a moment what they think about a young person who protests unfairness and injustice. Mark, what do you think about a young person who protests against injustice or unfairness?
Mark:	I think that Molly thinks we are being unfair when we want her to do more homework or watch less TV. And that's the problem. She gets angry then.
Kaethe:	So sometimes she sees unfairness where you judge there isn't any. So that can be a problem. But, in general, what do you think of a person who is sensitive to injustice?
Mark:	Well, I think it is natural to protest injustice at her age. And I think it's a hellavu lot better than being passive, which I don't think is healthy.
Kaethe:	Sharon, what do you think about a person who protests injustice and unfairness?
Sharon:	I respect it. I think it's a good thing.

Connecting Through Protesting Injustice

Kaethe:	Molly, are there any ways that your parents communicate to you that they respect your protesting what you believe is unjust or are there any ways they let you know they think it's a good thing?
Molly:	My mother encourages me.
Kaethe:	How does she do that?
Molly:	I talk about my teacher and how nothing changes. She agrees with me. Also, she's on the school council.
Kaethe:	She listens to what you say and she validates what you feel. Did I get that right?
Molly:	Yeah, she agrees with me. She's frustrated too. I was on the student council and we wrote five notes to the principal and he thanked us and told us he would work on these things and nothing has happened at all. We gave him ideas about lunches, time in the corridors, and backpacks. The school isn't fair for the kids who are too poor to pay for their lunches. That's about half the kids who come from downtown.

There's a rule in my school that you are only supposed to have 45 minutes of homework a night in any class and there is one teacher who gives the kids five hours of homework and they come into school with circles under their eyes. I could go on and on. There was a girl who was wearing a tank top and the principal made her put on a sweater, but it was boiling hot. Some kids told him it was unfair, and a teacher was there, but he didn't listen. It's not just the kids they don't listen to; it's the teachers, too. The only people who count are the School Board members and the people higher up. |

Molly comes from a middle-class, Jewish family and both of her parents work full time. In her own language, she is putting forth a class analysis of the problems within her suburban middle school. I interpret her speaking as confirming that it was helpful for me to bring out what she is angry about rather than keeping the focus on the anger per se.

Kaethe: Does your Dad show he thinks your protest is a good thing?

Molly: I don't know. I don't think so.

Kaethe: Maybe that is something you and he could work on, helping him show you more support. You know, your Dad has a lot of experience from his work developing strategies to make systems—like a school—change. I wonder whether he would have any ideas about strategy for you?

Molly: (Grumpily) He never does anything at school. He's too busy.

Kaethe: Sounds like you wish he were more active at your school. Maybe he could be active with *you* by talking about what happens at school. Maybe he would have some ideas for you?

Mark: (Nods)

Kaethe: Actually, let me get clear about something. Do you always express your anger when you feel it?

Molly: Definitely not.

Kaethe: What happens to the anger when you feel that your mother, or father for that matter, support you? Does the anger get smaller or bigger?

Molly: Smaller.

Kaethe: Is that a good or a bad thing for you?

I want her to be the judge of whether or not experiencing less anger is a positive or negative situation for her life.

Molly: Good.

Challenging the Cultural Idea of Anger as a Single Entity

Kaethe: So let me just see if I understand this. You have a lot of anger about injustice, and sometimes the anger gets expressed and sometimes it doesn't. Let me just make a box here. Anger Kept In   Anger Let Out and I'm going to add two words that we haven't talked about yet. Anger Constructive and Anger Destructive. Do you know what I mean by that?

I often draw pictures or diagrams to make points. I find that many people remember ideas better if they are also presented graphically. It also creates a literal opportunity to put our heads together, as we bend toward each other to study the page.

Molly: (Gives an equivocal shake of her head.)

Kaethe: I mean that there are ways of managing anger that are constructive, helpful, and ways that are destructive, harmful. I'll explain how I'm using them in a moment. You sound to me like you are really sensitive to injustice, unfairness, and ineffectiveness. It also sounds to me like you are aware of class and power differences in your school. I mean, you've noticed that students have the least amount of power and that the teachers don't have much more. At the same time, some teachers don't follow the rules, like the one who gives the kids five hours of homework every night so that they come in to school the next day with circles under their eyes . . .

Sharon: She doesn't have that teacher.

Kaethe: So you notice what's unfair even if it doesn't directly affect you, like the girl who was told to put the sweater on. That bothered you even though nothing was said to you. So, can we all look together at these squares? Let's take them one at a time. If you had to rate yourself as low, medium, or high for each of these boxes, how would you rate yourself, Molly, in terms of constructive anger kept in?

Molly: That's high.

Kaethe: And constructive anger let out?

Molly: That's high also.

Kaethe: What about destructive anger kept in?

Molly: Middle.

Kaethe: And destructive anger let out?

Molly: Low.

Kaethe: OK. So let's look at each box. You rate yourself high on letting constructive anger out. Can you give an example of that?

Sharon: I can. We were driving and Molly saw a gun shop and she said, "I want to do something about that because I don't think people should be able to have guns."

Molly: But nothing happened. I didn't do anything. I just have the idea and get angry.

Kaethe: What happens when you get angry about something and then don't feel that you can do anything about it?

Molly: Get angrier.

Using Parents as a Resource for Change

Kaethe: Do you think that maybe at your age, for a while, you might need some help from adults to do something with your ideas about social justice? Would a phrase like "social activism energy" fit for you?

Molly: Yes.

Kaethe: Do you think that maybe you could work with a parent to do something that might make you feel more effective in using your social activism energy?

Sharon: Like working at a shelter or an animal shelter.

Molly nods.

Kaethe:	Do you think you could use any help with any of the other boxes?
Molly:	I don't know.
Kaethe:	Is it hard to figure out if you need help?
Molly:	Well, I would like the keeping destructive anger in to be lower.
Kaethe:	How might that happen?
Molly:	I can talk about it.
Kaethe:	What about that note you wrote? Where does that fit?

Long pause.

Sharon:	Could it be letting out your anger constructively because you expressed your anger and then we were able to talk about it?
Molly/Mark:	Yes.
Mark:	What about the anger toward us?
Kaethe:	Is that destructive or constructive?
Molly:	Some of both.
Kaethe:	Some of the anger you direct at your parents is constructive and relates to injustices you feel from them but some may be a kind of spraying of anger on them that comes from other angers?
Molly:	Probably.
Kaethe:	(To everyone). Do you think there is a lot of spraying or not so much?
Sharon:	I think it's quite a lot.
Kaethe:	Maybe there are ways you can work as a family to help with the spraying also.

They all nod.

Kaethe:	Good. So I think we accomplished a lot today. I feel that I've learned quite a bit about you, Molly. I've learned that you are a person who is sensitive to injustices and unfairness and that these make you very angry. You are also very aware of ineffectiveness in dealing with unfairness and this increases your anger. It seems like we came up with some ideas that at least for the moment might be helpful to you—to give you a little assistance, to help you feel more effective with your social activism energy. And also the idea that you may want some help from your parents in figuring out how to "spray" them less. That might help you all get along better too.
	I am happy to meet with you again if I can help you with this work. It's been a real pleasure to meet a person as concerned about justice and fairness as you, Molly. The world needs more people like you.

CONCLUSION

One of the driving concerns motivating my work with people of all ages is that we live in a culture that promotes stories of hardship and suffering and is bored by stories of ordinary courage. In particular, I am dismayed by recent best-selling books supposedly written to represent the "plight" of adolescent girls (Pipher, 1995; Shandler, 1999) but that contribute to pathologizing them instead of exposing their responses to a "sick" context. Other accounts, which highlight adolescents' resistance to destructive conditions (Robinson & Ward, 1991), receive less attention by the media.

In general, where it is fitting, I try to undermine interpretations of young people as destructive or self-destructive and listen instead for opportunities—*that are present in the material if one is attentive and attuned to it*—to conceptualize their intentions as constructive even if their initial articulation of these intentions or their acting on them appears muddled, misguided, or calamitous. I believe that all of us need to have our experience of the world validated in some way. Listening well, listening to allow the heart of another person's meaning to emerge even if that person does not fully or clearly appreciate what she knows is, to me, the heart of empowerment (Weingarten, 1995).

I hope that Molly left this interview feeling empowered in the way I have just described. Crucial to her empowerment is that her parents participated in the process. With other social constructionists, I believe that what we know, we know with others. Reality isn't fixed, but rather is negotiated within the communities of which we are a part; meaning is primarily socially constructed (Bruner, 1990). For now, Molly's parents are her primary community. It is crucial that together they participate in the creation of new meaning systems that allow for different feelings, thinking, and actions on all their parts. I believe that involving Molly's parents was the most efficient and caring way to keep Molly safe.

Molly's parents came into the appointment fearing that their daughter was a danger to herself, to others, and to them. By the end of the interview, I think that they better understood the role they could play in directing her anger outward in constructive ways. It would be my wish that finding productive outlets for Molly's social activism energy might moderate the toxic effects of the helplessness she feels at school.

Not everyone in Molly's school is as fortunate as she. Molly was distressed not only on her own behalf but also on behalf of other students, many of whom were recent immigrants and came from less privileged backgrounds than she. These young people, like Molly, would benefit were someone to validate their experiences of helplessness, render visible inappropriate uses of power by faculty and administration, and channel justified outrage to productive paths.

Robinson and Ward (1991) have written about two kinds of resistance in African American girls, that for survival and that for liberation. Resistance for liberation acknowledges the problems of, and demands changes in, environments that are oppressive. Work toward a resistance for liberation requires, among other qualities, looking frankly at oppressive practices, blocking the internalization of anger, and a willingness to join with others for change. I believe that parents can work with their adolescents toward a resistance for liberation. In this interview, I encouraged both Sharon and Mark to do so. By validating Molly's perceptions of the inequities in her school and by helping her develop strategies to point out, protest, and change the school's bias against immigrant and poor children, Sharon and Mark become allies in a resistance for liberation that promotes self-determination and collective action.

Work with adolescents and their parents provides wonderfully rich opportunities to forge durable alliances between them that can serve each of their interests as they grow toward a mature interdependence with each other. Therapists who work only on the task of separation with their adolescent clients forfeit the chance to construct the relationship between parents and their adolescent children as a potent resource for each other.

When parents of adolescents are not available to work with therapists or counselors to validate helplessness, make visible inappropriate uses of power, and channel anger, groups for adolescents can be organized to do the work together. They can become like "family" to support each other. If there are significant adults willing to join these meetings even for a single session, their care and concern can be brought into the conversation and used—"stored up for the future"—as a resource.

Each of us occupies multiple social locations at the same time, some of which undoubtedly make us vulnerable to disempowering experiences. Molly, a "privileged," middle-class, White Jewish adolescent girl, suffered from helplessness in school even though she was painfully aware that her classmates who spoke English as a second language, were Latino/Latina and African American, and were less well-off financially, suffered more abuses of power than she. While working specifically on her experiences of helplessness in the hopes of creating an experience of empowerment for her, I wanted also to connect her despair with the essence of *tikkun olam*—the repairing of the world. I hoped that she would no longer think of herself as a "messed-up" person but rather as a caring and concerned one whose own well-being was intimately connected to making the world more just.

To me, this is the essence of a feminist therapy: helping people connect private pain to political realities, and to understand that their personal growth is linked to social change. In her 1996 acceptance speech for the American Psychological Association Award for Distinguished Professional Contributions, Laura S. Brown (1997) passionately argued for the importance of psychologists practicing in ways that place "moral, political, relational, and ethical cores" at the center of their commitment to "individual and societal healing" (p. 452). She also proposed that in a feminist therapy, the "initial and ultimate 'client' " (p. 453) is always the culture, as it manifests in the lives of clients day in and day out. The therapist's task is to assist clients into full empowerment, with a voice of their own, by acknowledging, validating, and promoting resistance to oppressive practices. In this interview informed by these feminist family therapy principles, Molly entered the office a "troubled" young woman and left a "social activist."

REFERENCES

Bateson, G. (1972). *Steps to an ecology of mind*. New York: Ballantine Books.

Blos, P. (1962). *On adolescence: A psychoanalytic interpretation*. New York: Free Press.

Brown, L. S. (1997). The private practice of subversion: Psychology as *tikkun olam*. *American Psychologist, 52*, 449–462.

Bruner, J. (1990). *Acts of meaning*. Cambridge, MA: Harvard University Press.

Dickerson, V. C., & Zimmerman, J. (1992). Families with adolescents: Escaping problem lifestyles. *Family Process, 31*, 341–353.

Foucault, M. (1980). *Power/knowledge: Selected interviews and other writings, 1972–1977*. New York: Pantheon Books.

Freedman, J., & Combs, G. (1996). *Narrative therapy: The social construction of preferred realities*. New York: Guilford Press.

Madsen, W. C. (1999). *Collaborative therapy with multi-stressed families*. New York: Guilford Press.

Pipher, M. B. (1995). *Reviving Ophelia: Saving the selves of adolescent girls*. New York: Ballantine Books.

Robinson, T., & Ward, J. V. (1991). A belief in self far greater than anyone's disbelief: Cultivating resistance among African American female adolescents. In C. Gilligan, A. G. Rogers, & D. L. Tolman (Eds.), *Women, girls, and psychotherapy: Reframing resistance* (pp. 87–103). Binghamton, NY: Harrington Park Press.

Shandler, S. (1999). *Ophelia speaks: Adolescent girls write about their search for self*. New York: Harperperennial Library.

Strassfield, S., & Strassfield, M. (1990). *The third Jewish catalogue*. Philadelphia: Jewish Publication Society of America.

Weingarten, K. (1995). Radical listening: Challenging cultural beliefs for and about mothers. *Journal of Feminist Family Therapy, 7*, 7–22.

Weingarten, K. (1997). *The mother's voice: Strengthening intimacy in families* (2nd ed.). New York: Guilford Press.

Weingarten, K. (1998a). Sidelined no more: Promoting mothers as a resource for their adolescent children. In C. G. Coll, J. Surrey, & K. Weingarten (Eds.), *Mothering against the odds: Diverse voices of contemporary mothers* (pp. 15–36). New York: Guilford Press.

Weingarten, K. (1998b). The small and the ordinary: The daily practice of a postmodern narrative therapy. *Family Process, 37,* 3–15.

White, M. (1995). *Re-authoring lives: Interviews and essays.* Adelaide, Australia: Dulwich Centre.

6

LOYALTY TO FAMILY OF ORIGIN

ROBERTA L. NUTT

A common issue in family therapy is loyalty to the family of origin—often for many generations—that dictates current behavior. This loyalty to doing things a certain way or living life by particular principles is often not in the awareness of clients when they begin therapy. However, over time it becomes clear that their actions and beliefs fit strongly within family patterns. There may be both functional and dysfunctional patterns, such as an emphasis on personal strength and competence versus a tradition of alcohol abuse or violence. Family patterns can be even more firmly entrenched when the pattern is also expected and reinforced by the larger culture. Because the larger culture is sexist and patriarchal, the family becomes a major venue for teaching stereotyped expectations.

The case presented in this chapter involves a dual-career couple in a family business. The couple is struggling with the division of labor and power in their relationship. The wife is particularly struggling with being a superwoman: outstanding mother, worker, spouse, and so on. The couple has two children. As is often the case, a problem with one of the children initially brought the family into therapy. Before describing the case more fully, I state my theoretical assumptions.

THEORETICAL FRAMEWORK

My theoretical framework includes family systems, feminist therapy, and feminist family therapy. Many family systems theories postulate that one person in the family system will carry the symptoms of the family dysfunction and be the person who causes the family to present for therapy. Such a person is termed the *identified patient*, or IP. Often this person is a child. In these situations, the first challenge for the family therapist is to recognize that person's place and function in the family system rather than accepting that individual's problems at face value. The problems of the family system need to be assessed to determine whether the individual's problem is actually an expression of the system's problem.

A particularly useful technique from family systems theory to both assess functioning and create change is the genogram (McGoldrick & Gerson, 1985). The genogram is a graphic representation of the family tree using standardized symbols for each family member. Several generations are depicted to aid in understanding the multigenerational transmission of family emotions, values, behaviors, and problems (Bowen, 1978). The genogram includes specific information about births, deaths, marriages, divorces, important relationships, emotional alliances and cutoffs, illnesses, and any other dimension of interest. Multigenerational transmission refers to the phenomenon of parents passing attitudes, values, and characteristics to their children who then pass them on to their children. Genograms provide useful background information for most clients in family, couple, and individual therapy. (A further discussion of the use of genograms can be found in chapter 11 of this volume.)

I also use relevant strategies from feminist therapy and feminist family therapy, which include analysis of power and hierarchy in the family relationships; analysis of gender roles in the family, including adults and children; analysis of oppression in a patriarchal society and its impact on each family member; affirmation of the voice and experience of each family member; examination of the interplay among sexism, racism, economics, ageism, ethnocentrism, heterosexism, and ableism; and validation of the importance of autonomy, achievement, competence, nurturing, emotional expressiveness, and parenting for both women and men (Braverman, 1988; Goodrich, Rampage, Ellman, & Halstead, 1988; Hare-Mustin, 1978; Nutt, 1991, 1992; Rosewater & Walker, 1985; Worell & Johnson, 1997; Worell & Remer, 1992). These strategies may stimulate growth for all clients by releasing them from rigid, unquestioned gender roles and expectations and increasing personal options.

Of particular utility in feminist family therapy is the analysis of responsibilities for all members and the determination of the amount of gender role stereotyping that goes into each task assignment (Avis, 1986). It is also imperative that the therapist

> appreciate the heavy load of responsibility that women carry for family well-being and recognize feelings of guilt and responsibility that women in particular feel when family problems develop . . . realize that both men and women are victims of gender-role socialization and develop a nonblaming attitude towards the socialized behavior of both genders. (Wheeler, Avis, Miller, & Chaney, 1989, p. 143)

Wheeler et al. also pointed out the importance of recognizing "that traditional childrearing arrangements frequently contribute to dysfunctional families" by skewing the power differential between marital partners (1989, p. 144). Traditional arrangements do not honor the specific interests and capabilities of each partner, and each partner's contributions are not equally respected. Research about the impact of multiple roles on women and men has yielded conflicting results (Bianchi, Milkie, Sayer, & Robinson, 2000; Dempsey, 2000; Press & Townsley, 1998). Some studies suggest that multiple roles lead to better adjustment, more positive mental and physical health, and feelings of competence. Other studies have found increased feelings of fatigue, frustration, burnout, and role overload (Adelmann, 1994; Crosby, 1991; Lundberg, 1996; Williams, Suls, Alliger, Learner, & Wan, 1991).

One strategy for reaching equity in role responsibilities is the gender inquiry that leads a couple "to a point of understanding and empathizing with the gender world of each spouse" so that "a major cognitive shift occurs, which leads to reduction of conflict, more effective problem resolution, and greater emotional intimacy" (Philpot, Brooks, Lusterman, & Nutt, 1997, p. 183). People seldom take the time and energy to go back and understand how they became the adults they are by examining the gender role messages received from parents, extended family, peers, media, and religious and cultural institutions. Yet, "this learning of gender roles has a powerful impact on later functioning and relationships" (Philpot et al., 1997, p. 217).

Gender inquiry uses questions to identify gender messages clients have received from their families of origin and their culture. These questions clarify the way that gender messages are transmitted across generations and can lead to empathic knowing that is critical to improved relationships. As summarized by Taffel and Masters (1989), "empathic support is almost always necessary to help someone challenge gender definitions" (p. 123). To understand multigenerational transmission of values and roles, one must learn about gender role socialization and how it is embedded in family traditions as well as in ethnoracial and social class values (Philpot et al., 1997).

Gender inquiry can be introduced at nearly any stage of therapy depending on context. For example, if a husband is resisting his wife's desire to return to school to earn a degree, it is likely that gender role issues are significant factors in the discussion for both partners. Generally, it is wisest to proceed in a developmental fashion, inquiring about early gender messages rather than taking on the current problem at first. The developmental model allows for deeper understanding and begins with less emotionally loaded content. "A full understanding of the immediate problem usually requires an appreciation of the context of past gender-role socialization" (Philpot et al., 1997, p. 220). An outline for developmental stages that might be assessed includes messages from childhood, puberty, high school years, college or early work experience, and adulthood. A sample childhood question, for example, could be, "Do you think that your mother (father) treated you in some special and different way because you were a girl (boy)? How?" (Philpot et al., p. 221).

THE GOLDEN FAMILY

The Golden family entered family therapy because their 8-year-old son Jonathan was acting out in school and his grades were dropping. The family consisted of the 35-year-old father Matthew, the 32-year-old mother Mary, Jonathan, and the 5-year-old daughter Jennifer. Matthew and Mary worked together in the family auto parts business with Matthew acting as general manager and Mary running the office and all accounts. Jonathan and Jennifer attended the same elementary school. They lived in a suburban home near both work and school. The family's income provided enough for two cars, extramural activities for the children, and an annual vacation for the family.

The Child as Symptom Bearer

The family attended the first family therapy session together at the therapist's request. The therapist explained that when a child is having a problem, the whole family is affected. Thus, it is preferable that all family members attend the sessions. The parents began by describing Jonathan's "attitude problem." Their son was getting into trouble at school and at home, talking back to both parents and teachers. His grades had dropped from A's to C's and D's.

Both Mary and Matthew were very upset and had been fighting about how to solve Jonathan's problems. Mary claimed Matthew was too lenient on the children (and on their employees), and Matthew was uneasy with Mary's harshness and rigidity. Matthew played with the children, and Mary was the disciplinarian. Mary was clearly frustrated with all the family problems in general, Matthew in particular, and overwhelmed by all her responsibilities at work and home. When Matthew and Mary fought, they both ended up with hurt feelings and withdrew from each other. They were both nursing wounds and resentments and felt hostile toward each other. They also reported that even though they were together most of the time at work and at home, they had no couple time alone. They were always working, discussing work, and ferrying the children around to their various activities. Jonathan and Jennifer also fought frequently and vied for the attention of each of their parents.

The therapist viewed this family as one in which the child (as the IP) was displaying the symptoms that symbolized the family's need for help. However, the therapist took Jonathan's problems seriously. Focusing first on the IP's problems often "hooks" the whole family into therapy when they see some early improvement. Parenting skills concerning attention, reinforcements, and boundaries were discussed, and Jonathan was sent to a school psychologist to rule out any learning problems. Jonathan's test results were welcome: He was a bright boy with no learning problems. The school psychologist also met with the parents and instructed them in boundaries, encouragement, and providing stability in parenting for Jonathan. Jonathan's problems quickly dissipated; his grades and behavior in school improved significantly.

Marital Issues Underlying Family Problems

It was apparent that Jonathan no longer needed to display dysfunctional behavior now that he had gotten his parents into therapy. The parents had developed rapport with the therapist and now accepted the reframe (or alternative interpretation) from the therapist identifying family problems. They acknowledged that there were marital problems. The therapist explained to them that children often act out when a family system is stressed. They agreed to come for marital counseling without the children.

Mary and Matthew's marital relationship had deteriorated in recent years. They blamed the decline on stress. Mary thought that Matthew did not listen to her and respect her opinion in the workplace. She also thought that he did not do his share of keeping their home running. Matthew complained that Mary was angry, hostile, critical, and not much fun to be around. She suffered from frequent headaches and reported little interest in sexual activity. Mary and Matthew were clearly locked in a power struggle at both work and home. Also, Mary felt overwhelmed by trying to do everything and do it well.

Revealing Family-of-Origin Expectations

Genograms with both Matthew and Mary revealed that Matthew was reared in a family with three brothers (see Figure 6.1). His parents were still married and had retired to Florida several years earlier. He maintained contact with his brothers and their families, and the total family visited at the annual family reunion in Florida. The family did suffer from some financial problems when Matthew was young, but his father's career stabilized when Matthew was in his early teens.

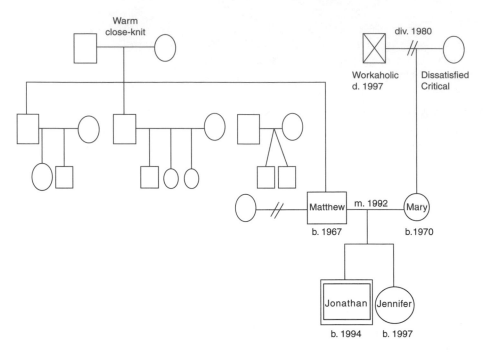

Figure 6.1. The Golden family genogram. Circles represent females; squares represent males; square within a square represents the identified male client; X inside a circle or square represents a deceased person;–//–represents divorce or split marital relationship.

Matthew had a brief early marriage before he met Mary. That marriage ended in divorce with no children. Matthew reported that he received 8 months of counseling after the divorce to "get his act together." He felt that the counseling had helped him understand his part in that marital dissolution and made him better able to recognize and express his feelings.

Mary reported more upheaval in her family of origin. She described her mother as extremely dissatisfied with and critical of both Mary and her father. Mary was an only child, and her parents divorced when she was 10. Mary was reared in her mother's home with infrequent contact with her father. She worshipped her father, describing him as a gentle man who always paid his child support, but he was a workaholic who traveled extensively and had little time for family activities. Mary grew up lonely and felt like she could never do anything right. Her mother compared her with her cousins who were always prettier, smarter, and more successful. Financially supported by her father, Mary left her mother's home to attend college and never returned. Mary's father died about 5 years ago. Although Mary is emotionally distant from her mother, the Golden family visits Mary's mother from time to time and maintains weekly telephone contact.

Rekindling of Goodwill

In an effort to counteract the negativity and blaming between Matthew and Mary, the therapist asked them to recall how they met and what first attracted them to each other. They enjoyed retelling stories from their dating history, and these happy stories reminded them of their affection for each other. Rekindling these positive memories did dispatch what Gottman and Silver (1999) termed the "four horsemen" destructive to marriages: "criticism, contempt, defensiveness, and stonewalling" (p. 27).

Analysis of Family Roles

Therapy proceeded to analyze the roles that each had played in the marriage and the origins of these roles in their individual histories and families (Pittman, 1985). Matthew and Mary were led to develop gender empathy with each other through understanding each other's individual experiences, expectations, desires, friendships, achievements, responsibilities, characteristics, stresses, strengths, devaluations, obstacles, and so on (Philpot et al., 1997; Taffel & Masters, 1989). Matthew was able to see how he had discounted Mary's opinions at work and did resolve to work toward sharing power in the family business. Matthew's previous experience in therapy was helpful. He was a fairly quick study in understanding the concepts of power inequity and the need for clearer, respectful communication. He was determined not to let this marriage end in divorce as his first marriage had.

Mary's stress was more complex. When we concentrated on her feelings of being overwhelmed, we investigated the division of labor in the household. Matthew was not shouldering half of the domestic chores as is fairly typical in U.S. and other families (Hochschild & Machung, 1989; Lerner, 1994). This inequity leads to family and couple conflict (Stohs, 1995; Wethington & Kessler, 1989). This family, however, did have the financial resources to hire household help. Matthew agreed to this expenditure easily. In fact, he reported that he had suggested it in the past, but Mary had resisted.

The therapist then asked each of them to describe how household duties were divided in their families of origin. The goal of this questioning was to discover the kinds of messages and expectations that had been passed down in their families (the multigenerational transmission). Matthew described a family in which roles had been flexible and negotiable, and the contributions of all family members were respected. In Mary's family, roles were rigid and traditional. As described earlier, her father was a workaholic who traveled frequently and whom she saw infrequently after the divorce. Her mother focused on the home and household chores.

After careful examination, it became clear that Mary's resistance to paid household assistance centered on loyalty, of which she was unaware, to her mother and her mother's standards. Her mother had been a meticulous housekeeper who had insisted that her daughter follow suit. As a teenager, Mary even had to clean the floor of her closet every week! Mary's mother had probably received similar expectations from her own mother and from the culture at large that in large part measured the worth of a woman by the cleanliness of her house.

Even though Mary's mother's life was much simpler than Mary's—she did not work outside the home and only had one child—Mary felt that she was not a real woman and certainly not living up to her mother's standards if she did not keep a spotless house by herself. This realization (an example of challenging the internalized sexism that blocks many women) helped Mary decide that it was all right to get help with the housework (including not cleaning before the cleaning service arrived). This decision freed time for work and for activities with her family. She no longer needed to try to please her mother or live up to her expectations.

Follow-Up

Upon 6-month follow-up, the Golden family reported more enjoyable family activities and less stress. Both children were doing well in school. The family business was thriving. Matthew and Mary had greatly improved their empathy toward and support of each other and had become stronger partners, coparents, and coworkers. They had also carved out small periods of "couple time" to spend together away from family and work.

BROADER IMPLICATIONS

Although the Golden family's problems fit a paradigm common in White, middle-class families in the United States, they might have also been related to their ethnic family origins. The Goldens had received messages typical for women and men about appropriate gender roles within the dominant culture. However, this family was also Jewish. Rosen and Weltman (1996) have cited the importance of a child focus in the Jewish family and of a strong connection with and obligation to previous generations. Such values may be related to Mary's unquestioned loyalty to her mother.

Rosen and Weltman also described Jewish families as having a tendency to "see suffering as an everyday occurrence" so that "enjoyment for its own sake, or the carefree expression of feelings, is sometimes questioned" (1996, p. 616). This theme fits Mary's struggle to enjoy herself and her family. These authors also reported that many Jewish families have expectations that Jewish women will achieve professional success in addition to excelling in their nurturing family roles. These conflicting demands have generated increased tension for Jewish women among their roles as parents, partners, and workers. Mary's attempts to be superwoman may be rooted here. The shame and disgrace that Jewish parents may feel if their child does not succeed financially may help explain Jonathan's dropping grades as an effective trigger for therapy.

Fortunately, this family had the economic resources to make the distribution of labor in the home easier. If this family had been from a different economic class, problems and solutions might have looked very different. For each cultural group, it is necessary to examine expectations regarding family roles. In particular, the wife's power in the system to request changes would need to be examined. It might be necessary for the therapist to provide support for the wife's voice during early discussions. The direction of a gender inquiry is always influenced by power in the family and by cultural expectations. Based on the multigenerational role definitions, the distribution of household labor has to be renegotiated. For example, it might be helpful to create detailed lists of household needs and have all family members (parents and children) describe preferences and negotiate responsibilities. Reevaluating family standards might also be useful.

Overall, this case provides one example of the negative impact of unquestioned loyalty to family-of-origin values. Mary adopted one of her mother's role expectations without questioning its fit for her own life and the cultural times. This type of multigenerational transmission can occur in many areas of life and can create disharmony in a family until the values and attitudes are examined. Once they are understood, personal choices can be made that fit present circumstances and relationships.

REFERENCES

Adelmann, P. K. (1994). Multiple roles and psychological well-being in a national sample of older adults. *Journal of Gerontology, 49,* 277–285.

Avis, J. M. (1986). Feminist issues in family therapy. In F. Piercy & D. Sprenkle (Eds.), *Family therapy sourcebook* (pp. 213–242). New York: Guilford Press.

Bianchi, S. M., Milkie, M. A., Sayer, L. C., & Robinson, J. P. (2000). Is anyone doing the housework? Trends in the gender division of household labor. *Social Forces, 79,* 191–228.

Bowen, M. (1978). *Family therapy in clinical practice.* New York: Jason Aronson.

Braverman, L. (Ed.). (1988). *A guide to feminist family therapy.* New York: Harrington Park Press.

Crosby, F. J. (1991). *Juggling: The unexpected advantages of balancing career and home for women and their families.* New York: Free Press.

Dempsey, K. C. (2000). Men's and women's power relationships and the persisting inequitable division of housework. *Journal of Family Studies*, 6(1), 7–24.

Goodrich, T. J., Rampage, C., Ellman, B., & Halstead, K. (1988). *Feminist family therapy: A casebook*. New York: Norton.

Gottman, J. M., & Silver, N. (1999). *The seven principles for making marriage work*. New York: Crown.

Hare-Mustin, R. T. (1978). A feminist approach to family therapy. *Family Process*, 17, 181–194.

Hochschild, A., & Machung, A. (1989). *The second shift: Working parents and the revolution at home*. New York: Viking Penguin.

Lerner, J. V. (1994). *Working women and their families*. Thousand Oaks, CA: Sage.

Lundberg, U. (1996). Influence of paid and unpaid work on psychophysiological stress responses of men and women. *Journal of Occupational Health*, 1, 117–130.

McGoldrick, M., & Gerson, R. (1985). *Genograms in family assessment*. New York: Norton.

Nutt, R. L. (1991). Ethical principles for gender-fair family therapy. *The Family Psychologist*, 7(3), 32–33.

Nutt, R. L. (1992). Feminist family therapy: A review of the literature. *Topics in Family Psychology and Counseling*, 1, 13–23.

Philpot, C. L., Brooks, G. R., Lusterman, D.-D., & Nutt, R. L. (1997). *Bridging separate gender worlds: Why men and women clash and how therapists can bring them together*. Washington, DC: American Psychological Association.

Pittman, F. (1985). Gender myths: When does gender become pathology? *Family Therapy Networker*, 9, 24–33.

Press, J. E., & Townsley, E. (1998). Wives' and husbands' housework reporting: Gender, class and social desirability. *Gender & Society*, 12, 188–218.

Rosen, E. J., & Weltman, S. F. (1996). Jewish families: An overview. In M. McGoldrick, J. Giordano, & J. K. Pearce (Eds.), *Ethnicity and family therapy* (2nd ed., pp. 611–630). New York: Guilford Press.

Rosewater, L. B., & Walker, L. E. A. (Eds.). (1985). *Handbook of feminist therapy: Women's issues in psychotherapy*. New York: Springer.

Stohs, J. H. (1995). Predictors of conflict over the household division of labor among women employed full-time. *Sex Roles*, 33, 257–275.

Taffel, R., & Masters, R. (1989). An evolutionary approach to revolutionary change: The impact of gender arrangements in family therapy. In M. McGoldrick, C. M. Anderson, & F. Walsh (Eds.), *Women in families: A framework for family therapy* (pp. 117–134). New York: Norton.

Wethington, E., & Kessler, R. C. (1989). Employment, parental responsibility, and psychological distress: A longitudinal study of married women. *Journal of Family Issues*, 10, 527–546.

Wheeler, D., Avis, J. M., Miller, L. A., & Chaney, S. (1989). Rethinking family therapy training and supervision: A feminist model. In M. McGoldrick, C. M.

Anderson, & F. Walsh (Eds.), *Women in families: A framework for family therapy* (pp. 135–151). New York: Norton.

Williams, K. J., Suls, J., Alliger, G. M., Learner, S. M., & Wan, C. K. (1991). Multiple role juggling and daily mood states in working mothers: An experience sampling. *Journal of Applied Psychology, 76,* 664–674.

Worell, J., & Johnson, N. G. (Eds.). (1997). *Shaping the future of feminist psychology: Education, research, and practice.* Washington, DC: American Psychological Association.

Worell, J., & Remer, P. (1992). *Feminist perspectives in therapy: An empowerment model for women.* New York: Wiley.

7

GENDER IN STEPFAMILIES: DAUGHTERS AND FATHERS

ANNE C. BERNSTEIN

As stepfamilies have become more common, so too have efforts to understand their complexities. Gender has often been omitted as a key explanatory principle. This chapter analyzes how gender prescriptions and expectations contribute to problems frequently seen in stepfamilies. In addition to feminist perspectives, the approach draws on family systems theory as well as narrative and social constructionist thinking about families. Included are examples from clinical work to illustrate how therapists can help family members discover ways of thinking, feeling, and behaving that are both more personally satisfying and more congruent with the changed context of family life. To achieve this end, therapists must help children resolve loyalty conflicts so that they can have positive relationships with both parents. Fostering positive relationships between fathers and daughters presents a particular challenge, largely because of impediments constructed by gender.

In the overwhelming percentage of families, mothers are the primary nurturers. Thus, when the parents separate, mothers generally retain primary custody of their children. Daughters whose parents divorce and remarry may feel distant, even estranged, from their fathers.[1] Fathers who have regular, frequent contact with their children following parental separation are a minority.[2]

---

[1] Throughout this chapter references are made to remarriage for the sake of brevity and style. All such references should be read in the more inclusive sense of any enduring relationship between someone who is already a parent and a new partner. It includes cohabiting heterosexual, lesbian, and gay couples.

[2] Cherlin (1996) reported that slightly more than half of the children living with their mothers whose fathers were living elsewhere saw their fathers once a month or more; 40% no longer had contact with their fathers. These and other statistics are based on figures collected between 1987 and 1990, when the U.S. Census Bureau discontinued providing estimates of marriage, divorce, and remarriage rates between decenniel census intervals.

Contact between fathers and daughters tends to be further reduced at remarriage (Buehler & Ryan, 1994; Furstenberg & Cherlin, 1991) when parents may entertain the fantasy—hazardous to the future viability of the stepfamily—that a new partner will replace the parent who resides elsewhere. A mother may see her new husband as a preferred coparent as well as a preferred partner, and a father may see his ex-wife's new partner as in a better position to provide fathering for their children. Shame about being unable to provide adequate financial assistance and dread about interacting with an angry ex-spouse contribute to fathers' absence in their children's lives. Children, however, are generally disinclined to see stepparents as replacements for parents, even when they can welcome them as loving and concerned caretakers.

Clinical experience, confirmed by research, tells us that women in stepfamilies experience more stress, less satisfaction, and more symptoms than their male counterparts (Bernstein, 1994, 1999). Due in large part to the unequal responsibility the culture puts on women for maintaining family relationships, stress results from unequal work compounded by unequal blame when problems arise. This means that family therapists are more likely to be consulted when a daughter is experiencing distress in her father's household (or when her stepmother experiences distress and identifies the stepdaughter as difficult, depressed, or acting out). Sometimes the request for intervention comes in girlhood, when the referring problem tends to be the quality of relationship between a girl and her father, a stepdaughter and her stepmother, or among stepsiblings. Family members—both within and between households—may differ as to whether the time allocated to the father's household is too much or too little.

Fathers not infrequently attempt to get more time with their daughters after remarriage, feeling more able to provide adequate care when they once again have a female partner. Daughters may seek more time with fathers so as to have the experience of having a father in a way that feels more like "real life." They may idealize the more absent father while the mother, left to shoulder more of the responsibilities, also collects more of the resentment.

Daughters may then seek relief from adolescent struggles with their mothers or, alternatively, negate their own desires to see their father for fear of hurting mother or abandoning her to loneliness. Both fathers and daughters will be influenced by how the girl gets along with her stepmother and stepsiblings and by how the father gets along with his new wife as both partner and coparent. Together fathers and daughters may seek therapeutic assistance to improve their relationship, either to effect a change in the parenting plan or to make the current plan more livable.

As daughters become young women, the desire to repair ruptured relationships with their fathers may bring them to therapy. Living independently allows a fresh perspective on the family story. It also allows the daughter to negotiate stepfamily relationships without her mother's participation. The young woman may feel more empowered to confront ongoing issues with her father. When young women prepare to become parents themselves, old resentments about their father being more available to step- and half-siblings may resurface.

Typically, clients come to therapy with troubled, hurt, or angry accounts of family life. Because parental separation and recoupling is at odds with the prevailing family ideology, family members find that stepfamily life conspires to detract from their sense of well-being and disrupts their illusions of "life as it ought to be lived." Daughters may want their parents, and most especially their fathers, whom they are more likely to see as "clueless," to understand the difficulties inflicted on them by marital transitions.

Adolescents and young adults may also be working through identity issues, attempting to integrate a sense of themselves as the child of both parents. If heterosexual, they may be puzzling over how their parents' marital history provides a template for their own, a template they typically want to discard. As one 20-something daughter seen in therapy with her father put it, "I'm like Mom, and I'm not like Jane; you divorced Mom and married Jane." Unspoken was the rest of the syllogism, "What does that mean about how you feel about me?"

In addition, the lower remarriage rates for women following divorce (Ihinger-Tallman & Pasley, 1987) and their subsequent greater economic disadvantage give daughters who live primarily with their mothers an intimate knowledge of the resulting hardships. Given that they hold their fathers accountable for their mother's and their own reduced circumstances, they may feel anger and resentment for past wrongs—personally or consensually defined—and at the same time long for an elusive closeness.

CLINICAL WORK WITH DAUGHTERS AND FATHERS

How then do feminist family therapists work to free clients from discouraging preconceptions about the limitations of postdivorce relationships? Three therapeutic interventions are illustrated in this chapter: (a) disassembling the "ungenerous attributions" and "underdeveloped patterns of empathic response" common to stepfamilies to repair ruptured relationships (Giles-Sims, 1994), (b) disentangling knotty relationships to resolve specific interpersonal problems, and (c) detriangulating stepfamily dyads so that fathers neither micromanage nor abdicate from engaging with the emotional nexus within their stepfamily. Although these techniques are often used together, cases illustrating primary use of one follow each description.

Deconstructing "Ungenerous Attributions"

Separation, divorce, and remarriage not infrequently leave in their wake a legacy of pain, as children and adults struggle to reorganize their lives while contending with physical and emotional dislocation, financial stress, and the rupture of their social networks. While adults often feel out of control during these transitions, children are required to accommodate to events entirely not of their choosing. Anger and resentment toward the parents whose choices occasioned these disruptions can linger into adulthood. As a balm to their pain, daughters, who typically express more concern about the quality of relationships than do sons, may seek their father's understanding of how his actions and inactions have affected them.

The therapist needs to maintain a "both/and" stance that allows empathy with both father and daughter, despite their unequal power in determining their joint circumstances. To do so, the therapist must hold the father accountable for the results of his actions and at the same time understand that he, too, has been navigating the uncharted seas of social change and has not emerged unscathed. Accepting ambivalence in relationships attenuated by family transitions is an important step toward disassembling the "ungenerous attributions" common to stepfamilies and working to cultivate the "underdeveloped patterns of empathic response" (Giles-Sims, 1994). The former refers to assuming the worst and withholding all benefit of doubt, and the latter to being unable or disinclined to understand the other's experience. Feeling "heard" empathically by the therapist helps open up the family story, inviting all to reconsider casting another as an intractable or oppressive opponent. Being accepted in the presence of one's family members as a basically well-intentioned person provides the basis for understanding that others might also be people of goodwill who deserve empathy, if not agreement.

"Mirror, Mirror, in Your Eyes . . ."

The Tylers are a White, Protestant family created by the remarriage of two teachers. In the year between college and medical school, Jeanne, 22, was living full time with her father, Jim, 45, for the first time since her parents separated a dozen years earlier. Father and daughter sought therapy to repair their relationship, strained by a conflictual divorce and the difficulties both experienced in making Jeanne a part of the family he had formed with his new wife, her son, now 15, and their twin daughters, 9. Tearfully, Jeanne reported that her needs had long been ignored or subordinated to those of the full-time residents. As a child, she had felt "lonely in a crowd" at Dad's. She often called her mother to retrieve her early, leaving over

Dad's objections to return to the quieter, less complex home she shared with Mom. Now, both feel that the old story of childhood hurt and paternal frustration is being replayed.

Much of the therapy consisted of working on the pattern of mutual defensiveness. Jeanne wants to feel that her father loves her and that she is important to him. Instead, she continues to feel unwelcome and peripheral, finding his actions unresponsive and his words invalidating of her experience. Jim wants his daughter to feel comfortably a part of his family and to find him a "good enough" person, imperfect certainly, but loving and not out to hurt her. Instead, he feels his efforts dismissed as inadequate. He expresses his hurt feelings by becoming curt. Each anticipates the other's response and attributes ill-will or lack of charity. Each feels negatively caricatured by the other. Seeing themselves reflected thus in the other's eyes, they both are less friendly than each would like to be The space between them is replete with negative inferences that become untested but tenacious beliefs.

Deconstructing those beliefs, and thereby slowing down the dialogue, allow the therapist to make the attributions transparent. Because each hears the other's experience as an accusation of one's own inadequacy, each acknowledges the other only briefly ("I know you were hurt") before going on to counter the implied or overt accusation (" . . . but I . . .") at greater length. What registers is the self-justification; the acknowledgment passes so quickly it fails to register.

I interrupted their dialogue to ask each to amplify their acknowledgment of the other and check in to make sure that this was recognized. The pattern of interlocking sensitivities may be such that a "button gets pushed," resulting in wholesale discounting of the message in which it was embedded. At one point, Jim made a heartfelt declaration of his continuing love and commitment, lamenting that he had not successfully communicated his caring to Jeanne. She responded that she felt disregarded and disrespected, that he was saying that she should not feel as she does. I asked her to entertain the possibility that both could be true—that he cares and that she does not experience him as caring—and invited their curiosity as to how that may have come about. Jim talked about how he had learned a typically masculine pattern from his own father: responding to hurt by adopting a "you're not getting to me" stance. He said that response might well be making her feel that he does not care.

Making direct statements about one's responses and needs is the reciprocal of being curious about those of the other. Long accustomed to seeing Jeanne as "too sensitive," Jim needed to differentiate reasonable requests that deserved accommodation from among what he perceived as a web of implied indictments. One pattern that he agreed to change was his response when he could not be immediately available to her. He agreed to mention a future time that he would be free to meet, rather than simply cataloguing what he had to do with whom—a response that always left Jeanne feeling that she came last in the family.

One obstacle to disassembling the ungenerous attributions and under-developed patterns of empathic response is the belief, whether conscious or not, that changing one's perceptions, recovering from one's symptoms, or repairing a relationship would be disloyal to one's history. *Accusatory suffering,* a concept defined by Glass (2000) in discussing therapy for marital infidelity, is based on the fear that full recovery, or doing too well, would invalidate the pain and suffering experienced earlier. This recovery would then allow the person one feels injured by to minimize the consequences of his or her actions.

Jim asked Jeanne to be direct in asking for attention, rather than looking for openings and angrily withdrawing when she saw none. She insisted that just because she has the potential to be more direct now does not mean that she had it in her power to get what she wanted when she was younger. Differentiating between what was possible for her in adulthood and what had been developmentally inappropriate for her as a child opened the way to creating opportunities for reparative experiences.

Disentangling Knotty Relationships

The quality of each relationship within the extended family network created by serial monogamy is highly contingent on each of the others. If a girl is very close to her mother, she may identify with mother, see father as choosing to divorce herself as well, and hold herself distant from father and anyone he chooses to add to the family. If she has been especially close to father, who, as is typical in the period between partners, has been a more indulgent and permissive parent to her than he was to her brother, she will have an especially difficult time welcoming a stepmother into the household in which she has been "the woman of the family." If father and stepmother are engrossed in an exclusive intimacy, her distress will be greater still. If he hands over her care to her stepmother, acceding to the cultural program-ming that defines nurturing children as "women's work," noncompliance, withdrawal, and rebellion are likely results.

The matrix is as complex for fathers, whose involvement with their daughters is highly dependent on their coparenting relationship with the girl's mother. Cooperation facilitates contact, thereby creating active, con-cerned fathering. Conflict, conversely, leads to amplifying tensions or with-drawal from the field. Within the stepfamily, each relationship is also highly dependent on each of the others. "I love you and would never abandon you," wrote one father to his 22-year-old daughter, "but I would be lying if I told you that your relationship with my wife doesn't affect my relationship with you." Struggles over who is favoring whose children lead to marital tensions. Guilty about not being available to his children, a father may hold himself back with his stepchildren, indulge his daughter during the limited time he has access to her, and fight with his new partner about his favoring his children over hers, leading each to adopt the stance of "you're not extending yourself to my child, so don't expect me to take care of yours." Just as negative relationships in one stepfamily dyad infect the others, positive relationships are also contagious. A cooperative coparental relationship between father and stepmother predisposes each to be favorably disposed, even generous, to the children of the other; and a friendship between stepdaughter and stepmother leads to the youngster's greater alacrity in being part of her father's household, increasing the opportunities for her to be close to her father.

As mentioned earlier, how to divide time between households is often part of the therapeutic work with daughters and their divorced/remarried fathers. Dealing with even so concrete a topic as the parenting schedule depends on sorting out the knotted relationships that underlie the decision. For example, here the therapist must address the following:

1. To what extent do family members share the desire to increase time together? To what extent is father's interest in more time with his daughter based on a desire for a more "normal" relationship, allowing for the kinds of day-in and day-out interactions that build intimacy?

2. Are there financial issues involved in the percentage of time the child spends in each household (as when child support is allocated based on residential pattern)? How are these influencing the decision? Can they be separated for the purposes of the therapy (e.g., by asking a father—for the sake of exploring the issue—to assume that child support obligations would not change; what, then, would he think would be the optimal allocation of time to each household?).

3. Are father and stepmother in agreement about increasing stepdaughter's time in the household? Can they discuss this openly between them?

4. To what extent does the daughter require stability in her living arrangements, preferring the comfort and familiarity of a primary household, perhaps with a single parent and full siblings only, thus requiring less accommodation to change?

5. To what extent is the daughter subordinating her own needs to avoid seeming disloyal to her mother, not voicing preferences that she fears would hurt her mother's feelings or expose her to loneliness? Are the possibilities for greater contact

among the children in the household an attraction or a deterrent to greater time together?

6. What is the work that needs to be done to improve all of
the family relationships prior to even discussing a change
in schedules?

"It's Not Just About You and Me"

The Lopez family was referred for family therapy because Daniel Lopez,
a Venezuelan professor, wanted to increase the time that his daughter,
Kathy, 10, is with him, his wife of 4 years, Lisa, a French American artist,
and her son, Jesse, 10. Jesse divides his time equally between his mother's
and his father's homes, whereas Kathy lives primarily with her mother,
Ellen, a Jewish occupational therapist, spending Wednesday nights and every
other weekend with her Dad's stepfamily. "Difficulties in communicating"
headed their list of what needed to be addressed, with both Lisa and Jesse
complaining that they cannot talk with Kathy. At the slightest hint of
criticism or displeasure with her behavior, Kathy "breaks down," unwilling
and seemingly incapable of discussing the matter at hand. Because these
episodes sometimes exacerbate her asthma, requiring medical intervention,
both stepmother and stepbrother have been silenced, "walking on eggshells"
and keeping their resentments to themselves, where they fester and grow.

I met first with the remarried couple, addressing differences in parenting
styles. "He brings in the tanks," Lisa said. "And she goes to the circus,"
Daniel chimed in. We began to work on how to parent more effectively
together by negotiating expectations and limits that both could support.
We explored how their models of parenting were shaped by both their
gender socialization as woman and man, as well as by having grown up in
very different cultures. For example, he had great difficulty in understanding
how she could allow Jesse to "talk back," whereas she saw herself as encouraging his assertiveness and self-expression. Later we worked on how they could
implement a cooperative strategy as unanticipated differences emerge and
on how to recognize—and directly engage as a couple—when they become
angry with the other's child because they are not getting along well with
each other.

Next, I met with each parent–child dyad, exploring the experience of
each child through the sequence of marital transitions. What was it like
when the parents separated? How had they gotten to know their stepparent
and stepsibling? What was working well and what needed improvement?
In the meeting with his mother, Jesse told her how she can overwhelm him
by piling on a litany of past complaints when telling him he has done
something that has angered her. He talked about tensions with his stepfather,
whom he experiences as "always having to be right." He talked about how

Kathy's tearful withdrawal when he is "a little bit mean" meant that nothing ever got worked out. In the session with her father, Kathy was cheerful and voiced no complaints, but she could hear from him how her closing off discussions leaves things "in the basement."

In talking with me about a conflict with Jesse, Kathy was able to understand his point of view as we speculated together about what might have been going on for him. I asked directly what would help her stay in conversation when things became tense, and she had two suggestions. First, she said it would be better if she and Jesse worked out their disagreements with one another, so that she would not feel outnumbered by what she experiences as the team of mother and son. Second, although she very much enjoys Lisa most of the time, Kathy talked about being scared by the tone in her stepmother's voice when angry.

In meeting with the stepfamily, we talked about how family members could talk with one another when tempers flared. We practiced having Lisa talk to Kathy about a tense topic she had been afraid to raise. I helped Kathy to tell Lisa what she could do to help Kathy to breath regularly and stay connected in the interaction, and Lisa agreed that "it sounds fair, and I'll try."

At one point I directed them to turn their chairs away from each other so that they could continue to talk without the visual cues to which each was reactive and which ordinarily triggered anger or withdrawal. In a later session, I had them switch roles, each taking the role of the other, and discuss an unresolved incident between them. As the therapy progressed, these conversations became less aversive for Kathy, so that by the last session she and Jesse could work out a grievance of his without the emotional intensity that had precluded resolution in the past.

Two other areas of work with the Lopez family were important. First, I helped the adults see the advantages of staying out of the children's conflicts. Each parent, fiercely protective of his or her own child, was seen by the other parent–child dyad as "unfair." Thus when parents got involved, what started out as a minor disagreement between the children ended up with the whole family up in arms. Second, I suggested that each parent–child dyad create time together without the enforced togetherness of "we're all one big happy family." It took some trial and error before a balance was struck between family time and one-on-one time, respecting both historical ties and stepfamily differences without being split down the middle.

This change was especially important for Kathy. Because the household division of labor was more or less along traditional gender roles, Lisa took more responsibility for both children than did Daniel. Increased access to her father increased Kathy's comfort in his home. The goal here is a parental system in which the partners may have differing responsibilities, but neither is powerless over the conditions of his or her own life. The challenge, to paraphrase Keshet (1989), is to work out a role division that respects *and* challenges both the biological ties of the parent and children and the gender roles for which men and women have been socialized.

I had spoken with Ellen, Kathy's mother, for a single session early on, and she had expressed her willingness to collaborate in the therapy. After stepfamily tensions abated, Kathy told me that she wanted to spend more time at her Dad's home but feared hurting her Mom. Once in the midst of a fight, she had said to her mother, "I don't want to live with you." Both were in tears, and Ellen had responded, "That's the worst thing you could say."

I told Kathy that words flung about in anger were received differently than when calmly discussing alternative plans. I asked what she would like if she could design an ideal shared parenting plan. She suggested that the school year schedule—Wednesday nights and every other weekend with her father—be reversed in the summer.

I helped her rehearse how to tell her mother, but in the end, she asked me to tell her. We worked together on what I would say to her parents: "It's hard for Kathy to tell you things she thinks you might not want to hear. She asked me to tell you, Daniel, that she hates going to Jesse's Little League games and wants to go to just a few. She asked me to tell you, Ellen, that she would like to spend more time with her father." "That's an A+," Kathy said, "but also tell my Mom not to give me twenty-hour lectures at home." "You want to be told in small doses," I said. "Yes," she said. I delivered these messages.

In a session with mother and daughter, Ellen told Kathy, "I won't feel bad if you spend more time with your father and Lisa; I'm glad you have a lot of people who love you." I asked if Kathy believed her mother, and she said she did. Ellen said she had also been thinking about how Kathy could spend more time with her father, and that Mom and Dad would talk about how to arrange that change.

Detriangulating Dyads in the Stepfamily

The remarried father in a stepfamily often feels like the rope in a tug of war, while stepmother and stepchild can feel marginalized by the other's closeness with him, a closeness that may appear to leave no room for their own needs and wishes. Because a stepmother and stepdaughter are in each other's lives by virtue of his relationship to both of them, a father is confronted with the task of demonstrating his love and loyalty to each, even when their interests are at odds.

His experience may well be that he can never please anyone when all are competing for his attention, affection, and allegiance. As the parent, he has more authority with and responsibility for his children and more power in making childrearing decisions. Jealous of his limited time with his children, he may forgo limit-setting in favor of maximizing fun and minimizing conflict, thereby inviting his new partner to criticize him as an overindulgent "Disneyland Dad." Fault-finding between father and stepmother is often reciprocal, with him criticizing her for not being sufficiently "motherly."

Although all parents have to work hard to make all family members—children and new partners alike—join them as "insiders" in the new stepfamily, fathers more easily drift to the ends of the continuum between withdrawal from the field and attempting to choreograph relationships among family members. On the one hand, they may attempt to micromanage, trying to impose preconceived ideas of how wife and daughter should relate, directing each how to behave. The therapeutic task is then to help each dyad take charge of its own relationship.

On the other end of the spectrum are fathers who abdicate all responsibility for maintaining relationships, drafting the women in their lives to do their emotional work for them, emerging unscathed as feelings fly fast and furious, only to complain (later and from a safe distance) about the irrationality of women. The therapeutic task is then to redistribute the emotional division of labor, helping fathers who are slow to know their own feelings and unaccustomed to emotional expression to remain emotionally present, increase their capacity to tolerate conflict, and engage directly with wife and daughter.

"Getting Out of the Middle"

The Johnson family, headed by an African American couple, both professionals, presents an example of a father, Steve, 42, working too hard to manage the relationship between his wife, June, 30, and his daughter, Ellen, 19. Ellen and June had liked each other a lot to begin with, but as Ellen became a teenager, not long after the birth of her half-sister, relations had become strained between them. A recent vacation—and the question of whether Ellen would accompany the rest of the family—had brought things to a crisis point. In the months leading to therapy, Steve had served as a switchboard between the two women, who were not speaking with one another.

I met with Steve, June, and Ellen individually prior to seeing them all together. From Steve, I heard of his pain and frustration at his daughter's estrangement from his household. From June, I heard of her hurt that her interest in and care for Ellen seemed unappreciated and unreciprocated. From Ellen, I heard that she felt in a double-bind: asked by her father to relate to June, she responded as best she could, only to have her efforts dismissed as insincere and inadequate. She felt damned if she did not take initiative, and damned if she did. Ellen told me that her father had said to her that she and June did not like one another. I asked her, "If you thought she liked you, would you like her?" "Yes," she said.

I introduced the family session by reporting to all that each wanted the relationships among them to improve. We began by exploring each person's version of the sequence of events that led to the current crisis. Having examined how indirect communication, inference, and attribution create distorted and unflattering portraits of the Other, family members were able to hear empathically the experience of the others.

It became clear to all that one-to-one communication between June and Ellen was essential. We talked about how Steve's well-intended efforts were keeping them apart. Both women confirmed that they needed to feel free to develop a relationship based on who they are, rather than feeling pressured to implement his vision of who they should be to one another. June tearfully told Ellen that she saw them as being family forever, connected by their years of history and her younger daughter, even without Steve, whom she expects to predecease her. Ellen was moved by hearing, for the first time in a long time, that June likes and cares for her, and talked about how close she had felt to June in years past.

At the next session, Steve reported that, for the first time in months, Ellen had been at the house for hours at a time, and that the tension level was noticeably lower. Ellen confirmed that she had made direct contact with June and was feeling more relaxed and hopeful. June was more ambivalent, acknowledging some changes but focusing on hurtful lapses.

The remainder of the therapeutic work involved disassembling the ungenerous attributions and underdeveloped patterns of empathic response between stepmother and stepdaughter, as described in an earlier section of this chapter. The father practiced witnessing rather than directing their interaction. As one example, both adults had attributed Ellen's not spending nights in their home as resulting from her discomfort with her stepmother, but they were able to hear that for Ellen, that was one minor influence among many, including the lack of a designated space that was hers, unhappy memories of the house from the time of her parents' divorce, and having the decision of where to stay a constant source of pressure.

CONCLUSION

Maintaining or resuming a positive relationship between father and daughter following parental divorce and remarriage presents therapeutic challenges that require both an understanding of the dynamics of family transitions and an appreciation of how gender intersects with stepfamily life. A daughter often feels abandoned, experiencing her father as rejecting her as well as the marriage to her mother, or, in the tumult before he has restructured his postmarriage life, as distant, unreliable, or disinterested. A father's remarriage adds to the complexity and can aggravate her sense of loss.

Father, for his part, may feel punished for inconstancy or neglect, be it perceived or consensual. Whether intentional, contextual, or circumstantial, parental lapses require father to take responsibility for the pain inflicted. Repairing fractured father–daughter relationships in therapy requires fathers to listen nondefensively to their daughter's experience and to demonstrate their continued caring, a first step toward deconstructing ungenerous attributions and developing greater empathy between them.

Addressing the relational matrix of the father–daughter dyad is an essential part of the therapeutic work. Working through lingering loyalty conflicts enables children to allow the relationship with their father to improve without threatening the connection to their mother. Detriangulating stepfamily dyads and encouraging one-to-one dialogue permit father and daughter to reknit a fractured bond. With well-designed therapeutic support, relationship injuries, like fractured bones, can heal. The break is not erased in memory—diagnostic imaging would reveal it has occurred—but reparative experience strengthens the connection, allowing it to carry its own weight and to resume an active relational life.

REFERENCES

Bernstein, A. C. (1994). Women in stepfamilies: The Fairy Godmother, the Wicked Witch, and Cinderella reconstructed. In M. P. Mirkin (Ed.), *Women in context: Toward a feminist reconstruction of psychotherapy* (pp. 188–213). New York: Guilford Press.

Bernstein, A. C. (1999). Reconstructing the Brothers Grimm: New tales for stepfamily life. *Family Process, 38,* 415–429.

Buehler, C., & Ryan, C. (1994). Former-spouse relations and noncustodial father involvement during marital and family transitions: A closer look at remarriage following divorce. In K. Pasley & M. Ihinger-Talman (Eds.), *Stepparenting: Issues in theory, research and practice* (pp. 127–150). Westport, CT: Greenwood.

Cherlin, A. (1996). *Public and private families.* New York: McGraw-Hill.

Furstenberg, F. F., Jr., & Cherlin, A. J. (1991). *Divided families: What happens to children when parents part.* Cambridge, MA: Harvard University Press.

Giles-Sims, J. (1994). Comparison of implications of the justice and care perspectives for theories of remarriage and stepparenting. In K. Pasley & M. Ihinger-Tallman (Eds.), *Stepparenting: Issues in theory, research, and practice* (pp. 33–50). Westport, CT: Greenwood Press.

Glass, S. (2000). Infidelity. In *Clinical Update 2.* Washington, DC: American Association for Marriage and Family Therapy.

Ihinger-Tallman, M., & Pasley, K. (1987). Divorce and remarriage in the American family: A historical review. In K. Pasley & M. Ihinger-Tallman (Eds.), *Remarriage and stepparenting: Current research and theory* (pp. 1–18). New York: Guilford Press.

Keshet, J. K. (1989). Gender and biological models of role division in stepmother families. *Journal of Feminist Family Therapy, 1,* 29–50.

III

CONTEXTUALIZING RACIAL AND ETHNIC IDENTITIES IN FAMILIES

8

CONTEMPORARY AFRICAN AMERICAN FAMILIES

RUTH L. HALL AND BEVERLY GREENE

This chapter updates our previous article (Hall & Greene, 1995) and incorporates a case study to highlight the experiences of African American families. We hope to provide information that can guide the practice of feminist family therapy. The purpose of this chapter is to discuss the use of a feminist family therapy paradigm within a specific cultural context. We selected an African American married woman as a client because African American women are more likely to use therapy and are frequently the person in the family who brings other family members into therapy. We discuss Sarah's reason for referral, the interventions used, and the outcome of therapy. Sarah and her husband's family of origin histories as well as their immediate family are also examined to illustrate its relevance to the presenting problem.

What is the fabric of the African American family experience? First, a therapist must appreciate that race and gender are two central and socially constructed concepts and that these constructs are not hierarchical but are interwoven (Greene, 1997; Lorde, 1987). An effective therapist must be able to work skillfully with the intricacy and diversity within each family; recognize each family's resourcefulness in coping with racism, sexism, and classism; and appreciate how the collective need to address racial oppression binds the African American family together.

Glaring obstacles to the culturally competent treatment of African American families include the absence or inadequacy of cross-cultural training. The irony of this is that most undergraduate and graduate students begin their experiential training by working with low-income clients, usually people of color, frequently with little supervision on the specific issues and dilemmas that arise in work with class and race differences. We advocate that training in cross-racial clinical work should constitute a required and formal part of all clinical training (Hall & Greene, 1995). Furthermore, a cultural competence requirement (similar to the continuing education requirement for ethics) should be required for continued license renewal. Frequently, it is the absence of cultural sensitivity that often leads to premature termination of African American clients and their families.

The second obstacle is the negative perception of feminism, and therefore feminist therapy, within the African American community. Feminism is viewed as a White, middle-class, and antimale practice that fails to account for race in an analysis of gender issues. Clearly, some of the African American community's response to feminism represents a level of defensiveness and denial about the reality of sexism in the African American community. Moreover, some White feminist therapists fail to appreciate their White skin and class privilege (Greene, 1995). Feminist therapists also must appreciate that coveting a White middle-class lifestyle and accepting White middle-class norms are not everyone's ideal. Problems arise when an ethnic group's cultural values are in conflict with Western values. Finally, therapists must be cognizant of their own racial identity as well as the racial identities of their clients (Helms, 1995) because culture is not experienced homogeneously.

AFRICAN AMERICAN FAMILY THERAPY WITHIN A CULTURAL CONTEXT

Afrocentric values including holism, contextual relevance, and connectedness are evident in African American family systems. For example, a holistic (rather than a linear) perspective appreciates the interconnectedness of behavior, a philosophy that is supported by both feminist (Surrey, 1991) and Afrocentric (Nobles, 1980) constructs. Both Afrocentric and feminist theories emphasize the importance of the group and the need for connectedness. We see this in how women value relationships and how African American culture values the importance of the extended family. Unfortunately, the social disorganizational approach (Higgenbotham, 1982), which uses problems and weaknesses to define the group, is frequently used to describe the African American family.

Contextual relevance emphasizes two aspects of African American culture. First, one must appreciate African Americans in terms of Afrocentric culture. Second, similar to feminist therapy, a therapist must appreciate that African American clients may not adhere to "traditional" clinical norms (Hall, 1998). For example, a client may inquire about personal matters (e.g., location of family of origin, experiences with racism) to enhance the relationship with the therapist. From a feminist perspective, the therapist who makes such disclosures minimizes the power differential; from an Afro-centric perspective, sharing information in ways that maintain appropriate professional boundaries enhances one's trust and affiliation needs. We are not suggesting that inquiries about the therapist's life should go unexplored or should be automatically presumed to be of cultural origin. It is important to understand the nature, timing, and type of question in the context of a specific family or client. The source of the inquiry must be explored and considered before disclosures are made.

Shweder and Bourne (1984) posited that holistic cultures such as African American culture are based on connectedness, which is antithetical to the cultural norms of Western society that stress individualism and autonomy. The interconnectedness of African Americans, like other families of color, has been pathologized as "enmeshed." Enmeshment is a pathological lack of psychological individuation, not an appropriate descriptor of the interdependence that is culturally driven in African American families. For example, in dominant culture paradigms, working mothers may be perceived as neglectful even when work is not a choice but a necessity. This frequently means that older children must monitor their younger siblings while their mother works. However, family structure does not determine the quality of its function. Pathologizing non-Western family structures is therefore inappropriate. The role of the parentified child is not pathological unless the responsibilities delegated to that child exceed their developmental capacity or interfere with the child's development.

FAMILY CONSTELLATIONS AND FAMILY ROLES

Family is a contextual term. The diverse constellations of African American families include the single parent (both single and divorced mothers and fathers), teenage mothers (who may live with their extended family), grandparents, aunts, uncles, cousins raising a relative's children, common law marriages, lesbian and gay mothers and fathers, foster parents, as well as the traditional nuclear family (Boyd-Franklin, 1989; Greene, 1997). Female-headed households are not synonymous with the presence of family pathology. Similarly, living in female-headed households does not mean that children have no meaningful male role models. Male family members who are blood related or fictive kin provide male role models, as do many biological fathers who, for a variety of reasons, do not live with their children or whose mothers do not publicly reveal that their children's fathers do live with them (Boyd-Franklin, 1989; Schaefer, 1998). Thus, the variety of family constellations in African American families is descriptive but does not explain the presence of pathology.

Socioeconomic Status

Class differences create differences in available resources for a family, in realistic options available to family members, and in the intensification of stress within the family (Wyche, 1996). Although there has been an increase in the Black middle class, 26% of African American families (compared with 8.6% of White families) live below the poverty line (U.S. Department of Commerce, 1998). Moreover, middle-class African Americans are more likely supporting a greater number of family members who are not middle class and need financial assistance (Greene, 1997). Thus there are more demands on whatever finances are available.

Another dynamic of African American families is the prominence of dual-income (as opposed to dual-career) families. Dual-income households are the rule of thumb in the African American family where working, for women, is not romanticized (Greene, 1995). In these households, working women carry the majority of the household responsibilities either out of choice or out of necessity. Although African American households have the cultural predisposition to be more egalitarian, consistent with African cultural derivatives, the influence of Western norms as well as differences in gender egalitarianism in precolonial African tribes has eroded this practice in many contemporary African American households (Greene, 1995, 1997).

A disparity in earning potential between men and women is another issue that can create stress in a family (Greene, 1995). Because of racism, African American women may find it easier to find employment than African American men. African American women are often aware of this disparity and the reasons for it and some feel guilty about it. However, African American women are usually able to separate employment problems that result from discrimination from those problems that are really a man excusing his own deficits and subsequently placing blame on his family and partner.

African American women are, however, more likely to be affected by sexism in the workplace, to be underpaid, to have a glass ceiling compromise employment opportunities, and to have jobs deemed "women's work" (e.g., hairdresser, domestic work, child care, waitress). The notion that most working African American women have glamorous careers paying high salaries that take jobs away from African American men is highly overstated and not consistent with the statistics of the workplace. When partners are not aware of the reality of workplace conditions, the distress they experience may need to become part of the focus of treatment (Greene, 1997).

African American Women, Men, and Their Families

An African American cultural context provides African American women with a broader range of flexible gender roles (Greene, 1995, 1997;

Hall, 1998; Young, 1993). However, broader gender roles do not necessarily translate into more freedom for African American women. In fact, many African American women believe that because their strength has been a mainstay of the group's survival, ubiquitous strength is a requirement for cultural authenticity. As such, many women harbor the mistaken belief that they should be able to manage everyone's problems and give little attention to themselves (Greene, 1997). This leads many African American women to become overwhelmed and frustrated because they rarely attend to their own needs. Thompson (2000) has suggested that moral masochism, the tendency to give to others (e.g., her family or origin, her partner, and her children) to the point of self-depletion, characterizes some of the problems observed in therapy with African American women.

It is essential that African American women claim the right to have their own needs acknowledged and take a personal inventory of those needs. For many African American women, attending to their own needs is perceived as selfish and antithetical to being the "strong Black woman" (Greene, 1997). Thus, a therapist must distinguish pathological overfunctioning from an appropriate high level of functioning for each client (Greene, 1995, 1997). The term "softly strong" (Hall, 1998) aptly describes the client's capacity for self-care (i.e., have tenor but recognized her need for support).

There is a dearth of articles that address effective coping styles for African American men, the importance of the family, and their role as community leaders. The preponderance of literature on African American men focuses on problems and pathology. Given that African American men are targeted by the police and presumed to be incompetent, violence prone, and irresponsible both at home and in the workplace, it is staggering that African American men survive. Boyd-Franklin and Franklin's (2000) book on raising African American boys is a step toward examining how African American boys can be raised to become strong, psychologically healthy men.

Eurocentric norms construct the relationship between African American men and women as one that emasculates men and therefore undermines healthy family functioning. This notion does not recognize or understand African American men and women within a cultural context. Dual-income and single-family homes do not realistically threaten one's manhood. Rather, one must appreciate that African American men are denied access to the male privilege enjoyed by White men, and this factor alone may add to a family's stress. An unfortunate outcome of some African American men's understandable feelings of rage is their displacement of that rage onto African American women and children. Rather than seeing the family as a source of support and strength, the combination of denied opportunities and negative stereotypes make women and children vulnerable targets for displaced hostility.

THE ROLE OF THERAPY: A CASE STUDY

Because most clients who come into therapy are women, we selected a female client to illustrate some of the issues and concerns of African American families. Sarah illustrates the following dynamics common in African American families: being raised by a single working mother and extended family members, the dual-income family, flexible gender roles, the importance of interconnectedness, and contextual relevance. Raised in an African American community, Sarah learned how race, gender, and class affected the lives of African Americans. Sarah's family also provided her with skills needed to monitor, assess, and respond to racism, sexism, and classism. It is important to note that the immediate and the extended family are core features of African American families; however, there is variation among African American families in the extent to which the extended family constellation is prominent within them. Although an African American family may not have close ties to their family and the extended family, they are cognizant of the importance of family within the community and that they deviate from a cultural norm. Most African American families have some characteristics that are routine features of African American culture and others that are not. We will demonstrate how feminist therapy techniques can be used in culturally sensitive ways with African American families. Names and other identifying information have been changed to protect the confidentiality of the clients.

Sarah is a 29-year-old African American woman. She has been married for 10 years to James, 35. They have three children, Dianne, 6, Sean, 4, and Alex, 2. Over the past 3 years, Sarah and James started a successful limousine service. This past year, they have done extremely well and have financially achieved solid upper-middle-class status.

James sought out an African American therapist for Sarah. For Sarah and James, a shared African American culture between Sarah and her therapist was critical. Sarah was experiencing intrusive, recurring, and disruptive memories of being sexually abused by her mother's paramour, Calvin. Sarah wanted to address these issues so that they would not compromise her mothering, her marriage, or herself.

A second goal was to come to terms with her feelings about her mother. Sarah feared losing her mother if she acknowledged that her mother never met her emotional needs. For Sarah, the importance of connection and of her extended family was a part of her cultural context. Sarah was seen individually weekly for a year and a half. One session was conducted with Sarah and her mother and two sessions with Sarah and James.

Sarah and James were only children from divorced homes and both valued the importance of family. Both were seeking life partners and looked forward to having children. Both had strong ties with some family members and fictive kin (non-blood-related friends who are seen as family) who were used as a support system. They described their marriage as a solid one. Both also recognized James's controlling, "takeover" nature. They stated that their children came first and that family activities were their primary focus. Although there was some disagreement on punishment (James was harsher than Sarah was), they were able to discuss differences and compromise.

Although Sarah frequently felt torn between pleasing her mother, Ms. Fink, and pleasing James, she aligned herself with James, which Ms. Fink had trouble accepting. For example, Ms. Fink's desire to control Sarah's wedding ceremony resulted in a breach in their relationship. After Sarah's wedding, they had no contact until the birth of her first child 3 years later. Again, Ms. Fink became intrusive and was critical of Sarah's marriage, her parenting, and other personal matters. Clashes between James and Ms. Fink emerged, ranging from an amicable truce to heated arguments. Although sometimes painful, Sarah prioritized her marriage but did not want to alienate her mother. She wanted her children to have a relationship with their grandmother. Because Ms Fink had a boyfriend, Sarah did not permit the children to have unchaperoned visits with their grandmother. James was aware of Sarah's conflict and kept his contact with Ms. Fink to a minimum.

James's History

James's parents divorced when he was young. Although his mother raised him, James maintained contact with his supportive father. This is typical in African American families. Like Sarah, there was no stigma in being raised in a single-parent household. However, unlike Sarah, James's father remained involved with him, providing him with an available male figure. James described his mother as a "controlling" type who was critical of his marriage. James felt that his mother was competitive and envious of his marital and financial success. Over the years her criticism has put a strain on their relationship, and her visits to their home were minimal.

As a man who was raised by a single mother who had been financially abandoned by her husband, James was determined that his children would never be raised in the same manner. He loved his children, his wife, and being a family man. He felt that he could handle all of his own emotional baggage and denied that his issues had any impact on his marriage. Consequently, he attributed their marital problems to Sarah's preoccupation with her "baggage" from childhood. James readily admitted that he did not "process" feelings and felt that Sarah needed to just let go of her feelings about her abuse and move on with her life.

Sarah's History

Sarah was primarily raised in a religious home by her maternal great aunt, Tess. Although Sarah's mother lived with them for some periods of time, Aunt Tess was Sarah's primary caretaker. Here, we see an example of a different family structure—an extended family member as a primary caretaker. Sarah felt that she had no positive role models in parenting. "I felt loved but never really noticed," she said. Sarah never had a birthday party or gifts. Sarah stated that she would sit in her room and wonder why no one loved her and could not understand what she had done to deserve this treatment.

Aunt Tess died when Sarah entered puberty and Sarah moved in with her mother. Sarah described her mother as a woman who prioritized men over parenting. Sarah thought that her mother had been emotionally neglected as a child. Sarah even speculated that her mother might have been abused by one of her maternal grandmother's paramours. Although Sarah initiated contact with her father as a young adult, he was unresponsive to her overtures. Characterologically, Mr. Fink was just as self-absorbed as Sarah's mother.

Calvin, Ms. Fink's paramour, dated Ms. Fink for several years and provided extensive financial assistance to both Ms. Fink and to Sarah's maternal grandmother. Calvin and Ms. Fink did not include Sarah in their social lives, leaving her to fend for herself. When Sarah entered adolescence, Sarah told her mother that Calvin had fondled her breasts for the first time. Her mother's response was that Sarah must have misinterpreted his gesture. Soon after Sarah's revelation to her mother, Calvin began regularly coming into Sarah's room at night. After 3 years, Sarah intuitively felt that Calvin's abuse would escalate and that penetration was imminent. Once again, Sarah told her mother of the abuse, which he denied. Ms. Fink believed Calvin. Sarah confronted her mother and Calvin and stated, "He and I know what happened and as long as it stops, I don't care who you believe." Fortunately, the abuse stopped but her mother continued to date Calvin. Sarah described her early adolescence as a time when she hated herself and everyone else, feeling betrayed and unloved. Although Sarah maintained her good academic performance, she began to act out.

Intervention

Sarah stated that having an African American therapist made it easier for her to discuss race-based issues. She felt that she did not need to monitor her thinking or protect the therapist when she wanted to discuss race or racism in her life. Some issues that Sarah raised included the racism that she has faced in previous jobs, the skepticism that others express about a young African American couple being self-employed, and issues about skin color and hair texture. African American women must negotiate racism as well as sexism and in so doing are forced to maintain a level of vigilance that can be both emotionally and physically draining. It is clear that Sarah made certain assumptions about the therapist, based on their shared ethnicity, that enhanced the creation of a safe space for her.

Goals in therapy were (a) to work through issues of the abuse and (b) to increase Sarah's confidence in herself and in her relationships to important people in her life, including her husband and her mother. Therapy began by processing her experience of sexual abuse. Interwoven in this process was Sarah's appreciation that the abuse was not her fault and that her own resilience protected her. In essence, Sarah was motivated to exchange her moral masochism (Thompson, 2000) to a softly strong stance (Hall, 1998).

Early on in therapy Sarah read *The Courage to Heal* (Bass & Davis, 1988). Sarah reported feeling relieved knowing that there were other women who shared her feelings about the abuse and felt comforted knowing that she was not alone. Bibliotherapy in this instance was clearly a useful tool. At one point, however, James became threatened by Sarah's immersion in reading about other abused children as she worked through her own abuse. Sarah was able to share with him the importance of support that came from her reading and reassure him that he was very much a part of her healing process. Both Sarah and James recognized that Sarah had to experience a period of emotional distance from him to work through her feelings. James understood and gave Sarah the space and support that she needed to heal. He did, however, feel rejected at times.

Therapy also assisted her in learning to accept her decision-making strength, even when she was at odds with James or her mother. One of Sarah's biggest decisions was to schedule a session with her mother to discuss the impact of her abuse on herself and on their relationship. In preparation for this session, Sarah and her therapist discussed the reality that Ms. Fink might not acknowledge that she did not protect her daughter because of her own need for a man.

After much preparation, Sarah invited her mother to a therapy session. Sarah was able to tell her how she felt betrayed and controlled. Her mother was candid and told Sarah that she had become a mother at a very young age and had prioritized her own needs over her being a parent. However, she took no responsibility regarding the betrayal of Sarah surrounding the abuse. Although her mother requested additional sessions, Sarah suggested that her mother enter therapy herself. Sarah stated that she would consider additional joint sessions only when her mother was able to acknowledge her own issues as well as her contribution to Sarah's problems. Setting a boundary around her own therapy is another example of Sarah's improved capacity for self-care.

In subsequent sessions, Sarah was able to discuss her disappointment with her mother's response. However, she was also able to appreciate her own strength in confronting her mother and feeling more at peace with the past. This sole session was not a remedy for the problems within their relationship. However, Sarah felt that she had let her mother know how betrayed she felt rather than continuing to protect their relationship at a high cost to her self. Sarah also realized that Ms. Fink was jealous of her success (i.e., a loving husband, three loving children, an upper-middle-class lifestyle, etc.). Sarah wanted her mother to appreciate and be proud of her accomplishments rather than to feel competitive with her. However, she was no longer willing to sacrifice her own needs for their relationship.

Sarah questioned her own competence and strength in all areas of her life except her unconditional love for and protection of her children. Sarah realized that she strove for perfection at home and in the business and saw herself as a Superwoman with no needs and unlimited resources. Sarah began to accept that it was appropriate to have her own needs met. However, having her needs met was generating changes in her relationships with her mother and with James. Sarah began to realize that her moral masochism, rather than empowering her, actually enabled others to underfunction, which, in turn, created a pattern that left her questioning herself and her own judgment.

Moreover, she realized that James's need to be in control reinforced her distrust of her own judgment. Sarah used therapy to discover what she wanted from her mother and from James, how to let them know what she wanted, and her options when her needs were not met. Sarah realized that she was not subordinate in her relationships with her mother or with James and that she brought strengths to these relationships. On an emotional level, Sarah "reclaimed" gender role equity, a culturally supported value, within her marriage.

In the sessions with James and Sarah, James's controlling nature and his commitment to family and to Sarah were explored. Therapy initially focused on examining what each found attractive about the other, what each of them brought into their relationship, and why they remained together. Sarah wanted James to accept her strengths and respect her decisions without making her feel guilty or inadequate when she disagreed with him. Therapy also explored how family decisions were made and the types of strains that are placed on relationships when a couple creates and runs a family business. Because James had been a supervisor in his previous job, he was used to delegating and expected Sarah to be his subordinate, to acquiesce on business decisions, and to absorb his "share" of the business or family responsibilities when he was "too busy." They were able to discuss his need to be in control even when Sarah neither required nor desired his supervision. Both acknowledged that more egalitarian roles were necessary.

James began to appreciate how counterproductive his behavior was to their business and to their marriage, as well as to appreciate that his dream of having a family business was realized and that Sarah was central (rather than secondary) to their business success.

Although James's devotion to his family was clear, as was his desire to seek help when he was in crisis, he felt uncomfortable and threatened by Sarah's assertiveness. James admitted that he did not anticipate that Sarah would change her behavior toward him, but he began to accept her (and his own) growth. He recognized that he feared losing Sarah and that he needed to listen to her needs. Although he was unable to articulate all of his fears, James stopped blaming Sarah for all of their problems. He became less controlling and critical of her and began to explore his role in their family and business conflicts. Sarah felt a point of unspoken contention was that her portion of the business generated more profit than the portion that James oversaw. Therapy helped her to raise this issue with James. They also discussed the option of resolving the discrepancy by renegotiating their responsibilities. This eventually resolved the dilemma. While the resolution of the balance of power in a marriage is not an uncommon issue for many couples, it may have special significance for African American families. African American men have historically been denied the opportunity to fulfill the male breadwinner role in their families because of racism. They may be particularly sensitive in situations when their spouse earns more or is more successful in a career. This requires an extra level of sensitivity on the therapist's part. While supporting sexism is not an appropriate response, reinstating the balance of power and helping the husband become more comfortable with his own successes without the need to compete with his wife is essential.

Conceptualization

Sarah's family illustrates many aspects of feminist therapy principles used within a cultural context. The relevance of relatedness from an Afrocentric and a feminist perspective, issues of empowerment within a cultural context, connections and disconnections, and the importance of extended family are all present in the rich fabric of the African American family (Greene, 1995, 1997).

Therapy built on Sarah's strengths and examined her presenting complaints in the context of her family of origin and her immediate family. Like many African American children, Sarah was raised by a relative. Her mother's psychological and emotional abandonment created problems for Sarah. Nevertheless, she fits the description of the "softly strong" African American woman. Such a woman recognizes her strengths as well as her need for support. Sarah did not feel that she gave up her femininity or womanhood by recognizing her strengths. In fact, her family became a stronger unit because she came to terms with her past. Sarah chose a life partner who complemented her desire for a family and for a life different from that of her mother. Through therapy, Sarah came to appreciate the appropriateness of meeting her own needs and could identify the moral masochism (Thompson, 2000) that had prevented her from doing so.

Sarah and her husband also fit neatly into Hill's (1971) description of African American families: strong achievement motivation, strong work orientation, and strong kinship bonds with fictive kin. Sarah maintained a strong relationship with a best friend and was invested in establishing a closer relationship with a maternal uncle. In addition, the important African American value of direct experience as the optimal means of acquiring wisdom and personal growth (Nobles, 1980) is also evident in Sarah's interactions with her family. She relied on and valued her "mother wit" and her life experiences. She realized that making appropriate demands in a relationship was not synonymous with being a shrewish, castrating Sapphire (West, 2000). Although she lost a companion with the loss of her mother, Sarah realized that their relationship was never on mutual terms, nor did it take her own needs into consideration.

Both James and Sarah functioned within a cultural context that is typical of many African American families. Both came from single-parent families and were involved in a dual-income nuclear family. Both recognized the importance of the extended family and of fictive kin. Both now function within a higher socioeconomic class than their families of origin. As a couple, they dealt with the disparity of earning potential between them and resolved the issue. Both came to recognize that Sarah carried the brunt of the responsibilities in the business and at home and made progress at modifying this pattern. James and Sarah were able to create a family structure with egalitarian gender roles that allowed each of them to grow independently and together.

Although her marriage is central in her life, Sarah wanted to maintain her newfound confidence and wanted her marriage to grow with her. She appreciated that concessions have to be made and she and James must remain willing to work on change. She also realized that James, as well as she, was accountable for their marriage's survival. James's control issues were not only gender role related but complement the control issues Sarah had faced with her mother.

Although James valued Sarah's strength as it was directed toward others, he was also affected by society's racial and gender role stereotypes. Stereotypes of American men dictate that they are in charge of family decisions because they are the primary wage earners in the family. However, African American men, blocked from being able to enact the primary provider role by societal racism, are viewed as failures. This failure that is caused by societal pressures is often experienced as a loss of personal power in their family. Thus husbands may experience a wife's demand for gender equity as further emasculating them.

Although James found it challenging to support gender equity within his own family, he realized that he would have to help more with household and parental responsibilities if their marriage was to work, particularly given the pressure that they both felt in making their business profitable. He also realized that he would have to assume more of the responsibilities in the business. James began to acknowledge the consequences of his own behavior and to accept the changes that Sarah made as positive rather than threatening. Both realized the need to build in time for each other and for other relationships as well. Not only did this adoption of gender equity impact their marriage, but it is a position that is supported by African American culture. Both James and Sarah received support from family and friends for making modifications in their family structure.

This case illustrates how one can practice culturally sensitive feminist family therapy without formally labeling it as such. African American clients do not have to accept the feminist label to benefit from feminist principles. In many instances, Afrocentric values (e.g., being interdependent and softly strong) complement feminist values (e.g., connectedness, empowerment).

Sarah was treated within an appreciation for her cultural context. For Sarah, working in therapy with an African American female therapist allowed her to address some of the more difficult aspects of her treatment earlier than perhaps she may have with a White therapist. White therapists must be willing to tolerate an initial period of skepticism and distance that racial difference can generate. Most importantly, if a therapist appreciates the cultural context of the client's life, feminist family therapy can be a useful tool in work with African American families.

REFERENCES

Bass, E., & Davis, L. (1988). *The courage to heal: A guide for women survivors of child sexual abuse*. New York: Harper & Row.

Boyd-Franklin, N. (1989). *Black families in therapy: A multisystems approach*. New York: Guilford Press.

Boyd-Franklin, N., & Franklin, A. J. (2000). *Boys into men: Raising our African American teenage sons*. New York: Dutton.

Greene, B. (1995). African American families: A legacy of vulnerability and resilience. *National Forum: Phi Kappa Phi Journal, 75*, 26–29.

Greene, B. (1997). Psychotherapy with African American women: Integrating feminist and psychodynamic models. *Journal of Smith College Studies in Social*

Work—*Theoretical, Research, Practice and Educational Perspectives for Understanding and Working With African American Clients, 67*, 299–322.

Hall, R. L. (1998). Mind and body: Toward the holistic treatment of African American women. *The Psychotherapy Patient, 10*, 81–100.

Hall, R. L., & Greene, B. (1995). Cultural competence in feminist family therapy: An ethical mandate. *Journal of Feminist Family Therapy, 6*, 5–28.

Helms, J. E. (1995). An update of Helms White and people of color racial identity models. In J. G. Ponterotto, J. M. Cascas, L A. Suzuki, & C. M. Alexander (Eds.), *Handbook of multicultural counseling* (pp. 181–198). Thousand Oaks, CA: Sage.

Higgenbotham, E. (1982). Two representative issues in contemporary sociological work on Black women. In G. T. Hull, P. B. Scott, & B. Smith (Eds.), *But some of us are brave: Black women's studies* (pp. 93–98). Old Westbury, NY: Feminist Press.

Hill, R. (1971). *The strengths of Black families.* New York: National Urban League.

Lorde, A. (1987). I am your sister: Black women organizing across sexualities. *Practice, 5*, 83–87.

Nobles, W. W. (1980). African philosophy: Foundations for Black psychology. In R. L. Jones (Ed.), *Black psychology* (2nd ed., pp. 23–36). New York: Harper & Row.

Schaefer, R. T. (1998). *Racial and ethnic groups* (7th ed.). New York: Longman.

Shweder, R. A., & Bourne, E. J. (1984). Does the concept of the person vary cross-culturally? In R. A. Shweder & R. A. LeVine (Eds.), *Culture theory: Essays on mind, self and emotion* (pp. 158–199). New York: Cambridge University Press.

Surrey, J. L. (1991). *Women's growth in connection.* New York: Guilford Press.

Thompson, C. L. (2000). African American women and moral masochism: When there is too much of a good thing. In L. C. Jackson & B. Greene (Eds.), *Psychotherapy with African American women: Innovations in psychodynamic perspectives and practice* (pp. 239–250). New York: Guilford Press.

U.S. Department of Commerce. (1998). *Statistical abstract of the United States 1998* (118th ed.). Washington, DC: U.S. Bureau of the Census.

West, C. (2000). Developing an "oppositional gaze": Toward the images of Black women. In J. C. Chrisler, C. Golden, & P. D. Rozee (Eds.), *Lectures on the psychology of women* (2nd ed., pp. 221–235). New York: McGraw-Hill.

Wyche, K. F. (1996). Conceptualizations of social class in African American women: Congruence of client and therapist definitions. *Women & Therapy, 18*, 35–43.

Young, C. (1993). Psychodynamics of coping and survival of the African American female in a changing world. In D. R. Atkinson, G. Morten, & D. W. Sue (Eds.), *Counseling American minorities: A cross-cultural perspective* (4th ed., pp. 75–89). Dubuque, IA: Brown & Benchmark.

9

RELATIONSHIPS BETWEEN WOMEN IN FAMILIES: VOICES OF CHIVALRY

LESLYE KING MIZE

There is a story that has been told for some time about the lives of women. It reveals structures of experience under which most women, unlike men, have nearly universally existed. These structures include political oppression, specific divisions of labor, lack of financial gain, and childbearing challenges. In the view of many scholars, these structures have formed a particular consciousness, epistemology, ethic, and narrative that tend to support a less valued experience of one's self as a woman and of women in general. Society reflects women's low value. This story may be especially reflected in the family in which women do not value themselves and their relationships with one another. Given this perspective, we might contend that relationships between women that are healthy and supportive represent "voices of chivalry" that have prevailed against conditions that actually support the opposite experience.

Why use the term *chivalry*? As defined by *Webster's Third New International Dictionary* (p. 393), chivalry means "having the qualities of courage, courtesy, and loyalty." It is defined as the sum of the ideal qualifications for medieval knighthood: courtesy, generosity, valor, and dexterity in arms. Most feminists would shiver at the word because it suggests that men need to protect women. I propose, in contrast, that we take back the term to describe the gallant acts of courage and loyalty that women display in connecting with one another rather than competing for male favor. Redefining the term reminds us that for the most part, women have been written out of the histories of culture and literature produced by men. Women have been silenced or distorted in the texts of philosophy, biology, psychology, family therapy, and medicine. However, there is a group of embodied beings socially positioned as women who now are trying to learn about themselves and their contributions.

In these postmodern times, we need a story more complicated than the original. Indeed, an array of stories needs to be told through lenses of race, class, ethnicity, age, sexuality, and other currents, which contribute to the formation of cultural identity. Such stories tend to be a matter of alliances rather than one story around a universally shared interest or identity (Fraser & Nicholson, 1990). They recognize that the diversity of women's needs and experiences may mean that no single solution or truth will work for all women. Further, although some women share some common interests and face some common foes, such commonalities are by no means universal and are interlaced with differences and conflicts. We see it as critical to explore through conversations with one another the conflicts and alliances that we share, and to make room for the patchwork of overlapping alliances that may not be circumscribable by a single identity (Fraser & Nicholson, 1990). Such explorations may be especially volatile and, therefore, chivalrous for women in family life because of expectations of shared context and solidarity.

This chapter highlights the struggles among women in family life and develop the idea that family therapy can aid in these struggles. It also describes how a feminist family therapist can hold herself in that process so that she may participate fully and not be an obstacle to the experience.

THEORETICAL CONSIDERATIONS

Narrative Contributions

The therapeutic process is an especially rich arena in which women may struggle with their stories of alienation from themselves and one another. In helping to develop with clients a context for exploration of these experiences, therapists from a combined feminist/narrative perspective can support a broad array of ideas. Merger of the narrative views with a feminist philosophy has solid common ground. First, both can share the view that human beings are interpreting beings, that we are all active in giving meaning to our experiences (White & Epston, 1990). This idea can help women restory their interactions with one another and themselves. Given imposed power differentials, such acts of restorying are courageous achievements.

Second, both narrative and feminist approaches support the notion that sharing one's story in a nonhierarchical way creates the possibility of reshaping all participants' lives, including the therapist's (Freedman & Combs, 1996). This inclusion of the therapist affirms the value of connection by emphasizing that the therapist may be "touched" by the client's story.

Third, both approaches can affirm that interpretations of ourselves that we know as personal stories are not invented inside our heads. These stories are negotiated throughout our lives in the relationships we live and draw on views distributed in our various communities and in the institutions of our culture (Weingarten, 1991; White & Epston, 1990). For instance, the stories Black women hold about themselves have been shaped not only by the gender bias that goes with living in a male-shaped culture but also by the racism of a White-shaped culture.

Finally, both feminist and narrative views support the idea that our personal story determines which piece of our lived experience we select for expression. Thus, it is the story that we have about our experiences that actually shapes us (Freedman & Combs, 1996). So as we sit in the therapeutic moment together as sisters or mothers or daughters or therapists, our relationships with each other are being shaped as we speak.

Feminist Contributions

Feminism has not stood still but rather has been shaped by culture and politics over time. Contemporary feminists often deconstruct feminism into many "feminisms" and write about the failures of Whiteness, White feminism, Westernization, and competitive individualism (Narayan, 1997). King (1990, p. 69) has reminded us that "many feminists too easily believe 'we' already know the 'history' or even histories of feminism even in the U.S. What is taken as truth are some privileged and published ideologies of feminism, which have been all too quickly naturalized." Similarly, bell hooks has written,

> The overall impact of postmodernism is that many other groups now share with black folks a sense of deep alienation, despair, uncertainty, loss of a sense of grounding even if it is not informed by shared circumstance. Radical postmodernism calls attention to those shared sensibilities which cross the boundaries of class, gender, race, etc., that could be fertile ground for the construction of empathy-ties that would promote recognition of common commitments, and serve as a basis for solidarity and coalition. (1990b, p. 27)

Because feminists speak differently at different times and in different locations, chronologies tend to erase the heterogeneity of feminisms at any given moment. Any historical narrative that collapses the diverse activity of a movement into generalizations results in a portrait that leaves out marginalized voices. The question of whose story gets told is particularly loaded for women, for women's stories have historically been excluded from the master narratives. Thus, family therapists with feminist understandings need be wary of exclusions and omissions during therapeutic conversations with families.

Further, family therapists informed by feminist/narrative thinking as well as postmodernist and multiculturalist views may want to negotiate among multiple feminisms and their challenging discourses. At the same time, they should continue to speak in a collective voice that articulates political demands on the basis of women's half of the human experience. This is the paradox that faces us: to avoid the recreation of a "master" narrative or "dominant" discourse as happens by thinking of one truth, and yet push for the well-being of women of all ages, races, classes, and cultures.

In the following case, I illustrate my struggles with the foregoing challenges. As I worked to understand the multiple experiences of the women in this therapeutic conversation, I also gained an important understanding of myself as a participant/therapist in the process.

AN EXAMPLE: SISTERS, DAUGHTERS, AND MOTHERS TOGETHER

Sandy called our university clinic wanting her family to be seen in therapy as soon as possible. She jumped at the chance to be seen in exchange for making teaching tapes. Her stated concerns were for her 15- and 13-year-old daughters and for changes in the family.

Sandy arrived at the clinic alone because she wanted to "see how things would go." A 42-year-old African American woman who worked as a chemist, she greeted me warmly. Eager to begin her story, she said that both girls had been raised by her sister and her mother. Two years ago, "I was finally able to convince my mother and sister that I am capable of taking care of my own daughters." She had had cancer 12 years prior and had almost died. She had turned her daughters over to her mother and sister for care while she recovered. They lived in a small town close by.

Sandy had been living with her husband Tom—the girls' stepfather—at the time, but "he was not able to care for the girls with my illness taking such a prominent role in our lives." Over time, the girls made their home with their aunt and grandmother. Sandy believed her mother and aunt "needed the girls as much as the girls needed them."

For many years, Sandy fought a great battle with cancer while holding a job and trying to make her marriage work. Tom worked long hours. Sandy said that she and Tom fought a lot about the girls and the other pressures they were under. She added, "I blamed Tom for the family not being together and finally asked him to leave. I thought of him as weak."

After the divorce, Sandy lived on her own for several years. Then, "I began the process of getting my girls back, and my mother and sister didn't like it!" One day, she picked up the girls and moved to Houston. Her relationships with both her mother and sister deteriorated, and Sandy thought that the girls had been caught in the middle. Formerly, both girls had done well in school, but in Houston, they began to have problems with grades and friends. "They fight a lot also," revealed Sandy, "where before they moved to Houston, they seemed to get along well."

I asked Sandy what she would like to get out of therapy. She answered that she wanted her family to get along again and the girls to do better in school. She said that she was considering reconciling with Tom and was concerned about the impact of that decision on the girls. She and Tom had been meeting secretly because she did not want to upset the girls, who were "mad at their stepdad for the way he handled everything." I asked her what her daughters would say if they knew about the reconciliation. She thought that they would not be happy about it and she wanted help with this issue in therapy. Further probing revealed that she feared that the girls might think that Tom would come before them once again and that then they would be asked to move away.

At the end of our session, I asked Sandy if there was any reason that we might not be able to work together. She laughed and said, "You mean because you are White?" I smiled and said that that might be one of many reasons, but if that were the case, I would understand and do my best to find her another therapist. She stated that she felt comfortable with me and that she thought that we could probably work well together. I asked if she thought a session with the girls present would be helpful. She arranged a meeting for the next week. I also asked if she wanted sometime to invite her mother and sister to a session. She said that she would think about that idea but was not ready now.

Treatment Plan

I wanted the plan for treatment to evolve through the process of therapy itself because I wanted the participants to be a dynamic part of setting the direction. However, as a systems therapist, I needed to make some assumptions about my work. These assumptions were as follows:

1. I wanted to see as many members of the family together as possible so that they would benefit from the interaction. My task was to hold the conversational space and support the therapeutic direction by asking questions that would not have been asked otherwise. These questions would be more about process than content. That is, I saw myself as the expert on the therapeutic process and them as the experts on the conversational content and what they wanted to get across to each other.

2. Gender and race had shaped the lives of these women and that fact needed to inform the questions that I introduced in therapy.
3. I wanted not my desires but theirs to determine the outcome of the process.

Second Session and Beyond—Mother and Daughters Together

Sandy arrived the following week with her two daughters, Tyrina, 15, and Jade, 13. Both girls were quick to share their ideas about why the family was attending therapy. Tyrina felt that Jade had been having too many behavior problems in school and that Jade and Mom fought a lot. She also mentioned that Jade was immature for her age. Jade pointed the finger at Tyrina and said she had a bad temper and made everybody at home miserable with her "bad moods." She denied that she and Mom fought a lot and charged that it was really Tyrina and Mom who fought. At this point, I followed the narrative approach of so-called deconstruction questioning. I questioned each member of the family about her own story of the development of the problems and about their favored version of the outcome of therapy. As a result, a consensus surfaced that therapy would be most helpful if everyone got along better at home. All hoped for more cooperation. Sandy spoke about her concerns about school and her desire to support the girls in making school a better experience.

Near the close of the session, I reframed the conflict in the family as a process of adjustment and possibly a way in which each woman was getting to know the other again in a new way. Here I was attempting to focus the challenge at the systems level rather than at an individual one. I could see the stress lift from each woman's shoulders. Jade even remarked, "You mean our fighting might not be a bad thing?" They all smiled.

Over the course of several weeks, Sandy, Tyrina, Jade, and I shared some moving moments in therapy. My feminist/narrative stance supported me in thinking through the notion that gender socialization was a significant factor in shaping the lives of these women. For example, they voiced their struggles with such dilemmas as financial status for Sandy and participation in sports activities for both Tyrina and Jade. All three felt that being female had set the tone for many challenges that they faced and that they were beginning to learn to work together by speaking about their concerns and encouraging one another to move through the obstacle.

This case also challenged me to recognize and embrace difference. I acknowledged race as a significant variable shaping our conversations. My "Whiteness" in experience and language became a subtle theme. I struggled with whether to make this issue explicit by acknowledging the difference myself, but this approach seemed artificial. Instead, I waited for the conversational moment. It came during an early session when Jade was talking, from my view, very rapidly using several unfamiliar words to describe a friend. When I asked her for an explanation, she very patiently explained that these were words that some Black kids used to describe someone that was acting like a jerk. That comment gave me an opportunity to note my "Whiteness."

This acknowledgment of pluralism opened up a conversation that was extremely helpful, and a new level of therapy emerged. Sandy described the tough times she had had as an African American girl in east Texas in the 1960s as one of two Black teens in her school. She had been discouraged from taking science classes because she was Black. In fact, she had to try harder and make better grades than White kids just because people believed that Black kids were not as smart. Because of such experiences, she worried that Jade and Tyrina were experiencing discrimination.

I asked Sandy questions to help elicit her narratives concerning discrimination: What experiences did you have that prompted your concerns about the girls in school? In what types of situations did you most expect these issues to be present when you were in school? How do you think you were affected by the discrimination against you as a child?

In response to her mother's concerns, Tyrina revealed that in her old school, there had been many Black kids but that here, there were not so many. She felt like she was "not as pretty as the White girls." At this school, it was important to be pretty. Questions deconstructing "pretty" developed the view that "pretty" meant "White with long straight hair." Jade said that there were more Black kids in her class, but they did not want to be friends with her. They would rather be friends with the White kids. I asked such questions as: How would you know when someone wanted to be your friend? Has there ever been a time when, even for a moment, you were hopeful that someone wanted to be your friend? Have the two of you ever stood up to some of these tough situations and decided to do something your own way? Have the two of you ever had moments when you were really proud to be Black? As you look back at this accomplishment, what do you two think were the turning points that made it possible?

Opening up a conversational space for these important issues revealed some unique outcomes and resilience. For example, Sandy revealed that she had taught Tyrina how to braid her hair. Then, Tyrina began to teach braiding to some girls at school, and now many girls braid their hair like Tyrina. Tyrina also remembered when she had made the highest grade on a difficult test. Even though her grade was barely passing, no one else did pass. Jade remembered several times that she had been asked to parties recently and even though she was too afraid to go, she was thinking about going the next time.

Another important moment in therapy was when both daughters remarked on how much they missed their grandmother and aunt and how important they had been. Jade added how much she missed her friends and the experience of going to school with a lot of Black students. Both girls spoke about how much they wished that they all got along once again so that they could spend time at their grandmother and aunt's house. Sandy acknowledged her appreciation of what her mother and sister had done and her difficulty struggling with cancer.

At the end of the session, Sandy suggested that the girls call their grandmother and aunt and say hello. They had not spoken since they had left their home. Also I pointed out the strength and courage the girls had shown in facing gender and racial discrimination. They said that they had not thought of their experience from that perspective. Then Tyrina described Jade as especially brave to consider going to a party where most of the kids would be White. She offered to go with her.

Grandmother, Mothers, Sisters, and Daughters Together

Soon a session was scheduled with grandmother, aunt, Sandy, Tyrina, Jade, and me. Sandy had had contact with her mother and sister on the phone prior to the session and all had gone "surprisingly well." Several themes emerged in the session that seemed relevant to women's relationships with one another in the family.

First, the women were troubled about how to disagree without disconnecting. Second, they each had experienced not being valued by the other women in the family. Third, they viewed men rather than women as carrying more value in the family. Fourth, they all had faced discrimination but felt that no one should talk about it. The contribution of the family therapy session might be a conversation between women in which these themes were discussed and negotiated in a new way.

"Disagreement" Theme

In the session, we laughed when Jade asked me what I thought of being in a therapy session with "five Black women who get mad at each other a lot." I replied that I had a lot to learn from them, especially about how they agreed and disagreed. All the women acknowledged having known some form of hurt from the others. All acknowledged having wondered if their feelings were important to the others. For instance, Grandmother revealed that she had been hurt because Sandy had not shared the girls with her recently and that she did not feel appreciated for all she had done. Further, she revealed that she was hurt that Sandy did not come home very often and had not come home when she had been sick with cancer.

This deep hurt of Grandmother's would take some time to heal. As hooks has written,

Since sexism delegates to females the task of creating and sustaining a home environment, it has been primarily the responsibility of black women to construct domestic households as spaces of care and nurturance in the face of the brutal harsh reality of racist oppression and social domination. . . . This task of making a home place was not simply a matter of black women providing service, it was about the construction of a safe place where black people could affirm one another and by so doing heal many of the wounds inflicted. . . . this task of making a home place a community of resistance, has been shared by black women globally. (1990a, p. 42)

Sandy was able to listen intently to her mother's words and respond in a caring way. She said that she had heard for the first time how hurt her mother had been by her decision to fight the cancer alone rather than to come home. In fact, she acknowledged that she had felt very alone in her battle with cancer and could have used her mother's love. She also had been raised by her grandmother and had thought that grandmothers raising children was "normal" for the family. As a result, she had not felt it necessary to express appreciation for all her mother had done.

This theme about difficulty with disagreements continued with remarks by Pam, Sandy's sister. She said, "You always take a risk of being cut off when you disagree with Mama or Sandy." Sandy agreed with Pam about their mother but had not thought of herself as difficult in that way. Both daughters added that it was difficult to disagree with Sandy.

Jade furthered the theme, saying that she wanted to be closer to her sister but "our fights keep us apart." Pam described struggles with Sandy as a younger sister whom she had much admired as a role model. Grandmother described struggles with her sister as well and reported that she had never found a way to disagree with her sister without years of "not speaking." Her sister died "not speaking to me." Both sets of sisters agreed that they did not want such separation and were willing to discuss ways to disagree while staying close.

"Valuing Each Other" Theme

Grandmother and Pam noted their fear that Sandy was ashamed of them because they were housekeepers. Since Sandy had moved to the city and had a "professional job," they thought that she thought them less important and did not appreciate what they valued. As Pam put it, Sandy thinks that "she is too good for us" and that we are just "country folk whose feelings are not important." She added that Sandy felt that the two of them were not "good enough" to raise the girls or even be a part of the girls' lives. Sandy responded by expressing how lonely she was and how much the girls missed their family and their community. Both Jade and Tyrina emphasized how much they missed "their home."

Further discussion led to the discovery that the values held by all the women were not markedly different. West (1985) helps us understand what prompted this discussion:

> There is increasing class division and differentiation, creating on the one hand a significant black middle-class, highly anxiety ridden, insecure, willing to be co-opted and incorporated into the powers that be, concerned with racism to the degree that it poses constraints on upward social mobility; and on the other a vast and growing black underclass, an underclass that embodies a kind of walking nihilism of pervasive homicide, and an exponential rise in suicide. Now because of deindustrialization, we also have a devastated black industrial working class. (p. 21)

"Men Being Valued More Than Women" Theme

Pam charged that whenever Sandy was in a relationship with either of her husbands, she and her mother felt abandoned by her. I asked more generally if they felt that men were more valued in the family (Greene, 1994). Although Jade and Tyrina said no, Pam said that women were the "workers" in the family and men were "scarce," so as a result, more valuable. Grandmother pointed out that in her family growing up, her brothers had been important for farming. Everyone in her community had always felt "blessed" when they had sons to work on the farm. But the men in the family were not very dependable. The women were the ones who did all the work around the house, raised the children, and often worked for White families in the town near home.

Pam revealed disappointment with Tom's decision to turn the daughters over so readily when things began to get difficult. She had thought Tom was a "different kind of guy," but he had been like "all the rest she had known and turned it all over to the women to do all the work of the family." Sandy countered that it had been her decision as well, but she also expressed disappointment with Tom's readiness to turn the girls over to her family. After further discussion, the women agreed that perhaps they did not value each other because women had not been as valued. Pam wondered if this situation had changed in the family with Jade and Tyrina's generation because they both had said that they felt loved and valued.

"Fighting Discrimination Alone" Theme

The last part of the session revealed an important theme that gave the family a chance to practice staying connected while disagreeing. Sandy wanted the others to know why it had been so important for her girls to leave their small town. She did not want her daughters to have the limited opportunity a Black woman would have in the small community. Although Grandmother and Pam agreed that the girls should have more opportunity, they said that life had been good in their home and the girls needed to be children first. Sandy described the discrimination she had felt as a child growing up in the community and how hard it had been for her. Grandmother replied that she had never experienced much discrimination in her life. She said that she "didn't see color in people and that people is people." She further stated that "it wouldn't have done much good thinking about that all the time and that there was more important things to do with my time." Pam put in that she had experienced feeling "less than" as a Black woman and agreed with Sandy that it had been hard growing up in a White community. Sandy and Pam remarked that discrimination was not a subject one could bring up "in our home so we just kept it to ourselves." "We did not even talk about it with one another," added Pam. After we discussed what discrimination meant to each member, Pam requested that the family members agree to talk with one another if anyone had that "feeling where you just don't feel as good as White folks or if you were White, things would be different for you." All agreed except for Grandmother.

Greene (1994) has suggested that psychotherapy with African American women should include helping them in "identifying the conscious and unconscious methods they employ in confronting and responding to racial as well as other personal difficulties" (p. 24). Our conversations concerning discrimination had revealed that the family members used very different strategies for handling these challenges and would likely continue to see these issues differently. Grandmother had not felt compelled to respond to these issues actively, explaining that she would have had little energy left to address other issues in her life. Further, questions were asked such as: How did other women in the family deal with the issues of discrimination and racism? How does managing racism show itself in the family generally?

What I learned from these women and girls was that managing discrimination seemed to be a multifaceted process, the importance of which varied from woman to woman. Many environmental factors contributed to the differences, but those factors interacted with the individual stories of how each woman thought of herself (Boyd-Franklin, 1989). Further, this family taught me that it is important to avoid using racial or gender oppression to explain all of a woman's difficulties. To do so could prevent both therapist and patient from understanding any role she may play in her own story and thus limit her options for making changes. At the same time, the family members challenged me not to romanticize their successes in overcoming their multiple oppressions without being aware of the costs.

CONCLUSION

Working with these family members by no means reveals generalizations automatically relevant to any other family of Black women or any group of female family members. However, common themes may emerge with other families as well. While African American women may seem to share many group characteristics, individuals are unique and often develop ways of thinking that are specifically their own. Each woman develops stories of coping with life stressors such as racial discrimination in the same manner that she meets other challenges in her life.

It may be important to see race simply as a dimension, particularly in the context of our racist society, along with the challenge of gender. The challenge for me as family therapist was to see the difficulty of coping with issues of gender and race, as well as the richness of each woman's identity, and the ways in which each had met these challenges. I came away believing that living in a "therapeutic conversation" that only preserved the status quo was not enough for me to maintain my sanity and human dignity.

I wanted to be part of a conversation that was personal and engaged while maintaining my role as therapist. I found myself experiencing a type of hybrid thinking that marked part of my own critical agenda, that is, to participate in creating a place of discussion and disagreement that was also a place of community. I wanted to engage the possibility of rethinking and reshaping. I hoped that this position would help me to expand comfortable cultural, gender, and age polarities and situate the conversation squarely within lived therapeutic space. As feminist family therapists, we may be better able to do so because of the feminisms that have come before us. Further, we can be grateful for the ways in which feminist family therapy with a narrative approach has made it possible for us to still have hope, to keep the faith, and to survive.

REFERENCES

Boyd-Franklin, N. (1989). *Black families in therapy: A multi-systems approach*. New York: Guilford Press.

Fraser, N., & Nicholson, L. (1990). Social criticism without philosophy: An encounter between feminism and postmodernism. In L. Nicholson (Ed.), *Feminism/postmodernism* (pp. 19–39). New York: Routledge.

Freedman, J., & Combs, G. (1996). *Narrative therapy: The social construction of preferred realities*. New York: Norton.

Greene, B. (1994). African American Women. In L. Comas-Diaz & B. Greene (Eds.), *Women of color: Integrating ethnic and gender identities in psychotherapy* (pp. 10–29). New York: Guilford Press.

hooks, b. (1990a). Homeplace—a site of resistance. In b. hooks (Ed.), *Yearnings: Race, gender, and cultural politics* (pp. 41–49). Boston: South End Press.

hooks, b. (1990b). Postmodern blackness. In b. hooks (Ed.), *Yearnings: Race, gender, and cultural politics* (pp. 23–31). Boston: South End Press.

King, K. (1990). Producing sex, theory, and culture: Gay/straight remappings in contemporary feminism. In M. Hirsch & E. Keller (Eds.), *Conflicts in feminism* (pp. 65–91). New York: Routledge.

Narayan, U. (1997). *Dislocating cultures: Identities, traditions, and Third World feminism*. New York: Routledge.

Webster's Third New International Dictionary of the English Language Unabridged. (1971). Springfield, MA: G & C Merriam.

Weingarten, K. (1991). The discourses of intimacy: Adding a social constructionist and feminist view. *Family Process, 30*, 285–302.

West, C. (1985). *Post analytic philosophy*. New York: Columbia University Press.

White, M., & Epston, D. (1990). *Narrative means to therapeutic ends*. New York: Norton.

10

CONFUCIAN PAST, CONFLICTED PRESENT: WORKING WITH ASIAN AMERICAN FAMILIES

LIANG TIEN AND KARI OLSON

"It is the context that fixes the meaning." (Bateson, 1988, p. 16)
"Families are embedded in and shaped by culture and society . . . individual behavior can be seen as reflecting progressively wider social influences depending upon the focus of observations." (Kluckhohn & Spiegel, 1968, p. 36)

Americans of Asian ancestry have immigrated, lived, married, and raised families on United States soil since the middle 1800s. When they seek psychotherapy, it is easier for both the client and psychotherapist if the latter is aware of the cultural and immigration context of the family. To the extent that psychotherapists understand a family's Confucian-based philosophical/cultural stance, they are better able to formulate interventions that are culturally congruent for the family. Moreover, the framework of the therapy itself should be culturally congruent for the Asian American. Here we argue that it is more efficacious to adopt a family therapy orientation when working with families with ancestry from Confucian cultures because family systems theory is more congruent with the beliefs of the Confucian cultures than is an individual therapy paradigm.

We outline family migration patterns to increase awareness of possible issues related to acculturation. We highlight cultural features and beliefs of Confucianism related to features of the family systems orientation. The cultural congruency of interventions based on the family systems orientation for Confucian families is illustrated in a case vignette.

MIGRATION PATTERNS OF AMERICAN FAMILIES
WITH ASIAN ANCESTRY

In the work of a multicultural feminist family therapist, the knowledge of cultural values of the client family and the level of the family's acculturation and assimilation is critical to understanding the issues of major concern to the family. Effective work with Confucian-based Asian American families can be vastly enhanced with some background knowledge of the group's migration and adjustment pattern in the United States. We present a brief overview of the generational migration patterns of the Asian American families from Confucian-based cultures.

The term *Asian Americans* commonly refers to individuals who originate from countries on the Asian continent. These can include countries bordered on the east by Tajikistan, on the west by the Philippines, on the north by China, and on the south by Indonesia. Yet Asians are not of one monolithic cultural background. This chapter addresses only those Asian Americans with ancestry from Confucian-based countries.

Generally, American families with Asian ancestry are either recent immigrants or fourth- to sixth-generation Americans. Chinese American families are either sixth-generation descendents from the first railroad workers or first-generation immigrants primarily from Taiwan or Hong Kong. Korean American families are either sixth-generation descendents from the plantation fields of Hawaii or first-generation families looking for a place free from political upheaval. Vietnamese American families are first-generation refugees. Japanese American families are fourth- and fifth-generation descendents from agricultural workers.

Because of the different political situations in their countries of origin, their length of time in the United States, and the reason for migration, Asian American families seek psychotherapy with a variety of presenting problems. Regardless of the specific issues presented for therapy, there are some common patterns shared by families with ancestry based on Confucian codes of conduct. A few features relevant to working with these families are highlighted below.

CONFUCIAN PRINCIPLES

Confucian-based cultures are found predominately in the countries of Japan, Korea, China, and Vietnam. Confucianism is a code of ethics that prescribes behavior. It originated in the writings of Confucius, a Chinese scholar who lived between 551 B.C and 479 B.C. Confucius lived in a time of political instability when several kingdoms were fighting for dominance in China. Thus, his writings were primarily concerned with the maintenance of stability and order through strict observation of social hierarchy. Confucianism spread from China to Japan, Korea, and Vietnam and has held a strong influence in these societies and cultures.

Interpersonal Focus

The Confucian code is characterized by the fundamental assumption that human beings exist in relationship to others. "The Western starting point of the anomic individual is alien to Chinese considerations of man's social behavior, which see man as a relational being, socially situated and defined within an interactive context" (Bond & Hwang, 1986, p. 215). Confucianism focuses on and emphasizes the *proper* relationship among people of different social positions, such as those between ruler and subject, father and son, elder brother and younger brother, husband and wife, friend and friend. All these relationships are hierarchical, the former in each pair being superior to, and having considerable power over, the latter.

Harmony

Confucianism codifies the Taoist emphasis on harmony. Taoists believe that when all members follow the proper conduct, society then achieves a state of perfect harmony with nature and humanity. Confucianism prescribes the proper conduct of individuals within their social positions to achieve the Taoist harmony.

The structure of Confucian relationships—by extension of society, inclusive of families—is hierarchical and collectivistic. The proper conduct by superiors calls for conscientious, just, and compassionate behavior. Such behavior is encoded in the *li,* or rules of conduct. The *li* specifies rights and responsibilities of both parties in the relationship.

Patriarchy

The Confucian family is hierarchical and patriarchal. Wives are subordinate to husbands, and fathers are dominant within family systems (Guisso, 1981). Women's roles are prescribed in the Book of Rites by the Three Obediences and the Four Attributes. The Three Obediences state that women are subject to their fathers before marriage, to their husbands within marriage, and to their sons after their husbands die. The Four Attributes of womanhood are virtue, speech, carriage, and work. A virtuous wife shows obedience and subservience to her husband. Her speech and manner should be pleasing and docile. She should be skilled in all types of household work such as cooking, weaving, preparing ancestral sacrifices, and serving her elder in-laws. Her responsibility is to manage and keep harmony in the domestic arena. The Book of Rites states that mediating the critical filial bond, tying father to son, and the regulation and harmony of families are the responsibilities of women. Such harmonious relations are seen as vital to the perpetuation of the family line. Especially during periods of rapid social change in China as elsewhere, women are named the guardians of morality and stability, charged with protecting the sanctuary of the family (Mann, 1991). This practice may be particularly relevant in the case of recent immigrants, who are experiencing rapid and intense social change.

American families of the Chinese diaspora do not maintain an unchanging Confucian culture across time and space (Ong & Nonini, 1997). We apply Confucian philosophy to a woman's role as delineated in the Book of Rites and the Analects of Confucius, and we outline general guidelines regarding family roles. To work within a highly patriarchal system like the Confucian culture, it is necessary to acknowledge the limitations that this culture places on the activities of women.

We do not suggest that feminist family therapists should advocate for the continued subservience of Asian American women to advance the coherence of the Asian American community. Nor do we believe that feminist family therapists should contribute to the estrangement and marginalization of Asian American women within their Confucian-based community, however oppressive it may be as a patriarchal system. We do suggest that feminist family therapists may be able to help Asian American women and men assume the role of "cultural transformer." This role can help the Confucian culture evolve toward greater equality between women and men and toward greater freedom for both sexes in choosing their roles in their adopted land of the United States of America.

FAMILY THERAPY AND CONFUCIANISM

The treatment of emotionally troubled persons in Western psychology has a long tradition of focusing on the individual. Freud's psychoanalysis as practiced in this century, Rogers's client-centered therapy, and Beck's cognitive–behavioral therapy all share in common the belief that psychological problems, though rooted in previous unhealthy interactions with others, are a result of current intrapsychic conflicts within the individual. These individualistic beliefs may not translate well to the collectivist-minded members from cultures that are Confucian-based.

A counter to the focus on the individual is family systems theory. Family therapists think of psychopathology as part of an ongoing, circular, causal sequence of behavior rather than something that exists independently in the individual (Nichols & Schwartz, 1998). Although many different schools of family therapy have emerged and evolved since the 1950s, there are a few basic assumptions shared by all schools of family therapy. The most basic assumption is that individual behavior is not solely based on internal representations but rather on interactions between individuals in the family.

Feminist family therapists would add the assumption that an individual's behavior is based on the interaction among the individual, the family, and the social milieu in which the family is embedded. The feminist family therapist would add the social context of the family as contributing a powerful force on the individual's behavior. The appearance of symptoms is thought to reflect disturbance in that individual's important relationship systems. The key to changing an individual is to change his or her relational context (Gurman & Kniskern, 1981).

The multicultural feminist family therapist acknowledges the influence of not only family members and the social context but also the cultural context. The Asian American multicultural feminist family therapist bridges Western family systems theory with the core values of the Confucian culture as she or he forms a more culturally friendly conceptualization of family therapy. The family therapist's emphasis on the interrelatedness of people's behavior mirrors the fundamental Confucian assumption that human beings exist in relationship to others. Families are conceptualized as having subsystems and boundaries. Family members concurrently hold roles in several subgroups—a woman may be a wife, a mother, a daughter, and an aunt simultaneously. In each of the subgroups (or subsystems), she is expected and required to behave differently (Nichols & Schwartz, 1998).

For Asian American clients, psychotherapy with a systems orientation may require less of a shift in worldview for the client. Interventions designed within the framework of systems theory thus may be more easily taken from the therapy relationship into the Asian American family and the Asian American community. However, using some key concepts and techniques developed within family systems theory does not mean the adoption of all aspects of Western family systems theory. Below is our blending of borrowed concepts in the service of treating families from Confucian-based cultures in the context of Western psychotherapy.

CONFUCIANISM AND FAMILY THERAPY

The idea of boundaries, enduring patterns, and hierarchical relationships may be translated and conceptually understood by Confucians as the rules of conduct prescribed by *li*. Confucius' writings are a collection of prescribed behaviors between subsystems: proper conduct between superiors to inferiors, between teachers and students, between emperors and subjects, between husband and wife, and so on. The *li* prescribes proper conduct that is to be repeated with such regularity that society is stabilized through these enduring patterns of behavior. Thus is a structure—in the family therapist's sense—created for a society.

The permeability of boundaries between subsystems can easily translate to Confucian thought regarding the degree of influence the superior is to allow the inferior. These rules are encoded in the *li,* the *I-Ching,* and numerous interpretive writings on Confucian proper conduct. In this Confucian hierarchy, a superior is to treat inferiors with respect and proper regard for their well-being. When the inferior's happiness is disturbed, it behooves the superior to examine his or her own conduct.

The harmony that is held in high esteem by Confucians is thought to occur when all subsystems within a social structure stay within their properly prescribed boundaries. The *li* prescribes behaviors so that the system is held in balance. In family systems theory, the concept of homeostasis, a state in which things are kept the same, is akin to the Confucian idea of harmony. The value placed by family therapy on homeostasis is somewhat negative because the tendency toward homeostasis is thought to maintain dysfunctional behavior in the family's interactions. In contrast, the value placed on harmony in the Confucian cultures is positive because harmony is thought to maintain a balance in which all members of the system are able to get their own needs met.

The function of the harmony derived from the *li* cannot be equated with the enmeshment of the members of a family in a dysfunctional homeostatic state. For Confucians, when a system has achieved harmony, all individuals within the system are having their basic needs met, all subsystems are functioning in proper relationship, and there is no cause for conflict. People acting in accordance with the *li* attain this homeostatic state.

When a therapist talks to an Asian American from a Confucian-based culture about family structure, the Asian American does not have such a wide conceptual gap to cross. Most structures hold cultural assumptions regarding the relationship between family members. The structural family therapist ascribes the executive functions to the father and the mother, whereas Confucian thought ascribes the executive function exclusively to the father. This male-dominated hierarchical family structure poses grave consequences regarding the oppression of women and severely limits role flexibility for men. Establishing social harmony within a hierarchical structure restricts all members of the group. In the Confucian system, it requires women's obedience and subservience to the male members of the family (father/husband/son) and results in men's isolation from their children.

We recommend that the multicultural feminist family therapist be the instrument of cultural evolution by inviting the Asian American family to construct their own family system with the help of the therapist. The restructuring of the family may then be the vehicle to transform the Confucian family toward one that is more respectful of all family members. We recommend a culturally congruent reframing of family problems. For example, we might suggest that harmony has been disrupted by migration for the first-generation family or by adoption/assimilation for the fifth-generation family. We might also propose that therapy will help the family to create its own *li* to establish harmony in the United States.

TREATMENT FOR ASIAN AMERICAN FAMILIES

Below is a composite case illustrating cultural transformation in the treatment of an immigrant Asian American family. Stages of the therapy process are presented, followed by discussion of the content of therapy in light of the Confucian culture and the use of techniques and concepts borrowed from family systems therapy.

Presenting Problem

Linda's father, a Korean immigrant, requested treatment for his 9-year-old daughter. The presenting complaint was that Linda was defiant, lazy, picked on her little brother, and did poorly in school. The first session was scheduled with the whole family—paternal grandfather, paternal grandmother, mother, father, Linda, and a 7-year-old son.

Mother and father reported Linda got A's and B's in school and talked about having friends at school. In the office, Linda was attentive to the therapist, followed instructions without difficulty or defiance, and took care of her brother by reading a book to him. The 7-year-old son, in contrast, was disruptive: running out of the room, up and down the hall, and around the waiting room. He did not speak to the therapist and did not comply with requests from his parents to sit down. The parents reported that the teacher said he had few friends at school. Both his teachers and pediatrician had commented on his high activity level. The family blamed the mother for not having a good daughter.

Not unlike the situation in the United States, it is severely stigmatizing in a Confucian family for a member to have any mental or emotional problems (Honig & Hershatter, 1988; Pearson, 1995). The family would lose face if a male member were to present as a patient. For this family, focusing on the female with the least power, that is, the daughter, might have been the only way for the family to seek help from a psychotherapist.

For the second session the parents were asked to come without the children for the expressed purpose of giving a family history. Neither the father nor the mother could agree to any aspect of the family problem. The father complained that the mother was inept in handling the daughter, as shown in the fact that the daughter would not cater to the son. When his wife was inept, he had to step in with a firm hand. The mother, in turn, complained that the father had a temper, could not properly discipline the children, and thus allowed the daughter to be problematic.

It is within the Three Obediences for the mother to adopt her husband's and her son's conceptualization of the problem, that she herself is the problem when her daughter is problematic. The Book of Rites states that mediating the critical filial bond, tying father to son, and the regulation and harmony of families are the responsibilities of women. As with this family, the underlying assumption in such cases is that the mother has not fulfilled her duties because members of the family are in conflict. Any disturbance of the family members indicates that the mother has not done her job of creating family harmony. That is, she has not managed emotional tension, has not supported family members, and has not taught her children proper conduct.

This father thought that his problems of his wife complaining about him, and his daughter not catering to her brother, were caused by American cultural influences. Given that he had led his family from Korea to the United States, he considered that he was acting within his prescribed role as head of the household to bring his emotionally ill daughter and his deficient wife for treatment. Despite her resistance to being labeled, the wife considered it to be within her prescribed role as obedient wife to acknowledge her failings as a mother by coming to treatment.

Redefining the Problem

Concurrent separate therapy sessions for the mother and the father were recommended. They were told that because the problem appeared to be the interaction between the daughter and the son, the most efficacious method toward a solution was to have the therapist craft individualized interventions for each parent.

In the Confucian framework, the goal is to achieve harmony through restoring the family to the ways of the *li*. Similarly, in family therapy, the therapeutic interventions target the whole family system with the goal of restoring the family to a functional system. It is of little importance which family member introduces the therapeutic interventions into the family system. Nor is it important who the identified patient is within the family. In other words, it does not matter who is in the room with the family therapist. Family therapy is both an orientation and a method. As an orientation, it understands behavior in the context of significant emotional systems; as a method, it can work either with entire families or with a single member (Nichols & Schwartz, 1991).

The family therapist joins the family system to help its members change their structure. The feminist family therapist changes the structure to one that is nonhierarchical, recognizing the dysfunction of mother being subordinate and father being distant. For this family, the treatment of choice was to have the father, as well as the mother, enter into individual sessions. The demand for the father to be in therapy flew in the face of cultural ideas about men in therapy but was congruent with the Confucian patriarchal structure. The father was given the task of acting benevolent toward his wife, his daughter, and his son.

Intervention

The father's sessions focused on exploration of the proper conduct by superiors, that is, the duty of a father to exhibit conscientious, just, and compassionate behavior toward his children. The therapist recommended that in order to do so, he establish an independent relationship with each of the children instead of using the mother as the mediating agent between himself and the children. The mother's sessions focused on supporting her position that the father's temper was contributing to the family conflict. Part of the work with the mother was to examine the role that patriarchal and Confucian social roles (specifically, The Three Obediences and the Four Attributes) had contributed to the family conflict.

The family pattern had been for the father to complain that the mother was not doing her job when the children misbehaved. He would then tell the mother what to do about the children's misbehavior. The mother maintained harmony in the family by not directly arguing with the father but passively disagreeing with him by not doing what he told her to do about disciplining the children. The children, with the support of the mother, would resist the father's directives. The father would then adopt an authoritarian and punitive style of yelling at the children.

The father was encouraged to talk directly to his children. He was asked to spend time with each of the children listening to their problems. He discovered that his daughter needed help with her homework and that his son was sad about not having friends at school. The father was encouraged to help his daughter with her homework. He then went on to teach her how to fix things around the house. He was encouraged to talk to his son about how to be nice to people so that he could make friends. In the process, the father was advised to introduce family rules that effectively set limits on the son's behavior. The son's anxiety significantly decreased and his hyperactivity calmed down. He started to cooperate with the teachers and gradually became more liked by his peers.

In the mother's individual sessions, the feminist family therapist discussed the oppressive nature of The Three Obediences and the Four Attributes. The mother was encouraged to relax her sense of responsibility for the relationship between her husband and her children. She was urged to speak directly to her husband when he lost his temper instead of acting as a passive bystander. This new behavior resulted in useful dialogue between the parents and cessation of the father's angry outbursts. She was relieved of some domestic burdens by the father taking on more child-care responsibilities, more household chores, and being generally more involved in the family.

When the father marveled at the lessening of conflict in family interactions and the greater intimacy in the marriage, the feminist family therapist explained to him the oppressive nature of The Three Obediences and the Four Attributes. He came to understand that his previous authoritarian behavior had a part in creating the problems in the family. He was then able to work on the marriage with a full understanding of the consequences of the hierarchical power structure that they had both adopted.

CONCLUSION

The psychoanalyst modifies the structure of the patient's thinking; the family therapist modifies the structure of the patient's family (Nichols & Schwartz, 1998). We have proposed that (a) in comparison with individually oriented theories, the underpinnings of family therapy are more congruent with the beliefs of Confucian-based cultures, and (b) using a family systems orientation, interventions may be crafted to advance Asian American women's mental health while staying within culturally congruent family patterns.

Within Confucian cultures, women are named the guardians of morality and stability and are charged with protecting the sanctuary of the family (Mann, 1991). Although women's role in the Confucian code is dependent and subordinate, women's power to influence the family is preeminent. By recognizing this preeminence, a feminist family therapist can work with individual family members to create a *li* that empowers women, enables men to be more intimate with their children, and promotes harmony for the entire family.

REFERENCES

Bateson, G. (1988). *Mind and nature*. New York: Bantam Books.
Bond, M., & Hwang, K. K. (1986). The social psychology of Chinese people. In M. Bond (Ed.), *The psychology of Chinese people* (pp. 213–266). Hong Kong: Oxford University Press.

Guisso, R. (1981). Thunder over the lake: The five classics and the perception of woman in early China. In R. Guisso & S. Johannesen (Eds.), *Women in China: Current directions in historical scholarship* (pp. 47–61). Youngstown, NY: Philo Press.

Gurman, A., & Kniskern, D. (Eds.). (1991). *Handbook of family therapy* (Vol. II). New York: Brunner/Mazel.

Honig, E., & Hershatter, G. (1988). *Personal voices: Chinese women in the 1980s.* Stanford, CA: Stanford University Press.

Kluckhohn, F. R., & Spiegel, J. P. (1968). *Integration and conflict in family behavior.* Topeka, KS: Group for the Advancement of Psychiatry.

Mann, S. (1991). Grooming a daughter for marriage. In R. Watson & P. Ebrey (Eds.), *Marriage and inequality in Chinese society* (pp. 204–230). Berkeley: University of California Press.

Nichols, M. P., & Schwartz, R. C. (1991). *Family therapy: Concepts and methods* (2nd ed.). Needham Heights, CA: Allyn & Bacon.

Ong, A., & Nonini, D. M. (1997). Toward a cultural politics of diaspora and transnationalism. In A. Ong & D. M. Nonini (Eds.), *Underground empires: The cultural politics of modern Chinese transnationalism* (pp. 323–332). New York: Routledge.

Pearson, V. (1995). *Mental health care in China: State policies, professional services and family responsibilities.* New York: American Psychiatric Press.

11

THE BLACK MADONNA: THE PSYCHOSPIRITUAL FEMINISM OF GUADALUPE, KALI, AND MONSERRAT

LILLIAN COMAS-DÍAZ

> Yes, I am Black! and radiant—
> O city women watching me—
> As Black as Kedar's goathair tents
> Or Solomon's fine tapestries.
> Will you disrobe me with your stares?
> The eyes of many morning suns
> Have pierced my skin, and now I shine
> Black as the light before the dawn.
> And I have faced the angry glare
> Of others, even my mothers' sons
> Who sent me out to watch their vines
> While I neglected all my own.
> —Marcia Falk, *The Song of Songs*

Latinas are immersed in a collectivist context wherein identity and development are transformed through relationships. Their relational needs are best addressed by feminist family therapy because this approach is empowering, situates Latinas' realities within their sociopolitical and historical contexts, and acknowledges their diverse types of oppression. Because individual problems are considered a family affair among Latinas, family intervention is

I thank Louise Silverstein for stimulating conversations on feminism and theology.

often required for healing (Canino & Canino, 1982). Tools in family therapy such as genograms effectively address Latinas' multigenerational ethnic and gender dynamics. The cultural transitional map, a genealogy tool developed for working with people of color (Ho, 1987), is useful for charting cultural translocation and its effects on individuals and families. By collecting personal, psychological, social, and cultural data, the cultural transition map assesses the transitional position and developmental stages of the multigenerational ethnic family in a changing society. In addition to standard clinical techniques, the cultural transitional map uses folklore, photographs, art, literature, and music. As an ethnic clinical approach, the map facilitates cognitive, affective, and emotional change.

LAS MORENAS AND HEALING

Feminist family therapy provides a paradigm for Latinas that is cultural- and gender-sensitive, particularly in the assessment of racial and gender trauma. Because the incidence of posttraumatic stress disorder among urban young Latinas is reported to be statistically significantly higher than among other populations (Lipschitz, Rasmusson, Anyan, Cromwell, & Southwick, 2000), it is imperative to examine trauma among this population. Likewise, the family therapist needs to recognize the diverse types of trauma—ethnic, gender, personal, cultural, and historic—and their interaction in the lives of many Latinas. By recognizing cross-generational transmission of racial and gender-specific oppression, feminist family therapy effectively addresses the internalization and projection of racism and sexism. As an illustration, *las morenas*—Latinas with dark skin or African ancestry—is an ambiguous term sometimes denoting a racial description, other times a racial insult, and yet other times an endearing term.

Feminist family therapy speaks directly to the Latina ancestral heart in its emphasis on female-centered spiritual development. To be culturally relevant, however, feminist family therapy requires grounding in indigenous spiritual beliefs. Latina spirituality involves a syncretism of Western, Eastern, Native American, and African beliefs. Oppressed by gender, race, and class, many Latinas seek through spirituality a relief from cultural and historical trauma, as well as from internalized racism and sexism. In the face of discrimination from society at large, from their own community, and from their family of origin, many Latinas, especially *morenas*, embody endurance and resilience (Comas-Díaz, 1994). Consequently, it is crucial to therapeutically rescue female blackness and restore its radiance.

In struggling with the meaning of their darkness, many *morenas* resort to spirituality whereby the color black is associated with the culmination of a mystical journey (Begg, 1985). A gender-specific spirituality, the Black

Madonna facilitates reparation, healing, and transformation. As a spiritual mother, the Black Madonna offers love, protection, and acceptance. Accenting the feminist family work, she represents the ancient, battered, much loved, little understood archetype of the feminine principle (Begg, 1985). Within Jungian psychology the Black Madonna plays a crucial psychic role representing earth, matter, the feminine in man, and the self in woman (Galland, 1990). In Christianity she symbolizes forgiveness, compassion, and reconciliation (J. Rodriguez, 1996). The origins of the Black Madonna have been traced to ancient Black goddesses such as Isis and Kali (Begg, 1985; Galland, 1990). Analogously, the Black Madonna reenacts the ancient goddesses by yielding power, expressing love, and harmonizing the world. The therapeutic use of the Black Madonna extols power, healing, compassion, and reconciliation among Latinas.

Invoking the Black Madonna is a female psychospiritual approach for equity, justice, and liberation (Mato, 1994). All over the world people struggling for liberation favor the Black Madonna (Teish, 1996). Indeed, the Black Madonna is a liberation icon. Quispel (1979) believes that unless both men and women become conscious of the Black Madonna and integrate her within themselves, humankind would be unable to resolve the problems of racism, women's liberation, and materialism. Because the reaffirmation of indigenous beliefs subversively resists domination, the Black Madonna helps Latinas to endure, oppose, affirm, and liberate.

This chapter discusses Sara's story, illustrating the use of feminist family therapy combined with Latino psychospirituality in the healing of multigenerational racial and gender wounds. Treatment consists of family therapy with one person, in addition to dyadic and family sessions with Sara, her mother, and her daughter.

Guadalupe: Resistance and Affirmation

"Virgen de la Guadalupe has always protected me," announced Sara, a 40-year-old Latina single mother during her first psychotherapeutic session. Sara admitted to a strained relationship with her mother and stated that she had adopted Our Lady of Guadalupe as her spiritual mother. "I leave my pain at the Virgencita's mantel and then feel better. But not this time," Sara wept.

The therapist working with Latinas needs to unravel their spiritual labyrinth with respect. Virgen de la Guadalupe is a central spiritual figure among many Mexican American women. A Catholic figure, Guadalupe nonetheless transcends organized religion. Known as *La Morenita* or the Little Darkling, our Lady of Guadalupe is the patroness and Goddess of the Americas. Her mythic history relates that in 1531, Guadalupe appeared to the Aztec convert Juan Diego in the place of worship of the Mexican goddess

Tonantzin (our Mother). In asking that her temple be built in Tonantzin's holy summit, Guadalupe allegorically acknowledged her previous incarnation as an indigenous goddess (Castillo, 1996). For contemporary Latinas, Guadalupe provides sustenance, hope, a sense of belonging, and a reason to live (J. Rodriguez, 1996). Many Latina feminists embrace Guadalupe as the feminine face of God.

The precipitating event leading to Sara's entrance into therapy was an argument with her mother Marta while planning her birthday celebration. In brief, Marta refused to invite Robert, Sara's lover. "I wish I was never born," shouted Sara to her mother. After this altercation, Sara began to suffer from insomnia, irritability, depressed mood, and problems concentrating. To cope, she began to "drink more than usual and to smoke like a chimney."

Family therapy with one person was used to address Sara's strong relational ties. With no history of emotional difficulties, Sara was now experiencing a reactive depression. Although infuriated, Sara was not exhibiting destructive behavior toward herself or others. "I learned from my family to escape from sadness," Sara confessed. She also revealed that potentially destructive tendencies were modulated by her spiritual values: "La Virgen does not like killing." Despite her devotion to Guadalupe, Sara professed to be a lapsed Catholic, an area of concern for Marta who as a devout Catholic objected to Sara's naming the virgin Guadalupe-Tonantzin.

In taking the form of the most oppressed, that is, a dark indigenous woman, Guadalupe's appearance to Juan Diego speaks to the triple oppression of race, class, and gender. She appeals to the oppressed because she imparts dignity and renews their energy to resist assimilation into the dominant culture (J. Rodriguez, 1996). As noted above, people struggling for liberation favor the Black Madonna all over the world (Teish, 1996). As a warrior, guerrilla combatant, and freedom fighter, *La Morenita* allies herself with those who suffer (Randall, 1996). Emblematic of the struggle against oppression, Guadalupe's image graces the flags of liberation. Father Hidalgo held her banner during the Mexican independence war against Spain. César Chavez carried her image in the recent American struggle for economic justice for Mexican farm workers (Castillo, 1996).

Sara acknowledged Guadalupe's intercession in her struggles against oppression at work and in society, particularly against sexism and racism. "Guadalupe loves me because I am *morena*. But, she has been silent with respect to my conflict with Mami," she declared.

Because of the oppressive context of Sara's reality, I anchored the therapeutic interventions within feminist family therapy. In addition to individual sessions, we agreed on couple and family sessions involving Marta and Alba, Sara's daughter. However, we first decided to work on coping skills to address Sara's relational difficulties.

Kali: Anger and Transformation

A journalist working as a freelance writer for several Latina-focused magazines, Sara traveled frequently and left her daughter with Marta. This convenient arrangement turned into tribulation when Sara became engaged to Robert and Marta vociferously objected to the union. A successful African American sportswriter, Robert was bewildered by Marta's rejection. "I don't understand why my mother is racist against Robert if she has called me Black all my life," Sara complained. "You see, my mother is from Veracruz, a coastal region in Mexico where African slaves were taken to work in the intense heat. With a high prevalence of African ancestry among the population, my mother married a *jarocho*" (the son of a union between a Black and an Indian; Leon, 1924). "Although she claims not to have Black ancestry herself, Mami's skin is very dark."

Interestingly, Marta prided herself on being the daughter of El Andaluz, an immigrant from Andalusia, a region in the south of Spain. Antonio, El Andaluz, married Marta's mother, Rosa, a *mestiza*. The product of the union between Indian and Spaniard, *mestizos* comprise the bulk of the Mexican population (Paz, 1950). Consequently, Marta explained her dark skin as a legacy of *mestizaje*: "I'm pure Mexican," she affirmed. Nonetheless, Marta did not acknowledge the Black Moorish or North African racial influence in the Andalusian population. Like many racially closeted LatiNegras (Latinas with Black ancestry; Comas-Díaz, 1994), Marta projected onto Sara her internalized racism. Growing up under Marta's constant supervision to minimize her blackness left Sara with deep emotional scars. For instance, Marta pressured Sara to look less Black by passing and bleaching (*blanqueando*), involving wearing products and hairdos to minimize blackness (C. Rodriguez, 1998).

Bleaching and passing left Sara with a diminished self-esteem. A good-looking petite woman, Sara questioned her attractiveness. "Men seem to like me, but I don't know why," she wondered. Sara felt too *morena* to be beautiful. Having "suspicious" hair (not good but not quite bad hair) did not help her self esteem. "I have a hate-hate relationship with my hair. When I was growing up, my mother cursed every time she combed my hair. It kills me to see my mother happily combing Alba's hair," Sara admitted.

Sara's 13-year-old daughter, Alba—a light skinned adolescent with red hair—was the product of her marriage with Joe, an Irish American man. Even though Joe was an unskilled laborer, Marta approved the union because he was White. Sara's marriage ended in divorce when Joe was laid off and refused to look for another job. "I did not want to repeat my mother's marriage. My father was an *explotador* (exploiter). Although Papi worked, he threw away his money gambling and drinking."

Sara's awareness of being an adult child of an alcoholic helped to control her excessive drinking and smoking. A family session poignantly addressed these concerns when Alba described herself as a codependent in her mother's substance abuse. By changing her behavior and feeling less depressed, Sara became more in contact with her anger, particularly against Marta. We worked therapeutically on understanding her rage and on expressing it constructively. Additionally, we used culturally relevant assertiveness training, particularly in the context of her relationship with Marta.

During the middle stages of therapy, Sara traveled to India to research an article on the role of women in contemporary Indian society. It was during this visit that she was first introduced to Kali, the Hindu Goddess of death, rebirth, and transformation (Mitchell, 1998). Kali's iconography is horrific; at times she brandishes a blood-stained knife, holds a dripping human head, wears a necklace of human heads, and places one foot on Siva (her husband) who lies like a corpse (Hawley, 1996). She is also depicted naked on top of a corpse, devouring its intestines (Meile, 1965). So terrifying are these images that they are believed to ward off evil spirits (Mitchell, 1998). A Black goddess, Kali's name not only means the Black One but also Deathly (Hawley, 1996). Indeed, her name derives from Kali Ma, meaning Black Mother (Trobe, 2000). To promote transformation, Kali removes weakness and attachment, reconnecting her followers with their divine identity. Possessed by Kali's power, Sara returned from India with a spiritual bindi (a small ornamental dot on her forehead), signaling a numinous awareness through the bindi's allegorical meaning of inner vision.

Impressed by Kali's popularity among oppressed women (Trobe, 2000), Sara identified with her power through anger and transformation. She began to meditate using Kali's image when needing to gain access to her anger. "Kali helps me release," Sara conceded.

Kali meditation has been successfully used in psychotherapy to help women channel their aggression and learn to nurture (McDermott, 1996). The Hindu tradition acknowledges Devi (literally meaning goddess) as all goddesses in one (Hawley & Wulff, 1996). As dark Devi, Kali incorporates the ineradicable face of the Great Goddess from Neolithic times. A paradoxical deity, Kali represents the union of opposites, combining within herself the roles of creation and destruction, birth and death, love and fear (McDermott, 1996).

The Gypsies' exodus from India into Europe may have transformed Kali into a Black Madonna. The similarities are startling. For instance, during the Portuguese repression of the Hindu religion, soldiers witnessing a Kali ritual in colonial Goa mistook the ceremony for a sacrament to the Virgin Mary (Roberts, 1994). Since the 19th century, Gypsies have embarked on a pilgrimage to Provence to celebrate Mary and venerate their patron saint, Sara, the Black servant of both Mary, mother of James, and of Mary

Salome. On May 24 and 25, Gypsies carry Sara's statue through the streets of Saintes-Maries de la Mer, culminating in the sea (Michelin Green Guide, 1998). As the Gypsies dip Sara-la-Kali into the sea, they select their queen (Begg, 1985). Likewise, Tamil Indians go to the Chartres Cathedral and prostrate themselves in front of the Black Virgin during the month of May because they have nowhere to worship Kali (Boyer, 2000). These are examples of the syncretism of the Black goddess into the Christian Black Madonna (Begg, 1985). Analogously, Guadalupe has been identified with the African Yoruba goddess, Oya, the Wind Mother, and the Warrior Queen (Teish, 1996), thereby cementing the belief of the dark goddess as Black Madonna.

During a dyadic session with Marta, Sara compared Kali to Guadalupe: "They both are Black and fight for the oppressed, declare war against injustice and evil, and comfort their children." "Blasphemy," screamed Marta and turned toward the office door. "I must not be your daughter," replied Sara in a quiet scream. "Can you help us?" pleaded Marta to the therapist.

I opted for narratives to foster Marta's and Sara's understanding of each other's perspectives. Such narratives were examined within a family systems perspective, given that Latina identity is transmitted across generations and coconstructed through relationships. Indeed, Latinas' relationships to others—including family, community, and history—are central to their well-being and sense of continuity (McGoldrick, Garcia-Preto, Hines, & Lee, 1989). Surprisingly, Sara did not know much about Marta's history of losses. Through testimony, or the verbal healing journey to the past (Cienfuegos & Monelli, 1983), Marta recounted her traumatic experiences and how these affected her roles as a woman and a mother. The first tragedy was the loss of her 15-year-old brother Raúl, who died while trying to save her from drowning when Marta was 12 years old. Afterward, Marta confessed that she had a pregnancy at age 13 that ended in a self-induced abortion. Plagued by Catholic guilt, Marta was reminded of "her sin" every time she saw herself in 13-year-old Alba. Moreover, at 20, Marta's groom stood her up at the church's altar. She later found out that her fiancée's White family kidnapped him on the wedding day. "Being a Black woman means being cursed," cried Marta.

The intense pain, shame, and self-hatred evoked in Marta's tale culminated in an abreaction for both women. Because of this vehement emotion, I "prescribed" an ethnic psychological treatment, a purifying cleansing (un baño de purificación), a ritual consistent with Marta's spiritual practice. I asked Sara to participate in the ceremony by getting the ingredients for the cleansing. However, Marta's ritual was an individual endeavor, and she was to undergo the cleansing and later discuss it at our next therapy session. I instructed Marta to take a baño (bath) in the curandera tradition following Ana Castillo's (1994) instructions. Sara provided the drops of spirit of camphor and ammonia, leaves of eucalyptus and sage, Agua de Florida, lemons, and garlic cloves (Castillo, 1994). I provided the psychotherapeutic component, asking Marta to first take the purifying cleansing, then meditate on her losses, examine her contributions, and finally, identify the lessons learned. This cognitive–behavioral technique taught self-observation (Tanaka-Matsumi & Higginbotham, 1996) and aimed to increase Marta's sense of agency.

Afterward, Marta was to light candles to her favorite deity or saint. This ritual, similar to a spiritual ceremony, addresses unfinished business and releases regrets as well as negative influence of the wounds (Myss, 1996). As soon as Marta completed the ritual, she called Sara on the phone and discussed what she had learned. Marta also shared with Sara that she lit one candle to Guadalupe and another to Saint Martin de Porres, the patron saint of race relations (Farmer, 1997). The cleansing ritual was cathartic for both women, thus signaling a renewal.

After the purification, Marta's fear of passing along her "curse" as a Black woman to Sara was addressed with cognitive restructuring. Following a cognitive–behavioral treatment approach, I asked Marta to identify and record her negative thoughts. Then I asked her to challenge them by writing rational responses next to her irrational assumptions. Marta's negative cognition—"I am a Black sinner and Sara will inherit my sins"—was challenged with rational responses: "Sinners come in all colors," "Sinners can get forgiveness," "Mothers' sins are not visited in their daughters." I purposefully used Marta's spiritual language to communicate within her explanatory model. I then identified Marta's unlovability schema, in which feelings of shame and humiliation prevailed (Bennett-Goleman, 2001). Afterward, I cognitively reframed her sense of unworthiness as "You have survived suffering," "You have overcome adversity," and "You can teach resilience to your daughter."

In validating her personal experience through testimony, Marta transformed painful experiences, reformulated her identity, created a new present, and enhanced her future. The integration of feminist family therapy with indigenous psychology (testimony, purification, and cleansing) therapeutically relieved Marta's trauma. Although the mother–daughter bond began to heal, reconciliation was still absent.

Monserrat: Reparation and Reconciliation

In addition to enhancing communication, assertiveness, and negotiation, Sara and Marta also worked on racial healing. Given their spiritual orientation, I recommended an adjunct 12-step program of attitudinal healing circles. By drawing on the format of "A Course in Miracles," Abadio-Clottey and Clottey (1998) devised an approach to racial reconciliation

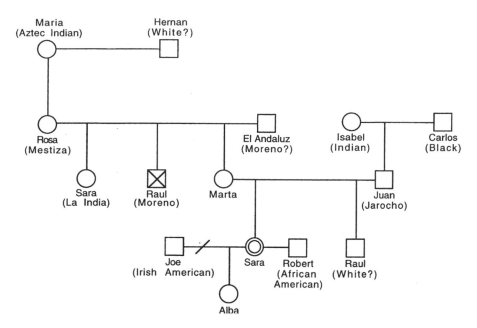

Figure 11.1. Sara's family's genogram. Women are placed on the left as a feminist stance. The genogram's symbols follow McGoldrick and Gerson's (1985) format. Circles represent females; squares represent males; circle within a circle represents the identified female client; X inside a circle or square represents a dead person; –/–represents divorce or split marital relationship.

involving 12 principles. Examples include the following: Healing is conquering fear; giving and receiving are the same; we are always learning and/or teaching; accepting others entails forgiving rather than judging. Sara and Marta attended several meetings, developed a common language, and began healing their racial wounds.

We completed a multigenerational genogram (see Figure 11.1) diagramming extended family relationships, kinship networks, and historical links (Boyd-Franklin, 1989). We emphasized Sara's family and ethnocultural identity by strengthening her connections, but we also identified disconnections. Given that many Latinas are named after family members, we identified Sara's namesake to uncover family scripts and expectations. Named after her mother's oldest sister, Sara better understood her mother's pain after hearing her namesake's story. A second mother to Marta, her sister Sara—who was known as La India—disappeared mysteriously after a trip to the United States. "She broke my heart," wept Marta.

While working on the genogram, I asked Sara and Marta to identify the skin color of their family members. Rosa, Marta's mother, was a *mestiza* who married Antonio, El Andaluz. However, since he was an immigrant in Mexico, there was no information about Antonio's family of origin.

Antonio was reported to have been *moreno*. Marta identified her maternal grandmother María as an Aztec Indian who "must have been very dark." María married Hernán, a "White" Mexican. Marta did not know about her grandfather or her paternal grandparents. She identified her own skin color as *café oscuro* (dark coffee). Marta married Juan, a *jarocho* with kinky hair. However, because of the blackness of Juan's family, Marta did not get along with them, and consequently, did not know much about them. She stated that while her mother-in-law Isabel was an indigenous woman, Carlos, her father-in-law, was Black.

Sara designated her own color as medium brown. However, she indicated that because of her suspicious hair, Marta felt that Sara was Black. A disagreement ensued and Sara confronted Marta on her favoritism toward Raúl, her brother. "Not only do you prefer Raúl because he is male but also because he is light-skinned," accused Sara. "By naming my son after my dead brother, I found redemption," yielded Marta. I asked whether Raúl could join us in family therapy sessions, but Marta responded that he was living in Mexico. Sara replied that she was not ready to include him.

We completed the cultural transitional map, assessing personal, familial, and community dislocations in Sara's family. This tool revealed that Marta immigrated to the United States to run away from her husband Juan, just a year after being married. Juan followed her and promised to stop drinking and gambling. Because she realized that Juan was unable to keep his promises, Marta continued to run away. He successfully followed her. Their marriage was characterized by "separations without adios," leaving Sara and Raul to uproot "several times too many." Marta and Juan permanently separated after 7 years of the marriage.

During the completion of the cultural transitional map, Alba visited Andalusia and Barcelona on a school trip. Upon her return, Sara and Marta were working on their multigenerational genogram, chronicling the historical, ethnic, racial, and cultural events affecting their lives. When asked to contribute, Alba identified the Moors as historical ancestors and recounted a story she learned in Barcelona about the Virgin of Monserrat. "She hid in a cave for centuries when the Moors conquered Spain. Because of this she turned Black and is called La Moreneta—the dark one," Alba recounted.

The Virgin of Monserrat has been venerated for more than a thousand years in Catalonia, the northeastern region of Spain. Her mythic history relates that her statue was found in a coal mine in the Monserrat mountains. What is particularly distinctive and evocative about Monserrat is that her skin and that of the Christ child remained "miraculously" black after cleaning. Pilgrims of all colors visit Our Lady of Monserrat's basilica located on a rocky mountain with steep peeks outside of Barcelona (Begg, 1985).

Monserrat's struggle against oppression signifies a return to her origins, to Mother Earth, as a symbol of rebirth and empowerment. She is so venerated that Monserrat is the most popular Catalan female name. La Moreneta's worship is prevalent in some Latin American countries, especially those with African ancestry. As an illustration, Monserrat is the most popular and Creole of all religious figures in Puerto Rico (National Museum of American Art, 1998). When Alba pulled out an image of Virgen de Monserrat, Sara and Marta stared at a Black Madonna holding her child on her lap and the sphere of the world on her right hand. "I've seen her in a vision," Marta whispered. "She looks just like your Indian goddess." "Tonantzin or Kali?" Sara inquired. "Both," murmured Marta.

FEMINIST SPIRITUALITY IN COLOR

Within the feminist psychospiritual model, Guadalupe helped Sara to resist oppression and reclaim her indigenous identity. Kali helped her fight internal racism and facilitated identity transformation. Monserrat promoted racial and gender trauma reparation, initiating mother–daughter reconciliation. Brought by Alba—herself a link between the two women—Monserrat became a connection between Guadalupe and Kali. In protecting herself and her child by returning to her origin (according to the Catalan legend by hiding in a cave away from the invaders), La Virgen de Monserrat modeled self- and maternal care and brought justice by balancing the world.

To augment therapeutic reconciliation, I suggested photographs, as an ethnic clinical tool (Ho, 1987). I have found photographs to be empowering and therapeutic against racial trauma. In particular, photographs appear beneficial for *morenas*' identity reconstruction. In addition to examining old pictures, Sara, Marta, and Alba were also asked to photograph each other in regular activities. This approach is consistent with the cultural transitional map.

Mother, daughter, and granddaughter examined their pictures, compared each other at the same age, looked back into the past, projected into the future, observing similarities and differences. To everyone's surprise, Alba's photographs had a professional quality. She became the anointed reality-tester, eloquently capturing the beauty of her female ancestors. When she put together the photos in a collage, Alba added the images of Guadalupe, Kali, and Monserrat. The collage became an *arpillera*, the artistic weaving that oppressed Latin Americans create as resistance, reconciliation, and liberation (Comas-Díaz & Jansen, 1995).

"Kali fights and liberates," declared Sara. "Guadalupe comforts and heals," Marta announced. "Monserrat balances and protects," Alba insisted.

EPILOGUE

Sara's story illustrates how feminist family therapy combined with indigenous spiritual beliefs can enhance reparation, healing, and reconciliation. As clinical ethnographer-archeologist, the feminist family therapist uncovers gems of wisdom under foundations of ethnocultural pillars. Acting as a guide, witness, and facilitator, the family therapist aided the healing of personal, family, and racial trauma by using narrative and testimony. While trauma work addressed racial and gender-related wounds, adjunct racial healing helped to repair the mother–daughter dyad. Moreover, the use of photographs became an empowering and self-affirming tool for Sara, Marta, and Alba.

Indigenous psychology embodies ancestral beliefs consistent with feminist therapy. In an innovative application of indigenous psychology, the Black Madonna was adopted as a spiritual mother offering consolation, protection, and healing. As an accent to feminist family work, the Black Madonna represents the ancient archetype of the feminine principle (Begg, 1985). In Christianity she symbolizes forgiveness, love, and reconciliation (Rodriguez, 1996). Analogously, in Indian cosmology Kali yields power, transformation, and harmony. The indigenous psychological approach extolled these virtues in the women.

The combination of feminist family therapy with Latina spirituality cemented the gender, racial, and cultural continuity among Marta, Sara, and Alba. This approach can help Latinas reclaim their ancestral identities, fight oppression in a culturally appropriate way, and transform their fates by safeguarding the collective future of their progeny.

PRELUDE TO THE NEXT GENERATION

Ensuring Latinas' collective continuity requires nurturing their offspring. Alba's participation in the feminist family therapy was both healing and transformative. In discussing her reactions to the family therapy, Alba declared, "I am Black, just like Mami and Abuela and her mother's mother. No matter her skin color, my daughter will also be Black."

REFERENCES

Abadio-Clottey, A., & Clottey, K. (1998). *Beyond fear: Twelve spiritual keys to racial healing*. Tiburon, CA: Kramer.

Begg, E. (1985). *The cult of the Black Virgin*. London: Arkana/Penguin Books.

Bennett-Goleman, T. (2001). *Emotional alchemy: How the mind can heal the heart.* New York: Harmony Books.

Boyd-Franklin, N. (1989). *Black families in therapy: A multisystems approach.* New York: Guilford Press.

Boyer, M. F. (2000). *The cult of the Virgin: Offerings, ornaments and festivals.* New York: Thames & Hudson.

Canino, G., & Canino, I. (1982). Culturally syntonic family therapy for migrant Puerto Ricans. *Hospital and Community Psychiatry, 33,* 299–303.

Castillo, A. (1994). *Massacre of the dreamers: Essays on Xicanisma.* New York: Penguin.

Castillo, A. (Ed.). (1996). *Goddess of the Americas/La Diosa de las Américas: Writings on the Virgin of Guadalupe.* New York: Riverhead Books.

Cienfuegos, A. J., & Monelli, C. (1983). The testimony of political repression as a therapeutic instrument. *American Journal of Orthopsychiatry, 53,* 43–51.

Comas-Díaz, L. (1994). LatiNegra: Mental health issues of African Latinas. *Journal of Feminist Family Therapy, 5,* 35–74.

Comas-Díaz, L., & Jansen, M. A. (1995). Global conflict and violence against women. *Peace and Conflict: Journal of Peace Psychology, 1,* 315–331.

Farmer, D. (1997). *The Oxford dictionary of saints.* Oxford, England: Oxford University Press.

Galland, C. (1990). *Longing for darkness: Tara and the Black Madonna.* New York: Compas/Penguin Press.

Hawley, J. S. (1996). The goddess in India. In J. S. Hawley & D. M. Wulff (Eds.), *Devi: Goddesses of India* (pp. 1–28). Berkeley: University of California Press.

Hawley, J. S., & Wulff, D. M. (Eds.). (1996). *Devi: Goddesses of India.* Berkeley: University of California Press.

Ho, M. H. (1987). *Family therapy with ethnic minorities.* Newbury Park, CA: Sage.

Leon, N. (1924). *Las castas de Mexico colonial o Nueva España* [The castes from colonial Mexico or New Spain]. Mexico City: Departamento de Antropología Anatómica. Talleres Gráficos del Museo Nacional de Arqueología, Historia y Etnografía.

Lipschitz, D. S., Rasmusson, A. M., Anyan, W., Cromwell, P., & Southwick, S. M. (2000). Clinical and functional correlates of posttraumatic stress disorder in urban adolescent girls at a primary care clinic. *Journal of American Academy of Child and Adolescent Psychiatry, 39,* 1104–1111.

Mato, T. (1994). *The Black Madonna within: Drawings, dreams, reflections.* Chicago: Open Court.

McDermott, R. F. (1996). The Western Kali. In J. S. Hawley & D. W. Wulff (Eds.), *Devi: Goddesses of India* (pp. 281–313). Berkeley: University of California Press.

McGoldrick, M., Garcia-Preto, N., Hines, P. M., & Lee, E. (1989). Ethnicity and women. In M. McGoldrick, C. M. Anderson, & F. Walsh (Eds.), *Women in families: A framework for family therapy* (pp. 169–199). New York: Norton.

McGoldrick, M., & Gerson, R. (1985). *Genograms in family assessment*. New York: Norton.

Meile, H. (1965). Mythology of the Tamils. In P. Grimal (Ed.), *Larousse world mythology* (pp. 267–270). Secaucus, NJ: Chartwell Books.

Michelin Green Guide. (1998). *Guide to Provence*. Greenville, SC: Michelin Tyre PLC.

Mitchell, A. G. (1998). *Hindu gods and goddesses*. New Delhi, India: UBSPD Publishers.

Myss, C. (1996). *Anatomy of the spirit: The seven stages of power and healing*. New York: Three Rivers Press.

National Museum of American Art. (1998). *Colonial art from Puerto Rico*. Washington, DC: Smithsonian Institution.

Paz, O. (1950). El laberinto de al soledad [The labyrinth of solitude]. Mexico, DF: Fondo de Cultural Económica.

Quispel, G. (1979). *The secret book of Revelations: The last book of the Bible*. San Francisco: McGraw-Hill.

Randall, M. (1996). Guadalupe, subversive Virgin. In A. Castillo (Ed.), *Goddess of the Americas/La Diosa de las Américas: Writings on the Virgin of Guadalupe* (pp. 113–123). New York: Riverhead Books.

Roberts, P. W. (1994). *Empire of the soul: Some journeys in India*. New York: Riverhead Books.

Rodriguez, C. (1998). *Latino manifesto*. Columbia, MD: Cimarron.

Rodriguez, J. (1996). Guadalupe: The feminine face of God. In A. Castillo (Ed.), *Goddess of the Americas/La Diosa de las Américas: Writings on the Virgin of Guadalupe* (pp. 25–31). New York: Riverhead Books.

Tanaka-Matsumi, J., & Higginbotham, H. N. (1996). Behavioral approaches to counseling across cultures. In P. B. Pedersen, J. G. Draguns, W. J. Lonner, & J. E. Trimble (Eds.), *Counseling across cultures* (4th ed., pp. 266–292). Thousand Oaks, CA: Sage.

Teish, L. (1996). The warrior queen: Encounters with a Latin lady. In A. Castillo (Ed.), *Goddess of the Americas/La Diosa de las Americas: Writings on the Virgin of Guadalupe* (pp. 137–146). New York: Riverhead Books.

Trobe, K. (2000). *Invoke the goddess: Visualizations of Hindu, Greek and Egyptian deities*. St. Paul, MN: Llewellyn.

IV

RECOGNIZING POWER
IN FAMILIES

12

HELPING MEN EMBRACE EQUALITY

GARY R. BROOKS

I first encountered John Smith after he was admitted to the inpatient psychiatric unit of a Veterans Administration Hospital where I functioned as a staff psychologist. John had sought admission after a minor physical altercation with Dwayne, his 13-year-old stepson. This had been the latest in a series of incidents between them. John felt strongly that Dwayne needed to be taught respect for authority, yet he reluctantly agreed to seek help for himself. John feared that he might overreact and hurt Dwayne.

An Army captain in Vietnam, John had suffered severe injuries to his head and upper torso in a land mine explosion. The explosion had caused permanent partial right-sided paralysis and diffuse brain injury. Although he retained most cognitive abilities, he was more emotional and less stress-tolerant.

With the explosion of the Viet Cong land mine, John's life radically shifted. John was driven to succeed and had been a star at everything he tried. He had been an all-state high school football player who married the head cheerleader (Becky) and won a full-ride scholarship to a military college. He excelled in college, started a family, and rapidly made rank in the military hierarchy. He fully expected to continue his military career to make General and raise sons who would continue his legacy. Everything had fallen apart for him. During his rehabilitation, Becky defied his wishes and completed nursing school. During her first training rotation, she was attracted to a young medicine resident and "ran off" with him, taking the children with her.

Everything had changed except John's almost superhuman commitment to repress his emotional distress, deny his losses, and tenaciously focus on achievement of his career goals. He became obsessed with the now-futile missions of making military rank and restoring his full physical capabilities.

Along the way he became a devout Christian and met Shannon while singing in his church choir. Like John, Shannon and her three children had been abandoned by her first spouse. At that time Shannon was minimally employed and solely responsible for parenting Jessica, age 13, Chuck, 11, and Dwayne, 8. On one level John saw Shannon and her children as needing his protection. At another level he saw an opportunity to relieve his loneliness and recapture his lost family.

To start afresh, John avidly took on fathering Shannon's sons (while ignoring her daughter). Over the next 5 years, John's poorly conceived effort to deny pain, both his own and the family's, was a disaster in all areas. The most visible symptom of systemic distress was the outbreak of hostilities between John and Dwayne. In part, these tensions were a product of a family struggling to integrate a new parent. In part, these tensions seemed a distraction from the uneasy relationship between John and Shannon. Because neither of them had fully recovered from the injuries of their earlier relationships, it had seemed safer to become overly focused on parenting concerns. As the youngest and most rebellious of the three children, Dwayne was the natural one to become an identified patient. Rambunctious and impulsive, he was simultaneously viewed as a family clown and a budding delinquent.

THERAPY WITH JOHN AND HIS FAMILY

I pressed for a family meeting to assess the system's most urgent needs. At the meeting, I could readily see that although Dwayne drew the most attention through his acting out and his conflict with his stepfather, he was certainly not the only troubled family member. Jessica, the oldest and most scarred by her father's abandonment, was visibly anxious and fearful of further loss and pain. Chuck claimed to be untroubled but seemed somewhat flat and depressed. Despite his role as family scapegoat, Dwayne seemed to be experiencing the least overt emotional distress.

This session allowed me to help the parents reassure Jessica, Chuck, and Dwayne that a commitment was being made to improve the situation. Because I felt that the family's greatest anxiety was tied to fears of marital dissolution, I chose to initially target the couple's shaky relationship. I assured the children, however, that future sessions would include them.

My first session with John and Shannon came 1 week after his hospital discharge. John and Shannon confessed that there had been a significant conflict on John's return home. During his absence, Shannon had decided to have her hair much shorter and more curly. She had expected a surprised reaction from John but was annoyed by his actual response. He was quite irritated that Shannon had initiated this "major physical change" without "consulting" him. Shannon had scoffed at his indignation about such a minor personal decision. A bitter argument had ensued, with each party feeling misunderstood. John felt betrayed and actually threatened to seek a divorce.

I weighed the situation carefully. As a feminist therapist, I consider it critical that I (a) challenge abuses of power and foster egalitarian marital relationships, (b) help clients recognize and alter destructive aspects of traditional roles, and (c) make overt value choices that maximize their human potential. As I have noted earlier (Brooks, 1991), I am especially cautious about the possibly inadvertent damage produced by marital therapy when a woman's power base is insecure and the therapy might undercut her position. In this situation, however, it seemed that Shannon's position was solid. She was comfortably employed and determined to make her own choices. Therefore, I felt I could turn my attention to John while continuing to support Shannon.

My Own Reactivity

It was very hard for me to keep from reacting strongly to John. John was similar to several men—powerful, White, heterosexual—who have provoked in me a confounding mix of anxiety and exhilaration by simply presenting themselves to me for therapeutic guidance. Such men have been so formidable because they embody the aspects of masculinity that evoke my deepest insecurities. More than just successful in their careers, each had mastered every challenge he took on. Many of these men have been physically imposing, either because of actual size or because they just *seemed* larger than most of us. Most had been accomplished athletes and maintained their aura of confidence, strength, and interpersonal dominance. They were accustomed to deference and to control of situations. I knew that they expected the therapy situation to be no different.

But what about my odd sense of exhilaration? Perhaps I realized that despite their façade of confidence, these men are somewhat uneasy entering a new environment that called for skills and postures they poorly comprehended. Because of their status, such men have been able to function through privilege and without needing to communicate, negotiate, and reveal insecurities. Could it be that in some not-too-terribly-mature way, I was taking gratification from seeing these men experience disequilibrium? Was I thinking such childish thoughts as "Wow, this pompous, big-shot neurosurgeon (military officer, corporate executive) is being deflated and is actually needing my help!"? Was I gratified that these seemingly omnipotent figures were being held accountable and their human frailties revealed?

There is some truth to this analysis. I have rarely escaped from the need to be "manly enough," "to impress my 'male chorus' " (Pittman, 1990,

1993). This situation provided a form of payback. These mighty and dominant men were now appearing far less imposing, and now they needed me.

However, there is another aspect to my excitement when meeting these men. Their appearance for therapy needs to be recognized as a dramatic indication that matters are changing in traditional marital relationships. The women's movement has been making a significant difference in women's lives and has laid the groundwork for reciprocal changes in men's lives. I viewed John's therapy as representative of the challenge to make the best of this opportunity.

Here was a man who had once personified many of the "masculine" characteristics I had most admired. He had accepted nothing but the best from himself and expected the same from those around him. I reacted to his stiff military bearing, only partially aware of my irrational needs to prove myself to him—to have him recognize not just my competence but the value of therapy itself. Although he intimidated me, I also felt a need to protect him. As I watched him drag himself across the therapy room, I was struck by the enormity of his losses, both real and symbolic.

In light of his lost dreams of military leadership, his unreasonable posture with Shannon took on new meaning. Deprived of real power and authority, John had attempted to compensate with hollow demands for blind obedience to his dictates. Although some contemporary families profess commitment to male authority (e.g., the Promise Keepers), this family was not so committed. Shannon expected shared leadership. My job was to help John back away from his position without further loss of face and self-respect.

Over the past decade or so, I have worked hard to understand the psyches and worldviews of traditional men. I have read avidly in the new literature of men and masculinity, talked openly with other men, and continued my own personal explorations into my reactivity. Although troubled by the darker side of traditional masculinity, I have also learned to appreciate the meritorious aspects of individual men. Many traditional men have been trying to do what they believe is the right thing. They have been devoutly loyal to a code of masculinity that emphasizes duty, courage, bravery, and even sacrifice of life and limb. Whether they functioned as soldiers, firefighters, or sewer workers, many have made sacrifices to fulfill deeply ingrained roles as good providers, protectors, and family leaders.

In addition to recognizing multiple abuses of patriarchy and male power, I have recognized how this system of turning young men into work machines and warriors has harmed men themselves. Despite the considerable political and economic power of men in the collective, most individual men feel relatively powerless. As I support and celebrate the empowerment of women, men of color, and nonheterosexual men, I have also become aware of how this important social shift erodes the power of White, heterosexual men. In recognizing how threatening this change is for traditional men, I have become more empathic and compassionate. Because I believe that these social shifts create an environment in which men have more to gain than lose, I have been able to help men move beyond their anxieties and begin to embrace the difficult job of revising their ideas of masculinity.

John's Perspective

I asked John to help me understand what it was about Shannon's haircut that unsettled him. After asserting that haircuts were one of the "significant life choices" that should spur a husband and wife to consult with one another (an argument so silly that it could not escape Shannon's further derision), John acknowledged that this was just the latest of several decisions that Shannon had made without him. She had recently become much more involved with her work as a salesperson for cosmetics. As her income increased, so had her "independence." He said "independence" as if it were a dirty word. John explained that Shannon had begun to remind him of the "girl" in the Virginia Slims commercials—"Miss Independence" and "the feminist of today." He noted that when he married Shannon, she had been "a nice little girl from Kansas," but now she was "eaten up with the drive to succeed."

In further exploration, John admitted to feeling upset about Shannon's decreased availability to him. He feared that Shannon's career would cause her to encounter attractive and successful men. His deepest fear was that Shannon would "replace" him with a "higher functioning" man. John described his fantasy of the man who would "win" Shannon away from him—a "tall, dark guy in a three-piece suit, with wavy hair and a pencil-thin mustache."

With that admission, the therapy took markedly different form. Shannon noted that she had realized that John feared abandonment similar to that experienced in his first marriage. John contended that his fear was realistic, because his war injuries had reduced him to being a mere shadow of his former self. Shannon challenged John's recall, stating that he had actually been injured *before they met*. "I fell in love with you as you are now."

Therapy now shifted to focus on John's standards of masculinity and his unrealistic ideas about relationships. Raised as a very traditional man in a highly competitive, hierarchical system, he had assumed that women are attracted to the highest performing men. More importantly, he assumed that women value status over commitment to relationship. Like many men, he feared that a woman partner will always want to "move up the ladder" to be with a higher functioning man or leave when the current partner does not perform.

Shannon moved to correct John's misconception. She explained that she had little interest in a relationship structured around John's patriarchal leadership and heroic performance. Rather than wanting the man he had fantasized, she craved a man who would support her career, encourage her, and take pleasure in her accomplishments. This was a stunning revelation for John, one that took many months for him to fully comprehend. Eventually he came to realize that a man's security in a relationship did not have to be based in unilateral performance and patriarchal leadership. He began to understand the many advantages of a relationship organized around sharing, cooperation, and mutual affirmation.

THE CHALLENGES OF FEMINIST FAMILY THERAPY FOR TRADITIONAL MEN

A major challenge in family therapy is engaging a reluctant husband/father. Because of the sometimes exaggerated efforts to involve male family members, some feminist theorists have cautioned against catering to male perspectives by idealizing and patronizing fathers while criticizing and blaming mothers (Avis, 1988; Bograd, 1986). I have also raised concerns (Brooks, 1991) about the need to proceed cautiously in seeking to incorporate a husband into therapy with a newly empowered woman. However, when the situation is appropriate, we must make psychotherapy more attractive to traditional men and sell them on the benefits of change.

The recent literature in men's studies is replete with descriptions of the traditional code of masculinity and its poor fit with the role of psychotherapy client (Andronico, 1996; Pollack & Levant, 1998; Scher, 1990). In previous writings (Brooks, 1998, 2000), I have described a model for therapy with traditional men and utilized the acronym MASTERY to represent its core components. I illustrate its use with the Smith family. The first letter of each of the section headings below spell out the acronym MASTERY.

Monitor Personal Reactions to Men and Male Behavior Styles

Brooks and Silverstein (1995) noted that the "dark side of masculinity" includes a wide range of negative behaviors that frequently appear in populations of traditional men: violence, alcohol and drug abuse, sexual excess, emotional flight or withdrawal, sexism, and inadequate behavior as relationship partners. Therapists working with the victims of men's dark-side behavior are quite likely to have a strong negative reaction to the perpetrators. Such a reaction is understandable and, to the extent that it alerts therapists to protect vulnerable parties, it is functional. However, in some extreme cases, men may evoke unnecessarily strong reactions, being labeled as "wife-beaters," "winos," "deadbeat dads," or "male chauvinist pigs." Sometimes, therapists must struggle to avoid generalizing their negative reactions to *all* men.

Already angry or defensive about entering the therapy situation, many of these men can be expected to be sensitive to a therapist's disapproval, and, if sensing it, may quickly exit. Some men may adopt a supplicant and self-condemning stance, heaping blame and guilt on themselves while idealizing loved ones whom they have mistreated. Others may present as overwhelmed, confused, or emotionally anesthetized. To establish rapport, the therapist must find a way to get behind aversive features of the client's pretherapy behavior and highlight the client's more positive characteristics. The capacity to monitor personal reactivity, to value traditional men, and to extend empathy to them is one of the core elements of treatment.

Assume the Male Client Is Feeling Pain

Pleck (1981, 1995) noted that gender role strain is a critical component of the lives of all men. That is, most men are plagued with anxiety about whether they are "man enough," whether they measure up to the next guy or to (unrealistic) public images of male heroes. Most men are susceptible to health problems related to the way men are taught to treat their bodies. Many men will die prematurely. Many men have satisfying sex lives, but a great many others are dissatisfied with the quantity/quality of their sexual activities or the physical appearance of their partner. Finally, many feel emotionally isolated and yearn for closer connections with others.

See the Male Client's Problems in a Gendered Context

Culturally sensitive therapy adjusts its diagnostic formulations and intervention style to the dominant value system of clients. With therapy for traditional men, it follows that "masculinity" should come under the microscope. Solomon (1982) proposed that most men benefit from "gender role psychotherapy" in which gender role issues are explicitly agreed on as a major focus of therapy. Many others have argued for "gender-sensitive" or "gender-aware" therapies, that is, those that make gender an integral aspect of counseling and that view problems within their social context (Good, Gilbert, & Scher, 1990; Philpot, Brooks, Lusterman, & Nutt, 1997).

At their heart, these context-aware therapies urge men to see themselves in social context, as products and sometimes victims of their upbringing in a gendered culture. This challenge to men's usual attribution system usually provides them with immense relief. Men often benefit when they see their failures as less personal and more as the product of a severe and unforgiving socialization. When they recognize that they have suffered because they have been loyalists to an anachronistic masculine code, they cannot help but experience a decrease in self-blame. This process provides comfort and may generate enough energy to begin the corollary investigation of how socialization has limited women.

Transmit Empathy and Understanding

Intense emotional pain is the shameful secret of traditional men. Experienced as humiliating weakness, it is so terrifying that men will go to great lengths to hide from it. Rage and frustration, because they are "manly" emotions, are the primary affective states men allow themselves. McLean (1996) stated that "the process of turning boys into men has, historically, been one of systematic abuse, both physical and emotional, designed to teach boys not to show most emotions, except in certain ritually prescribed situations, and if possible, not to feel them" (p. 21). Before significant change can take place, therapists must understand men's pain, develop skills at evoking its expression in therapy sessions, and show men how to use the resultant energy for growth.

Empower Men to Change

From Robert Bly's (1990) work to the controversial work of sociobiologists and evolutionary psychologists, there have been many calls for greater *understanding* of men's behavior and more *acceptance of male modes of being*. These works are helpful, but disappointing, even counterproductive, when they espouse essentialist philosophies and call for nothing more than improved understanding of men's behavior. Therapists cannot settle for mere understanding of men. We must commit to helping men *change*. Men must be challenged to reevaluate their values and assumptions regarding manhood to bring themselves into greater harmony with a changing world.

Respect Systemic Pressures and Resistance, Yield Some Control to the Family System to Determine Its Ultimate Course

Therapists face an enormous challenge when first encountering new male clients and their families. More than making themselves available, therapists must take full advantage of this opportunity to engage the reluctant man in therapy and demonstrate to the family that it can reshape itself. Therapists should describe the benefits of change to the resistant traditional man and simultaneously help the family counter its natural tendency to get men to "change back."

USING THE MASTERY MODEL WITH TRADITIONAL MEN

Because the Smith family originally sought help with the explosive interactions between John and Dwayne, this issue became a major focus for intervention. The initial progress made in the marital relationship was soon disrupted by another outbreak of conflict between John and Dwayne. It occurred when John insisted that Dwayne help him clean out the garage. When Dwayne resisted, John became enraged and threatening. As John became more insistent, Dwayne became more defiant and challenged John's right to order him to do anything. Because he feared another loss of control, John stormed out the house and again insisted that divorce was the only option.

In the following session, Dwayne was indignant about his stepfather's demands and righteous about his own position. Shannon and Jessica were annoyed with Dwayne but were far more concerned about John's "overreaction." Shannon was irked with John's reliance on unilateral actions and authoritarian parenting. Jessica feared another paternal abandonment. Chuck seemed overwhelmed and paralyzed about what to do. John was furious, both about Dwayne's defiance of his authority and the family's view of him as the bad guy. He challenged the value of the therapy and announced that this would be his last appointment.

In the face of such distress in the family, I needed to align myself quickly with Shannon and John as the parents and as those most able to provide family leadership and reassurance. This move would be difficult, of course, because John was taking a fairly extreme position—that he was a stalwart family leader hampered by the betrayal of his junior officer. Worse, he seemed to be rapidly losing confidence in me.

Although John was not the only troubled family member, it seemed likely that therapy would benefit if I could get him to a more reasonable posture. To do so, I had to see his situation in gender context, transmit to him that I understood his situation, and empower him to adopt a more adaptive family role. I turned to him and said, "John, it's clear to me that you sense serious danger here. You recognize the need for quick and decisive action. Over the past 20 years I have had the opportunity to work with a lot of combat veterans and had the chance to meet a lot of good men who have taught me a great deal. I've learned a lot about what they've had to face and how they've survived. Because of this, I think I can appreciate that as a military man you have assessed this situation and have decided that it is up to you to initiate the action needed. I can see that it frustrates you to do this analysis and then feel you aren't getting the support you need."

John said nothing for a moment, but his reflective expression suggested that there was definitely a reaction. I pressed on. "It looks to me like the inability to resolve this is pretty tough for you to take." John's eyes watered. I asked him, "Can you talk to us about this?" "Not right now," he replied.

John recognized that talking further would reveal more pain than he felt ready to show. The point was made, however, as the family could see another side of John's situation—the apprehension and self-blame that lay behind his demands and complaints. That realization set the stage for further exploration of the multiple sources of John's distress. Gradually, he provided a glimpse into his grief, shame, and bitterness about the "failure" of his military career. In an awkward, yet poignant fashion, he described his current motivations. "I know I'm not perfect. It's like the potter and the clay. I'm trying to remold this military guy. It takes time. I've messed up before but I'm not gonna mess this one up."

Encouragement from me and from a more receptive family made John more comfortable in revealing his disappointments and insecurities. As he did so, he softened and became more open to hearing other family members describe their own pain. Jessica was the most outspoken, tearfully describing her efforts to "keep this family from falling apart." She confronted her stepfather, "You have a family to raise—you can't throw in the towel and give it all up when things don't go well. We need you to care and to be there for us."

In future sessions, we unraveled the multiple strands of conflict rooted in gender dynamics and the unique challenges in the integration of stepfamilies. We identified how Jessica, as an only daughter, tended to be unfairly saddled with excessive responsibility for the emotional welfare of other family members. We clarified how Dwayne's acting out and Chuck's lack of emotional expressiveness were further representations of traditional gender patterns. Most importantly, the therapy empowered family members to change. John was the one least prepared to cope with the sweeping cultural changes in gender roles. His gender role strain had three major components: transitioning from the more traditional military culture to civilian culture, adjusting to the cultural shifts of the women's movement, and adapting to the idiosyncratic changes of gender roles in his own family life.

Initially, John had reacted to these changes with resistance and entrenchment. With destructive results, he had puffed himself up and demanded obedience to his manly (and God-given) authority. He had resolutely continued to think of men as valuable only when they were unilateral family leaders and primary breadwinners. When he failed to meet this standard, he had become demoralized and hopeless, not seeing other areas in which he could make crucial contributions. In therapy we worked to broaden his conceptual map to include multiple ways to be a worthy man. By providing him with some writings of the men's movement and enrolling him in a men's group, I helped him to see other men who had successfully navigated his crises. We spent time correcting his misconceptions about women and the results of sharing power. Gradually, he came to recognize that change did not mean he would be less manly but that he would be able to function more adaptively and flexibly with a far richer repertoire of behavioral and emotional skills

It would be inaccurate to say that John metamorphosed into a radically different person who became a profeminist activist. He maintained outspoken allegiance to many values inherent in military culture. He and his family continued to be active in their conservative Christian church.

Such an outcome is to be expected, because the MASTERY model acknowledges that change is frequently incremental and integrated into preexisting value systems. Still, the Smith family did become fundamentally different. Although John retained his belief that his masculine duty included family leadership, he eased his rigid ideas about the roles of women. He became more supportive of Shannon's career and took on household tasks he had previously disdained.

Both John and Shannon reconsidered their gender-typed expectations of Jessica, Chuck, and Dwayne. Efforts were made to free Jessica from excessive responsibility for monitoring family welfare so that she could turn her energies toward her own career. Chuck's stoic silence was relabeled from a strength to a shortcoming, and emotional expressiveness became a therapeutic goal. Finally, we searched for the many meanings of Dwayne's disruptive behavior. In addition to identifying the systemic meaning of his scapegoat role, we also distinguished subtle mixed messages given to young men about anger and reckless behavior.

A NOTE ON ETHNIC DIVERSITY

In the previous section on my reactions and reactivity to working with the Smith family, I emphasized the ways that I responded to John as a powerful and successful man. In my work on improving therapeutic approaches to traditional men, I have focused primarily on *gender* as a critical variable. Therapists must also be carefully attuned to the influences of race, ethnicity, social class, sexual orientation, age, and physical ability status. Although it would be impossible to explore here the entire range of influence of all these dimensions, it is possible to consider at least one: the role of ethnic diversity.

How then would I use the MASTERY model if John Smith and his family were of a different ethnic background? For example, what would be different if they were African American? Obviously, my "monitoring of personal reactivity" would need to be broadened to a careful consideration of my experiences living as a White man in a racist culture. This matter would include analysis of my concepts of Whiteness and examination of my own racism (Sue & Sue, 1999). Although I might have some success identifying with John as a fellow man, I would still be ineffective if I could not appreciate the fundamental differences rooted in our racial histories. Unless I had made significant progress in my own White racial identity development (Hardiman, 1982; Helms, 1995), I could not be fully effective in my work with this family.

In addition to viewing John in a *gendered* context, I would need to be able to see him in a *racial* context. The first step in racially sensitive work with African American clients is the recognition of the deleterious effects of racial oppression (Jones, 1985; Montague, 1996). In developing a working alliance, we would need to acknowledge the hampering presence of "historical hostility" (Vontress & Epp, 1997) and the adaptive phenomenon of "healthy paranoia" (Paniagua, 1998).

The suspicion and guardedness inherent in situations in which oppressed groups seek help from members of the oppressor group pose a major therapeutic hurdle. This is particularly critical because my MASTERY model emphasizes transmitting empathy and understanding. As a White man, I can say that I have walked in the shoes of many men (and no women). However, it is a significant mistake to assume that the experiences of *all* men can be understood without recognition of major differences rooted in racial heritage. For this reason, I need to be up front about our differences and especially open to discussing any problems these differences might pose.

Fortunately, in my 28 years of work with military veterans, I have had many rich opportunities for increased understanding of the lives of African Americans. Although this experience has helped me become more culturally competent, I still need to read extensively, continually monitor my work in therapy, and seek consultation from multicultural experts.

CONCLUSION

Compassionate, thoughtful, and gender-aware psychotherapists offer unique hope for challenging men to reach out to each other, to interact sensitively with women, to challenge regressive institutions, and to mentor the next generation of men. These therapies offer hope for developing couple relationships characterized by the feminist principles of mutual respect and empowerment. Psychotherapists must be alert to the destructive potential of the darkest aspects of traditional masculinity, yet we can also hold utmost confidence in the potential of men—men who want a better deal for themselves, their culture, and their loved ones. Therapists are uniquely positioned to provide leadership in the painful but ultimately exhilarating process of helping traditional men discover realistic and compassionate masculinities, helping couples develop egalitarian relationships, and helping family systems empower women and men.

REFERENCES

Andronico, M. (1996). (Ed.). *Men in groups: Insights, interventions, and psychoeducational work.* Washington, DC: American Psychological Association.

Avis, J. M. (1988). Deepening awareness: A private study guide to feminism and family therapy. In L. Braverman (Ed.), *A guide to feminist family therapy* (pp. 15–46). New York: Harrington Park Press.

Bly, R. (1990). *Iron John: A book about men.* New York: Vintage Books.

Bograd, M. (1986). A feminist examination of family systems models of violence against women in the family. In M. Ault-Riche (Ed.), *Women in family therapy* (pp. 34–50). Rockville, MD: Aspen Systems.

Brooks, G. R. (1991). Traditional men in marital and family therapy. In M. Bograd (Ed.), *Feminist approaches for men in family therapy* (pp. 51–74). New York: Haworth Press.

Brooks, G. R. (1998). *A new psychotherapy for traditional men.* San Francisco: Jossey-Bass.

Brooks, G. R. (2000, Summer). A six-step model for engaging men in psychotherapy. *The Texas Psychologist,* 34–36.

Brooks, G. R., & Silverstein, L. B. (1995). Understanding the dark side of masculinity: An integrative systems model. In R. F. Levant & W. S. Pollack (Eds.), *A new psychology of men* (pp. 280–333). New York: Basic Books.

Good, G. E., Gilbert, L. A., & Scher, M. (1990). Gender aware therapy: A synthesis of feminist therapy and knowledge about gender. *Journal of Counseling and Development, 68,* 376–380.

Hardiman, R. (1982). White identity development: A process oriented model for describing the racial consciousness of White Americans. *Dissertation Abstracts International, 43,* 104A. (University Microfilms No. 82-10330)

Helms, J. E. (1995). An update of Helms's White and people of color racial identity models. In J. G. Ponterotto, J. M. Casas, L. A. Suzuki, & C. M. Alexander (Eds.), *Handbook of multicultural counseling* (pp. 181–191). Thousand Oaks, CA: Sage.

Jones, A. C. (1985). Psychological functioning in Black Americans: A conceptual guide for use in psychotherapy. *Psychotherapy, 22,* 363–369.

McLean, C. (1996). The politics of men's pain. In C. McLean, M. Carey, & C. White (Eds.), *Men's ways of being* (pp. 11–28). Boulder, CO: Westview Press.

Montague, J. (1996). Counseling families from diverse cultures. A nondeficit approach. *Journal of Multicultural Counseling and Development, 24,* 37–41.

Paniagua, F. A. (1998). *Assessing and treating culturally diverse clients: A practical guide.* Thousand Oaks, CA: Sage.

Philpot, C., Brooks, G. R., Lusterman, D.-D., & Nutt, R. L. (Eds.). (1997). *Bridging separate gender worlds*. Washington, DC: American Psychological Association.

Pittman, F. (1990). The masculine mystique. *Family Therapy Networker, 14,* 40–52.

Pittman, F. (1993). *Man enough: Fathers, sons, and the search for masculinity.* New York: Perigee.

Pleck, J. H. (1981). *The myth of masculinity.* Cambridge, MA: MIT Press.

Pleck, J. H. (1995). The gender role strain paradigm: An update. In R. F. Levant & W. S. Pollack (Eds.), *A new psychology of men* (pp. 11–32). New York: Basic Books.

Pollack, W. S., & Levant, R. F. (Eds.). (1998). *New psychotherapy for men.* New York: Wiley.

Scher, M. (1990). Effect of gender-role incongruities on men's experience as clients in psychotherapy. *Psychotherapy, 27,* 322–326.

Solomon, K. (1982). Individual psychotherapy and changing masculine roles: Dimensions of gender-role psychotherapy. In K. Solomon & N. Levy (Eds.), *Men in transition: Theory and therapy* (pp. 247–274). New York: Plenum Press.

Sue, D.W., & Sue, D. (1999). *Counseling the culturally different: Theory and practice* (3rd ed.). New York: Wiley.

Vontress, C. E., & Epp, L. R. (1997). Historical hostility in the African American client: Implications for counseling. *Journal of Multicultural Counseling and Development, 25,* 170–184.

13

TREATING MALE ALEXITHYMIA

RONALD F. LEVANT

Male gender role socialization, through the combined influences of mothers, fathers, and peer groups, suppresses natural male emotional self-awareness and expressivity. Thus boys grow up to be men who cannot readily sense their feelings and put them into words. They are therefore normatively alexithymic. *Alexithymia* literally means the inability to put emotions into words. The term is composed of a series of Greek roots: *a* (without)-*lexus* (words)-*thymos* (emotions)—without words for emotions. Sifneos (1967) and Krystal (1982) originally used this term to characterize the severe emotional constriction that they encountered in their patients (primarily male) who are psychosomatic, drug dependent, and suffering from posttraumatic stress disorder. They were dealing with cases of severe alexithymia, which is at the far end of the continuum of this disorder. I have found that alexithymia also occurs in "garden-variety," or mild-to-moderate forms, and alexithymia in these forms is very common and widespread among men (Levant & Kelly, 1989; Levant & Kopecky, 1995). I have termed this widespread but milder condition *normative male alexithymia*.

Male gender role socialization further creates men who have an action-oriented variant of empathy but tend to have difficulties with emotional empathy. Men tend to channel their vulnerable emotions (such as fear, sadness, loneliness, feeling unloved) into anger, and to transform their caring feelings (such as fondness, love, attachment) into sexuality (Levant, 1998; Levant & Kopecky, 1995).

This chapter is adapted from "Desperately Seeking Language: Understanding, Assessing, and Treating Normative Male Alexithymia" (pp. 35–56) by R. F. Levant, 1998, in W. S. Pollack & R. F. Levant (Eds.), *New Psychotherapy for Men*, New York: Wiley. Copyright 1998 by Wiley. Reprinted with permission.

Simply put, as a result of the male role socialization ordeal, boys grow up to be men who are genuinely unaware of their emotions. When men are required to give an account of their emotions, they tend to be unable to identify them directly. They then rely on their cognition to deduce logically what they should feel under a given set of circumstances. As the following clinical vignettes show, they cannot do what is so easy, almost automatic, for most women—simply turn inward, feel the feeling, and let the verbal description come to mind.

One man (let's call him "Don") whom I was interviewing in a couples therapy intake session appeared to become so intensely anxious that his body was literally vibrating while his wife "Mary" discussed her many complaints about his lack of participation in caring for their infant son. When I asked him if the discussion was upsetting him, he said it was not. In fact, he stated that he was "glad that they were discussing these important matters."

Another man ("Joe"), also in a couples intake session, was describing without affect how his two school-age children surprised him one day and discovered his predilection for cross-dressing. I asked him how he felt about that. He turned to his wife "Judith" and asked her "How did I feel?" She responded: "You were embarrassed."

From a feminist perspective, this widespread inability among men to identify emotions and put them into words has enormous consequences. It makes it less likely that men who suffer from it will be able to fully participate in family life—in either the emotional nurturing of parenting or the emotional intimacy of marriage. It also blocks men who suffer from it from using the most effective means known for dealing with life's stresses and traumas, namely, identifying, thinking about, and discussing one's emotional responses to a stressor or trauma with a friend or family member. Consequently, it predisposes such men to deal with stress in ways that make certain forms of isolating, nonrelational, and antirelational pathology more likely. Examples of these patterns of managing feelings include substance abuse, violent behavior, and sexual compulsions. All of these nonadaptive coping strategies severely limit the possibilities for intimacy in family life. Finally, this inability to maintain an active connection to his own emotions and to the emotional life of the family places an unfair burden on women to provide the "emotional lubrication" of family life.

Alexithymic men tend to deal with vulnerable emotions by either passive-aggressively becoming mute or transforming these emotions into aggressive displays of anger. Don (in the first anecdote) became mute when he was planning to take a business trip that would leave his wife Mary alone with their infant son. He was aware that his plans would upset her, but he was unable to identify, much less process, his anxiety about discussing his plans with her. As a result, he delayed informing her of his plans until the very last moment, blurting them out the evening before departure as he began to pack. Feeling totally blindsided, Mary sunk deeper into her depression. Joe (in the second anecdote), in contrast, flew into a rage, when—embarrassed but not knowing it—his wife, Judith, confronted him on his furtive cross-dressing behavior.

Treating male alexithymia is a feminist intervention because it addresses two major facets of contemporary gender relationships: the closeness/distance reciprocity and the power-up/power-down imbalance (Levant & Silverstein, 2001). First, with regard to the closeness/distance reciprocity, popular culture (using the "Mars/Venus" metaphor) misunderstands male–female relationships by asserting that women "naturally" seek emotional closeness and men "naturally" seek emotional distance. A feminist perspective, however, focuses on the cultural construction of these contrasting behaviors in men and women. From a feminist perspective, the traditional gender role socialization of girls fosters attachment, emotional expressiveness, and caretaking—attitudes and skills that are functional in creating emotional closeness and maintaining relationships. Conversely, traditional masculine gender role socialization fosters alexithymia, discomfort with intimacy, and a competitive orientation—attitudes and skills that are functional in creating emotional distance. For example, Mary, like Don, had a high-powered job. However, all she had to do was look at her infant son to become convinced that she should sacrifice that job, if necessary, to care for him. Don, in contrast, rationalized his distancing behavior by thinking of himself as following in his father's footsteps by becoming the family breadwinner. He maintained this perspective, despite the fact that Mary earned considerably more money than he did.

Systems theory emphasizes the impact that relationships have on an individual's behavior. Individual behavior is thought to be *reciprocal*, that is, it responds to and influences the behavior of others. If one person in a couple is pursuing the other in an attempt to feel emotionally close, this pursuing behavior is thought of, in large measure, as a response to the other person's moving away from them. Similarly, the other person's distancing behavior is constructed, in part, as a response to this pursuit.

If we consider the story of Mary and Don, Don went on a 3-week business trip to Asia when his son was just 6 weeks old. This distancing behavior at a time when she was especially vulnerable dramatically increased Mary's sense of isolation and abandonment. As a result, she became much more demanding of his participation in family life. Thus women's tendency to pursue closeness is in part a function of men's tendency to distance.

Virtually every heterosexual couple enters therapy with gender-based complaints. The women complain that their husbands are too distant; the men complain that their wives want too much closeness. Couples often mention communication as one of their problems. For example, Karen expressed dissatisfaction that Richard did not talk about things that upset him, whereas Richard was annoyed by these demands and would say that his preferred way of coping with such difficulties was to "just go in my cave and try to forget about it." However, most couples are unaware that their failure to communicate effectively has been culturally constructed by their contrasting experiences with gender role socialization.

Teaching men how to take responsibility for their emotions counters the cultural pressure on women to fulfill the expressive function for the whole family, and thus changes the closeness/distance reciprocity. It also creates the possibility that men can become more emotionally empathic and expressive toward not only their wives but also their children. This increased emotional accessibility enhances their overall ability to participate in the intimacy of family life, which in turn may reduce the need for their wives to shoulder an unfair burden in terms of child care and housework.

Second, there is the dimension of power. Because we live in a male-dominant society, men are automatically awarded power. They are socialized to develop personality characteristics that are functional for attaining and maintaining power. Men are also reinforced for wielding power. In contrast, women are socialized to avoid power, excluded from positions of power, and punished for seeking power. Thus, men will seek power and women will avoid it, creating a power-up/power-down imbalance.

Hence it should be no surprise that men tend to deal with marital conflicts through the assertion of power, using such tactics as stonewalling, hyperrationality, gruffness, verbal bullying, and worse. Gottman (1991) has found that such men experience marital conflict as distinctly unpleasant and have high rates of autonomic arousal during such conflict. It is my view that many such men are normatively alexithymic. The subjective discomfort and autonomic arousal is the trace left by their unarticulated emotions. As noted earlier, alexithymic men have learned through their childhood socialization to deal with these emotions by either transforming them into aggressive displays of anger or by becoming passive-aggressive by going mute.

I have found clinically that alexithymic men who desire to repair their marital relationships benefit by learning how to access and discuss their feelings about a conflict with their wives. They also improve by learning how to see and feel things from their wives' points of view, thus becoming emotionally empathic. This often leads to reconciliation and the deepening of the intimacy of the relationship.

The psychoeducational program that I have developed is an active, problem-solving approach that relies on the use of homework assignments and is done in the initial phase of treatment (Levant, 1997). It thus can be thought of as a preparatory phase, designed to get the male client ready for the later phases of family therapy. I have found that many men find such an approach very congenial, because it is congruent with aspects of the male code, that is, the tendency to take charge and actively problem solve situations. In addition, men who are demoralized for one reason or another may find that it restores their sense of agency, by giving them something that they can *do* to improve their situation. Furthermore, helping men overcome normative alexithymia is useful at the beginning stages of therapy for many men, because it enables them to develop the skills of emotional self-awareness and emotional expressivity that will empower them to wrestle with deeper emotional issues in later stages of therapy.

ASSESSMENT

During the first interview with the husband/partner, in addition to taking a standard history, I also assess his ability to become aware of his emotions and put them into words, as well as his ability to accurately sense and articulate the emotions of others. I use the following format, using a mixture of structured and unstructured questions. (For more information, refer to Levant, 1997, 1998.)

1. To what extent is the client aware of discrete emotions as contrasted with the bodily sensations that often accompany strong emotions (e.g., tension in the forehead, tightness in the gut)?
2. What specific emotions does the client become aware of? Is he aware of his vulnerable emotions, such as worry, fear, anxiety, sadness, hurt, dejection, disappointment, rejection, or abandonment? If he is not aware of his vulnerable emotions, are these emotions transformed into anger and expressed as rage, violence, or disconnection (e.g., stonewalling)?
3. Is the client aware of his emotions in the caring/connection part of the spectrum, such as concern, warmth, affection, appreciation, love, neediness/dependency, closeness, or attachment? Is he limited in his ability to express caring/connection emotions? Does he express these emotions primarily through the channel of sexuality?
4. Is the client aware of his emotions in the anger part of the spectrum? Does he become aware of an emotion—such as anger—only when it is very intense?
5. At what intensities does the client experience his emotions?
6. Can the client identify any of his wife's or children's emotions? Does the idea ever occur to him that the emotions of family members are worth noticing? What does he experience and do when his wife or child is upset with him? Can he stay calm and reflect their feelings or does he become overwhelmed and either withdraw or become aggressive?

The program for the treatment of alexithymia that I have developed has five steps that progressively build on each other. It begins by working with the male partner alone from a psychoeducational perspective. It then moves to a more systemic focus, including family-of-origin work and analysis of the reciprocal pattern of family relationships in the client's current family of choice.[1]

Step 1: Psychoeducation About Normative Alexithymia

In order for the client to be able to make sense of his experience and utilize the treatment techniques, he needs to know what his limitations are in his ability to know and express his emotions, and how these limitations came about through gender role socialization. An important part of this is helping the client develop his ability to tolerate certain emotions (such as fear or sadness) that he may regard as unmanly and therefore shameful. It is also important to teach men about the reciprocal and systemic nature of gender roles and how women are socialized for emotional closeness and nurturance.

Step 2: Develop a Vocabulary for Emotions

Because men tend not to be aware of emotions, they usually do not have a very good vocabulary of words for emotions. This also follows from the research literature on the development of language for emotions (Levant, 1998). The next step, then, is to help the man develop a vocabulary for the full spectrum of emotions, particularly the vulnerable and caring/connection emotions. I ask my male clients to record as many words for feelings that they can several times during the week. This step often requires teaching men about the different kinds of emotions. Some men can benefit at this stage from being asked to compare themselves with their wives in terms of their use of language to express emotions. This additional step also has the side benefit of helping men become aware of gender-based disparities in terms of who bears responsibility for managing the emotional aspects of the relationship.

---

[1]To some, it may seem surprising that I am working with an individual in what I have identified as systemic therapy. However, systemic therapy is a paradigm defined by the theoretical orientation of the therapist, not by the number of people in the consulting room.

Step 3: Learn to Read the Emotions of Others

The third step involves learning to apply emotional words to feeling states. It is often less threatening to do this with other people than with oneself. Thus I recommend focusing on other people at this stage. This focus on reading other people's emotions has the added benefit of helping men see things from another person's perspective, and thus contributes to their development of emotional empathy.

I teach male clients to read facial gestures, tone of voice, and other types of body language in other people. I explain that these nonverbal behaviors are usually a sign that the person is experiencing an emotion. I encourage them to learn to identify the emotions of others, in conversations, while observing other people, or while watching movies. I instruct them to ask themselves questions during this process such as: What is he feeling? What does this feel like from her perspective? I particularly encourage them to do this with family members: children, spouse, parents.

Step 4: Keep an Emotional Response Log

The next step involves teaching men to apply emotional words to their own experience. Building on Step 3, I try to keep this in a relational context by asking my male clients to notice how they respond when they identify their wives' emotions. I ask them to keep an Emotional Response Log, noting when they experienced a bodily sensation, explaining that this is usually a sign that they are experiencing a feeling. I ask them to describe what the circumstances were that led up to the feeling or bodily sensation. The instructions for keeping an Emotional Response Log are as follows:

- Record the bodily sensation (or feelings, if you notice them) that you become aware of, and when you first started to experience them.
- Describe the social or relational context within which the emotion was aroused: Who was doing what to whom? How did that affect you? If this emotion occurred in response to identifying your wife's feelings, what do you think she was feeling?
- Go though the emotional vocabulary list that you have developed in Step 2, and pick out the words that seem to best describe the emotion that you were experiencing.

Step 5: Practice

The fifth and final step involves practice. Emotional self-awareness and emotional empathy are skills. Like any other skill, they require practice to become an automatic part of one's functioning. Under certain conditions, I have used role-plays, videotaped for immediate feedback, to practice the skills. In these situations, I teach men to tune in to their feelings and those of others through watching and discussing immediate playbacks of role-play situations in which feelings were engendered. By pointing out the nonverbal cues and asking such questions as "What were your feelings, Jack, when you grimaced in that last segment?" men learn how to access the ongoing flow of internal emotions. Although working with video feedback obviously has advantages, one can also practice this skill without such arrangements. By systematically keeping an Emotional Response Log and discussing the results in therapy, one can gradually build up the ability to recognize feelings as they occur, and put them into words. It is also important to continuously encourage men to take responsibility for their part of relationships rather than relying on women to do it for them.

For example, Don began therapy with a very limited ability to discern his own emotions. Initially he could not even say he was upset when he obviously was. Later, he could describe his emotional state as being "upset" but could not go much further. After a month of work, he brought in a notation in his Emotional Response Log that concerned his wife Mary. She had gotten very upset and was screaming in the shower. He noted that the best word to describe his emotional state was "fear." This analysis was an improvement over his earlier undifferentiated descriptions of his emotional states. With coaching, he was able to say that he felt helpless because he did not know how to comfort his wife. This realization allowed him to begin to deal with his helplessness by brainstorming things he might do to respond to her needs.

Some colleagues have expressed surprise that men can learn these emotional skills fairly easily. Yet young girls learn these skills as matter of course. Moreover, men might have learned the skills as well if they had not undergone traditional male socialization. When the men do learn these skills, they feel that a whole new world—the world of emotions—has been opened up to them. One man said that it was as though he had been living in a black-and-white television set that had suddenly gone to color. Others have reveled in the benefits and increased intimacy that they have experienced in their family relationships.

CASE STUDY: A NUMB EXPECTANT FATHER

Raymond, a 41-year-old successful software designer currently racing to bring a new, "preemptive" telecommunications product to market, called for an appointment (at the urging of his wife) because he "felt nothing" about the fact that he and Janet, his wife of 20 years, were expecting their first child. He and Janet met in high school and had postponed having a child because Raymond's work required many moves over the years. Raymond was a hard-driving guy who met or exceeded most of the requirements of the male code. The firstborn son of a rural family, responsibility was his middle name. He took care of various members of his family of origin and his extended family. Apart from the fact that his wife was pregnant and he thought he "should" feel something about that, Raymond did not find it particularly odd that he "felt nothing." He usually felt nothing. The last time he cried was when a car hit his dog. That was 10 years ago.

Raymond was assessed as normatively alexithymic and was treated with the psychoeducational program. As is typical of many men, he welcomed an action-oriented approach to therapy in which the client is asked to do something to get better. He willingly did the homework that was assigned. As a result of the psychoeducational treatment, long-buried issues about his father (who had died several years earlier) started to surface by the fifth session, and the family systems work began in earnest.

Using Raymond's emerging curiosity about the therapeutic process, I constructed a ritual in which he was asked to identify the questions he had about his father. He was asked to identify his emotional responses to the questions and to color code them using felt-tipped pens. I used this latter suggestion, which draws on right-brain processes, to bypass any defensive equivocation that might have come into play. Finally, I used family photo reconnaissance to stimulate memories and additional questions. The combined effect of these interventions was to bring the client face to face with his bitterness about his father's psychological absence. This confrontation with his feelings initiated a long-delayed grieving process, not only about his father's death but also about his emotional absence when he was alive.

Fortuitously, Raymond had an opportunity to visit his father's younger sister at a time when he was receptive to learning more about his father. This visit provided a wealth of information about the man that his father was. This helped him begin to see his father as a whole man, far from perfect, but doing the best he could with what he had, and quite well at that. However, it was not until a visit to his father's grave that he was able fully to grieve the father he never knew.

Having done a brief but significant piece of grief work, Raymond found his feelings about becoming a father had come unblocked. The first set of feelings he had was on the anxious end of the spectrum. He was worried about whether the baby would be healthy and concerned that his wife Janet would be okay. He began to express these feelings to Janet. After a visit to Janet's doctor, he was able to get his worries addressed, and also to hear the direct evidence of his baby's heartbeat. At that point his anxiety turned into excitement. Soon thereafter he reported that his relationship with Janet had improved. He was not only being able to recognize when she was upset but also able and willing to initiate a conversation about her upset. In this way he took responsibility for aspects of their relationship that had previously fallen to Janet alone. Shortly after that the therapy ended.

SUMMARY

In this chapter I considered the problem of normative male alexithymia and its role in contemporary family relationships. I noted that treating alexithymia is a feminist intervention because it addresses two major facets of gender relationships: the closeness/distance reciprocity and the power-up/power-down imbalance. I presented a method to assess the degree to which male clients suffer from normative male alexithymia using a five-step psychoeducational program. A case study illustrated the approach.

Is this type of therapy useful for all types of male patients? I certainly do not have enough experience to answer that question, but I can say that it does seem to work best with those normatively alexithymic male patients motivated to comply with treatment—that is, those who are motivated to follow a directive, homework-based form of therapy. It may be less useful to clients who tend to defy treatment, for whom the issue of resistance is a much larger matter.

To date, I have used this approach only with European American, heterosexual, middle-class men. For it to be useful for a more diverse group, issues of immigration, ethnicity, race, class, disability status, and sexual orientation would need to be incorporated in the same way that gender has been addressed in the current model. I will make some tentative suggestions about how to apply this model to middle-class African American men, on the basis of research that I have conducted in collaboration with Richard Majors (Levant & Majors, 1997).

African American men are caught in the jaws of a powerful dilemma: They strongly want the opportunity to perform the role requirements of traditional masculinity. However, because of impediments resulting from institutional racism, this opportunity is often not available to them on the same terms as it is to European American men (Dovidio, 2001). In response, some African American men have developed a distinct set of mannerisms and behaviors that serve to protect the self from the pain associated with oppression and stigmatization. Majors (Majors & Billson, 1992) coined the term *cool pose* to refer to this set of behaviors that attempt to cope with oppression but that ultimately are dysfunctional.

A different subset of African American men, those with the best prospects for employment (i.e., educated middle-class men), have had to overcontrol the expression of anger and aggression to survive in a racist society. However, these men have been allowed somewhat freer expression of their vulnerable and caring/connection emotions (Cazanave, 1984; Hunter & Davis, 1994). Hence their situation is somewhat analogous to that of European American women who have also been socialized to express nurturing feelings and to restrict their expression of anger and aggression (Levant, 1998). This pattern may also be characteristic of other oppressed minorities. For example, Olkin (2001) noted that restricting the expression of anger is an issue for people with disabilities.

Thus, alexithymia treatment for middle-class African American men may not need to emphasize learning to experience and express vulnerable and caring/connection emotions, but will require training in anger expression and management. It may be appropriate to use an approach that we use with European American clients in Step 1, where we help the patient develop his ability to tolerate certain uncomfortable emotions. However, we must take great care to validate a middle-class African American client's very real fears about the consequences of being openly angry and aggressive in a racist society. At the moment these suggestions remain clinical hypotheses that must be tested.

REFERENCES

Cazenave, N. A. (1984). Race, socio-economic status, and age: The social context of American masculinity. *Sex Roles, 11*, 639–656.

Dovidio, J. F. (2001, January). Why can't we get along? Interpersonal biases and interracial distrust. In L. Porche Burke & D. Wing Sue (Co-Chairs), *Race, racism and anti-racism.* Symposium conducted at the National Multicultural Conference and Summit, Santa Barbara, CA.

Gottman, J. (1991). Predicting the longitudinal courses of marriages. *Journal of Marital and Family Therapy, 17*, 3–7.

Hunter, A. G., & Davis, J. E. (1994). Hidden voices of Black men: The meaning, structure and complexity of manhood. *Journal of Black Studies, 25*, 20–40.

Krystal, H. (1982). Alexithymia and the effectiveness of psychoanalytic treatment. *International Journal of Psychoanalytic Psychotherapy, 9*, 353–378.

Levant, R. F. (1997). *Men and emotions: A psychoeducational approach* [Video]. Hicksville, NY: Newbridge Professional Programs. (Out of print, available from author)

Levant, R. F. (1998). Desperately seeking language: Understanding, assessing and treating normative male alexithymia. In W. S. Pollack & R. F. Levant (Eds.), *New psychotherapy for men* (pp. 35–56). New York: Wiley.

Levant, R. F., & Kelly, J. (1989). *Between father and child.* New York: Viking.

Levant, R. F., & Kopecky, G. (1995). *Masculinity reconstructed.* New York: Dutton. (Out of print, available from author)

Levant, R. F., & Majors, R. G. (1997). An investigation into variations in the construction of the male gender role among young African American and European American women and men. *Journal of Gender, Culture, and Health, 2*, 33–43.

Levant, R. F., & Silverstein, L. (2001). Integrating gender and family systems theories: The "both/and" approach to treating a post-modern couple. In S. McDaniel, D. D. Lusterman, & C. Philpot (Eds.), *Integrating family therapy casebook* (pp. 245–252). Washington, DC: American Psychological Association.

Majors, R. G., & Billson, J. M. (1992). *Cool pose: The dilemmas of Black manhood in America.* New York: Lexington Books.

Olkin, R. (2001, January). *What psychotherapists should know about disability.* Paper presented at the National Multicultural Conference and Summit, Santa Barbara, CA.

Sifneos, P. E. (1967). Clinical observations on some patients suffering from a variety of psychosomatic diseases. In *Proceedings of the Seventh European Conference on Psychosomatic Research.* Basel, Switzerland: Kargel.

14

WOMEN'S SECRETS IN THERAPY

EVAN IMBER-BLACK

No woman wakes up in the morning saying to herself: "I think I'll create a secret today." Secrets have their origin far beyond any given woman, her intimate relationships, her family position as a mother, daughter, sister, spouse, or lover. We must take a broader perspective and consider the historical period, and the cultural/political context within which she finds herself, to understand what a woman chooses to conceal or reveal. Often this larger arena is hidden from view, thereby adding further layers of the unspoken and the unknown.

Many secrets involve power imbalances. Those with power over others—male over female, White over Black, rich over poor—often assume they have the right to conceal information, whereas those with little or no power are intimidated into silence. Thus, men, who have more power, often feel entitled to keep secrets to maintain privilege and control. Women, who have less power, may keep secrets either to protect men's position or to protect themselves from the punishment that may follow a secret's discovery.

Gender, social class, race, religion, and ethnicity braid together to shape what is silenced, hidden, or taboo in the lives of women and their families. This chapter explores examples of these forces at work and then addresses them in therapy.

GENDERED SECRETS

A few years ago, a journalist called me to get ideas for an article she was doing on "Women's Secrets." I asked her what she had in mind. She replied, "Oh, you know, when a wife buys an expensive new dress, clips the price tag off, and tells her husband she found it on sale." When I asked her if she thought a husband would make a secret and tell a lie about the purchase of a sport jacket, she told me, "Certainly not." Suddenly we were in the realm of secrets kept because of fear and power inequities in intimate relationships.

The secrets that many women feel compelled to keep are far more profound than a recent purchase or a fender bender. Until very recently, in the United States nearly all women kept physical and sexual abuse secret. Although abuse is now spoken of in the wider culture, many women still remain silent about being beaten by their partners or about their daughters being sexually abused. In many parts of the world, women are degraded, humiliated, and blamed following a rape, and so keep the violation a secret. The continuity of these secrets is supported by the deeply rooted and only recently challenged assumption that women and children are the property of men. Working with women in therapy who are struggling to open such secrets requires dealing with shame, self-blame, community stigma, centuries of training to protect men, and the ever-present uncertainty regarding the responses of extended family, police, courts, and social agencies.

To protect their jobs, women may keep sexual harassment a secret. When Anita Hill came forward to declare that Clarence Thomas had sexually harassed her, a spotlight suddenly was turned on this national secret. This spotlight faded quickly as we watched a highly educated attorney endanger her reputation and her future by speaking out. Senator Barbara Mikulski remarked,

> To anybody out there who wants to be a whistle-blower, the message is: Don't blow that whistle because you'll be left out there by yourself. To any victim of sexual harassment or sexual abuse or sexual violence either in the street or even in her own home, the message is nobody's going to take you seriously, not even in the United States Senate. (Phelps & Winternitz, 1992, p. 127)

Sexual harassment quickly moved from a secret that certain working women kept to a secret that we all know but pretend not to know.

The television program *NYPD Blue* portrayed the effects of two gendered secrets on a newly married couple. The secrets that women keep involving assault, violence, and sexuality intersect powerfully and reciprocally with the secrets that men keep involving vulnerability, competency, and physical weakness. The relationship of police detective Andy Sipowicz and Assistant District Attorney Sylvia Costa erodes under the weight of secrets each is keeping from the other. Recently mugged on the street, Sylvia begins to have flashbacks from a rape years earlier. She has kept this rape a secret from her husband, a decision driven both by her own shame and her fear that he would not love her if he knew. She experiences the dilemma of many rape victims regarding whether to tell anyone about this trauma.

Simultaneously, Andy is keeping a secret: He fears that he may have prostate cancer. As a man, Andy believes he needs to hide any vulnerabilities, particularly medical ones, from his wife. Not knowing her husband's secret, Sylvia musters the courage to tell him the secret of the rape. Although he is emotionally supportive, he withdraws from her sexually because of his own medical problem. Not knowing his secret, Sylvia believes that her worst nightmare about revealing her secret has come to pass—her husband is turned off to her. Only much later, after discovering that he does not have cancer, does Andy reveal his secret.

This carefully crafted subplot shows the deleterious effect of gendered secrets on a relationship. Sylvia's secret is a secret of rape, and like women throughout time, she fears her husband will think less of her or blame her for being raped. Andy's secret is connected to male sexuality and his fears that his wife will think less of him if he has cancer.

Many men feel entitled to keep secrets from the women in their lives. Secrets may protect men at the expense of women. In the first recorded example of donor insemination in 1884, a couple consulted a physician about their struggle to conceive. Unbeknownst to the woman, while under anesthesia she was inseminated with the sperm of a medical student. In an act demonstrating clear belief men were entitled to keep such a secret, the doctor informed only the husband. The wife gave birth and raised a child she believed to be her husband's. Behind this secret was another secret kept from the wife—the cause of the infertility was the husband's syphilis (Orenstein, 1995). Although this particular secret would not occur today, the belief in male power and privilege that underpinned this secret over a century ago still continues. For one illustration, in 1992, Dr. Cecil Jacobson was convicted of 52 counts of fraud for secretly inseminating his women patients with his own sperm (Chartrand, 1992).

Secrecy and Privacy

A quarter of a century after the start of the women's movement, many men keep secrets from their wives about money, conveniently redefining such secrets as "private matters." Men also keep secrets from women to enhance an insupportable image or cover vulnerabilities and weaknesses that our gender definitions regard as "unmanly," including work insecurities, lack of competence, or failure.

When Alan, 42, and Mona, 40, came to see me for couples therapy, their marriage was in crisis. An upper-middle-class White couple, Alan and Mona had been married for 17 years. Unknown to Mona until just before they consulted me, Alan's business had been failing for many months. To maintain his secret, Alan began using their children's college fund to keep his business afloat. Further, he secretly secured a loan that jeopardized their home ownership. For months, Mona had noticed that Alan seemed withdrawn, dismissing her inquiries about his work and staying at the office later and later. A week before our initial meeting, Mona had opened a letter from the bank and discovered her husband's secret.

At the beginning of our session, Alan seemed arrogant, furious with Mona for what he called "snooping and violating my privacy." Later in the session, however, he broke down and began to cry, saying, "I'm the man. I'm the husband. I'm supposed to take care of you. I didn't want you to know I was failing." Alan's father was a successful entrepreneur who taught Alan the cultural message: "Men take care, women are taken care of." Mona came from a family with similar beliefs. Our work together in therapy focused on challenging those beliefs and the untenable secrets to which they lead. The initial crisis quickly abated as a result of exploring three themes: (a) locating what appeared to be Alan's betrayal of Mona to a broader social level, (b) linking what each one learned in their families of origin about men's and women's gendered roles, and (c) tracing where such ideas came from in the culture.

In my work with Alan and Mona, we talked over the differences between secrecy and privacy. When Alan initially insisted that it was his right to keep his financial dealings from Mona, calling them "private," I asked him if Mona had the same right. He quickly recognized that what he was designating as "private" for his own behavior, he would name "secret" if Mona had done it. We talked over the idea that definitions of what is secret and what is private change across time, cultures, and sociopolitical circumstances, depending on what a given family or culture stigmatize or value. I pointed out that those with more power in relationships often invoke "privacy" to protect a toxic secret, whereas those with little or no power have relatively little privacy, even in areas that should be so protected. Secrets affect another person's right to know information, whereas truly private matters do not. Secrets are often marked by shame; privacy is shame-free (Imber-Black, 1998).

Alan and Mona's therapy allowed them to reconstruct their relationship to make it a partnership in which each was responsible for the family's financial and emotional well-being.

Secrets From Oneself

Secrets sometimes appear to reside inside one person. In fact, their maintenance requires the silent collusion of others in a social network.

Nowhere is this more true than with women's "secret" eating disorders, a seemingly individual secret that requires a systemic perspective in therapy.

Sara, 24, and her fiancée, Carl, 26, a White upper-class couple, came to see me 3 months before their wedding. Carl began the session insisting that they had no problems but had come at the suggestion of their minister. They quickly began to speak of their wedding plans, a wedding that sounded like it had leaped off the pages of *Bride* magazine. What they did not speak of was a visible secret: Sara, 5 feet 11 inches, weighed less than 100 pounds. When I inquired about her weight, Sara responded that she knew she was too fat and that she planned to lose 5 more pounds before her wedding. Carl smiled at her as she spoke. Her severe anorexia was both a secret that Sara kept from herself and an open secret with her fiancée and family, none of whom said a word as this young woman was disappearing.

At the time of her engagement 1 year earlier, Sara weighed 130 pounds. Both her mother and mother-in-law criticized her weight and expressed the hope that she would slim down for her wedding. Everyone regarded this couple as "perfect." Carl was a stockbroker and Sara had graduated from a prestigious women's college but was not expected to work outside the home. Paradoxically, as Sara became thinner and thinner, she both conformed to her family's quintessential model of womanhood and silently demonstrated the grotesqueness of this ideal.

Early in our work, Sara and Carl presented an impenetrable united front. "All of our friends say we're the best couple they know. We never fight. We agree about everything," Sara said. After she spoke, Carl patted her on the head as if she were a small child or a pet.

I asked if I might have one meeting with each, separate from the other. This request sent our therapy into a tailspin. Each canceled the individual appointment. When we rescheduled, each "forgot" to come. Finally, the two showed up together, telling me this arrangement was just "easier and better." Clearly, my request to see them separately powerfully threatened the myth that they had no differences and that Sara's weight was of no concern. I decided to move in a different direction, widening our therapeutic system. I asked to see them with their minister, hoping to hear and have them hear a different version of their lives from the one they kept telling each other.

When Sara, Carl, and Reverend Giuseppe met with me, I asked the minister what had prompted his concern for this couple. Haltingly, he began to speak about standing by helplessly as Sara starved herself this past year. His attempts to raise this concern with Carl's or Sara's parents had been dismissed. He spoke of knowing Sara from her birth, of christening her and watching her develop into a bright, capable young woman. Sara began to sob, "My life is over. I wanted to become a veterinarian. I'll never do anything except make dinner parties, go to charity dinners, and not eat."

Carl looked furious. "I thought you wanted what I want. You lied to me," he yelled. Carl started to walk out of the session, but I gently stopped him and asked him to listen.

As we talked, it became apparent that Sara had lost all track of what she wanted in life. All of her attention was focused now on her weight, on what was "wrong" with her. As she became thinner and thinner and no one protested, Sara became increasingly convinced of her worthlessness. As her life felt out of her own control, food and eating became her last refuge of seeming control. With actions rather than words, Sara expressed her pain. When no one listened or commented or tried to stop her, she grew increasingly unaware of what she was doing to herself and lost all sense of what she wanted in her life. Until our meeting, Sara's dangerous anorexia was a secret from herself, a secret supported by her fiancée, her family, the values of her social world, and everyone's belief about what it meant to be a "good" woman.

I worked with Sara and her family for many months. As in many families where eating disorders emerge, real individuality and painfully unacknowledged desires had long been hidden under a veil of "feminine" perfectionism, social status, and propriety. I had to remind Sara and her family many times that she nearly chose death rather than depart from her family's expectations of her.

Anorexia has many complexities. Indeed, opening the "secret" of Sara's anorexia was just the beginning of our work. Truly defeating anorexia required that Sara directly challenge her parents' plans for her life. She broke her engagement to Carl, moved out of her parents' home, and began veterinary school.

Like many women, Sara had tried to live a life that did not fit for her. As she tried harder and harder to accept a life that eroded her own integrity, she lost more and more knowledge of herself, until finally the most essential parts of her life were a secret from her. When no one in her family and social network protested, the knot of secrecy was pulled tighter. Once the secret opened on its many levels, Sara was able to regain her self.

PLACING A SECRET IN A BRAIDED SOCIAL CONTEXT

Whenever I work with individuals, couples, or families who are struggling to make informed decisions in their lives about secrets, I start by examining the multiple systemic and interactional contexts in which the participants and their secrets reside. Decisions about creating, keeping, or opening a secret are an individual responsibility, but these decisions are constrained or enabled by the sociopolitical context, historical events, institutions, families of origin, current household groups, and friendship networks.

I ask my clients and myself about the ways that gender patterns and beliefs in the wider culture affect the secrets in their lives. Together we question how positions of men and women in their particular culture and social class influence their decisions about secrecy and openness.

When I first met Alice, 46, she was struggling with the impact of a secret shaped by race, racism, cultural beliefs about child rearing, social class, elitism, and gender. Although she had known the content of this secret for 30 years, she had held it in a context of individual blame and bitterness. Our work together would free her from this legacy and enable her to heal two decades of cutoffs.

"One Sunday when I was 16, my mother went with me to our neighbor, Mrs. Stone, with some cookies she had just baked. Mrs. Stone thanked me and said offhandedly, 'I haven't seen your mother for a while, when is she coming?' 'What do you mean?' I asked, 'You see my mother everyday.' 'You mean they've never told you that Gertie is your mother?' she said. With that, Mrs. Stone turned away from me and fled into her house."

With this brief and shattering talk, Alice discovered the secret of her adoption. Raised in Barbados by a middle-class Black family, Alice grew up the younger of two sisters. I asked what she sensed about the secret before its actual revelation, and Alice replied that she always felt something was being kept from her. "I was always told I asked too many questions, that I was too outspoken. I had a lot of curiosity about Gertie, a light-skinned woman who often visited. She was always bossy to me, but not to my older sister. She used to change my hairdo, take down my braids, put a big bow in my hair and announce, 'There, this has much more class.' I hated it, but if I protested, I got into trouble. I learned to just let it be, but inside me, I knew it made no sense."

I asked Alice what she did when she discovered the secret of her adoption. She confronted her adoptive parents, who angrily denied it and refused any further discussion. "You have to understand," Alice told me, "In Barbados, children were raised the British way: to be seen and not heard. Children were like cats, you picked them up, you put them down where you wanted them. You owed them no explanation and they had no right to ask or feel. My parents would say 'Little pitchers have big ears,' and usher me out of the room."

Discovering the secret of her adoption in her mid-teens, in a context where no one would speak to her about it, seemed to disrupt Alice's young adult life. Alice ran away from Barbados at 18 and moved to New York. "I came to see you because it's time to figure out how to go back. I'm tired of living angry. I miss my family. I just need to understand it all," Alice told me.

We began our work by constructing a genogram of Alice's adoptive family. I wondered with Alice who might give her information. "I know where Gertie is now. She lives in Miami. I've written her a few times and she wants to see me." I coached Alice for her visit with her biological mother. We began with her writing several letters that she did not send. From these, Alice constructed several questions that she wanted Gertie to answer. Then on her visit, as she listened to Gertie's story, she understood that the secrets that shaped her life were far larger than the individual people involved. They included dimensions of women's limited roles, men's entitlement, skin color, religion, and social class. She came back from her visit with Gertie and told me this story:

Gertie's father, Michael Rose, was a White Barbadian whose grandfather was a slaveholder. Gertie's mother, Ruth, was Black and descended from slaves. Michael Rose was a highly placed landowner and deacon in his church; he, nevertheless, fathered several children with many different women. Alice discovered relatives she never knew she had.

Gertie was her father's favorite child. When she got pregnant with Alice and Michael Rose discovered that the baby's father was a working-class Black man, he was furious. He forbade Gertie to see this man and demanded she give the baby up for adoption. Fearful of her father's wrath, and having no alternatives as a young unmarried woman, Gertie gave Alice to her cousins, the Jarvis's. During their talk, Gertie, who never married, would not tell Alice who her biological father was. "She said that he was dead, but I'm not convinced. I don't suppose I'll ever know." I talked with Alice about the fact that some secrets remain so.

As we started to put together all of the information Alice had discovered from her biological mother, I urged Alice to connect the secrets to the complex social context of Barbados in the 1940s. Still a British colony at the time, Barbados was a society steeped in incongruities related to gender, race, and class. As a very successful White man, Michael Rose married a Black woman, kept her in a one-down position, and felt no compunction about his many extramarital affairs, including one with his sister-in-law. These liaisons were not unusual and comprised an open secret in the culture. However, although a highly placed White man's sexual behavior was tolerated, his daughter's similar behavior was not. A powerful double-standard regarding women's sexuality, combined with the race, skin color, and social class of Gertie's lover, led to the secret of Alice's birth origins. "I never before understood all of the forces that shaped this secret," Alice declared.

I helped Alice examine the ways that arrogance and shame combined to make this secret. In any society, community, or family in which beliefs in the superiority of some people over others abound, little, if any, thought is given to keeping secrets that affect a person who is considered "less worthy." Making and keeping secrets maintains the social order and amplifies the power of the secret-keeper. Shame is surgically removed from the secret-bearer and reattached to the person whose life story is hidden from her. As a child, Alice was always made to feel something was wrong with her: Her skin was too dark, her hair was too curly, her manners too unruly "for a girl."

Reconnecting with Gertie was just the beginning of Alice's journey. "I want to understand why my parents, my adoptive parents, kept the secret from me. I haven't seen them for 20 years. I'm scared to get in touch with them, but I must," Alice said.

Although Alice had not seen or spoken to the Jarvis's for two decades, she had seen her older sister, Bernice, on a few occasions. Bernice was living in Philadelphia. I urged Alice to invite her to a session, and Bernice agreed.

"What were you told when your parents brought Alice home?" I asked. Bernice responded, "They just came home with her one day. I was 13. No one told me anything and I knew better than to ask. We all just loved her a lot and that seemed enough at the time." When Bernice spoke of how her parents loved Alice, and how hurt they remained at the cutoff, Alice began to weep. "I know they want to see you," Bernice said softly.

Toward the end of our therapy, Alice made her first trip back to Barbados in over 20 years. She discovered that her parents had had to promise Gertie that they would keep Alice's origins a secret from her. They had so wanted a second child and had not been able to have one. Like many women, Mrs. Jarvis blamed herself for not being able to conceive. They also wanted to protect her from feeling stigmatized. It turned out that they knew little of Gertie's actual story, of how ashamed she had been made to feel in her own family.

"I feel like I've connected so many pieces of my life," Alice told me after her trip to Barbados. "There are still some mysteries, but I feel forgiving and I can live with what I may never know."

CONCLUSION

Secrets never reside solely within an individual, couple, or family. Although each secret is its own unique instance, every secret springs from social rules about gender, culture, and social class. Making sense of secrets and doing effective therapeutic work addressing concealment and revelation require a wide-angle lens, one that is capable of helping our clients erase shame, gain knowledge, and derive courage.

REFERENCES

Chartrand, S. (1992, March 15). Parents recall ordeal of prosecuting artificial insemination fraud case. *The New York Times*, p. A16.

Imber-Black, E. (1998). *The secret life of families: Truth-telling, privacy and reconciliation in a tell-all society*. New York: Bantam Books.

Orenstein, P. (1995, June 18). Looking for a donor to call Dad. *The New York Times Magazine*, pp. 28–35, 42, 50, 58.

Phelps, T. M., & Winternitz, H. (1992). *Capitol games*. New York: Hyperion.

15

GENDERED CONSTRAINTS TO INTIMACY IN HETEROSEXUAL COUPLES

CHERYL RAMPAGE

To say that one practices feminist marital therapy is to assert that the distribution of power, privilege, and responsibilities between men and women in intimate relationships must be thoroughly addressed in both assessment and treatment. Aside from the belief that men have historically held rather more than their fair share of power and privilege, and that this imbalance has had deleterious effects on both women and men, there are few universally held beliefs among therapists who attempt to bring feminism into the therapy room. Feminist therapists may practice within a psychodynamic model, family or origin model, behavioral model, or a score of others. This chapter focuses on issues related to intimacy in heterosexual couples. Although lesbian and gay couples may also seek therapy to explore issues of intimacy, the power dynamics stimulated by the gender difference in heterosexual couples are sufficiently distinct to warrant addressing them separately.

My approach to therapy is consistent with a model that has been developed by my colleagues and myself at the Family Institute (Breunlin, Schwartz, & Mac Kune-Karrer, 1992; Goodrich, Rampage, Ellman, & Halstead, 1988; Pinsof, 1995). The Family Institute model proposes that human problems are best understood and addressed in the relational context in which they occur, and therefore couples therapy or family therapy is generally preferred over individual therapy. The model is focused on the present and on interpersonal interactions. The therapist is a guide or coach rather than an "expert."

Clients bring problems to therapy because they are constrained from solving those problems by one or more factors that they may or may not be aware of. For example, a couple who comes to therapy for help in managing conflict may be constrained by a large number of issues: their gendered beliefs about conflict, stylistic differences emanating from their cultural or ethnic backgrounds, rules about conflict they absorbed from their families of origin, or different temperaments. The task of the therapist is to help the clients identify and remove whatever constraints are preventing them from solving their problem.

Often multiple constraints operate at different levels of the system (e.g., intrapsychic or interpersonal) and combine to hold a problem in place. The problem of marital intimacy is usually constrained on multiple levels by the time a couple decides to seek therapy. Gender issues usually comprise at least part of the web of constraints that keep heterosexual relationships from achieving intimacy, although often other constraints must be identified and removed as well before the couple can reach their therapeutic goals.

Whatever model of change the therapist has, the *sine qua non* of successful therapy lies in a strong alliance between client and therapist. Clients report more improvement when they regard their therapist as genuine, caring, and empathic, no matter what the therapist's theoretical orientation. Alliance is notoriously tricky when working with couples, as each partner may feel concern that the therapist is more interested in what the other partner has to say, or believes the other partner is more "right." Working with couples requires that the therapist pay exquisite attention to balancing attention, care, and validation between the partners.

Practicing as a feminist makes this task even more challenging, because the very premise of feminism—that men as a group have been privileged over women—may draw the therapist into challenging the male partner or working directly to change the power balance in the couple to favor the woman more and the man less. Such interventions, although they may be necessary to solve the problem, put an undeniable burden on the alliance. Most feminist therapists who work with heterosexual couples address this dilemma by attending overtly to the costs that privilege have exacted from the man, and by attending to the ways in which he has been injured or hindered by patriarchy.

The translation of a political reality such as gender inequality into a clinical conversation about a marital dilemma requires care and subtlety. The fact that *some* men exploit women is not a sufficient explanatory concept to understand the experience of any particular male client. Similarly, the notion that women are disempowered by the institution of marriage is not sufficient for understanding how a particular female client perceives and uses power within her marriage. Feminist couple therapy will attend to the details and daily practices that determine how privilege and responsibility are allocated and enacted within the relationship. This exploration requires a careful, specific kind of inquiry into such things as who takes care of what in the relationship, when agreement and support can be assumed and when these must be explicitly secured, and what methods partners use to persuade each other to be cooperative.

ACHIEVING INTIMACY: EQUALITY, EMPATHY, AND COLLABORATION

Many couples today come to therapy complaining about the lack of intimacy in their relationship. Exactly what they mean needs to be fully explored, because intimacy has multiple connotations. Possibilities include lack of closeness, a dull or mechanical sexual relationship, and an inability to connect in activity, in attitude, or in feeling. My own preferred definition is that intimacy is the experience of personal and relational affirmation resulting from interactions demonstrating reciprocal knowledge and validation between partners. Intimate interactions are typically described as collaborative, empathic, intense, accepting, and validating of the relationship as well as of the self. At best, such interactions are recurrent transitory states within a relationship that also contains many nonintimate interactions. Nonetheless, if such interactions do occur regularly in a significant relationship, participants are likely to describe the entire relationship as intimate.

Achieving intimacy in a marriage or other long-term relationship depends on three conditions: first, equality between partners; second, empathy for each other's experience; and third, a willingness to collaborate about both meaning and action. The requirement of equality between partners means that intimacy cannot be imposed, coerced, or demanded. At least in the intimate moment, each partner must feel that participation is intentional and voluntary. Empathy requires knowing, accepting, and honoring the other person's experience. Collaborating about meaning and action requires a willingness to give up, at least temporarily, the primacy of the self, to negotiate with one's partner about what should happen and what that action means. Clearly, intimacy is a sophisticated and higher order relational accomplishment, and even to consider it as a therapeutic goal is a privilege reserved for those who are not occupied with issues of basic survival and safety. Many people would probably be happy to settle for courtesy, affection, respect, and safety as the goals of their closest relationship. Yet for many of the couples who make the effort to get into therapy together, intimacy *is* a goal, and its absence is often the source of great longing and pain.

Couples who enter therapy to "become more intimate" tend not to realize what is constraining them. Each partner often has a theory, but their theories may not be particularly helpful, often because they are drenched in gender role stereotyping. For example, women often believe that men simply do not *want* intimacy or that they are not capable of it. Conversely, men may think that women want an endless stream of intense conversation about the relationship. Such theories are unhelpful, because they render the problem unsolvable and draw attention away from more interesting and useful descriptions.

OBSTACLES TO INTIMACY

Although many things can derail an intimate moment (the baby cries, the phone rings, a misunderstanding between partners about what each means by "connected"), there are some redundancies in the major obstacles to couple intimacy that are worth noting. The first and most important of these is a lack of equity in the relationship. Inequity exists anytime a partner judges there to be a discrepancy in the amount of effort expended in the relationship and the amount of reward received. Some inequities are glaring and obvious (such as all marital assets being in one person's name). Others are much more subtle (Whose overall contribution to the family is greater? How should blowing the leaves be weighed against cooking the dinner?). Ultimately, the overall sense of equity anyone has about a relationship requires a subjective judgment; the *perception* of equity in a marital relationship is probably more important than any external measure.

One of the tricky things about determining equity is that whatever the domain under consideration, whoever has more is likely to feel a situation is more equitable than one who has less. Because statistically men still have more (status, salary, education, age, physical size), they tend to be less sensitive to issues of inequity. Larson, Hammond, and Harper (1998) noted that husbands' perceptions of intimacy were unrelated to equity. That is, husbands are able to feel intimate with their wives even if they believe there is significant *in*equity in the relationship. Wives, in contrast, felt significantly less intimate with their husbands when they felt less equity in the relationship.

A related obstacle to couple intimacy is a kind of relational hubris demonstrated mostly by women, which frequently takes the form of a declaration that "she knows him better than he knows himself." That position makes intimate conversation impossible, because it is based on a belief in inequality between the partners. Deprived historically of the opportunity to matter in the public world, women have laid claim to a special competence about emotional relationships. Many men have been all too willing to sign on to such an ideology, because it locates relational incompetence on the Y chromosome, and thus seems to remove all personal responsibility from their shoulders.

Such beliefs poorly serve the interests of either men or women. Feeling relationally superior is a hollow victory for women when it also leaves them feeling isolated and despairing. Although it might be tempting for men to claim that they just cannot do or are not interested in an emotional life (their own or anyone else's), such a stance leads to the same isolation and despair that the women in their lives feel (Real, 1998).

Gendered Understandings of Intimacy and Relational Dread

One of the more observable differences between men and women is the level of enthusiasm that each brings to certain relational experiences. Men are apt to like *doing* things with people they are fond of. Taking walks, making love, playing poker, hitting golf balls are a few of the things that men enjoy doing with people they care about. To be intimate with men requires that women accept and participate in those ways of being close, and not judge or demean them.

Women like doing things too, but from about the time they learn to speak, the real heart of most female relationships is talk—about feelings, relationships, wishes, and needs. Because emotional talk is something in which boys receive far less training than girls, it is a domain in which men are often uncomfortable. This discomfort is sometimes so acute as to constitute relational dread (Bergman, 1991). To satisfy their wives' intimacy needs, men often need to build up a tolerance for and competency in emotional conversation. To do so frequently requires addressing the underlying dread. For example, the therapist may have to probe for "catastrophic expectations" that a male partner holds about the consequences of letting himself be emotionally vulnerable.

Female Anger

Another obstacle to couple intimacy is female anger. Women have plenty of reason to be angry if they have been disadvantaged by long-term marital inequities. Some women feel this anger quite intensely. Indeed, their anger may have been the stimulus that finally persuaded their otherwise reluctant partners to participate in couples therapy at all. They may enter into the therapy with the agenda of improving the relationship or even increasing the level of intimacy in it, but until that anger gets addressed and validated, not much else may be possible in the therapy room. A clue that this constraint to intimacy is operative is a sequence in which a woman asks her partner to share something he feels vulnerable about, and then shows derision, impatience, or disbelief when he does. At such a moment it is critical for the therapist to intervene by blocking that response and directing the woman's attention to the mismatch between her request and her response.

PURSUING INTIMACY IN THE THERAPEUTIC CONVERSATION

Conversations About Equality

All these caveats are meant to suggest that intimacy is elusive, demanding, and not for everyone. Intimacy is constrained by factors operating far outside the boundaries of any particular relationship. These factors have to do with broad, well-established social patterns and rules that are sometimes wholly out of awareness. Given this complexity, where can therapists begin?

First, we must practice what we preach. That is, therapeutic conversations *about* intimacy must themselves conform to the requirements for intimacy already outlined here. In other words, intimacy is not a goal that therapists can or should *impose* on clients. We must demonstrate respect for our clients' decision to choose whether or not they want to work on increasing intimacy in their relationship. We must believe that men and women are equally capable of intimate connection, although the constraints they face may be different. We must have empathy for the constraints that make it difficult for them to understand and empathize with each other. We must be willing to work collaboratively with our clients, to cocreate meaning and coordinate actions.

The therapist must also be sensitive to how the racial, ethnic, and religious identity of the couple will inform their beliefs about their relationship. For example, a couple practicing a fundamentalist religion may have an explicit belief in the subordination of women. An African American woman may be reluctant to challenge the privilege her male partner exerts in their relationship because she is sensitive to the oppression he experiences in the outside world. In such situations the therapist must work with the clients to determine how equality and intimacy can be construed within their relationship.

An inquiry into the nature of marital intimacy draws attention to how much of the mythology of intimacy is tangled up with notions of romance, notions that are based on gender stereotypes. The vast majority of the familiar images of intimacy in this culture are based on a model of male dominance and female submission. Both men and women have been trained to see inequality as romantic. To the extent that clients stay in the thrall of this vision of romantic love, their capacity to collaborate to create intimacy will be impaired. There are even darker consequences to the pairing of domination and romance, such as the rendering of violence as romantic and loving (Benjamin, 1988).

An adequate conversation about marital intimacy must be political, in the sense that it must address the socially determined and socially reinforced patterns of relationship between men and women, patterns which operate to reinforce inequalities between husbands and wives, even when their preference is for equality. Engaging clients in political analysis in the therapy room is very different from doing so at the dining room table or at a political rally. The only therapeutic way to analyze the politics of heterosexual relationships is at the very personal and specific level. For example, the therapist should bear in mind that 22% of married women feel that they have been forced to have sex by their husbands, and yet only 3% of husbands admit to having used force as a means of getting sexual satisfaction (Schulhofer, 1998). This disparity suggests that there is an enormous gender gap in what constitutes forced sex. The range of behaviors included under this heading spans the distance from ignoring gentle refusals all the way to forcible rape. Sex that is forced, even if the force is implicit, cannot be intimate, because whoever feels forced is not freely consenting.

When a couple expresses dissatisfaction with their sexual relationship but does not have a clear understanding of what keeps sex from feeling more satisfying, one avenue to explore is how free each of them feels to withhold their consent for sexual contact. If the woman never refuses her partner's request, even though she does not enjoy sex very much, the therapist ought to wonder *why* she never refuses an activity that brings her so little pleasure. The couple could then be invited to reflect on their beliefs about the importance of satisfying their partner, asking for what they want for themselves, understanding their partner's needs, and so on. The therapist could ask them to share with each other what they know about what kept sex from being more gratifying. Such a conversation would be deeply political as well as deeply personal.

Whatever the specific area of concern, helping married couples look at obstacles to intimacy will necessarily involve drawing attention to behaviors and beliefs that are inconsistent with equality. Gender-based privilege must be challenged on the ground that it prevents intimacy. For example, a couple came to therapy in the midst of a major conflict over the husband's wish to relocate to a warmer climate. The wife wanted to stay in the city where their children and extended families lived. The husband believed that, because he was the one who had earned most of the family income, he should have a greater say in deciding where to retire. Therapy provided a forum to explore the consequences of this logic for the marriage. With support from a therapist, the wife challenged her husband's linking of income with marital privilege, and insisted that their plan for their retirement honor *both* of their wishes. Eventually he was persuaded that trying to impose his will on such a major decision would have disastrous effects on the intimacy of the marriage.

However, what if a couple seeking greater intimacy does not raise gender issues as a topic? Perhaps they even believe that they have no gender issues. Therapists should be especially cautious about such couples, because research has shown that those couples are most likely to believe in a myth of marital equality that is belied by their actual experience (Knudson-Martin & Mahoney, 1996). Most educated, middle-class adults believe in equality between partners *in the abstract*. Their awareness of the extent to which their lived experience contradicts this ideal may be vague or wholly absent. Drawing attention to the gap between equality as an abstraction versus a lived experience is a crucial component of feminist therapy. The only way to accomplish this is by specific inquiry into how responsibilities and resources are allocated.

It is often not helpful to ask abstract questions such as "Do you share equal responsibility for maintaining your relationship and household?" Rather, the therapist needs to ask specific questions along the lines of "How do you decide to purchase a new automobile?" or "How do you divide up responsibilities regarding the care of your children?" It is not helpful to ask *whether* gender matters to them. Rather, one must ask *how* it figures into their daily lives.

Creating Empathy

Given the considerably different expectations that men and women have of each other, increasing empathic understanding between them can play a critical role in improving their relationship. A number of gendered issues can block the expression of empathy within the relationship, including ignorance of each other's experience, premature problem solving, negative expectations, and timing differences. Each of these obstacles requires therapeutic management.

Many women (and even some therapists) believe that men are not as capable of an empathic response as women are. Research has shown, however, that men are as capable of demonstrating empathy as women when they are motivated to do so (Lott, 1990). Men and women often differ with respect to their belief about what constitutes an adequate response to a conversational partner. When women listen to their partner's problems, they are more likely to assume that what is called for is a response that demonstrates their concern, caring, and understanding of the other person. Men, on the other hand, tend to listen to problems with an expectation that they should provide *solutions*. These different expectations lead to conversational impasses in which the wife feels angry because she wants to solve her own problems and experiences her husband's suggested solutions as patronizing and unhelpful. He feels frustrated that his caring and helpfulness are being misconstrued and rejected unreasonably.

Helping a couple define what they want from each other is often a valuable process in increasing their experience of conversational success. Because they have learned from early childhood that they are valued as problem solvers, men frequently believe that simply listening, understanding, and facilitating their partner's efforts to solve a problem is an inadequate response. When reassured that this is exactly what she wants, most husbands are able to provide this sort of mirroring for their wives.

Often a woman enters couples therapy hoping for greater emotional responsiveness from her partner but is discouraged that she has not been able to get the response she desires. In conversation, she attempts to stimulate him by sharing an experience of her own or by asking him questions. If his response is not immediately forthcoming, she may interpret his silence as a lack of interest and give up, either withdrawing from the relationship or becoming angry and precipitating a fight. Encouraging her to be patient with the silence, not to interpret or speak for him, but to give him time to find his own response can be helpful in interrupting this cycle and allowing an empathic bond to be deepened.

Another facet of increasing couple empathy involves breaking down the barrier of ignorance and mistrust that each partner has about the other's experience. None of us raised under patriarchy is free of sexist bias. This bias inevitably creeps into the beliefs we have about our partners as well as about ourselves. This bias sometimes gets expressed directly in the form of statements that characterize one's partner as a typical member of his or her gender ("guy vision" is an example of this, as are epithets about "crazy women drivers" or "men who can't talk about feelings").

More frequently, gender bias is experienced and expressed in more subtle ways, for example, in the form of assumptions that are made about the other gender without even being articulated. Gender bias infects clients' notions about themselves as well as about their partners and can create tremendous constraints to change. Information is an antidote to bias. Encouraging partners to challenge their own gender assumptions and to be curious about each other's feelings, thoughts, beliefs, and attitudes can be critical elements in creating empathy.

Collaboration and Coordination

The principle of behavioral saliency is behind the most useful intervention that I have ever known to come out of behavioral therapy, and it is one that I routinely use with couples early in marital therapy, both as a diagnostic tool and to produce change. The intervention is a variant of Stuart's (1980) "Caring Days" exercise and consists of asking partners to each make a list of 15 actions their partner could take that would make them feel cared for. The items on the list must be specific, positive, and behavioral and take no more than a few minutes to do. After exchanging lists, the couple is sent home with the instruction to begin doing at least three things each day off of their partner's list, and to notice how it feels to be both on the giving and the receiving ends of these transactions.

This exercise is a way of addressing the final requirement for increasing couple intimacy: increasing the experience of shared meaning and coordinated action. Calling home when one is going to arrive late, making the bed while your partner showers, cooking his or her favorite meal, or filling the car with gas before the other person takes it are just a few of the ways people in committed relationships take care of each other. In and of themselves, none of these actions may feel intimate, but when they occur routinely, these attachment and caregiving behaviors create a cushion of trust and goodwill that is the precursor of intimate interaction (Wynne & Wynne, 1986).

Intimacy occurs when two people can collaborate in the creation of meaning between them, whether that meaning concerns sex, conversation, the best way to raise children, or whether eating broccoli is crucial to one's health. If the interaction is emotionally charged and the meaning is reached collaboratively; if each partner feels heard and visible and the couple can act in coordination, then they are likely to regard the encounter as intimate (Weingarten, 1991).

DEREK AND SUSAN

The rigor, self-discipline, understanding, and generosity of spirit required to create intimacy are high-level personal skills. They take effort and patience to develop and, as the following case illustrates, they have very little to do with the notions of romantic intimacy that we are constantly exposed to in this society.

Derek and Susan entered therapy because their 20-year marriage had grown cool and detached in spite of their continued claims to love each other. Early conversations in therapy revealed that both partners believed Susan to be the more emotionally sophisticated of the two. In fact, one of the constraints that kept the relationship from deepening was Susan's conviction that Derek was incapable of greater emotional responsiveness. That conviction was challenged by structuring several therapeutic conversations directing the partners to reveal their feelings about the relationship and their role in it.

Initially, these conversations provided support for Susan's hypothesis that Derek was not capable of greater emotional response. He was pleasant and eager to please, yet also superficial and emotionally flat. He looked to Susan for guidance about his feelings, and she tried to cooperate by explaining

Derek to himself, finishing his thoughts for him, and filling his silences. Susan allowed me to block her attempts to be "helpful," and both allowed me to push Derek for more emotional response. Although clearly anxious and unpracticed, Derek demonstrated some recognition of his deeper feelings (as well as those of his wife) and was tentatively willing to expose them if he believed that they would be accepted and not judged. Over a period of several sessions, Derek said more about himself than he had shared for a long time. Initially, Susan was relieved and hopeful at this turn of events. Gradually, however, she became more depressed.

At this point I suggested separate meetings with each partner. In the meeting with Susan, she disclosed being consumed with guilt for having had what she called an affair with her former therapist several years before. Like most victims of a boundary violation, she blamed herself. Every potential sexual encounter with Derek retriggered her guilt (and her trauma). His relative lack of expressed emotion provided a convenient rationale for maintaining distance from him. As therapy demonstrated his capacity for greater emotional engagement, she became more aware of her own feelings of shame and guilt as barriers to intimacy in the marriage. With my encouragement, she agreed to talk to Derek about the experience with the therapist.

Susan told her story in great pain and with clear sorrow for the hurt and confusion she had caused Derek. He responded by expressing deep empathy for her, reaching out to soothe her physically while engaging her in a conversation that accepted her feelings. He encouraged her to consider the culpability of the therapist in the boundary violation. He was able to suggest that Susan's loneliness in the marriage had made her more vulnerable to the overture of care and concern by the psychiatrist that had inducted her into a sexual relationship. The conversation marked a dramatic turn in their marriage, as they were able to cocreate new meaning about why their relationship had been suffering, and to act in ways that positively affirmed their commitment to each other.

CONCLUSION

We live in a world that saturates us with stimulation. Yet loneliness and despair haunt many of us, even when we live in close relationship to others. Committed relationships almost always begin in hope, with each of us believing that we have found someone who will understand, accept, and enrich our life. When that hope is unrealized, some couples give up the relationship, some give up hope, and some find their way into our offices. Many couples realize they do not inhabit a "happily ever after" paradise and yet refuse to settle for a "war between the sexes." For these couples, therapy must offer a vision of an intimate relationship that adheres to the rigorous demands of equality, empathy, and collaboration that make intimacy possible.

REFERENCES

Benjamin, J. (1988). *The bonds of love: Psychoanalysis, feminism, and the problem of domination*. New York: Pantheon.

Bergman, S. (1991). Men's psychological development: A relational perspective. In *Works in Progress* (No. 48). Wellesley, MA: Stone Center Working Paper Series.

Bruenlin, D., Schwartz, R., & Mac Kune-Karrer, B. (1992). *Metaframeworks: Transcending the models of family therapy*. San Francisco: Jossey-Bass.

Goodrich, T. J., Rampage, C., Ellman, B., & Halstead, K. (Eds.). (1988). *Feminist family therapy: A casebook*. New York: Norton.

Knudson-Martin, C., & Mahoney, A. (1996). Gender dilemma and myth in the construction of marital bargains: Issues for marital therapy. *Family Process, 35*, 421–437.

Larson, J., Hammond, C., & Harper, J. (1998). Perceived equity and intimacy in marriage. *Journal of Marital and Family Therapy, 24*, 487–506.

Lott, B. (1990). Dual natures or learned behaviors: The challenge to feminist psychology. In R.T. Hare-Mustin & J. Marecek (Eds.), *Making a difference: Psychology and the construction of gender* (pp. 65–102). New Haven, CT: Yale University Press.

Pinsof, W. (1995). *Integrative problem-centered therapy*. New York: Basic Books.

Real, T. (1998). *I don't want to talk about it*. New York: Fireside.

Schulhofer, S. (1998, October). Unwanted sex. *The Atlantic Monthly*, 55–66.

Stuart, R. (1980). *Helping couples change: A social learning approach to marital therapy*. New York: Guilford Press.

Weingarten, K. (1991). The discourses of intimacy: Adding a social constructionist and feminist view. *Family Process, 30*, 285–305.

Wynne, L., & Wynne, A. (1986). The quest for intimacy. *Journal of Marital and Family Therapy, 12*, 383–394.

16

GENDER, MARRIAGE, AND DEPRESSION

PEGGY PAPP

During the past decade, a spotlight has been thrown on depression as the number one psychiatric disability of our time. Amidst the avalanche of information in professional journals and mass media, there has been a startling lack of attention to the interpersonal aspects of depression. Most of the research has been biologically oriented, with antidepressants as the major form of treatment. Yet even the most biologically oriented researchers agree that depression occurs in an interpersonal context and is profoundly affected by the quality of intimate relationships.

Twice as many women as men suffer from depression (Kessler et al., 1994). Numerous theories propose explanations including biological factors, lower socioeconomic status, developmental and temperamental factors, and stereotypical gender role expectations. Complex and reciprocal interactions among these components are likely, and researchers are developing models that integrate them (Mazure, Keita, & Blehar, 2002).

Research on depression and the marital relationship has found that negative affect in one partner is one of the most consistent predictors of relationship difficulties (Karney & Bradbury, 1995). Not surprisingly, the relation between depression and marital conflict has been found to be reciprocal. Marital distress can lead to increased negative behaviors that in turn precipitate clinical depression (Gollan, Gortner, & Jacobson, 1996; Gotlib & Beach, 1995). Similarly, depression often involves negative behaviors such as lowered motivation, self-focus, and irritability, and these strain the marital relationship (Beach, 2000).

Marital strain, whether in any given instance caused by depression or resulting from it, distresses both men and women. There are, however, important distinctions. One of the most consistent differences reported by researchers comparing men and women is a greater interpersonal orientation in women (Helgeson & Fritz, 2000; Nolen-Hoeksema, 2000). This along with the 2:1 gender difference in depression between women and men suggests that relational troubles may have a greater impact on women than on men. Indeed, some researchers propose that marriage provides a "buffer" against depression for men but has the opposite effect for women, and that relational distress increases women's vulnerability to depression (Hammen, 1991; Koerner, Prince, & Jacobson, 1994). These statistics have profound implications for the diagnosis and treatment of depression. However, they are often ignored in treatment.

The Depression Project of the Ackerman Institute for the Family in New York City was established to develop a multidimensional approach for treating depression within the context of the couple relationship, highlighting gender differences and taking into account interpersonal, psychological, cultural, and biological factors. We began by addressing the following questions: Do women and men become depressed for different reasons? Do they react differently when depressed? What part do traditional gender roles play in depression? Is the adaptive behavior of husbands and wives to a depressed spouse different? Are there certain stereotypical gender beliefs and practices that contribute to depression?

We decided that these questions could best be explored by treating couples in which one partner is depressed together in marital therapy. In our work, we found that men and women had become depressed for very distinct reasons, coped with depressive symptoms differently, and were responded to differently by their spouses.

GENDERED DIFFERENCES IN DEPRESSION

It is impossible to separate one's self-image from one's identity as a woman or man. The self does not exist in a vacuum but in a relational and social context. Gender norms and expectations that prescribe how we are supposed to behave as women or men profoundly influence this context. Failure to live up to these expectations can be damaging to one's view of oneself as competent and worthy. As Virginia Goldner (1985, p. 19) so aptly stated, "Personhood and gender identity develop together, co-evolving and co-determining each other. As a result, one could no more become de-gendered than de-selfed." Yet, much of the diagnosis and treatment of depression is "de-gendered."

As noted earlier, women's sense of self is still built largely around relatedness and emotional connections in their professional as well as domestic life (Helgeson & Fritz, 2000; Nolen-Hoeksema, 2000). Typically for women, and especially in contrast to men, self-worth is associated with being responsible for and giving to others. Women with this characteristic often put their own needs second, inhibit their anger, take responsibility for the physical and emotional well-being of those around them, and blame themselves if anything goes wrong (Mazure et al., 2002). The centrality of relationships for most women means that disruption in an important relationship can lead to depression.

Crowley-Jack (1991) interviewed a cross-section of women with depression regarding their beliefs about themselves in intimate relationships. She described depressed women as experiencing a divided self: "an outwardly conforming, compliant self, and an inner, secret self who is enraged and resentful. . . . By silencing their voices, the women kept themselves from expressing their anger openly and their mates were unaware of its source" (Crowley-Jack, 1991, p. 168). She concluded that the women had silenced their voices and become depressed, not because they were "passive and dependent" but because they did not trust their perceptions and feelings and were afraid of isolation or reprisal if they expressed them openly.

In our work, we have noted a difference in the ability of men and women to recognize and acknowledge depression. In general, we have found women quicker to seek help and better able to connect their depression with certain events or relationships in their lives. Further, we have found that they are nearly always acutely aware of an emotional distance in their marital relationship and reach out for more contact and closeness. When they feel safe enough to express their underlying feelings, we hear statements such as, "I feel I'm living on an emotional desert." Other examples include "He's not interested in my feelings" and "We never talk to each other."

Traditional norms for men affect their view of self just as women are affected by theirs. Such norms for men emphasize achievement and success in the workplace, earning money, sexual performance, status and power, excelling in sports, and other externally socially validating experiences. To live up to these standards, men are required to deny dependency, repress personal emotions, guard against intimacy, and avoid any feelings that incapacitate them or make them feel weak and helpless. Men can become prone to depression when they fail to live up to these cultural expectations and cut themselves off emotionally from intimate relationships.

Unlike women experiencing depression, men experiencing depression in our project often seem unaware of their need for intimacy and may have difficulty reaching out to their partner for comfort or more contact. They rarely connect their depression with any aspect of their relationship, even though when they develop a more open and supportive relationship with their partner, they are better able to handle the stress and competition of the workplace. Many men are reluctant to share their feelings of disappointment, anxiety, anger, and frustration that are generated at work. We often hear, "I don't want to bring problems home" or "I've always believed in handling my problems myself." By doing so, they deprive themselves of the support and comfort they might gain from their partners and at the same time deprive their partners of an opportunity to share their lives.

We have found that, generally speaking, the caretaking practices of men and women differ markedly. When women are depressed, men typically try a problem-solving approach replete with talk of "fixing it," "analyzing the situation," and "mapping out a plan of action." Women with depression generally experience these efforts as dominating and controlling. Women tend to want more verbal exchange and sharing of feelings rather than advice and solutions. Men have great difficulty understanding what it is the women are asking for because they experience themselves as having made every effort to "help" their wives. An exasperated husband, after a weekend of unsuccessfully trying to raise his wife's spirits, exclaimed, "I took you boating, didn't I?" to which his wife wistfully replied, "Yes, but you never talked to me."

We have found that women react differently when men are depressed. They tend to protect, placate, and appease, cater to their moods, shield them from telephone calls, keep the children away, and protect them from their extended families. Although the men rely on this caretaking, they often resent it because it makes them feel dependent and controlled.

Despite all the changes that have taken place in traditional male–female roles, stereotypical beliefs and patterns still tend to dominate a couple's lives in important ways and are intricately interwoven into the patterns of depression. Of course, depression is an individual response to these traditional beliefs and expectations. Everyone who holds them does not automatically become depressed. However, it is important to become aware of the different ways in which these gender-based patterns might be contributing to a person's depression.

TREATMENT APPROACH

The Ackerman Project views the couple relationship as a potential source of healing and prevention, and we involve the nondepressed partners in the recovery process from the very beginning of therapy. We learned early on the importance of acknowledging the effect of the depression on the partners, who feel left out and rejected not only by their depressed mate but also by the mental health system in which they have often been ignored and excluded from treatment plans. We convey to the partners a sense of confidence in their ability to do something that will make a difference. At the same time, we sympathize with their despair and acknowledge their fortitude and commitment.

Our referrals come primarily from psychiatric hospitals. Most of the depressed spouses have a long history of depression with numerous hospitalizations and some serious suicide attempts. All of the depressed partners take antidepressants that are being monitored by the outside psychiatrist who referred them and with whom we maintain a collaborative relationship. The antidepressants have initially provided varying degrees of symptom relief but have had little or no effect on the couple's relationship. In our experience, antidepressants are helpful in alleviating the most severe symptoms of depression and enabling people to begin to face life's problems, but they do not solve life's problems. The members of the project staff—Jeffrey Seibel, Gloria Klein, Paul Feinberg, Sandra Rolovich, and myself—work in male–female cotherapy teams. While one team interviews the couple, the other team observes behind the one-way mirror and serves as a consultation team.

The first stage of therapy is focused on identifying the precipitating event for the most recent episode of depression, dealing with the aftermath of the hospitalization, and exploring the effect of the depression on the couple's relationship over the years. This is usually the first opportunity either partner has had to express their pent-up feelings of anxiety and confusion in a safe setting.

We cast a wide net in searching for the experiences or situations that may be creating a depressed person's sense of hopelessness. We look for triggers in the couple relationship, extended family, work, or social situation. We then examine the beliefs, attitudes, and interactions that activate the depressive response and for the hidden strengths and resources available for changing these. Special attention is paid to those beliefs involving power, dominance/submission, equality, and responsibility, and the effect of those on the couple's decision making about crucial issues such as sex, money, work, and parenting.

Being Heard

A sense of emotional connection is essential in alleviating depression in both men and women, but just as the source of the disconnection is generally different for each, the approach to reconnecting must be tailored to individual needs. Whatever else is bothering the women with depression, their major complaint is not "being heard" by the men they live with. Outside therapy, the men often feel overwhelmed by the women's complaints and either dismiss them as part of their "sickness," invalidate them with defensive justifications, or become angry and leave the room. The sessions provide a safety zone for raising and discussing these forbidden subjects.

In one case, a wife's desire to throw herself out of a window came from her despair over her inability to "get through" to her husband concerning a desperate financial situation. Every time she attempted to bring it up, her husband diverted the conversation to his complaints about their sex life. Finally, trembling and crying, she announced she could no longer remain silent about what was happening in their life. She then revealed that her husband, who had been fired from his job, was involved in illegal activities. She lived in constant fear of his being caught, thereby implicating her and jeopardizing her job.

The husband had refused to discuss these issues because, he said, his wife became "irrational" and "hysterical." He believed her worries to be "excessive" because of her "illness." The wife was left with no recourse and felt trapped in an intolerable situation. Once her fears were out on the table and validated by the therapists, her husband could no longer dismiss them as "excessive." He eventually conceded that there was some risk involved for his wife and family in the present situation and agreed to take responsibility for working out a different financial plan. When the wife felt heard, her hope returned and she saw alternatives to throwing herself out of a window.

Becoming Connected

Men who were depressed had little awareness of what led up to their breakdown in functioning. They seemed to be in a vacuum disconnected from their own feelings as well as from those of everyone around them. Because much of their identity was tied up in the workplace, they had not developed close relationships at home. Helping them to connect emotionally with their wives often served as the first step out of the void.

One depressed man discovered a new facet of himself when he was able to comfort his wife when her father died. This was the first time in his life he had ever comforted anyone. "I'm the kind of person who's always kept everything inside. I felt I wasn't worthy of letting anything out. If I did, whomever I was letting it out to would think I was stupid or something like that. So in order to shield myself I put up this barrier." Taking on the caretaking role was a validating experience that made him feel needed and competent in an area in which he generally felt incompetent. It activated the part of himself that he had learned to shut down, the caring, emotional part. As a result of developing a more open and supportive relationship with his wife, he became more confident in facing the pressures and competition of the workplace.

We consider it crucial to explore the meaning of work in the lives of men experiencing depression. It is not unusual for men to stifle their unique abilities and talents to conform to the societal mandate for status and money, or in some cases, simply a viable living for themselves and their families. They often find themselves locked into jobs they dislike, which they perform routinely without enthusiasm or hope. Life becomes meaningless and drab.

As their dreams go down the drain, their sense of identity and purpose goes with them. Whenever we discover a man's work situation is a factor in his depression, we ask him to examine his priorities, values, and options and, in some circumstances, encourage him to consider a different life plan.

Prior to entering our project, one husband had admitted himself to a psychiatric hospital after having been promoted to a managerial job. In the first session we discovered he had become depressed several times before as a result of a promotion. He had been told by a succession of previous therapists that he was "afraid of success" and had been persuaded each time to return to the jobs and "face his problem." When we explored his work experience, it became clear he had valid reasons for not wanting to be promoted. He loved the hands-on work on the lower rung of the ladder and felt awkward and uncomfortable in the role of manager or supervisor. In his most recent supervisory position, he was required to side with management on employment practices that he believed to be exploitative. He had accepted the promotion because "that's what a man is supposed to do—climb the ladder, be ambitious, get ahead, make more money." He was convinced that his inability to conform to these values was a "fatal flaw."

We offered an alternative explanation to the previous "fear of success." Rather than a "fatal flaw," we saw his panic and depression as a natural reaction to his going against his values and trying to wear a mantle for which he was unsuited. One of the therapists told the story of a famous acting coach who, after sitting through a painful rendering of a scene from *Medea*, turned to the student and said, "If Frank Sinatra had tried to sing opera, he would have been a dismal failure. Stick with what you do best." The husband then hinted, somewhat embarrassed, that he would really like to return to his old job but felt his wife would object because to do so would lower their income. His wife, who had been listening intently, said that until now, she had never understood his reactions to the promotions. She had always assumed that his running away from them was a sign of weakness. Her new understanding enabled her to support him in returning to his old job, feeling it was a small price to pay for his mental and emotional well-being.

This case points up the importance of having the partner participate in the treatment. Had the wife not been present, she may never have understood the connection between her husband's depression and his frustrated desire to devote his life to the kind of work he loved and for which he was best suited.

Changing Belief Systems

When two people come together to form an intimate relationship, they bring with them a whole set of beliefs regarding love, marriage, intimacy, sexuality, gender roles, and the way men and women should relate to one another. They are generally unaware of the way that these beliefs, which are implicit rather than explicit, govern their lives and relationships. We believe it is important to understand the beliefs of each partner and the way these interlock to form the foundation of the couple's relationship. When these belief systems are understood, they can be used as a code for deciphering the interactions that set off episodes of depression.

The following three cases are examples of the way in which we identify and challenge the underlying beliefs of each partner on several different levels, including their beliefs about work, extended family, and stereotypical cultural myths.

"I Don't Want a Father Figure"

Upon her release from the hospital where she had spent a month for a severe depression, Sonya, a 40-year-old European woman, requested marital therapy. However, the hospital staff told her that she needed individual psychiatric treatment. She complied with the hospital's assessment and saw a psychiatrist for the next 6 months. However, she continued to believe that her depression was connected with marital problems. She finally left the psychiatrist and applied to Ackerman for couples counseling.

During the first session, it became clear that Sonya was extremely dependent on her husband, Tom. She sought his approval constantly but failed to attain it, as he was extremely critical. Tom saw his criticism as "helpful advice" in the service of "keeping her from going down the tubes." He was deeply invested in his role of parental guide to his wife. On one occasion when he criticized her for a mistake she had not made, he refused to apologize, "If I apologize, she is going to think I'm weak and not capable of taking care of her." This deeply embedded masculine belief—that criticism and coercion equal strength, and empathy and support equal weakness— kept Tom in the position of the authoritarian father and Sonya in the position of a child who could not take care of herself.

Sonya, in contrast, believed an apology would be a sign of strength. "I would cry out of happiness realizing how strong he is that he had grown to understand how to relate to a woman. I'd like an adult discussion with him person to person. I don't want a father figure. I don't want a police figure. I don't want a superior figure talking to me." Sonya experienced Tom not as a protective father but as a "police figure" and a "superior figure." This unequal power defeated her hope for the egalitarian relationship she longed for and led to feelings of desperation and depression.

The idea that his wife could respect him as anything but a stern authoritarian father figure was new to Tom. In exploring the origins of this belief, we discovered that Tom's practice of using intimidation to exert control was learned early in his life. As the eldest son in his family of origin, he felt compelled to control a "crazy and chaotic" family. The only option that seemed open to him was to use strong-arm tactics. This practice served him well as a teenager growing up in a tough neighborhood and was later reinforced in the business world where it brought him status and financial success.

Eventually Tom was able to see that there were better ways of helping his wife than his strong-arm tactics. He learned to tolerate the anxiety that accompanied his letting go of the expert position as he began to experience the rewards of a closer relationship with Sonya.

Sonya's desire for an "adult" relationship required a continuing effort on her part to avoid lapsing into the helpless victim position. This was difficult for Sonya because she had no model of an assertive woman. She saw her mother as weak and passive, succumbing to her father's abusive and domineering behavior. An important part of our work lay in helping her to perceive her mother differently and to reconnect with her on a new basis. She had not spoken to her mother for 2 years because of an argument on her last visit home. Although she claimed she wanted nothing more to do with her and had written her off as "cold and uncaring," she became despondent every year on Mother's Day.

To understand more about her mother's social context, we began asking Sonya questions about the culture of her country and women's place in it. She stated that men ruled the home and were considered to have the final authority. As we continued to explore the conditions of her mother's life, she began to realize it must have taken a great deal of strength and courage for her mother to survive under such oppressive conditions and concluded, "I see I have not given her enough credit." Through the exchange of a series of letters that we encouraged, Sonya forged a new relationship with her mother, developing a kindlier, more forgiving attitude toward her mother and thus toward herself. At the end of therapy she stated tearfully, "For years I have had this nightmare of standing over my mother's grave and feeling remorseful and guilty. Now I know I won't have to do that, and it is such a relief!"

As a result of no longer feeling cut off from her husband and mother, Sonya's depression lifted and she was able to turn her attention and energy to her business pursuits. These comprised the central focus of the last phase of the therapy.

"Performing Romance"

Depression and antidepressants can have a dampening effect on the libido, often resulting in decreased sexual desire or impotence. It is sometimes difficult to untangle the side effects of the medications from the couple's long-standing interactions around sex. It is not uncommon for the couple and therapist to blame the sexual dysfunction entirely on the effect of the antidepressants rather than addressing the relationship problems that contribute to it.

Masculine and feminine identity is never more vulnerable than in the bedroom where the meaning of a "real man" or a "real woman" is thrown into sharp relief and enacted in both symbolic and graphic terms. Male and female sexual needs, fantasies, desires, and expectations crisscross in a complex dance that can either lead to a blissful fusion or to alienation, frustration, and disappointment.

Such a dance had been going on for 47 years with Ben and Ruth when Ben was hospitalized for depression at the age of 73. He believed his depression was due to, among other things, his unsatisfactory sex life. He had always equated his masculinity with sexual potency. He had problems with impotence during their entire married life, but his impotence had increased after a prostate operation a year earlier. Sex had always been extremely important to him, but he complained that his wife had never been interested in sex. "She is like a refrigerator. I feel I'm only getting the appetizer out of a possible big meal." Ruth, his 71-year-old wife, complained that Ben was not affectionate or romantic. "I might as well be a hole in the wall. There's never any kissing, touching, talking. I feel lonely and unloved."

According to Ruth, despite her feelings of deprivation, she had put her own needs aside and devoted herself to trying to turn her husband on. She brought home erotic literature, rented pornographic videotapes, read many sex books, and tried every technique, but Ben had remained dissatisfied. Ruth was left with a great sense of failure. Asked where she got her idea that she was responsible for her husband's orgasm, she said, "I suppose from movies, television, women's books and magazines, Marilyn Monroe. A real woman knows how to turn a man on."

Ben said that he understood what Ruth needed when she complained about his lack of affection but felt unable to meet her needs because he had never been good at "performing romance." He felt guilty and inadequate and often thought she should find another man who knew better than he how to give her what she longed for.

Sex had now become the symbol around which their whole relationship revolved. For Ruth, it represented 47 years of frustration trying to satisfy and please her husband. For Ben, it represented 47 years of feeling incompetent in the relationship and impotent in bed. Neither was living up to the myth of what a "real man" or a "real woman" should be.

The major focus of our therapy was in dispelling these myths. We suggested to Ruth that rather than trying to turn her husband on, she might focus instead on her own enjoyment and pleasure. We challenged Ben's notion that he was unable to "perform romance." We discovered that he had been an actor when he was young, playing romantic leads, and that he was still involved in amateur productions and took great pride in his acting ability. To focus on this area in which he saw himself as a romantic figure, we wondered if he might use his acting ability to "perform romance" with his wife. We invited him to envision himself as a leading man in a scene in which he seduced his wife. How would he go about it? There was much humor and laughter in imaging all the various possibilities.

The couple entered the session a few weeks later, smiling coyly. Ruth reported that Ben had surprised her on their anniversary by arranging a "romantic" weekend in a country inn, replete with candlelight dinner, soft music, and roses. They giggled and blushed as they described their romantic tryst in which Ben had "performed romance."

Ruth said that it was not so much the roses and candlelight that made her feel loved and sexual but the fact that Ben had stopped at a mall on the way to the country and sat in the car and waited for her while she went shopping. Previously, he had refused her request to stop, leaving her feeling that everything was always centered on him and his needs. His willingness to wait for her to do something she wanted to do was experienced by her as an act of love and caring. As a result, sex became a pleasurable experience for her rather than an ordeal, and Ben—perceiving her pleasure—responded with masculine verve.

This experience allowed them to envision different possibilities in their relationship. Ben was no longer in the passive role of waiting for his wife to turn him on and then blaming her when she did not succeed. Ruth, no longer shackled by a sense of duty and responsibility, was able to relax and respond to her own bodily desires. Ben began taking more initiative in other areas of their relationship, suggesting walks, making dinner arrangements, buying concert tickets, and visiting friends.

As a more open communication developed between them, he was able to bring up some touchy issues that had been upsetting him for a long time but that he had been reluctant to broach. He told Ruth of his hurt and resentment over her excluding him from important decisions regarding the children. Ruth explained that she had tried to protect him from painful encounters because she was afraid they would depress him. He managed to convince her that protection was no longer necessary. She agreed to stop running interference. Expressing the many resentments he had harbored over the years further released Ben from his passive role. His depression lifted in direct proportion to his feelings of mastery over his life.

"I Can Be Loved by My Wife and Family"

The effect of any kind of social discrimination, whether based on race, class, ethnicity, or sexual orientation, can play a significant role in a person's depression. Many therapists feel confounded about how to approach these broad social issues in therapy because they cannot eradicate them. However, therapists can help the person with depression avoid personalizing discrimination in a way that corrodes his or her self-esteem.

In our work with an African American couple, the depressed husband, Charles, stated that when he was growing up, his father kept telling him he would have to be three times as good any White person in order to succeed. This belief led him to isolate himself from his coworkers in a job that required close collaboration. In his attempt to protect himself from the unfairness of racism, he strove for an unattainable perfection, the strain of which eventually led to his becoming immobilized in his job.

In an unprecedented discussion, Charles and his wife Loretta were able to share their experiences of living in a racist society and the impact on their lives and relationship. Acknowledging and discussing their humiliating experiences, their pervasive fears and feelings of powerlessness helped to make the pain of these daily experiences more bearable. Charles found comfort and safety in the thought he expressed at the end of therapy, "I couldn't be loved by White society for who I am, but I am learning that I can be loved for who I am by my wife and family."

CONCLUSION

This chapter has described a multidimensional approach to treating depression in couples therapy with a focus on gender differences. The approach attempts to integrate the biological, interpersonal, social, and cultural aspects of depression. In our work, we observed that men and women become depressed for distinctly different reasons, cope with depressive symptoms differently, and are responded to differently by their spouses. Women's depression is most often related to a disruption in a close personal relationship, whereas men's depression is most often related to a performance failure. These differences require a different therapeutic understanding and different methods of intervening.

We in the Ackerman Depression Project view our work on gender and depression as a beginning and hope our colleagues in the mental health profession will join us in developing new ways of understanding and treating this mysterious and devastating condition.

REFERENCES

Beach, S. R. H. (Ed.). (2000). *Marital and family processes in depression: A scientific foundation for clinical practice*. Washington, DC: American Psychological Association.

Crowley-Jack, D. C. (1991). *Silencing the self*. Cambridge, MA: Harvard University Press.

Goldner, V. (1985, December). Warning: Family therapy may be dangerous to your health. *Family Therapy Networker*, 19–23.

Gollan, J. K., Gortner, E. T., & Jacobson, N. S. (1996). Partner relational problems and affective disorders. In F. W. Kaslow (Ed.), *Handbook of relational diagnoses and dysfunctional family patterns* (pp. 322–334). New York: Wiley.

Gotlib, I. H., & Beach, S. R. H. (1995). A marital/family discord model of depression: Implications for therapeutic intervention. In N. S. Jacobson & A. S. Gurman (Eds.), *Clinical handbook of couple therapy* (pp. 411–436). New York: Guilford Press.

Hammen, C. (1991). Generation of stress in the course of unipolar depression. *Journal of Abnormal Psychology, 100,* 555–561.

Helgeson, V. S., & Fritz, H. L. (2000). The implications for unmitigated agency and unmitigated communion for domains of problem behavior. *Journal of Personality, 68,* 1032–1057.

Karney, B. R., & Bradbury, T. N. (1995). The longitudinal course of marital quality and stability: A review of theory, methods and research. *Psychological Bulletin, 118,* 3–34.

Kessler, R. C., McGonagle, K. A., Zhao, S., Nelson, C. B., Hughes, N., Eshleman, S., et al. (1994). Lifetime and 12-month prevalence of *DSM–III–R* psychiatric disorders in the United States: Results from the National Comorbidity Study. *Archives of General Psychiatry, 51,* 8–19.

Koerner, K., Prince, S., & Jacobson, N. S. (1994). Enhancing the treatment and prevention of depression in women: The role of integrative behavioral couple therapy. *Behavior Therapy, 25,* 373–390.

Mazure, C. M., Keita, G. P., & Blehar, M. D. (2002). *Summit on women and depression: Proceedings and recommendations*. Washington, DC: American Psychological Association. Retrieved from www.apa.org/pi/wpo/women&depression.pdf

Nolen-Hoeksema, S. (2000). The role of rumination in depressive disorders and mixed anxiety/depressive symptoms. *Journal of Abnormal Psychology, 109,* 504–511.

17

BRINGING POWER FROM THE MARGINS TO THE CENTER

LYNN PARKER

Power disparities, although they underlie all relationships, are at best unsettling. These are the issues we collude to deny both in personal and in professional relationships. If we were to raise them for analysis, they might mean trouble. Think for a moment about an intimate relationship of yours. Contemplate how power operates in that relationship. For instance, who tends to be the decision maker? Who accommodates more or has less strong opinions? Is there one of you who does the greater share of housework, child care, elder care, relationship care? Whose moods dominate? Does one of you have the power to threaten the other (e.g., to "out" your closeted partner, to withdraw financial support, to reveal lack of citizenship status)? Do both of you have the financial ability to leave the relationship? Can you support yourself and your children should you need to? Has one of you cut down on work hours to care for children, elders, or home? Does anyone use physical or verbal force or violence as a means of intimidation or control? Look closely, because power issues will be there, and you will not want to acknowledge that they are there. You will want to be an exception, and you are not.

My primary purpose in this chapter is to build the reader's awareness of issues of power and privilege in couples' relationships. My plan is first to elaborate several examples of power issues that exist in relationships. Then I describe strategies that therapists can use in counseling with couples. The challenge for the therapist is how to raise these issues when none of us want to admit they are there.

It is said that fish do not see the water they swim in. Similarly, we do not see power issues because they so completely shape our environment. To raise power issues with clients, and thereby promote more equitable and just relationships, therapists need to identify the pertinent issues. Here I describe four categories that depict how power can be used covertly in relationships. This list is not complete. Rather, these four challenge readers to think more broadly when they are searching for power disparities.

Power misuse does not show up just in the extremes of physical, mental, and verbal abuse but also in everyday, socially accepted behaviors and arrangements. The four categories I present here are The Unfair Bargain, King of the Castle, Don't Worry Your Pretty Little Head, and Different Standards.[1] My premise is that therapists who work with couples without addressing the broader social scene that defines the category of "couple" may reinforce inequitable roles that have captured men and (especially) women for centuries

The Unfair Bargain

The way most heterosexual relationships are organized day to day requires women (or the partner with less social power) to carry the bulk of relational and household responsibilities (Blair & Lichter, 1991). Division of labor in relationships is a fundamental issue of power and privilege that underlies many partners' complaints. Roles resulting from the division of labor are often gendered across racial and class distinctions. Although women tend to be more egalitarian in their beliefs than men are, they are not successful in getting male partners to assume domestic roles, nor do they appear to expect them to take equal responsibility. For many women, these roles are "simply" part of the bargain—what comes with relationship. That is, in return for the partnership (even though it is unequal), sex, social status, presumed safety, and usually enhanced financial position, they will do most of the domestic work to keep the relationship afloat.

What is unfair about this bargain, in addition to the unequal division of labor necessary to maintain it, is that the husbands are getting similar rewards (i.e., sex, enhanced social status, financial resources, and so on) without doing the same amount of work. As documented in *The Second Shift* (Hochschild, 1989), husbands and wives alike go to great lengths to hide the unfairness of this arrangement from themselves. Although most

---

[1] These categories were derived from a qualitative study in which I interviewed 15 prominent feminist family therapists in 1995 (Parker, 1998b).

women today have assumed financial responsibility, most of their male partners do not carry corresponding responsibility for caring for house and people. Most women across ethnic and racial boundaries have two jobs, one in the market place and one in the home. When there is a woman in the picture, caregiving tends to fall disproportionately to her. "Peer men" are still in the minority (Schwartz, 1994).

Interestingly, lesbian and gay male couples "tend to show much greater equality and gender-role flexibility than heterosexual couples do," contrary to the stereotypes of "butch/femme" roles (Green, Bettinger, & Zacks, 1996, p. 197). In general, both lesbian and gay male couples have been found to be more cohesive and more flexible than heterosexuals in their ability to make changes in "power structure, role relationships, and relationship rules" (p. 195).

Therapists working with couples must be alert to how categories such as gender and sexual orientation intersect with various adversities. For example, a lesbian partner who is also a Puerto Rican immigrant may have less power in her relationship on several accounts: financially (e.g., obtaining a work permit may be difficult), as a person of color in a racist society, and as an immigrant without citizenship status. Each of these issues could militate against an equitable distribution of power within the relationship, with caregiving and housekeeping roles potentially landing in the realm of the less powerful person. Therapists should assess what are the "unfair bargains" operating in the relationship. Access to resources, financial viability, and distribution of labor must be evaluated, as well as external influences imping-ing on the couple such as societal homophobia and racism. All are issues of power that profoundly affect the relationship.

King of the Castle

Because all cultures are male dominant, men are privileged in many relationships. More often than not, they determine conversational topics; they escape responsibility for caring for children and house; they earn the most and control the money; and they keep their own names as well as have family members named for them (Goodrich, 1991).[2] Male privilege is so widespread that it is considered normal to most of us. For example, when members of a heterosexual couple are interacting, often both partners think that when he is through talking about a topic, the discussion is at an end.

---

[2]Of course power dynamics in relationships do not necessarily follow a simple male-dominant pattern. Some heterosexual relationships may present the opposite pattern. The point is to begin illuminating taken-for-granted behaviors and roles to reveal issues of power and privilege that may go unnoticed because they seem so ordinary.

Therapists might not identify that move as a power issue because it is so common. Failure to change that pattern, however, will block realignment of other power imbalances by the couple, because the therapist is now colluding with the man's privilege. Communication difficulties are not just rooted in seemingly benign gender differences (e.g., "men are from Mars, women are from Venus"). Instead, very often, someone (usually the man in heterosexual relationships) has more power. This fact can be revealed by who controls the terms of the conversation.

Yet, most men do not experience themselves as kings. In fact, they have lost ground economically and face job insecurity. The issue for therapists is how to address male privilege and still acknowledge the individual man's sense of personal vulnerability. While their more powerful and affluent employers may oppress White working-class men, they are generally not vulnerable to daily assaults based on skin color or gender (Almeida, Woods, Messineo, Font, & Heer, 1994).

Most of us are not aware of our privilege. Whites are not aware of the automatic door- opener their light skin gives them. Men are unaware of the privilege their gender affords them. Therapists need to assess who has more privilege in the relationship, how, and under what circumstances. Places to look include who has been given the ability to name (e.g., does one partner take the other's last name), make the major decisions, escape caring for house and people, control finances, and establish the level of emotional intimacy.

Don't Worry Your Pretty Little Head

For many couples, money is a significant power issue. It buys privilege in the world and at home. Schwartz (1994) wrote, "The person who makes the buck makes the rules, or at least the contested rules. If we could measure each partner's ability to get his or her own way, the provider would win" (p. 112). This circumstance is compounded in heterosexual relationships in which there is strong social and psychological conditioning that keeps both men and women uncomfortable with the notion of equal economic responsibility (Schwartz, 1994).

Particularly when couples have children, if someone needs to reduce his or her workload, in heterosexual relationships, it is most often the woman who does so. Women who are out of the job market are particularly vulnerable. They are likely to be much less well off financially if they become divorced than their male partner, and in that case will frequently support their children with little, if any, financial help from the father. They also experience asymmetrical vulnerability in their relative ability to withdraw from a relationship. This vulnerability is accentuated by the rate of domestic violence estimated to occur in 30%–50% of all relationships (National Coalition Against Domestic Violence, 1997). All people must have financial means to leave battering relationships. Accordingly, economic viability needs to be part of the assessment process. The romantic myth of the traditional family is especially dangerous to women and children (Okin, 1989).

What happens when the woman earns more? Does it follow that she wields more power in the relationship? Ironically, a woman also may suffer in heterosexual relationships if she makes more money than her male partner does. She often downplays the reality by taking on more responsibilities at home. "Even if the wife has more money because of a job, or windfall, or inheritance, both her husband and she may feel it does not entitle her to more power in the relationship" (Schwartz, 1994, p. 112).

Different Standards

An appeal to holding different standards means that one partner claims to care less about an issue such as having a bed made or having a clean bathtub. On the surface the issue looks harmless, like a difference in opinion. However, when examined more closely for consequences, the claim to "different" (i.e., lower) standards looks more like a strategic power maneuver in couples with women or others who are socialized to be primary caregivers for house and children.

The partner who cares less or has lower standards for what is needed regarding child/house care has effectively removed himself (or herself) from carrying equal responsibility. For example, one partner may claim to like a messy house: "It looks more lived in." Or one partner may claim, "The children do not need a babysitter." That partner not only does not take responsibility for house cleaning or arranging babysitters—a frequent complaint of women in heterosexual relationships—but also establishes a rationale for refusing to share responsibility. In a sense, with this pattern, further discussion is closed with the implied message: "It's your problem." Different standards can also be played out in what defines a clean kitchen or bathroom, or how often one believes the house needs vacuuming. Usually, the person who declares lower standards wins (i.e., gets a vacuumed house but does not have to work to get it).

Power and Social Location

Elaborated above are four ways power disparities can be expressed in relationships. Therapists must always situate their analysis of these and other power disparities in a broader context. They must be cognizant of how partners' various social locations (i.e., their gender, class, race, sexual orientation, physical ability, age, citizenship status, and other attributes) intersect and how social location influences each person's power and privilege in the relationship. For example, Beth, who is experiencing violence in her relationship with Ann, is reluctant to seek help from police or therapists. Doing so would "out" herself and her partner, potentially submitting both to homophobic responses from "helpers" who may take the report less seriously because of beliefs that women do not resort to violence (Elliot, 1996). If Beth is out of work or underemployed, she is also at a disadvantage in her ability to leave the relationship. Consequently, the intersection of various social locations of partners determines the relative power each has—with each other and in society. If both partners are from a nondominant group (e.g., not White, male, heterosexual, or at least middle class), relative disadvantage multiplies.

WHAT CAN THERAPISTS DO TO RAISE THESE POWER ISSUES?

Most importantly, therapists must recognize power issues. They must use a contextual lens sufficiently broad to identify the multiple and interacting social locations of partners to see how power and privilege operate in the relationship. Once the issues are identified, therapists need methods for getting them on the table with clients. Here the therapist's task is to induce partners to begin thinking about their dilemmas as having a basis in power relations. This perspective is critical if political and social dimensions of couples' dilemmas are to be introduced into partners' awareness, then into therapeutic conversation.

Therapists must somehow bring what is unseen, and perhaps unpleasant, to the surface, and make it available for conversation. This is the hard part: how to raise power when it is the last thing partners want to acknowledge to themselves. Raising the issues, then, is *the* challenge: to raise the issues and not lose the clients, particularly the partner with more power and privilege who is not so anxious to give it up; to make what has been invisible, visible; what has been comfortable, less comfortable; and what has been absent, present. Raising difficult issues for scrutiny is, of course, not unique to feminist family therapy. What is unique is the topic: issues of power and privilege. In feminist family therapy these issues are regarded as central to therapeutic concerns and outcomes rather than simply marginal issues addressed only when clients raise them.

Below I discuss three strategies therapists can use to situate power more centrally in sessions with couples: Structuring the sessions for consciousness-raising; boldly naming power issues, and indirectly raising the power issues.[3] The strategies help therapists raise these difficult issues as well as keep them alive in therapeutic conversation once raised. (For other strategies, see Parker, 1997, 1998a.) These strategies induce partners to begin thinking about their dilemmas as having a basis in power disparities. The strategies are not mutually exclusive. Implicit in each is that couples' problems have roots in patriarchy. To begin to unravel the problems, the social and cultural system impinging on the couple has to be illuminated and brought to bear.

Structure the Sessions for Consciousness-Raising

The way a session is initially organized sets the feminist course. Structure conveys what issues are relevant. Consequently, feminist therapists intentionally ask questions and sequence events so that a connection is made between partners' concerns on one hand, and the distribution of power and privilege in the relationship on the other. A first session may be structured by questions that raise power issues for discussion and analysis. Examples are questions that surface such data as how much money each partner earns, how resources are allocated, who makes decisions, who accommodates, and how household and people-care responsibilities are distributed. The specifics of these arrangements help partners begin to move beyond what is likely a denial of power disparities in their relationship. In-session exercises, education, and homework assignments are other structural means for eliciting power issues and raising partners' consciousness of such issues in their relationship.

For example, in a first session, along with other identifying information such as clients' names, ages, and children, a feminist therapist might ask about how much money each partner earns. This question requires courage because most people would rather talk about everything else (e.g., troubles with their mothers or even their sex lives) before they want to speak about how much money they earn. Most of us have learned that it is impolite to talk, much less ask, about money.

Although this first step seems simple enough, it is radically different from most traditional couples' sessions in which incomes would never be questioned. Traditional counseling has therapists follow the client's lead. In contrast, feminist therapy introduces money as relevant to the couple's concerns. By way of a simple question, power and privilege are brought into conversation.

---

[3] These categories were derived from the same 1995 study mentioned earlier (see Footnote 1). Portions of this section come from a previous article (Parker, 1997) that reports on strategies for raising power in couples' sessions.

Once incomes are on the table, discrepancies can be questioned. If one partner is making far more than the other, I might say, "How does that affect your decision-making process?" Often the partner making more money will say, "It doesn't affect it at all." The partner making less may elaborate several ways the disparity does affect decision making. Again, potential power issues are on the table.

If the couple has children and both parents work, I ask, "How is child care managed?" This question encourages discussion about who does it, who has cut back their work to be able to handle it, and or who arranges it. Further questions might include: "What happens if your child is sick and can't go to child care, or what happens if your child-care worker is sick and doesn't show up? Who stays home or leaves work to handle the situation?" Connecting these issues to the issues the partners brought to therapy helps to deepen the conversation. For example, "How does the way you currently divide household tasks and child-care responsibilities affect your intimacy?" "How does your arrangement for handling finances affect your sense of trust (or how autonomous you can be)?"

This line of inquiry delivered in the initial information-gathering phase introduces partners to the notion that all of their domestic arrangements (including family roles) are important and reflect how power and privilege are structured in the relationship. In a sense, the organization of the session provides a kind of power-issues literacy training for clients. Such training can occur by way of specific, concrete questions that raise power inequities. It can also occur in genograms in which therapists examine with partners the transmission of power issues down the generations. Hardy and Laszloffy's (1995) cultural genogram and Halevy's (1998) "genogram with an attitude" provide the reader with good examples of this process.

Homework assignments can also be used to get issues of power and privilege on the table. For example, partners may be asked separately to list what each actually does regarding household/child-care tasks in a given day. Inequities become apparent in the concrete lists each brings to the next session.

As described in a chapter in this volume (see chapter 22), Rhea Almeida's Institute of Family Services in Somerset, New Jersey, offers a dramatic example of an entire family therapy program structured to address issues of power and privilege. Three striking features are the use of community sponsors, same-gender consciousness-raising groups, and social education for all clients who seek help there. Each of these structural components serves to dismantle power and privilege. Even couples counseling occurs in the context of a larger group, thus providing both partners with empowerment tools and group accountability (i.e., others who will actively support and hold partners answerable for making changes). This approach is radically different from traditional couples counseling in which accountability is mostly absent. Research done with this program suggests that clients report not only behavioral and relationship changes but also increased consciousness regarding power and control issues (Parker, in press).

Boldly Name Power Issues

Rather than structure a session at the outset to elicit power issues, another strategy is to confront issues directly as they arise. Therapists may speak about or question what it means to be powerful in the relationship, or redefine behavior or expectations as issues of power and privilege. Because this strategy is potentially threatening, it depends on careful relationship building.

In a recent premarital counseling session, a woman said that she had difficulty discussing with her male partner the issue of name-changing. I replied by asking *him*, "Are you thinking about changing your name?" He laughed at what he considered to be a ridiculous notion, because of course *that* was not the issue. He wanted *her* to change her last name to his when they married, or second best, for her to take on a hyphenated name. He, however, would not alter his. He proclaimed, "I guess I am just a traditional guy." Because I have a sound therapeutic relationship with him, I was able to tease out (with some humor) the blatant inequality of this position. Further, we unpacked other "traditional" notions that resulted in both partners privileging his career, his preference about where the couple should live, and his ways of doing things.

A therapist identifies problematic power issues as she or he sees them in the moment with the couple. This strategy requires that the therapist be able to recognize "power-over" behaviors, that is, dominating or controlling behaviors. Power-over behaviors may be contrasted with what Surrey (1991) has called "power with" or "mutual power" behaviors (p. 165). Thus, therapists must be watchful for how power and control are exerted, and abnegated, both actively and covertly in couples' arrangements and must straightforwardly bring these observations to the couple's attention. The therapist must swallow hard, garner courage, then name the issues, firmly yet kindly.

Indirectly Raise the Power Issues

In contrast to the two previous direct strategies for raising power issues, many therapists choose a more indirect route. The therapist starts with the partners' concerns, asking them to unfold events step by step, very specifically. The therapist listens for how problems are related to power issues and may offer gentle probing questions that point in that direction. The therapist then gives feedback or tasks that help partners make a connection between the problems that concern them and underlying power issues.

The idea here is that if power issues can be related to issues about which clients are already distressed, clients will be more cooperative and less resistant. Hence, the therapist waits quietly as clients describe their concerns, listening and watching for hints of power disparity or privilege in the relationship. Then, the therapist invites partners to consider new or alternative meanings for their dilemmas.

For example, the therapist may invite partners to examine the consequences of current arrangements: "How did the two of you decide who would be the major income provider, and what effect does that designation have on your decision making?" "What are the consequences of one of your incomes being twice that of the other's?" "What are the repercussions of one of you doing the majority of the house/child care?" "What will be the consequence if the two of you decide to part ways and you have no economic viability?"

Therapists need to be attentive to potential power issues (e.g., division of familial and household responsibilities, economic viability of partners, and dominance of one partner over another in decision making) to know what questions to ask. Questioning results of behaviors and costs and benefits of current arrangements puts power on the table, not as "givens," but as choices made, either consciously or unconsciously, which can be reconsidered. Examining consequences further illuminates who has the power, in what situations, how that came to be, and what are the repercussions.

CASE EXAMPLE

Jay and Rose, a heterosexual German couple in their mid-30s, initiated counseling with me because they were experiencing "horrendous" conflict."[4] Jay complained that Rose was "always angry." Rose was upset that "Jay's work always comes first. Our children and I come second or third. Jay seems to have no time or much desire for me or our children."[5]

Jay is a liberal, small-town minister revered by his parishioners and the larger community. Rose is a midwife with a local family medical clinic. When I asked each about how they had come to these career choices, Rose said her career choice complied with her parents' traditional gender imperative: If wives "have to work it should be 'women's work' since women are more caregiving." Although she "loves her work," for Rose, work is not the central passion that Jay's work is for him, a passion he refers to as a "spiritual calling."

---

[4] This case was previously published with slight alterations in Parker (1999).
[5] An example of "The Unfair Bargain."

Both express having integrated the notion that, although it is all right for a wife to work, the husband's work is primary.[6] It is his work that requires support and accommodation from family members. Rose worries that her "double-shift" complaints seem petty and unimportant next to the "significant" issues Jay faces. Yet, she is increasingly angry and dissatisfied with his lack of involvement with her and at home.[7]

In the initial information gathering, I asked them to describe their broader societal, church, and family socialization concerning "appropriate" gender roles.[8] Both became aware of strongly held social messages (at the time it felt to them more like truths) concerning the role of a minister's wife. A "good" minister's wife plays the organ on Sundays, teaches Sunday school, and arranges potluck dinners. She is at church each Sunday in one of the front pews with well-behaved children listening attentively to her husband's sermon.[9]

Rose, however, did not want to *have* to go to church on Sundays, nor did she want to be expected to carry any of the other "unpaid" minister's wife roles. As they discussed these expectations and their ramifications, I suggested, "Imagine what it might look like were your roles reversed. For example, what if Jay was expected to be involved weekly in a subordinate, unpaid role at Rose's place of work?"[10] Both Rose and Jay were struck that when reversed, the expectation seemed strange. Indeed, Jay was not expected to come to Rose's place of work. Rampage (Rampage & Goodrich, 1995) has suggested that such reversals help to illuminate behavioral expectations that do not appear as reasonable when the gender roles are reversed.

Church members grumbled about Rose's lack of attendance on Sundays and felt sympathy toward Jay for having a "women's libber" wife. Thus, her predicament required careful unpacking. That her feelings could be legitimate was an idea foreign to them both. As Jay came to understand that, if reversed, the expectation would appear silly, he became willing to support Rose's independence—her freedom to choose how she wanted to spend Sundays and what functions she wanted to attend. He also started to do some "consciousness-raising" with church members regarding Rose's role and, more broadly, women's roles.

I then gave them a homework exercise in which I asked each to list the responsibilities they carried daily for home and people care.[11] When

---

[6] An example of "King of the Castle."
[7] An example of "The Unfair Bargain."
[8] An example of "Structuring the Sessions for Consciousness-Raising."
[9] An example of "The Unfair Bargain."
[10] Exploring consequences of expectations and role reversals are examples of "Indirectly Raising the Power Issues." Raising the issue of "minister's wife" as an unpaid job is an example of "Boldly Naming Power Issues."
[11] An example of "Structuring the Sessions for Consciousness-Raising."

they compared their lists, Jay was able to acknowledge that the current arrangement was unfair to Rose. I encouraged both of them to notice other behaviors that could be limiting them. For example, I asked Jay, "What are the consequences of the long hours you put in at work to your relationship with Rose and your family life?" Further discussion revealed that they both assumed it would be Jay who would take on extra work (e.g., weddings and speaking engagements) to bring in additional income.[12] Neither had considered downsizing their expenses so that both could be more available for family life.

Rose and Jay also learned to make requests of each other (see Stuart's, 1980, "caring-days technique" [p. 197] and "constructive request-making" [p. 228]). Rose expressed her need for Jay to be more proactive concerning family and relationship issues and responsibilities. Jay requested that when he was assuming a domestic responsibility, she allow him to take it. Jay finally was able to see that the choice to escape child/house care was only available to him. Rose had no such choice.[13] He agreed to my suggestion that he request coaching from a good friend of his, a single father, to improve his domestic abilities. It was important here that Jay take responsibility for improving his domestic skills. Also, connecting more intimately with other men takes some of the emotional burden off of the female partner to meet all of her male partner's emotional needs and allows them to become more equal in their emotional relationship (Parker, in press).

The issues presented by Rose and Jay required a redistribution of power in the relationship. Previously, both partners, though philosophically "liberal," had quite traditional gender ideologies. Both regarded Jay's job and time as more important than Rose's. Moreover, church members who held traditional expectations for their minister and "his wife" reinforced these ideologies. As Jay and Rose became aware of the constraints of their socially mandated roles, they were more willing to enact change. Because they were "liberals," they began to take on educator roles with members of their community—Jay becoming something of a model and spokesperson for "liberated husbands." Admittedly, there was acclaim afforded him in this role, thus making it more attractive to him. Nonetheless, a change occurred.

In retrospect, I wonder whether power issues were addressed or simply dressed in new clothing? Rose probably still carries the brunt of the domestic responsibilities. Although Rose joined a women's group and had the women's support to keep examining her place in the relationship, there was no corresponding social support to ensure that Jay remained accountable. Newly found awareness and behavior are celebrated in the short run. However,

---

[12] An example of "Don't Worry Your Pretty Little Head."
[13] Examining consequences of current arrangements is an example of "Indirectly Raising the Power Issues."

without the benefit of social support like that which is offered in Almeida et al.'s (1994) program, it is difficult to keep partners accountable in the long run, especially the partner whose position offers more privilege.

CONCLUSION

Power issues are central to the problems that bring couples to therapy. If they are not addressed, problems persist. Patriarchy exists in families, it tends to be invisible, and it is not benign. Quite the opposite, it structures and animates subordination and oppression. Those with less power (e.g., all those who are not White, male, heterosexual, or citizens) are often maintained in subordinate roles without viable means to negotiate change in the relationship.

Feminist therapeutic work embraces the tenet that people should be equal. How can family therapists address power issues in their work with couples? First, they must be aware themselves of what the issues are. Then, they must get the issues on the table where they can be examined. Skill and courage are needed both in perceiving potential power arenas in relationships and in surfacing those issues in the awareness of the partners. It is a feminist family therapist's responsibility to raise partners' consciousness about the issues, so that partners themselves have knowledge about the consequences (to themselves, the relationship, and more broadly to society) of current arrangements and therefore the tools to construct a more equitable relationship.

REFERENCES

Almeida, R., Woods, R., Messineo, T., Font, R. J., & Heer, C. (1994). Violence in the lives of the racially and sexually different: A public and private dilemma. *Journal of Feminist Family Therapy, 5*(3/4), 99–126.

Blair, S., & Lichter, D. (1991). Measuring the division of household labor. *Journal of Family Issues, 12,* 91–113.

Elliot, P. (1996). Shattering illusions: Same-sex domestic violence. *Journal of Gay and Lesbian Social Services, 4,* 1–8.

Goodrich, T. J. (Ed.). (1991). *Women and power: Perspectives for family therapy.* New York: Norton.

Green, R.-J., Bettinger, M., & Zacks, E. (1996). Are lesbian couples fused and gay male couples disengaged? In J. Laird & R.-J. Green (Eds.), *Lesbians and gays in couples and families: A handbook for therapists* (pp. 185–230). San Francisco: Jossey-Bass.

Halevy, J. (1998). A genogram with an attitude. *Journal of Marriage and Family Therapy, 24,* 233–242.

Hardy, K., & Laszloffy, T. A. (1995). The cultural genogram: Key to training culturally competent family therapists. *Journal of Marriage and Family Therapy, 21,* 227–237.

Hochschild, A. (1989). *The second shift: Working parents and the revolution at home.* New York: Viking Penguin.

National Coalition Against Domestic Violence. (1997). *NCADV fact sheet.* Denver, CO: Author.

Okin, S. M. (1989). *Justice, gender, and the family.* New York: Basic Books.

Parker, L. (1997). Unraveling power issues in couples therapy. *Journal of Feminist Family Therapy, 10,* 17–38.

Parker, L. (1998a). Keeping power issues on the table. *Journal of Feminist Family Therapy, 9,* 1–24.

Parker, L. (1998b). The unequal bargain: Power issues in couples therapy. *Journal of Feminist Family Therapy, 9,* 17–38.

Parker, L. (1999). Bridging gender issues in couples work: Bringing "Mars and Venus" back to earth. *Journal of Family Psychotherapy, 10,* 1–15.

Parker, L. (in press). *A social justice model for clinical social work practice.* New York: Affilia.

Rampage, C., & Goodrich, T. J. (1995). *From ideology to practice: A feminist clinic* (Cassette Recording No. 715-408). Washington, DC: Family Therapy Networker Annual Symposium.

Schwartz, P. (1994). *Peer marriage: How love between equals really works.* New York: Macmillan.

Stuart, R. (1980). *Helping couples change.* New York: Guilford Press.

Surrey, J. (1991). Relationship and empowerment. In J. Jordan, A. Kaplan, J. Miller, I. Stiver, & J. Surrey (Eds.), *Women's growth in connection* (pp. 162–180). New York: Guilford Press.

V

ANALYZING SERVICE DELIVERY SYSTEMS

18

INCARCERATED AFRICAN AMERICAN WOMEN

JANET BRICE-BAKER

The world, both external and internal, of incarcerated women has long been overlooked. Yet this population represents the intersection of two very intricate systems: the prison system and the woman's family system.

The American Heritage Dictionary defines a *system* as "a group of interrelated elements forming a collective entity" (Davies, 1972, p. 704). Family systems resemble biological systems in many ways: They are always in a state of change; the action or behavior of one individual has a domino effect on the behavior of other family members; the family adjusts itself for accurate and proper functioning; the family is a small system that interacts with others in a larger social system; and stabilization is achieved through the use of negative or positive feedback loops (Gladding, 1995). In a broad sense these same characteristics define a prison system. In addition, racial oppression, gender oppression, and class oppression reverberate off the metaphorical walls of both the correctional system and the family system.

The goal of this chapter is to explore how prisons operate like dysfunctional family systems and to provide an example of how to work with an African American woman in that setting. Finally, the issues and divided loyalties for therapists are enumerated. Because of the goals and objectives of this book, I do not address the intrapsychic system here.

DEFINING THE POPULATION

Female inmates make up approximately 6% of all state and federal prisoners (Metzner, Cohen, Grossman, & Wettstein, 1998). Almost half of the women in prison (46%) are African American and 14.2% are of Latino descent (Chesney-Lind, 1997). Incarcerated women who have minor children make up two thirds of the prison population. Half of these mothers have never been visited by their children during their incarceration. Poor women of color are overrepresented in these prison systems.

There are very real differences between male and female prisoners. Male prisoners are more likely to be incarcerated for convictions on violent offenses and often have a history of prior arrests or convictions. Female prisoners, in contrast, are more likely to be serving time for nonviolent offenses (Chesney-Lind, 1997). At this time, one will find women most frequently incarcerated for drug-related offenses. Incarcerated women have a longer history of drug use prior to imprisonment than their male counterparts. Moreover, the women are more likely to have been under the influence of an illegal substance during the commission of a crime. Drug-related offenses can include simple possession of a controlled dangerous substance (CDS), possession of CDS with intent to distribute, CDS manufacturing, sale of CDS to an undercover police officer, possession of CDS with intent to distribute within 1,000 feet of a school zone, and possession of drug paraphernalia.

The majority of incarcerated women are poor. Poverty is the result of the interplay of various factors, including little to no education, lack of job skills, low-paying employment that does not cover living expenses and child care, sexism and racism in the job market, and lack of child support from the fathers. The women with non-drug-related convictions often have committed these crimes to secure money necessary to support their drug habits.

Additional factors that set the female inmate apart from the male inmate is the age when they first used drugs and their reasons for using drugs. The causes of drug abuse are multidimensional. However, it is worth noting the significant numbers of women who first became involved with drugs as a way to medicate themselves after an incident or repeated incidences of physical and sexual abuse. Once the women are incarcerated, and by default detoxed, the symptoms of posttraumatic stress disorder more readily emerge. The ongoing experiences of abuse, coupled with the traditional socialization of the sexes in our society, leave these women with confusing messages about when it is appropriate to be angry, and how to deal with their anger and with the anger of others.

The behaviors labeled and connected with anger in women in prison fall into three broad categories. The first category is self-abuse and mutilation. Examples of this are pounding their heads against the walls, pounding their fists against their forearms and thighs, picking scabs on past scars, using drugs when they can get them, setting fires in their cells, and cutting themselves superficially. The second category is the ultimate self-abuse: a suicide attempt. The third group of behaviors that reflect their anger and frustration are fights with other inmates. The inmates often refer to these fights as "beat downs." Threatening actions against custody officers are another manifestation of their frustration, impotence, and anger.

PRISON: A VERY STRUCTURED SYSTEM

A prison is a penal institution utilized for the purpose of incarcerating individuals who have been convicted of committing crimes. An individual will serve time in prison when his or her sentence exceeds 364 days. There are various subsystems within this metaphorical family. At the executive level there is the administrative subsystem composed of a superintendent and associate and assistant superintendents. The custody subsystem exists at the next rung of the hierarchy. These are the correction officers. Within their membership there are ranks: captain, lieutenants, sergeants, and officers. The business office, classification department, commissary, education, food services, health services, housekeeping, human resources, maintenance, parole, recreation, and social services all form the next level. Finally, the last tier is composed of the inmates. They are divided according to levels of security or levels of proposed threat: maximum, medium, and minimum.

The prison system most closely resembles an abusive family system. Abusive families are hierarchical systems characterized by the abuse of power, rigid and porous boundaries, the denigration and isolation of lower status members, and the encouragement of affiliation or loyalty through fear. Prisons function in much the same way. Members of the bottom tier are constantly reminded of their lowly status by the numerous rules and regulations. According to Minuchin and Fishman (1981), the family subsystems of greatest significance are the spousal subsystem, the parental subsystem, and the sibling subsystem. Within the prison family, administration and custody are the spousal and parental subsystems. The staff members and the female inmates are the siblings. However, because of the power differential between these "siblings," probably the best family template is the stepfamily. In this stepfamily the inmates take on the role of the unfortunate, unloved stepchildren, and the staff members are the natural or biological children.

The potential for dysfunction in the prison family lies in the nature of its boundaries. For the most part, the boundaries between the parental subsystem (custody and administration) and the inmate subsystem are clear and rigid. There is no mistaking who has the power. In some cases, correctional officers may abuse their power. It is difficult to know just how often this occurs because women are afraid to come forward for fear of not being believed and receiving further sanctions. Fellow correctional officers are also hesitant about coming forward when they have witnessed an abuse of power out of fear of what will happen when they break the "blue wall of silence."

An officer may abuse his or her power by writing an excessive number of charges or writing unsubstantiated but serious charges. The more serious charges result in a hearing where a determination of guilt or innocence is made and sanctions are doled out. A record of those sanctions is available to the parole board and certainly plays a role in the decisions they make. An inmate could lose credit for good behavior or be denied parole when the inmate goes before the board.

At other times the abuse may be emotional and take the form of verbal harassment and humiliation. This includes, for example, name calling or cursing; making fun of someone crying; making fun of someone who is scared, anxious, or ill; or giving someone a particularly debasing kind of work assignment. Although all of these are awful, the most heinous abuses are still physical and sexual assault. It is no less an assault if an officer tells a woman that she needs to provide him with sexual favors or risk certain deleterious consequences.

Similar violations occur in other parts of the system. At times the boundaries between civilian staff and inmates have been diffuse. Social workers and medical staff, as well as others, have been known to develop personal relationships with women. These women are their clients. The fact that the professional service takes place in a prison does not give one license to behave unprofessionally and take advantage of these vulnerable women. In some ways, these violations are even more heinous than those of the custody staff because the women expect helping professionals to have a level of caring and a desire to be helpful. Inmates do not have that same expectation of custody personnel.

My role as a consulting psychologist in this prison stands on ever shifting sands. On the surface I seem to have power in the reports I write. These reports and their recommendations are supposed to have ramifications for some administrative decisions. However, the walls of confidentiality around my client and myself are very porous. There are many instances in which prison administrators and others have access to mental health files. Similarly, I can speak up about many things. However, if I become too much of an irritant to the administration, they cannot fire me, but they can bar me from entering the prison. My client seems to be the prisoner at times and the prison administrators at other times. Within these constraints, if one wants to effect change, it needs to be done subversively.

I turn now to a description of my work with an African American woman. This woman's story illustrates both the frustrations and rewards of doing feminist family therapy within the prison system.

J'S STORY

J is a 30-year-old, Black female of African American descent. She is the oldest of five sisters in her family of origin. J's mother was in a nursing home specializing in neurological rehabilitation; she died during J's incarceration. One of the reasons she was there was because of her inability to speak. J's father is 65 years old, and his current whereabouts are unknown.

J was raised primarily by her mother. Her father was a frequent visitor but only seemed to stay around long enough to impregnate his wife. J's father sexually abused her from the age of 8. He considered J his favorite and would often "volunteer" to watch her on his all too infrequent trips home. While her mother was out and the babies were sleeping, he would insist that she arouse him. When she got older, he insisted on intercourse. Her father bought her silence by threatening to harm her mother and her sisters. This was quite believable because he had been physically abusive to J's mother for as long as she could remember.

J tried on several occasions to tell her mother, but her mother did not want to hear about it. She changed the subject or told J that she was misreading the situation. All of this enraged J, because she had often stepped in to help her mother when her father was beating her unmercifully. J ran away many times but always returned home. Her mother had repeatedly told her that there was nowhere for a woman to go, especially if she didn't have a man. J reported that it was her guilt about leaving her younger sisters behind that kept her coming back.

J finally left home at the age of 25. On that particular day her father came to the house. He was clearly drunk (his eyes were red and bloodshot, his gait was unsteady, he smelled of alcohol, and his language was unusually vulgar). He began to fight with his wife. J was out working and her sisters were in school.

J walked into the house to find her mother lying unconscious on the living room floor and her father passed out on the couch. She found a big gash on her mother's forehead and tried, without luck, to revive her. She called 911 and waited for the ambulance to come. In the meantime her father woke up and asked what had happened. J beat him with everything she could get her hands on in the house. When the police arrived at the house they had to tear her off her father. She was charged with aggravated assault, and her father was never seen or heard from again.

Although it seems, at least on the surface, that J coped very well as a sexual abuse survivor, there is another side to her struggle that should not be missed. J abused drugs for years beginning at the age of 16. It started out with prescription pain medication. The more she tried to suppress her anger, the more pain-related ailments she developed. When the doctors warned her that she was using too much medication, she turned to illegal drugs. Despite her involvement with drugs, she completed 2 years of college during this time. However, she continually interrupted her education, dropping out whenever she believed that her mother needed her. At those times she would get a job and contribute to the family finances. She dated but her relationships never lasted long. She admitted that she had a basic problem with trust.

J never saw a mental health professional prior to her incarceration. At the time that she requested to see me, she had done some time in prison and was looking at considerably more. The administration was concerned about her aggressive behavior. J was serving time on a conviction of aggravated manslaughter. The victim was her common law husband of 10 years. She had stabbed him to death and received a sentence of 30 years. J must serve the 30 years before she is even eligible for parole. She had numerous disciplinary charges against her. Administration and custody claimed that she was always looking for a fight. She was seen as unpredictable, quick to use her hands, and having total disregard for authority.

When I saw J, she presented "the problem" in a different way. She framed things in terms of her desire to get paroled and start a new life. She was worried about what she saw as the system's reluctance to see the changes in her behavior. She took responsibility for her violent past and stated that she had been spending the past year trying to change all of that.

SPECIAL CONSIDERATIONS FOR PROVIDING THERAPY IN PRISON

The therapeutic relationship begins at the moment of contact, before any problems or issues are discussed. Therefore, it is incumbent on the therapist to inform and help the client understand the multiple roles and multiple obligations you have as a therapist. Bruns and Lesko (1999) have done an excellent job of outlining the salient areas of such a discussion. Confidentiality is one of those issues. The client should have knowledge regarding what type of notes are written, where those notes go, and who has access to the records. These issues are particularly complex when working within a prison environment. The client should know specifically which representatives of the department of corrections and the criminal justice system have access to her therapy records. She should be encouraged to consult a lawyer; because this is the only way that one can really have informed consent for treatment. Besides record keeping, you must explain when you are obligated to report something that she says to custody or administration.

Another area of discussion is the structure of therapy. Feminist therapy encourages the active and real participation of the client in the decision-making process. The therapist needs to find out where is the safest, which in this case could also mean the most private, place to have therapy. It is wrong to view the client as someone who is literally "doing time" and subsequently place no value on her time. Inmates have job assignments, go to school, and attend various programs. It is not in their best interests to schedule therapy appointments that pull them out of other responsibilities.

Discipline is not a word or image I would ever associate with psycho-therapy. However, in some penal institutions, mental health practitioners are not only allowed but also encouraged to give inmates disciplinary charges. Sometimes the charges are directly related to therapy, as in the instance of giving a charge for failure to show up for a therapy session. Inmates are well aware of this practice and may often expect the therapist to participate in this. For this reason the client should be informed of the therapist's stance on this issue. From my point of view, making a decision to give an inmate charges only reifies the client and the therapist in an already hierarchical, power imbalanced, and oppressive system. I refuse to do this. Therefore, it is up to the therapist to explain this to the client and to make sure that no one else in the institution is shadowing the therapy and taking it on himself or herself to proffer charges against the inmate on your behalf.

A final issue concerns report writing. The therapist and the client must explore who might request a report and ascertain how that report might be used. In J's case there would be at least two times when the department of corrections would need psychological input: (a) when deciding on whether or not J could move from maximum custody to grounds and (b) when she became eligible for parole.

J'S THERAPY

In Bowenian family therapy, the goals of therapy are (a) to have the individual/couple/family understand intergenerational relationship patterns and the stresses that have shaped their coping mechanisms, and (b) to help each member of the family increase her or his level of differentiation of self. Gibson and Donigan (1993, p. 28) defined differentiation as "the degree to which a person is able to distinguish between the subjective feeling process and the more objective intellectual process." The goals in this case were similar: (a) to reconnect J with her family of origin to help her identify and change negative coping patterns, and (b) to analyze how triangular relationships in prison were reenacting emotional triangles in her family. Understanding these repeating relationship patterns would help her decrease her emotional reactivity and thus increase her differentiation of self.

In J's situation one of the most important relationship patterns was that women in the family were less valued than men. This pattern was manifested by the physical, emotional, and sexual abuse J suffered at the hands of her father, and the fact that it was condoned by everyone's silence. There were also subtler forms of this message around the issue of women not being encouraged to establish economic independence and parity with men. Another family myth was that women could not do certain things because they are "too emotional." Negative emotions like sadness, anger, or fear were not tolerated. Passive expressions of anger were much more likely to be tolerated than aggressive acts of anger. Women were definitely considered "out of line" if they were physically aggressive, even if the aggression was in the defense of self or others. Overall, in J's family, women were not allowed to be in control of themselves.

In addition to the patterns observed around the idea of gender, there were also patterns associated with race. J struggled with external racism from society and internalized racist messages from her family. One particular example of this was the role that skin color played in the family. J was substantially lighter in skin tone that her sisters and mother. Her father frequently told her and other family members that she was the prettiest of the five girls. For years her sister, and even at times her mother, failed to acknowledge her sexual abuse at the hands of the father as abuse. Rather they chose to paint J as the "light skinned seductress who was always daddy's favorite." The unspoken implication of this interpretation was that she deserved what she got.

Another aspect of the treatment was devoted to identifying some of the key triangles in her family of origin. One of the most powerful triangles was that formed by J, her mother, and her father. This triangle worked against J's development of a solid sense of self in several ways. From one perspective, her mother allied with her father against J in terms of refusing to protect her from his sexual abuse. Her father's abuse and her mother's refusal to acknowledge it put J in the position of having her body violated over several years. From another perspective in the same triangle, J gave up self by physically fighting her father in an effort to protect her mother. This position in the triangle resulted in J's first incarceration.

J, her mother, and any one of her sisters formed another very sensitive triangle. Within this triangle, her mother and her sisters were the insiders, resenting her light skin and her position as her father's "favorite." Yet, J gave up self by postponing or relinquishing her own needs, for example, dropping out of college, to help her mother with her sisters. She was also in a triangle with her sisters, with each one of them trying to get her to side with them against one or more of the other sisters.

I coached her to dismantle some of the triangles. Specifically, J was coached in establishing what Bowen referred to as a "person-to-person" relationship with her half-sister. J, her sister, and their mother had formed a powerful triangle for many years prior to their mother's death. Neither sister could talk to the other without triangling in the mother. Because J was able to use the phone and write letters, we worked on J communicating personally to her sister, using "I" statements, talking about her own feelings and inquiring about her sister's feelings—all without mentioning their mother.

J did similar work in detriangling from relationships with her other sisters. She would talk on the phone to a sister and keep the conversation focused on the two of them. J learned to refuse to engage in those talks when one sister tried to tell her something about another sister. When those moments arose, she suggested that the three involved parties get together. At times she has been able to accomplish this during visitation.

Because J's mother had not been capable of communicating, it was difficult for her to work on this relationship in or out of prison. At different times in the therapy, I asked J to compose letters to her mother, telling her of her anger and resentment. One of the advantages of this letter-writing exercise was that it provided J with the opportunity to get out some of her anger in a way that was not going to get her into trouble. Working on the anger she harbored toward her father was much harder. At this stage in the treatment, we have only gone so far as to pinpoint people who knew him at different times in his life and put her in touch with them.

J and I established several goals for her treatment:

1. To take inventory of how the different facets of herself—gender, race, ethnicity, age, prisoner, and client—increased or decreased her power.
2. To stop her physical or verbal challenging of others, particularly when it led to punishment for herself. One way for her to achieve this goal was to learn to be less emotionally reactive, to distinguish emotions from intellectual process. This would help her learn to respond to anger with words rather than physical aggression.
3. To brainstorm about how to be powerful in an indirect way.
4. To mend the relationship with her sisters so there was some balance between her need for total fusion at times and total cutoff at other times.
5. To mourn the loss of her mother. This would involve developing a more realistic and more balanced picture of the woman her mother really was.

Another aspect of this treatment involved teaching and showing J the similarities between what she had experienced in her family and what she was currently experiencing in the prison. The triangles formed by J, other inmates, and a female guard often mirrored her relationship with her mother and sisters. Placing herself in a position to protect other female inmates from male guards was very similar to the relationship she had assumed as she tried to protect her mother and her younger sisters from her father. Similarly, putting herself in the middle of a controversy between female administrators and male custody chiefs paralleled her triangulation in her parents' marital relationship.

One aspect of detriangling is the ability to be in contact with others while being emotionally separate and nonreactive. This was key for J in the triangles she had established in prison. A discussion of the triangulation process helped J resolve some of her anxiety over these prison relationships. Ultimately, she was able to interact with other inmates without becoming the focus of their tension. In many instances she managed to avoid becoming a scapegoat.

J's story illustrates the ways in which family patterns are reenacted in the context of the prison "family." However, above all, her story is one of incredible resilience and hope. In the face of the incredible complexities and constraints that she faced as a long-term inmate, she was able to make significant progress in improving her family relationships, her prison relationships, and her sense of herself.

THE THERAPIST'S JOURNEY

Just as the goals of therapy for the client are to increase self-knowledge and decrease emotional reactivity, these goals are also relevant for the therapist. Thus, the work is equal parts theoretical knowledge and knowledge of self. This is particularly true in an environment as complex as the prison system. The journey toward self-knowledge requires that the therapist continually question her motivation and behavior. Here is a sampling of some of the questions that I struggled to answer:

1. Why do I want to work in this setting?
2. What appeals to me most about the setting: the women, the job?
3. What don't I like about it?
4. How much do I really understand about the oppression of women?
5. What do I know of the oppression of people of color?
6. Am I aware of the disparities that exist in this country along socioeconomic lines?
7. Have I examined my feelings about same-sex relationships?
8. Am I conscious of the impact of homophobia on lesbians?

9. Do I fully understand my role in the correctional system as a mental health caregiver?
10. Are the ethical dilemmas I could be faced with clear to me?
11. How familiar am I with the American Psychological Association Code of Ethics and the Feminist Code of Ethics?
12. How subversive am I willing to be within the correctional system?
13. Am I aware of how I use the power ascribed to my position as a therapist with those who have less power?
14. Are my needs for power being met elsewhere?
15. Am I a culturally competent therapist? How have I made that determination?
16. Can I cope with a multiplicity of diversity that now includes what it means to be an "inmate"?

SUMMARY

As the years go by, it becomes increasingly apparent that in order to help women, we must be aware of the diversity of their roles and the multiplicity of their oppression. If we can take anything away from our attempt to treat women in prison, it is how miserably we can fail them if we do not make changes in our roles as therapists. It is insufficient to say that sexism exists in society and leave it at that. We have to examine closely each individual institution in which women live and work and be willing to "get our hands dirty." A prison is an example of one of these institutions. Although it is far from glamorous, working in a prison is worthwhile if we empower even one woman on one day in one situation.

REFERENCES

Bruns, C. M., & Lesko, T. M. (1999). In the belly of the beast: Morals, ethics and feminist psychotherapy with women in prison. *Women & Therapy: A Feminist Quarterly, 22,* 69–85.

Chesney-Lind, M. (1997). *The female offender: Girls, women and crime.* Thousand Oaks, CA: Sage.

Davies, P. (1972). *The American Heritage dictionary of the English language.* New York: Dell.

Gibson, J. M., & Donigan, J. (1993). Use of Bowen theory. *Journal of Addictions and Offender Counseling, 14,* 25–35.

Gladding, S. T. (1995). *Family therapy: History, theory and practice.* Englewood Cliffs, NJ: Prentice Hall.

Metzner, J., Cohen, F., Grossman, L., & Wettstein, R. (1998). Treatment in jails and prisons. In R. Wettstein (Ed.), *Treatment of offenders with mental disorders* (pp. 211–264). New York: Guilford Press.

Minuchin, S., & Fishman, C. H. (1981). *Family therapy techniques*. Cambridge, MA: Harvard University Press.

19

A VENN DIAGRAM: FEMINISM, FAMILY THERAPY, AND FAMILY MEDICINE

LUCY M. CANDIB

A Venn diagram is a set of circles that overlap in one or several places. Both the overlapping areas and the areas where there are no overlaps are areas of interest. In this chapter I discuss some of the ways that family medicine and family therapy overlap and how feminism intersects with these overlapping areas. After considering the intersecting history of collaboration between family therapy and family medicine, I show how a feminist approach is essential for addressing the common problems of somatization and past abuse, and also for preventing a repetition of prior trauma in the medical setting. Finally, I point out the reasons why family medicine is the appropriate specialty to work with feminist family therapists on women's health care.

Feminist family therapists have reason to be wary of medicine, given the long history of abuse and neglect of women as both patients and providers of care. Despite the fact that upward of 45% of students graduating from medical school now are women, and despite the academic efforts of feminists within medicine, woman-centered values have been slow to penetrate the medical academy (Candib, 1995; Wear, 1997).

Viewed from the position of the client-centered feminist family therapist, most doctors are remarkably poor communicators, with little awareness of the power dynamics at work between the patient and the doctor. Moreover, most doctors have little understanding of the family dynamics leading up to a medical consultation or illness and minimal cognizance of the impact of their recommendations or of the illness itself on the family constellation. Additionally, most doctors have had no exposure to family therapy and are terrified of the word *feminist*.

On the other side, although family therapists inevitably work with families with chronic medical problems, they have a varied exposure to medical practitioners. Some have little or no connection with the physicians treating their clients; others have weekly or even daily contact with physicians concerning their patients. Regardless of their understanding of the relationship between mind and body, feminist family therapists often retain mechanistic ideas about medicine and negative views of doctors.

This negative "take" on physicians and medicine may cause therapists to view doctors as technicians who are useful only to obtain workups and medications. Insofar as they see doctors only as practitioners of reductionism, their potential to work collaboratively with doctors is restricted. We have all, in fact, been trained in separate compartments, and there is no overlap even in training sites except for those few fortunate practitioners who train and practice in collaborative settings. No wonder there is such poor communication between disciplines and such lack of respect.

WHERE WE HAVE BEEN: FAMILY MEDICINE AND FAMILY THERAPY

Despite the constraints mentioned above, some practitioners of medicine *do have* a deep interest in psychological work. In some areas of medicine, particularly in family practice and pediatrics, there is strong awareness of the connection between family relationships and illness. Family medicine and family therapy share a common history of emerging as alternatives to prevailing models of individual treatment, models in which the individual was the bearer of the pathology rather than a participant in a system subject to various internal and external stresses (Candib & Glenn, 1983). During the 1970s and 1980s in a few special settings (e.g., Rochester, New York), teaching and treatment programs for family practice and for family therapy developed together, thus demonstrating a model of collaboration that is unfortunately still too rare.

In the same period William Doherty and Macaran Baird (1983) published a book demonstrating their creative collaborative work between a family physician and family therapist. A journal dedicated to this collaborative vision, *Family Systems Medicine*, was born in 1982 through the efforts of Don Bloch, a psychiatrist, family therapist, and editor at that time of *Family Process*; Don Ransom, a pioneer family researcher; and Michael Glenn, a doubly trained family physician/psychiatrist with a commitment to collaboration. In 1996 this journal was renamed *Families, Systems & Health* and rededicated to collaborative work between the health care fields and family therapy, under the joint editorship of family therapist Susan McDaniel and family physician Tom Campbell.

In the early 1990s, Susan McDaniel of the Rochester group spearheaded publication of two texts fostering collaboration: one for physicians about family systems (McDaniel, Campbell, & Seaburn, 1990), and another for therapists working with families with health problems (McDaniel, Hepworth, & Doherty, 1992). The latter book is a veritable handbook for therapists working with physicians. In it McDaniel and her coauthors outline the kinds of collaboration that have developed between family therapists and primary care doctors for patients whose problems cause them a great deal of contact with the medical care system—families with a member with chronic illness or with somatization.

Further collaboration in clinical settings has been championed by the growing Collaborative Family Healthcare Coalition (www.cfhcc.org), an organization of health care professionals spanning primary and tertiary care, nursing, medicine, psychology, social work, family therapy, and administration. Within family medicine itself, the academic organization of Society of Teachers of Family Medicine holds a yearly conference on families and health that attracts those teaching and practicing with the collaborative vision. Thus, a shared history, scholarly books, a journal, a multidisciplinary organization, and a growing number of dedicated scholars and practitioners now strengthen the connection between family systems thinking and primary medical care practice.

HOW FEMINISM OVERLAPS

Separately and largely independent from the collaborative movement, second and third wave feminism was making its impact on family medicine and family therapy. Silverstein has outlined the history of feminist family therapy in this volume (see chapter 2), so here I cover only the connection between feminism and family medicine. Family medicine and second wave feminism both burst forth in the late 1960s and 1970s as energetic forces critical of the status quo. They shared a criticism of how medicine had been treating people and yearned for a new vision. At that time, feminist health concerns focused on women gaining control over their own bodies. Feminist health activists did not know about family medicine. Likewise, family medicine was struggling for academic legitimacy and knew nothing about feminism.

In 1976 in a two-page article, Lynn Carmichael (a man), a key founder of the family practice movement, stated that the "family" in family medicine referred to the characteristics of the relationship between the doctor and the patient: affinity, intimacy, continuity, and reciprocity. Carmichael identified relational thinking as central to family medicine in the same year that Jean Baker Miller published the beginnings of self-in-relation theory (1976). A prophetic voice in family medicine, G. Gayle Stephens (another man) located the commonality between feminism and family medicine in his landmark article, "Family Medicine as Counterculture" (1989), which was republished 10 years later, equally as relevant. I introduced the parallel between feminist thinking and knowing in family medicine (Candib, 1988). I outlined a shared epistemology and showed how "connected knowing" is integral to the daily practice of family medicine.

Despite these potentially feminist philosophical underpinnings, family medicine shared several biases with conventional specialties: a male-centered understanding of growth and development, a traditional view of the individual and family life cycle (based on conventional women's and men's roles), and a self-serving misconception of the damage done to women by the family through sexual and physical abuse (Candib, 1995). Like family therapy, family medicine was only too ready to accept "systemic" views of "family violence" in which the concepts of homeostasis and complementarity allowed clinicians to ignore abuse of power and gender violence in families.

Feminist family therapists first identified these issues (Bograd, 1984, 1986; Goldner, 1988), and I attempted to highlight them for family medicine (Candib, 1989, 1990, 1995). Carole Warshaw, an internist at Cook County Hospital in Chicago, was likewise trying to educate physicians about the limitations of the medical model for addressing violence against women (Warshaw, 1989, 1993). Awareness about the harm done to girls in families through incest and sexual abuse was even more abhorrent for physicians to recognize, yet research efforts in family medicine increasingly demonstrate the burden of suffering resulting from such abuse (Dickinson, deGruy, Dickinson, & Candib, 1998, 1999).

All of these critical areas for women patients in family medicine are being reinterpreted as waves of women trainees enter the field bringing with them some prior knowledge and understanding about women's experience of gender oppression. These privileged young women do not usually define themselves as feminists (Wear, 1997). Nevertheless, they carry the potential to understand power inequities that they have lived through before and during medical training as they learn to care for patients who experience even more layered versions of that oppression. This coming generation of practitioners holds the possibility of bringing feminist practice to the many fields of medicine.

WORKING TOGETHER

Family therapists who work with physicians are likely to see families whose problems are dominated by chronic illness or by somatization (Mc-Daniel et al., 1992). Many women from families who ultimately seek help from feminist family therapists have already weathered many health problems, yet continue to have a variety of symptoms. Therefore, therapists need to have a way to help patients think about their medical care. Therapists need a working understanding of physical symptoms: Not everything that hurts has a specific biomedical explanation (probably more than 80% do not). Conversely, not everything that hurts is in the patient's head (or family system). Yet regardless of what causes the symptom, family relationships strongly affect its course.

So where does feminism apply? Families with chronic illness may have deep imbalances in caregiving, coupled with strongly gendered ideology about the caring roles. Women in these families, especially low-income or single women and women of color, face structural and social injustices outside the domestic and medical arenas that further constrict the resources available to them for their families. Clinicians working in settings dedicated to the underserved are likely to be aware of the economic and social realities that these women face as they try to deal with chronic diseases like diabetes and hypertension while they care for their families. Those working in the private sector may be relatively protected from awareness of the multiple layers of gender oppression affecting women's abilities to persevere as caregivers.

The tired and sometimes desperate African American grandmother caring for boisterous grandchildren whose mother or father is addicted to crack or sick with AIDS is a frequent attendee in many inner-city health centers. A support group to help with access to scarce services may be key to her ability to carry on (Okazawa-Rey, 1994). Practitioners who work with the underserved—family doctors, family therapists, indeed, any clinicians—need to understand the dynamics of power, small and larger systems, and women's gendered realities. In fact, I would argue that the only way for them to make sense of their work and their patients' lives is to integrate both the feminist and systems approaches.

As with chronic illness, family therapists will also be highly involved with families with somatization. Somatization represents a special area of concern for doctors and therapists because, by definition, the designated patient has multiple symptoms that do not have a defined biomedical cause. By the time of referral to a therapist, the patient's physician is likely to have reached a stage of frustration, if not desperation, about the unremitting and protean symptoms. Patients likewise may have reached the end of the road with their frustration with the medical system and may accept the therapy referral primarily because of how distraught they and their families feel about their lack of improvement.

Despite their relative power, doctors feel victimized and trapped by these patients at the same time that these patients feel victimized and mistreated by doctors. The feminist contribution to this impasse lies in promoting the understanding among physicians and therapists alike that patients with many somatic symptoms have usually had prior experiences of physical or sexual abuse. (The rate of combined prior physical and sexual abuse for women with more than 13 symptoms is 65%, and for women with 6–12 symptoms, 49%, compared with a control group with fewer than 6 symptoms whose rate is 33%; Dickinson, Dickinson, & deGruy, 1999).

This background of abuse means not only that women with many symptoms are among the most problematic of medical patients but also that they are among the most vulnerable. Qualitative study with these women shows that their relationships with their doctors likely recapitulate dynamics from childhood—secrecy, not being believed, denial of their symptoms and experience, and not being able to trust an authority figure (Morse, Suchman, & Frankel, 1997). Among refugees, somatization may be the presenting feature of previous political persecution, torture or witnessed atrocities, and even ongoing threats by powerful military forces (Waitzkin & Magaña, 1997). Feminism has prompted the exploration of these core issues about the abuse of power over women and children in families, issues that should change how family doctors and family therapists practice and collaborate.

The high likelihood of prior abuse in patients with somatization requires a specific clinical approach using the following strategies: respectful inquiry into the possibility of past abuse, recognition of the experience of suffering, putting the patient in control of interactions, permission-based examinations, recognition that "body memories" can trigger hypervigilance, and consistent use of an integrated mind–body approach and sensitivity to the inherent power imbalance in the relationship (Candib, 2003). These strategies become even more important when trauma is central to current symptoms and relational dynamics.

TRAUMA AND RETRAUMATIZATION

Feminists critical of the dynamics of power in medical care are likely to understand the potential for abuse in medical interactions in which class, race, gender, education, and control over medical knowledge and resources are so skewed between doctor and patient. Therapists familiar with the effect of power inequities on vulnerable patients know that such interactions with doctors, even when they are routine and otherwise unremarkable, can be traumatic. Brusque or impersonal treatment of a Black or Latino patient by a harried White health care worker appears racist to the patient even when there is no conscious intent. The details of these interactions need to become well understood by medical providers.

Less well recognized is the fact that medical testing and procedures can also be traumatic, especially for patients who have been previously victimized. Given the high frequency of prior physical and sexual abuse among women with many somatic symptoms, as well the fact that about one third of women have had some experience of intrusive childhood sexual abuse, the potential for medical retraumatization is very high. Despite the growing awareness among physicians about the frequency of past sexual abuse, doctors are desensitized by their training to how traumatic medical exams and procedures can be for patients in general and for this group in particular.

The relational dynamics that are problematic for sexually abused children—powerlessness, betrayal, stigma, and traumatized sexuality (Finkelhor & Browne, 1985)—are exactly the same dynamics in medical settings for adult survivors of abuse. The issue of powerlessness is always present from the minute the patient comes into the office. Betrayal is an impending issue whenever the physician does not come through for the patient, even in small ways (a phone call not returned, a prescription not phoned in). Fear of betrayal also leads to preoccupation with the confidentiality of medical records. Survivors may feel betrayed by routine exchanges of information among medical providers in the course of consultation and may desire control over exactly what the clinician puts in the record for every visit. Patients feel stigmatized by their symptoms and their diagnoses, whatever they may be, but particularly if the patient thinks that the doctor thinks "it's all in her head."

Traumatized sexuality may lead patients at times to sexualize medical relationships. Identification of this last dynamic has been used to blame the patient for being "seductive" and further stigmatize her. Finally, women who have been abused are likely to avoid routine women's health care like pelvic exams and mammography. Thus, sexual victimization overlaps with other forms of oppression—class and race—to keep women away from preventive health care. A typical example is that of a Black woman, sexually abused in childhood and physically abused in marriage, who delays seeking help for a breast mass (Lawson, 1998). The result is that the most disempowered group in our society, minority women, who are more at risk for cervical cancer and for late diagnosis of breast cancer, if they have also experienced sexual victimization, are even less likely to obtain the necessary screening Pap smears and mammography.

When the dynamics of prior abuse are in play, medical procedures are likely to be highly traumatic. For instance, an incest survivor reluctantly permitted a routine pelvic exam and Pap smear done carefully with attention to her feelings and ability to "stay present in the room." Subsequently, she suffered intrusive flashbacks for months. Similarly, a previously sexually abused woman suffered from chronic pelvic pain. Despite caring preparation by her physician, having a pelvic ultrasound done with the insertion of a vaginal probe by a previously unknown technician proved to be highly charged. Another patient whose childhood abuse involved being forced to manipulate her own feces found that bad memories made it impossible for her to obtain samples of her stools to test for blood. Such "routine" procedures have the potential to retraumatize vulnerable patients and trigger flashbacks and dissociation.

When medical care requires more than routine care, clinicians are best advised to remember that painful procedures bring up painful memories. Patients with a history of prior physical and sexual abuse may have prolonged and painful recovery from surgical procedures or other medical interventions. For instance, a lesbian woman with a history of brutal physical abuse as well as sexual abuse suffered intractable chest wall pain and abdominal wall pain after breast reconstruction surgery postmastectomy for breast cancer. The patient found her flashbacks to be more intrusive and disruptive during this period. Referral and ongoing consultation with a systemic therapist was able to reduce the problem with flashbacks although the pain persisted. Therapists and physicians alike need to be aware of the power of medical settings and medical interventions to recreate such dynamics. They must not only think clearly about the need for such procedures but also work through with the patient the details and potential impact of any proposed test or procedure before deciding to go ahead.

It should be no surprise that survivors of prior sexual abuse often avoid medical care precisely because of these troublesome power dynamics as well as the potential for restimulation of traumatic memories. Therapists, using both personal experience and professional legitimacy, can assist clients in getting routine exams. First, a therapist can verbally "walk" the patient through the steps of making and keeping an appointment, and telling the clinician what kind of exam she wants and what her concerns are about having it. The therapist can remind the patient of the specific steps. For example, for a Pap smear: taking off her clothes, then having her perineum inspected, a speculum inserted in her vagina, samples taken, and a bimanual exam. (If uncertain, the therapist may want to find out exactly how these steps are accomplished in a particular provider's office. This preparation will enable a patient to know where the stumbling blocks will be and help her, at a minimum, keep the appointment, meet the medical provider, and go as far in the process as she can.)

A therapist can help a patient choose a provider likely to be sensitive to the patient's vulnerability and willing to put the timing and conduct of the exam as much as possible under the patient's control. Therapists can develop a list of collaborative physicians and nurse practitioners in their locale who are receptive to working with low-income women, women of color, and lesbians, and who have flexible policies about insurance and fee schedules. Therapists can encourage patients to interview a prospective clinician before having an exam, to bring a friend along to help her assess whether this particular practitioner would be appropriate for her, and to bring a friend to accompany her for exams expected to be difficult.

Therapists can also discourage patients from continuing to see a medical provider who, through tactlessness or deliberate abuse of power, replicates the patient's past experience of abuse. With the patient's permission, a therapist can speak directly to the patient's medical practitioner about the implications of any upcoming examination or treatment. I was able to help a patient get to a much-needed dental appointment by talking with the dentist in advance about the patient's terror of the exam because of repeated abuse from a dentist during childhood.

A tactful but explicit phone call from a therapist to the patient's health care provider can change the conduct of treatment from a routine, run-of-the-mill, impersonal interaction to a careful and gentle evaluation. Patients are often too intimidated by physicians to advocate for themselves. A phone call from the therapist can enlighten the medical provider about unexpressed fears. In one instance I was able to have an otorhinolaryngologist (ear, nose, and throat specialist) approach very gently the treatment of a tongue lesion in an abuse survivor who otherwise would not have consented to treatment. Too often the only transaction between therapists and health care providers is the mandatory request for documentation of a primary health care exam. With the patient's permission, direct communication can lead to far more effective health care.

Medical providers need to accept the limits that previously abused patients may put on having physical and pelvic exams and mammograms (McKegney, 1993). Patients may want to stay healthy but cannot tolerate the idea of such exams. Together with their patients, providers have to weigh the real risks of not having the exam versus not having an experience that will cause flashbacks and dissociation. An incest survivor in my practice spent 5 years working up to having a pelvic exam and Pap smear but dissociated through the entire procedure. Her new goal several years later was to have a follow-up exam and remain "in the room."

Many physicians are not ready to enter into this slow process with patients because they are unaware of the impact of routine procedures on patients. Therapists can help physicians gain this understanding and clarify that gaining control over powerlessness may be more important for a survivor's view of her health than engaging in cancer detection. For highly complex cases—for example, a previously abused patient with multiple personality disorder who developed inflammatory bowel disease—such collaboration is essential (Ruddy, 1994). The feminist contribution to medicine and family therapy is the absolute requirement to attend to past and present issues of power and abuse. Together, feminist therapists and physicians can remind each other of the damaging power of medical interventions and can work together to minimize them.

COLLABORATION WITH WHOM?

If feminist therapists are to collaborate with physicians, with whom should they start? Given medicine's historically poor treatment of women, some feminist therapists will wonder why we should not embrace a women's health specialty, in which women patients could see a woman-oriented physician. A movement in that direction has been growing during the 1990s, and feminist therapists may find it appealing. I believe this solution is unsatisfactory for both feminists and family therapists.

First, women hold up half the sky—there are just too many of us. A specialty for half the people is not a specialty, which by definition serves a select group. Because only small numbers of physicians would be trained in such a field, only a very few women would have access. Because such clinicians are unlikely to work in sites for the underserved, the women having access will likely be those with financial and educational resources. Yet it is exactly the women without such resources who need medical care that is empowering. All medical clinicians, be they nurse practitioners or doctors, need to be educated to address the power imbalance that prevails in medical care. A feminist solution needs to be one that is open to all women.

Second, health care spans a lifetime, yet a women's health specialty is likely to address only the medical problems of adult women. Women during all phases of their lives need clinicians aware of the abuses of power that women experience and of women's need for empowering rather than disempowering clinical relationships. As women get older and develop chronic diseases or even terminal illnesses, they will be exposed to a variety of specialists who likewise need to be thinking about how to conduct relationships with patients in ways that do not rob them of their power.

Third, because women are in charge of the health care of their families, they arrange the visits and accompany their family members to receive medical care in innumerable settings. Clinicians in all these settings, and in all the potential disciplines involved (family medicine, pediatrics, geriatrics, internal medicine, surgery, and all the subspecialties), need to understand about the power dynamics in health care and about the role of women providing care in families. All of these clinicians must be taught about women's needs for safe, respectful, collaborative care as they go about getting health care for their families.

All of medicine needs feminist health practitioners, in every discipline, working to provide care to women, men, and children, within the context of their families, recognizing the larger sources of disempowerment in the wider society as well as within families themselves. We need to be directing feminists into the health care field so that they can make a difference in every discipline. When young women professionals approach the decision of which specialty to choose, I tell them that they can practice good care for women in any field. However, only one field allows them to care for women throughout the life cycle in the context of their families: family medicine.

Family medicine also allows the care of the whole family by one clinician, thus permitting multiple agendas to be addressed at office visits. As a discipline, family medicine has the potential to integrate both the somatic and emotional concerns of the individual patient, recognize the contributing support and stress from the family, and interpret the way the family system functions with this particular person's symptoms as the presenting feature. Of course, family medicine is not for all patients, nor for all doctors. Some patients do not want to be seen by the physician caring for the rest of their family, and some doctors have specialized interests or are not interested in certain age groups or kinds of problems. Sometimes the specific family physicians available may not be right for this person or this family. However, to address women's health care needs in context, family medicine has the most potential.

CONCLUSION

Feminist family therapists need to be able to help empower clients to work with medical clinicians. That group of family therapists who have had some exposure to family medicine will know areas of the country where family medicine is being taught with a systemic focus. They will know where residents and faculty take seriously the understanding of power at work, as well as the impact of economics, race, class, and gender on the doctor–patient relationship. At times it is possible to identify clinicians who focus on empowerment and who shape a clinical site where underserved patients are welcomed, respected, and integrated into the treatment system as collaborative participants. These therapists can help such medical consultants develop further along feminist and systemic lines.

Likewise, feminist family doctors can collaborate with family therapists in the mutual care of families struggling with chronic disease and somatization. When the contributions of feminist theory are integrated into family medicine and family therapy, the potential for emancipatory personal and professional practice will be realized. Both feminist family doctors and feminist family therapists raise the bar for medicine and therapy to develop and practice strategies for empowerment with women in the context of their families. Let us hope we can all rise to the challenge!

REFERENCES

Bograd, M. (1984). Family systems approaches to wife battering: A feminist critique. *American Journal of Orthopsychiatry, 54*, 558–568.

Bograd, M. (1986). A feminist examination of family systems models of violence against women in the family. In M. Ault-Riche (Ed.), *Women and family therapy* (pp. 34–50). Rockville, MD: Aspen Systems.

Candib, L. M. (1988). Ways of knowing in family medicine: Contributions from a feminist perspective. *Family Medicine, 20*, 133–136.

Candib, L. M. (1989). Editorial: Violence against women: No more excuses. *Family Medicine, 21*, 339–342.

Candib, L. M. (1990). Naming the contradiction: Family medicine's failure to face violence against women. *Family & Community Health, 13*, 47–57.

Candib, L. M. (1994). Self-in-relation theory: Implications for women's health. In A. Dan (Ed.), *Reframing women's health: New paradigms for multidisciplinary research and practice* (pp. 67–78). Thousand Oaks, CA: Sage.

Candib, L. M. (1995). *Medicine and the family: A feminist perspective*. New York: Basic Books.

Candib, L. M. (2003). *Clinical implications of the Mobile study on somatization in primary care*. Manuscript in preparation.

Candib, L. M., & Glenn, M. (1983). Family medicine and family therapy: Comparative development, methods, and roles. *Journal of Family Practice, 16*, 773–779.

Carmichael, L. P. (1976). The family in medicine: Process or entity? *Journal of Family Practice, 3*, 562–563.

Dickinson, L. M., deGruy, F. V., III, Dickinson, W. P., & Candib, L. M. (1998). Complex PTSD: Evidence from the primary care setting. *General Hospital Psychiatry, 20*, 1–11.

Dickinson, L. M., deGruy, F. V., III, Dickinson, W. P., & Candib, L. M. (1999). Health-related quality of life and symptom profiles of female survivors of sexual abuse in primary care. *Archives of Family Medicine, 8*, 35–43.

Dickinson, W. P., Dickinson, L. M., & deGruy, F. V., III. (1999). *Family characteristics of moderate and severe somatizers in primary care*. Paper presented at the North American Primary Care Research Group Annual Meeting, San Diego, CA.

Doherty, W. J., & Baird, M. (1983). *Family therapy and family medicine*. New York: Guilford Press.

Finkelhor, D., & Browne, A. (1985). The traumatic impact of child sexual abuse: A conceptualization. *American Journal of Orthopsychiatry, 55*, 530–541.

Goldner, V. (1988). Generation and gender: Normative and covert hierarchies. *Family Process, 27*, 17–31.

Lawson, E. J. (1998). A narrative analysis: A black woman's perceptions of breast cancer risks and early breast cancer detection. *Cancer Nursing, 21*, 421–429.

McDaniel, S. H., Campbell, T. L., & Seaburn, D. B. (1990). *Family-oriented primary care: A manual for medical providers*. New York: Springer-Verlag.

McDaniel, S. H., Hepworth, J., & Doherty, W. J. (1992). *Medical family therapy*. New York: Basic Books.

McKegney, C. P. (1993). Surviving survivors: Coping with caring for patients who have been victimized. *Primary Care Clinics of North America, 20*, 481–494.

Miller, J. B. (1976). *Toward a new psychology of women*. Boston: Beacon Press.

Morse, D. S., Suchman, A. L., & Frankel, R. M. (1997). The meaning of symptoms in 10 women with somatization disorder and a history of childhood sexual abuse. *Archives of Family Medicine, 6*, 468–476.

Okazawa-Rey, M. (1994). Grandparents who care: An empowerment model of health care. In A. Dula & S. Goering (Eds.), *"It just ain't fair": The ethics of health care for African Americans* (pp. 221–232). Westport, CT: Praeger.

Ruddy, N. (with commentaries by Farley, T., Nymberg, J., & Hayden, K.). (1994). Multiple personality disorder in primary care: A collaboration. *Family Systems Medicine, 12*, 327–338.

Stephens, G. G. (1989). Family medicine as counterculture. *Family Medicine, 21*, 103–109.

Waitzkin, H., & Magaña, H. (1997). The black box in somatization: Unexplained physical symptoms, culture, and narratives of trauma. *Social Science and Medicine, 45*, 811–825.

Warshaw, C. (1989). Limitations of the medical model in the care of battered women. *Gender and Society, 3*, 506–517.

Warshaw, C. (1993). Domestic violence: Challenges to medical practice. *Journal of Women's Health, 2*, 73–90.

Wear, D. (1997). *Privilege in the medical academy: A feminist examines gender, race, and power*. New York: Teachers College Press.

20

GENDER, COUPLES, AND ILLNESS: A FEMINIST ANALYSIS OF MEDICAL FAMILY THERAPY

SUSAN H. MCDANIEL AND KATHLEEN COLE-KELLY

Serious illness or trauma can be a crash course in consciousness-raising about gender for couples. The demands of an illness can raise and sometimes challenge already agreed-on, complementary gender roles that have been adopted consciously and unconsciously by a couple. Illness can be an existential correction. It often suddenly pulls people out of their daily routines, forces reevaluation of priorities, deflates any sense of personal importance, penetrates defenses, and robs the individual and family of a sense of ultimate control. In this situation, patients are faced with biological, psychological, and interpersonal challenges. The depth of this challenge inevitably heightens people's sense of identity, connection, and disconnection.

Research has documented that negative aspects of marital functioning have indirect influences on health outcomes through depression and health habits, and direct influences on cardiovascular, endocrine, immune, neurosensory, and other physiological mechanisms (Kiecolt-Glaser & Newton, 2001). These findings underscore the importance of understanding couple dynamics and relationship contributions to the development, treatment, and prognosis for serious illness. This chapter explores those dynamics and the impact of gender socialization on couples facing illness. We describe medical family therapy, an approach to psychotherapy with these couples, and provide a feminist analysis of its principles and techniques. Then we address life-cycle issues, sexuality, caregiving and couples' roles, and the importance of balancing agency and communion.

FAMILIES, GENDER SOCIALIZATION, AND ILLNESS

The family has always provided the majority of health care to its members. This situation has become even more pronounced with the downsizing of health care, the reduction in hospital stays, and the reduction in health benefits. The home is now the primary site for gathering information about an illness and for providing care. For adults, it is often a spouse or significant other who helps the ill person to understand symptoms and arrive at an informal diagnosis of the problem. Once a physician or nurse practitioner is consulted, the couple will decide together whether and how to implement the health professional's suggestions. Then, it is often the partner who implements the treatment, reminds the loved one to take medication or not, and generally helps or hinders the ill person's healing (McDaniel, Campbell, & Seaburn, 1990).

As children, men and women learn how to be sick in their families along with many other skills modeled by their parents. Typically, men learn that being sick is not masculine. Men need to be strong, productive, and instrumental. None of these attributes goes along with being ill. Women, in general, learn that being sick can be syntonic with the feminine role. Women are often encouraged to be passive, receptive, and openly emotional. These attributes are consistent with being ill. This socialization has widespread implications for patienthood and for caregiving. What Virginia Goldner (1991) has called "the cultural insistence on gender polarity" can have differential effects for men, women, and their individual and relational health. For example, adult women tend to go to the doctor, and as a rule, men do not (Commonwealth Fund, 2000). Adult women, rather than men, tend to be the primary caregivers of older adults. Women tend to express more feelings about their illness.

Illness can evoke conflict about roles, even in couples that prefer nonstereotypic gender roles. For example, in one couple the husband did most of the child care while his wife, a lawyer, was the primary source of the family's income. This arrangement worked well until the wife became ill with multiple sclerosis. Although the couple was pleased with the roles they assumed in their relationship, they found their roles challenged as they encountered other systems with traditional gender expectations. Health professionals spoke to the wife about her loss of parenting abilities, rather than her loss of worth as an attorney, as she became more and more debilitated. Extended family members expressed biases they kept in check prior to the illness about the way the couple had split the family workload. Illness can create dissonance when the family or community pressures a couple about their roles.

Family health psychologists may be consulted when the gender-socialized responses to illness contribute to problematic behavior in a patient or a caregiver. Whether heterosexual or homosexual, the same relationship that has the potential to offer support during an illness also can be a source of stress. Two clinical examples will illustrate this point.[1]

> A Catholic couple experiencing primary infertility had been working with infertility specialists for almost a year. Lynn, from an expressive Italian American family, had all the usual blood tests and invasive diagnostic procedures to rule out female infertility. Mike, from a stoic Irish American family, could not seem to remember his appointments with the urologist. The one time he did make it, he was unable to leave them a sperm sample. It was clear that Lynn would endure almost any pain or procedure that might enable her to become a mother, which she considered the ultimate validation of her femininity. Mike, on the other hand, was terrified that this undiagnosed infertility was a marker for his inadequacy as a man, and so did not go to the doctor to have this confirmed.

> Greg and Jeanne, an Ashkanazi Jewish couple, illustrate a common gender-based pattern with caregiving. When Jeanne was diagnosed with a rare form of lymphoma, Greg went into management mode. He dealt with insurers, managed the many appointments to the specialists, and read everything he could find on the Web. He ran the family. This instrumental approach to the illness threat was enormously helpful and comforting to Jeanne during the diagnostic and treatment crisis. Once the diagnosis was clear and a treatment plan was established, there was little more action to take as they moved into a chronic phase. Jeanne then wanted Greg to comfort her and to talk about the illness and the possibility of her death. Greg withdrew and became depressed. Jeanne became angry. The illness came between them.

Both these cases illustrate situations when a couple may consult a medical family therapist. Medical family therapy is a biopsychosocial approach to helping couples and families who face significant health problems (McDaniel, Hepworth, & Doherty, 1992, 1996). This psychotherapy is implicitly feminist in its theory and its approach to intervention. The next section provides a feminist analysis of medical family therapy, to make explicit its feminist foundation and to discuss the challenges of working with feminist sensibilities in a male-dominated health care system.

A FEMINIST ANALYSIS OF MEDICAL FAMILY THERAPY

Medical family therapy is a metaframework for psychotherapy, meaning that it provides overarching principles within which any form of psycho-

---

[1] All case examples are factual but camouflaged to protect the confidentiality of the patients involved.

therapy can be practiced. Medical family therapy is based on a biopsycho-social systems theory. This theory, unlike biotechnical medicine, is expressly systemic and sensitive to the effects of context, including such variables as gender, race, culture, and class, on health and illness. The goals of medical family therapy are to increase agency and communion for the patient, the family, and the health professionals involved (Bakan, 1969). These goals reflect the feminist goals commonly described as empowerment and connection. Vicki Helgeson (1994), in a review of the research on agency and communion, concluded that both agency and communion are required for optimal health. She found that unmitigated agency (often associated with masculinity) or unmitigated communion (often associated with femininity) is associated with negative health outcomes.

A discussion of a few medical family therapy techniques illustrates how this approach lends itself to feminist psychotherapy. We also comment on the pitfalls and challenges of working within this framework. The first technique is to attend to the biological dimension of any problem. This is fundamental to a biopsychosocial approach. Avoiding the biological dimension of a problem can lead to misattributions such as "this problem is all in your head," a dismissive comment experienced all too often by female patients. However, women must also beware of the use of inappropriate biological diagnoses for what is actually a social problem.

Several techniques focus on the development of a collaborative (rather than hierarchical) relationship between the health professional, the patient, and the partner. In this way, we attempt to right the well-described power problems that can occur for patients in the doctor–patient relationship. Techniques include eliciting the illness story and feelings, asking about family illness history and illness meanings, and documenting transgenerational health beliefs and coping strategies. Those must be understood if a partnership is to develop for health care.

Women and men may approach this collaboration in different ways. Because of the power differential, women may need to develop a trusting relationship with their health care provider before being able to share their illness story. For men, an illness story can be difficult to elicit because exposing vulnerability (whether physical or emotional) goes against many men's socialization. This technique may require patient, supportive questioning by the therapist.

A respectful therapeutic stance also includes understanding individual and family developmental issues (including biological markers like childbearing and menopause in women and cardiovascular and sexual function concerns in men). It also includes respecting the patient and partner's defenses, diminishing blame and guilt, and accepting unacceptable feelings in reaction to illness. Unacceptable feelings may arise, for example, related to ways in which men or women respond to illness that run counter to their gender script. In response to a new diagnosis, a man who is tearful or a woman who is angry may feel the additional burden of criticism from others. Medical family therapy works to counteract the oppressive experience of these gender scripts.

Increasing agency through empowerment is accomplished through providing psychoeducation and information for men and women, encouraging the patient and family to maintain individual and family identities, developing flexible roles in caring for the illness, and drawing out individual and family strengths and resources independent of gender scripting. Connection (or communion) between the patient and the family, and the patient and the health care team, is strengthened through attention to clear communication. This technique often involves understanding idiosyncratic and gender-based styles of communication regarding illness and treatment. With one couple, for example, therapy focused on negotiating a balance between the wife wanting to share her fears regarding her husband's heart attack and her husband's desire to focus on the future.

One of the largest challenges to feminist medical family therapy is interacting with the traditionally androcentric, heterosexist medical system. Biotechnical, reductionist medicine does not take into account context, does not value relationship or connection, and does not attend to psychological or interpersonal aspects of a problem or a solution. The collaborative stance that is the cornerstone of medical family therapy involves respecting the patient's agenda, supporting the patient's goals, and providing empathy and emotional support from a consultative rather than authoritarian position.

Like physicians who practice biopsychosocial medicine, medical family therapists offer a clear alternative to the traditional medical approach to illness. Medical family therapy points to a different way to manage power among health professionals, collaborating by determining leadership depending on the expertise most needed by the patient. Successful collaboration avoids the profound power problems that can characterize the traditional medical system (McDaniel & Hepworth, in press) and encourages clear communication between the couple and the health professionals. Sometimes this collaboration involves coaching the patient (and sometimes the physician) to deal directly with an acknowledged problem in the doctor–patient relationship.

Given the expert stance of the traditional health care system, health professionals are often concerned with patient "noncompliance" to treatment. This noncompliance may reflect disagreement by the disempowered patient or partner (often a woman) with a medical expert (often a man). Studies by Deaton and Olbrisch (1987) have shown that noncompliance by mothers of sick children is often reasoned and reasonable. Medical family therapy focuses on the importance of a mutually agreed-on treatment plan, in which patients' and families' voices are heard. "Concordance" rather than "compliance" becomes the goal of these interactions. To facilitate this outcome, the medical family therapist may also coach the patient and family to make the best use of time with their physician: preparing for the session ahead of time, writing down questions, and encouraging the couple to see the physician together so they both provide input and hear treatment suggestions.

ILLNESS, COUPLES, AND THE LIFE CYCLE

When couples confront chronic illness, identifying the stage of their family life cycle can be useful in helping them address the developmental issues affecting how they cope with chronic illness (Candib, 1995; Rolland, 1994). Most life-cycle stages have gender-socialized roles associated with them. For example, when a chronic illness strikes one partner with young children, the impact on parenting roles and responsibilities can be devastating. If before illness one of the partners has agreed to do more of the child rearing while the other is doing more out-of-home work, these differences will be a source of strain when the illness hits.

> Joe and Sue were an Irish American Catholic couple who had been married for 14 years and had 2 sons: Seth, 10, and Jacob, 13. Joe taught physical education at a local high school. He also coached basketball for the high school team. After a prolonged series of diagnostic expeditions, Joe was diagnosed with multiple sclerosis. A very proud, physical, and independent man, Joe could not tolerate the image of his being so "weakened" in front of his children.
> He left the family and insisted that they not see him. Sue begged Joe to get involved with counseling so that they could address his worries, his changing role in the family, and his feelings about himself. Joe finally relented and got involved in medical family therapy. The epicenter of his concerns was his worry about the impact of his being a physically debilitated role model for his adolescent children. Joe lived so much in the land of his body that he struggled to be more conversant with the world of his and his family's emotions. Had it been Sue who had the multiple sclerosis, the impact on the family might have been quite different, given the roles and expectations assigned in this couple's relationship.

Medical family therapy in this case focused on grieving the losses brought about by Joe's illness, increasing honest communication with his wife, and increasing his sense of connection with his sons through coaching them on their homework and developing a shared coin collection.

In addition to gender roles that couples develop in their relationship, culture often influences the assignment of roles with illness.

In a Puerto Rican family, a father with HIV found it very difficult to acknowledge to his wife and young children that he was terrified about what the future held for him. He had constructed very clear rules of how a father of young children behaves when confronted with difficult situations: Plow ahead and don't let anyone know it hurts you. In this case, the male therapist in the cotherapy team worked to offer an alternative view of what is manly, in general and in coping with HIV.

The confluence of gender expectations, cultural influences, and life-cycle stage must be understood when treating a couple confronting a chronic illness. For example, in an older couple with many years to solidify family roles, if the woman has been expected to be the caretaker and it is she who becomes sick, the husband often can have great difficulty making the transition to caretaking. The wife can be as unwilling to give up her caretaking role as the husband is unwilling to take it on. A scene in the movie "Dad" aptly portrays this dynamic when the mother has just had a heart attack and is still trying to direct the housekeeping action from her hospital bed while her emotionally overwhelmed husband is fumbling to reassure her that everything will be taken care of.

Medical family therapists need to explore the following with couples at each stage of the life cycle: what the roles are for all tasks in the family, how they can get redistributed, and how each partner can make a transition to a new role. Providing support for both partners in making this transition and acknowledging the potential barriers to it (including family of origin and cultural expectations) can be very useful.

ILLNESS AND SEXUALITY

Vivian struggled with her decisions about treatment for her breast cancer and decided, with support from her husband and others (including her oncologist), that she would have a bilateral mastectomy. She then underwent the months of radiation and chemotherapy. During this ordeal, a sexual relationship was the furthest thing from her mind. However, once Vivian was out of the woods with her treatment, her husband was feeling more optimistic and gently started talking to her about breast implants. Before her treatments had begun, Vivian had stated that she never wanted breast implants. At the time, her husband had cautioned her not to make that decision yet. Now he was ready for that to be revisited. Throughout their relationship, both raised in Italian American families, Vivian had adjusted to Alan's strong need for control. She had been able to make her own choices in her work, her house, and raising their children. She chose her battles carefully and was usually not too disturbed by his forceful nature. However, when the discussion of breast implants reoccurred "so that we can have a more normal sex life," Vivian was astonished. She was already depleted by the months of struggle against the cancer and was beginning to abandon her former resistance to implants. But she knew she wasn't ready for this decision to be his about her body. Vivian decided it was time for them to return to their medical family therapist. "Whose body is it, anyway?" she thought.

It was important for the therapist of this couple to help Vivian articulate what she wanted for her body after the mastectomy. Before the illness, Vivian was somewhere between comfortable and resigned to Alan taking a dominant role in decision making about most everything, including her body. However, her illness changed that dynamic. Vivian then felt the need for a therapist's support, to focus and express what she really wanted after the mastectomy. The therapy required sensitive steps to embolden Vivian, amplifying her strength and her confidence. At the same time, Alan needed considerable support while confronting his assumptions about Vivian, her needs and desires, and learning what it was like for Vivian to feel so little control.

Vivian made it clear in the therapy that she desperately wanted Alan's support during this crisis. Given her goals, a more openly challenging approach—having Alan publicly acknowledge that many of his motives met his own needs, apologize for his controlling nature, and turn all decisions about Vivian's body over to Vivian—might result in relationship strain or separation right at the time that Vivian most wants Alan to support her through the physical and emotional changes occurring in response to the illness. Not infrequently, an illness may challenge a couple's commitment to change together. In this case, the therapy challenged Alan's use of power and domination in their relationship by amplifying Vivian's voice and Alan's responsiveness to it.

Many chronic illnesses have disfiguring or dysfunctioning impact on parts of the body that are identified with sexual behavior and attractiveness. Family therapists working with couples coping with a chronic illness need to be particularly attentive to the shifts in sexual behaviors, attitudes, confidence, and identity that occur during the phases of a chronic illness. With Vivian and Alan, a thorough discussion of both partners' needs, desires, and comfort in their sexual relationship was essential if their intimacy was to survive. Alan, who had been frustrated with his lack of being able to do anything for Vivian to relieve her pain and suffering, felt that now he could help her do something to regain her confidence—have her look "normal." But Vivian was not at all sure this was what she wanted. She definitely wanted to regain a sexual relationship with Alan but was not sure the implants were for her.

Family therapists working with couples in which one partner has a chronic illness need to explore the ramifications for that particular illness on their sexual relationship. If the illness has caused a physical change to the patient's body, there needs to be discussion between the partners about how their sexual relationship can integrate these changes. Both partners should be encouraged to talk about the loss, the adjustments, and the fears of sexual/physical rejection or discomfort.

One of the most powerful developments in the treatment of sexual dysfunction related to chronic illness is the introduction of the medication, Viagra, to treat male erectile dysfunction. For some couples, Viagra has offered a cure for the mechanical problems that prevented a fully enjoyable sexual encounter. However, for many others, the medication raised both hopes and relational problems.

> On a recent day in a medical family therapy practice, three of six sessions involved some focus on Viagra. In the first, a Polish American Catholic woman expressed deep disappointment because the man she recently fell in love with had erectile dysfunction secondary to treatment for prostate cancer, and Viagra was not effective in treating the problem. In the second session, Viagra was effective some of the time for a man with diabetes. However, the Jewish couple's communication was tentative and strained any time it was not successful. Both were trapped by destructive gender prescriptions: The wife felt the problem might be her obesity; the man rejected this idea and felt he should be able to maintain an erection if he was stronger as a man. The couple began to avoid sexual contact in order to avoid these uncomfortable feelings. Both said their relationship suffered from this lack of intimacy.
>
> In the third session, a German American man with muscular dystrophy suffered from significant disabilities, having trouble standing or walking. He presented to therapy with his Italian American wife because she refused to have sex with him after discovering he had been using Viagra for the past 2 years against her wishes. Once she discovered the pills, she refused to have sex anymore, stating, "I feel like Pavlov's dog: He rings the bell and I pant. I'm not doing it anymore." Clearly, the medical intervention is only part of a larger biopsychosocial intervention that is needed with some couples who use Viagra.

Some chronic illnesses cause internal changes that can affect a sexual partner, such as depression and dementia. In any chronic illness, it is important for the family therapist to help each partner define what she or he is wanting in a sexual relationship with the changes in the couple's dynamics. For the patient with dementia, there still might be great enthusiasm for a sexual relationship. For the partner, that might be very difficult to consider. A skilled medical family therapist can help the partner of the demented patient talk with her or his loved one to try to ease the hurt or sense of sexual rejection. Given the physical, emotional, or cognitive changes that can result from chronic illness, it is critical to increase communication and help relieve patients' or partners' guilt that they are not fulfilling expected sexual roles.

CAREGIVING AND COUPLES' ROLES

Men and women generally are socialized differently to cope with the uncertainty and fear associated with illness. Many women seek support and may have trouble taking action; many men may take action or become angry to avoid the grief and fear that characterizes serious illness. Because women are often expected to take a caregiving role, they may experience a lack of support when they themselves are ill. Women with diabetes, for example, report significantly lower marital satisfaction than men who are ill. Cigoli, Binda, and Marta (1994) stated: "The low scores on the quality of marital relationships in diabetic wives show that these women feel they receive no support or protection from their husbands at a time when they are also more prone to suffering the anxieties that come with bringing up children" (p. 311). These researchers come to the stark conclusion that, "For the most part, men seem capable only of consuming, rather than providing care" (p. 312). We suggest that this conclusion is an oversimplification; that it is not men's "capabilities" that determine behavior when it is negligent, rather it is their gender role socialization. The conclusion of Cigoli et al. also grossly underestimates the instrumental care that many men provide so effectively.

When roles are consonant with expectations, illness does not require significant role change.

> Grace and Ernest were married for 40 years when Ernest began to show early signs of Parkinson's disease. Ernest had been a successful physician, admired by his peers and his community; Grace was a community and Jewish activist, as busy as her husband. As Ernest became more and more symptomatic, he retired and Grace began to cut back on her community leadership roles. Soon they were both confined to their home, dealing with the grueling and never-ending demands of Ernest's disease. Grace had difficulty accepting help from their adult children and especially from professionals outside the family. However, her role as caregiver for her husband fit comfortably with her view of herself and she embraced it as a meaningful, if painful, task for this stage of her life. Medical family therapy helped her to see that she was more effective as a caregiver for her husband if she took care of herself; that accepting outside help would allow her to stay in charge of her husband's care better and longer.

This situation was quite different from that of Angela and Bill.

Angela, from an Italian American family, had a long history of chronic illness and developed what looked like petit mal seizures. She was hospitalized for tests and found to have nonelectrical seizures (pseudoseizures). Referred for medical family therapy, she came to the first session with her German American husband. It became clear that she worked very hard to care for her husband and her adult children and was trapped by her gender socialization. She said, "I don't let my husband get the salt and pepper at dinner. It's my time to care for him." As Angela became more symptomatic from her kidney disease, her seizure activity increased. Over time, it emerged that whenever Angela became ill, Bill became intensely verbally abusive. He was enraged when she could not take care of him and was frightened of her illness.

The therapist diagnosed depression in Bill and persuaded him to begin an antidepressant medication. With the medication, support, and behavioral suggestions, Bill's abuse was eliminated, followed by Angela's seizure symptoms. The work then focused on Angela's difficulty with advocating for herself in the patient role, and Bill's allergy to his wife's illnesses. The therapist (Susan H. McDaniel) identified the illness, rather than the individuals, as the appropriate target for Bill's anger and Angela's frustration. She asked questions to understand what Angela and Bill each learned from their families and their culture about how men and women respond to illness. The couple's relationship improved significantly as they began to pull together to tend to the illness, rather than having the illness come between them. Both Angela and Bill achieved greater role flexibility. (McDaniel, 1997)

Balancing this dedication to communion with a sense of personal power and an acceptance of personal limitation is a goal for many women in medical family therapy. It is also important for her partner to come to see this new behavior as an asset to the relationship.

BALANCING AGENCY AND COMMUNION

Achieving greater role flexibility is essential to the goals of increasing and balancing agency and communion for both members of the couple in medical family therapy. Setting limits on caregiving and focusing on self-care is often a challenge for women who experience illness as well as women who are caregivers. Resentment over the demands of an illness, or a partner, can build over time without the woman feeling permission to acknowledge the difficulties or the burdens. Balancing this dedication to communion with a sense of personal power and an acceptance of personal limitation is a goal for many women in medical family therapy.

Men like Bill, in contrast, need to work on increasing communion and caregiving skills. Because there is not a societal imperative for men to talk about feelings of vulnerability, both patient and caregiving roles challenge male role socialization. Men may attend to the practical demands of an illness but feel less permission to process the experience. Being in touch with and expressing feelings is important to coping with both patient and caregiving roles. A man may need coaching about how to be a patient who both advocates for himself and listens to input from health professionals and caring family members. Also, men who take a primary caregiving role (like men who take a primary childrearing role) may receive an unusual amount of social support for being self-sacrificing while performing the very same tasks that go unnoticed by a female caregiver. Generally, the challenge for men is increasing openness to communion, and for his partner also to come to see this new behavior as an asset for the relationship.

Rigid gender roles will be challenged as a chronic or terminal illness progresses. It can be useful for the medical family therapist to list the demands of illness and who can best take care of what. This effort can help people play to their strengths and their own sense of agency rather than to some cultural script. Communication across the family can be another area of difficulty during a serious illness. It can be useful to explore what information is shared with whom, and who is in charge of the communication. Encouraging both members of the couple to have a few individuals with whom they can be honest is part of the self-care of patient and caregiver. Communication with extended family may need to be negotiated. When a husband's father is ill, for example, does the husband check on his father, or is it his wife who calls or helps with caregiving? There is no one right answer to these situations; much is embedded in the nature of these relationships. Medical family therapy offers an opportunity to examine how caring is expressed and by whom, ensuring these decisions are made based on love and commitment rather than because of socially prescribed roles.

Just as role flexibility is important to couples' successful adaptation to illness, flexibility is also important for the feminist medical family therapist. Direct communication with the physician or nurse practitioner is an essential part of systemically oriented medical family therapy. This involves managing any actual or perceived power imbalances through competence, flexibility, relational sophistication, and occasional constructive confrontation. The medical family therapist always works to build collaborative relationships and may use the traditional medical protocol for consultation and communication—requesting input regarding assessment, communicating clearly the need for the physician's involvement in the collaborative care of the couple, and making suggestions for the comprehensive treatment of the patient.

Finally, the feminist medical family therapist must attend to his or her own sense of agency and communion. It is challenging and difficult work to help people face illness or death and to work within a traditionally sexist, hierarchical medical system. In addition to the usual self-care strategies, medical family therapists must attend to issues about their own health and illness histories and the gender scripting they themselves have experienced. A consultation group of supportive colleagues is essential in sorting out difficult clinical issues and about problems regarding gender and power for couples and for the health care team.

Medical family therapy allows us to integrate the mind and the body with sensitivity to gender similarities and differences that can enhance or diminish the experience. The impact of chronic illness not only threatens a couple's former sense of equilibrium but can also provide an opportunity for positive change. Gender-informed coping strategies can be tested, questioned, and modified. Opportunities for resolving old rifts, establishing new priorities, and forging new intimacies for a couple facing biological threat become available if the couple is motivated and supported in making these changes. Feminist medical family therapists are conscious of the dimensions gender, power, and privilege that can enhance or diminish the experience of coping with illness for patients, couples, and the health care team.

REFERENCES

Bakan, D. (1969). *The duality of human existence*. Chicago: Rand-McNally.

Candib, L. M. (1995). *Medicine and the family: A feminist perspective*. New York: Basic Books.

Cigoli, V., Binda, W., & Marta, E. (1994). Marital relationships and Type II diabetes. *Family Systems Medicine, 12*, 295–314.

Commonwealth Fund. (2000). Many men dangerously out of touch with the health care system. In *The Commonwealth Fund 1998 survey of men's and women's health*. New York: Author.

Deaton, A. V., & Olbrisch, M. E. (1987). Adaptive noncompliance: Parents as experts and decision makers in the treatment of pediatric asthma patients. *Advances in Developmental and Behavioral Pediatrics, 8*, 205–234.

Goldner, V. (1991). Toward a critical relational theory of gender. *Psychoanalytic Dialogues, 1*, 249–272.

Helgeson, V. S. (1994). Relation of agency and communion to well-being: Evidence and potential explanations. *Psychological Bulletin, 116*, 412–428.

Kiecolt-Glaser, J. K., & Newton, T. L. (2001). Marriage and health: His and hers. *Psychological Bulletin, 127*, 472–503.

McDaniel, S. H. (1997). Trapped inside a body without a voice: Two cases of somatic fixation. In S. H. McDaniel, J. Hepworth, & W. J. Doherty (Eds.), *The shared experience of illness* (pp. 263–273). New York: Basic Books.

McDaniel, S. H., Campbell, T. L., & Seaburn, D. (1990). *Family-oriented primary care: A manual for medical providers*. New York: Springer-Verlag.

McDaniel, S. H., & Hepworth, J. (in press). Family psychology in primary care: Managing issues of power and dependency through collaboration. In R. Frank, S. H. McDaniel, J. Bray, & M. Heldring (Eds.), *Primary care psychology*. Washington, DC: American Psychological Association.

McDaniel, S. H., Hepworth, J., & Doherty, W. J. (1992). *Medical family therapy: A biopsychosocial approach to families with health problems*. New York: Basic Books.

McDaniel, S. H., Hepworth, J., & Doherty, W. J. (1996). *The shared experience of illness: Stories of patients, families, and their therapists*. New York: Basic Books.

Rolland, J. S. (1994). *Families, illness, and disability*. New York: Basic Books.

21

THE WOMEN'S CENTER: FEMINISM IN THE TREATMENT OF AIDS

ANITRA PIVNICK

Just as family therapy expanded the focus of psychotherapy from the individual to the family system, this chapter describes a model of treatment that expands the system of care from the treatment of individual families to the provision of services to a broader community. I describe the ways in which feminist culture shaped the inception, the services, and the spirit of The Women's Center, a program in the Bronx, New York, for HIV-positive women, their children, family members, and friends. The Center's program illustrates how, for disempowered women, support from a larger feminist community may be a prerequisite before feminist family therapy can be effective.

The Women's Center was created by a team of professional and community women and is therefore distinct in many ways from a typical mental health institution. Today the Women's Center is a mental health and primary health care clinic serving more than 500 people a year. The array of services evolved from the stated needs of women attending the program rather than from people identified as experts in the field. These services include the following: individual, couples, and family therapy; case management; primary and prenatal care; Adult Day Treatment; peer support groups; an Outreach/HIV Prevention Program; Permanency Planning; transportation; child care; daily nutritious meals; emergency food and funds; The Children's Center, a therapeutic after-school and summer program for HIV-infected and -affected children; and job training of participants as counselors and AIDS educators who subsequently become paid staff in the Center.

As an anthropologist I assume that individual behavior originates in and is perpetuated through social activities and cultural contexts. Anthropologists also assume that all knowledge is constructed, including science and medicine. Culture, as a system of shared meanings, is seen as having a fundamental influence on behavior. To understand the effects of culture on behavior is to understand the social, economic, and political contexts that influence meanings. Therefore, I begin with the sociohistorical climate that existed when the Women's Center was founded. I then describe the Women's Center, from its inception in 1987 as a modest research project to its current form as a comprehensive and integrated service center for HIV-positive women and their families. Throughout, I highlight the feminist philosophy and family focus that defined the evolution of the Center.

CONSTRUCTIONS OF WOMEN IN THE AIDS DISCOURSE

In 1987, at the time the Women's Center was created, public discourse about children with AIDS constructed the disease in a way that held the mothers of such children as the direct source of infection, solely responsible for the illness and the deaths of their children. In opposition to this view, some researchers suggested that institutionalized sexism and the stigma of drug use were the implicit factors governing the construction of drug-using HIV-positive women as conduits for the infection of their children and their sexual partners. However, once these mothers were designated vectors of transmission, they were considered undeserving of discrete attention (Anastos & Marte, 1989; Mitchell, 1988).

Throughout the 1980s, public discourse about the births of "AIDS babies" proliferated. Drug-using women were portrayed as selfish, drug-stupefied individuals who lacked moral character and, only secondarily, education about AIDS (Arras, 1990; Levine & Dubler, 1990). Criminal cases were brought against drug-using pregnant women for child abuse ("The Most Tragic Victims of AIDS," 1989). During this period of heated public debate, health care providers observed that providing women with knowledge about the possibly fatal infection of their offspring did not appear to deter them from bearing children (Mitchell, 1988; Wofsy, 1987).

As medical researchers prepared to investigate how HIV-positive women made the decision to have a child, political factions gathered momentum for a national battle over reproductive rights. Public agencies (funding sources for research and direct care) produced guidelines for counseling HIV-positive women. These guidelines included the suggestion that pregnancy be postponed in an effort to reduce perinatal transmission (U.S. Department of Health and Human Services, 1985). Discussion of termination of pregnancy was avoided in the guidelines because of the public debate about abortion. However, according to women who were attending the Women's Center at that time, HIV-positive women who had already conceived were urged to terminate their pregnancies.

There was much discussion about why HIV-positive women decided to have children. Within the social domain of *morality*, public discourse implicitly conveyed the notion that drug- using, HIV-positive women who bear children are child abusers, and as such ought to be subject to punishment under law. Within the social domain of *medicine*, these same women were characterized as conveyors of health risk to their children and to their sexual partners. Within the social domain of *finance*, women who chose to bear children in the context of HIV infection were identified as a source of excessive health care expenditures, and therefore guilty of draining the public coffers.

These outcries all held to the notion that HIV-positive women were responsible *as individuals* for child abuse, health risks, and escalating health care costs. Even the most benign explanations assumed that these women did not comprehend the principles of perinatal transmission; or that they were victims of drug abuse, and therefore morally weak; or that they lacked self-esteem, and therefore aspired to the positive cultural and social identifications available to them only through the bearing of children. In all of these explanatory models, the men with whom these children were conceived were omitted almost entirely from analyses. Similarly forgotten were the structure and processes of poor, ghetto-dwelling families described long before the AIDS epidemic by anthropologists, sociologists, political analysts, and mental health professionals (Liebow, 1967; Minuchin, 1967; Piven & Cloward, 1971; Stack, 1970).

THE WOMEN'S CENTER

In 1987, the Centers for Disease Control funded a modest research project to be added to two ongoing medical research projects. As a part of the effort to understand the social and cultural aspects of HIV transmission, the Women's Center was conceived as a field station for social science research, structured as a peer support group and located in a methadone clinic. Project staff members were charged with (a) conducting research to identify social and cultural aspects of HIV transmission and (b) providing women participants with an opportunity to speak freely about drug use, HIV infection, and any other matters they wished to bring to group meetings.

The results of this research contrasted dramatically with the views that demonized HIV-positive mothers. The research found that women's decisions about whether or not to carry a pregnancy to term were related to whether they had been forced to give up children in the past (Pivnick, Jacobson, Eric, Mulvihill, & Drucker, 1991). All of the women attending the Center had a history of drug abuse, thus most of them had been forced to give up one or more children for some period of time by the legal system.

The study revealed that all terminations of pregnancy occurred among women who had been in residence with at least one of her children for the child's entire life. Of the pregnancies occurring among women who elected to bear, 75% were among women who had not lived with any child for the entirety of the child's life ($p = .005$). Decisions to terminate were also found to be significantly associated with the length of time the woman had been aware of her serostatus ($p < .02$) and the number of prior abortions she had had ($p < .02$). In this study, historical residential separations of mothers from their children were found to affect women's subsequent reproductive decisions. Thus, if a woman had never lived with any of her children, she was more likely to carry her child to term, despite the risk of infecting that child. These women reported that they saw their current pregnancy as a last chance to "do it right this time."

FROM RESEARCH TO SERVICE

The research agenda was soon eclipsed by the women's needs. Their problems ranged from threats of incarceration in the struggle to regain custody of their children to the painful experience of dying of AIDS. At the time, clinical medicine had little to offer. Facing their final months of life was made even more unbearable by histories of separation from children and intensified conflict with family members. In addition to their own suffering, these women experienced many deaths among members of their larger community now devastated by AIDS.

In another study conducted in the Women's Center, female methadone patients reported significant numbers of HIV-infected members in their social networks (Pivnick, 1996). Of the total of 715 siblings (all participants plus their siblings), 9.7% were reported to be HIV positive. One hundred twenty-six participants reported lifetime knowledge of 105 persons living with HIV infection, 63 AIDS deaths, and 44 deaths by violent means among a total of 5,053 known relatives of all ages. These statistics illustrate the tragic toll that the HIV epidemic has taken on this community of people in the Bronx.

Kathleen Eric, a nurse and psychodramatist, was the first director of the Women's Center. Her original mandate was to convene a support group for female methadone patients whose drug use was most uncontrolled. She was joined by Dooley Worth, an anthropologist; Brenda Chabon, a psychologist; and myself. At first the group was attended by a small number of women. Following the first 6 months of group meetings, three additional Women's Center groups were formed: a group of drug-using female methadone patients and community women, a group of Spanish-speaking HIV-positive women, and a group of HIV-positive and AIDS-diagnosed drug-free women and men.

Gender had been the principle of inclusion in the formation of the Center, and as the culture of the Center evolved, gender became a unifying force transcending race, ethnicity, class, and occupational status. This change occurred as a result of the combined efforts of the staff and a group of highly motivated and competent HIV-positive women, including Ruth Figueroa, Carmen Rotger, Nora Candelario, and Verna Palmer. These community women initiated outreach, identified problems and their solutions, and collaborated on the content and structure of the evolving program.

The banding together of women of different ethnic/racial backgrounds, different socioeconomic circumstances, and different drug-use histories— in a context of public vilification of HIV-positive women—expressed the supremacy of common feminist concerns and culture. The putting aside of race and class differences was also no doubt influenced by the urgency of the AIDS epidemic. HIV-positive group members communicated needs related to entitlements for services, therapy, case management, and the reeducation of spouses about safer sex and condom use. Staff responded, and grants were written to fund services.

The willingness to divert attention from research to service contributed significantly to the methadone community members' willingness to share experiences and information about sensitive personal matters, including contraceptive practices, drug use, illegal activities, and HIV infection. Although I believe the absence of emphasis on race and class was strongly influenced by the extremity of the circumstances in which the community residents found themselves, there were qualities specific to the women who founded the Women's Center that also profoundly determined its direction.

Notions of nurturance predicated on women's traditional roles were reflected in the recognition that child care and food were fundamental to the formation of the group and its ability to retain its members. Because drug treatment has not been historically delivered with the needs of women in mind, there was no child care in the methadone clinic despite the fact that women were required to meet regularly with their counselors.

Because Kathleen Eric was a trained psychodramatist, it was her clinical perspective that provided the foundation for the initial group process. Psychodrama, conceived by Moreno (1946), has two principal requisites: activity and spontaneity. The requirement for activity means that instead of *describing* a relationship or a problem, participants *enact* it through the assignment of roles and dialogue derived from life circumstances. This enactment or performance encourages the actors to feel and then observe their own behavior. The notion of spontaneity requires an emotionally authentic expression of feeling.

Sociodrama is an additional aspect of psychodramatic enactment. Sociodrama utilizes themes that are common to group participants rather than concentrating on individual circumstances as the material for enactments (Moreno, 1953). These themes are elicited by the director and presented to the group for enactment in the form of improvisations. Kathleen Eric decided to focus on sociodrama because all of the participants shared the social context of HIV infection.

As the group process evolved, the HIV-positive women soon suggested a coeducational group so they could include their male partners. The women realized that, within a male- dominant culture, many did not have the power to change the men in their lives. The Center enlisted responsible men who could then hold other men accountable. Together, staff and group members decided the principle of participation would continue to be one of incorporation rather than division into groups defined by gender, sexual preference, or stage of HIV infection. Such divisions characterize many HIV/AIDS peer support groups.

The group offered men the opportunity to participate, but the invitation had several provisos. One was the unspoken acknowledgment that the activity was directed by feminist concerns. Women were running the show. Accordingly, they specified principles of conduct such as nonviolence, a commitment to communication as a means of change, and the persistent effort to understand the ways in which gender influenced activities such as sex, needle-sharing, relationships, and parenting.

From the beginning, female members expressed an interest in learning sociodramatic techniques. This educational enterprise was encouraged as a means of retaining members, as a means of training peer facilitators, and as a therapeutic activity. Participants and leaders-in-training learned to tolerate silence, to recognize that even when nothing appears to be happening, *something is*. They learned not to censure participation. A participant whose enactment seemed to lack authentic feeling was understood to be potentially awakening feelings in others. The facilitators-in-training learned that squelching any mode of participation conveyed the message that participation is a test, that a member had to find something to enact that the facilitator and the group valued rather than searching out his or her own feelings.

The exercise of personal agency was also expressed through an emphasis on governance. That is, members insisted that they learn to facilitate groups themselves. The therapist was required to share the power of the therapeutic role not only with the group as the agent of change but also with members who wanted to learn how to become leaders themselves. The participation of some women in Narcotics Anonymous provided another level of influence and was expressed through consciously formulated group-determined rules of operation read aloud at the beginning of each group and enforced by members.

Based on both theoretical and personal convictions, Kathleen Eric insisted that actions, enactments, and exchanges must be resolved positively. Constructive integrations were to be encouraged. She promoted the reduction of anxiety. In these circumstances, there was a significant increase in spontaneity, insight, understanding, and the desire to find new ways to deal with old situations. It became clear that people, particularly drug-free young people who faced imminent death, were in need of help to structure and understand feelings. They were not in need of someone to control their feelings or behavior. The idea was to be as flexible as possible, to direct the content as little as possible, and to use enactments to teach technique to interested members.

In contrast to other efforts at HIV education and prevention, our program soon found that the constant repetition of the need to use condoms was unnecessary. The open discussion of sexual, personal, and social matters in a group of people whose commonality was their HIV infection, not their gender, sexual preference, or marital status, was awe-inspiring. No topic was considered taboo. Because the group was heterogeneous, participants were called on to find a means of relating to the problems and issues of others whom they might not have previously perceived as having anything in common with themselves. For example, a female member's painful experience with a gynecologist who was fearful of HIV infection and insensitive to her pain became the topic of group interaction for 2½ hours. Men listened, moved by her story, and found ways to relate to her dilemma.

A decision was made to provide a full, nutritious meal after the group. In addition to the nutritional requirements of immune-compromised people, members felt that the intense group process needed to be continued and resolved in a more relaxed manner through the sharing of a meal. Because child care had been provided for group members from the beginning of the program, children also participated in the meal.

Because the group was open, participation was not limited to a predetermined number of people. Consequently, the size of the group varied considerably. In some sessions there were 15 people; in others there were as many as 60. People were not penalized if they were not present for reasons of illness, hospitalization, or just because they had temporarily tired of the process. A staff person telephoned participants if they did not attend group and had not communicated their reasons. They were not ostracized from future groups and were always welcomed warmly when they returned, as they would have been as members of a family or a close group of friends. Kathleen Eric believed the opportunity for reentry should be guaranteed. This policy was (and is) facilitated by the fact that the Women's Center was (and is) grant-supported rather than dependent on third-party reimbursement.

Finally, because of women's focus on familial concerns, and because of the presence of women's partners in the coeducational groups, Kathleen

Eric decided to invite two family therapists to attend group. One of the two, Nellie Villegas, is now the clinical director of the Women's Center. The presence of the family therapists in the groups provided participants with an opportunity to get to know the therapists and to make appointments. The therapists were provided with the opportunity to observe participants' issues in a group setting, thereby extending their understanding of the social and cultural context of drug abuse and HIV/AIDS among this group of people.

Inviting family therapists rather than therapists focused on individuals had a profound impact on the history of the Women's Center. Family therapy became the central therapeutic perspective in the Women's Center. The construction of the client as a parent and family member, rather than as a decontextualized individual, greatly influenced the content and design of programs. From the outset, children were included in treatment. More recently, the Children's Center was created for orphaned and HIV-infected and -affected children and adolescents.

Young people's participation in the Children's Center has proved to be a positive incentive for their mothers' engagement in family treatment. Nellie Villegas notes that mothers whose children participate in the Children's Center are highly motivated to engage in family therapy initially on behalf of their offspring, and ultimately on behalf of themselves and other family members (Villegas, 2000). This outcome speaks to the value of comprehensive, *integrated* family-based services as well as the advisability of addressing the social and academic needs of young family members from a therapeutic perspective.

Our programs for prevention are similarly family-based. In a recent study of Children's Center participants, Nellie Villegas and I observed a course of influence from parents who were (are) Women's Center clients to children, a course that illuminates the importance of family services and a family orientation in the context of HIV infection (Pivnick & Villegas, 2000). Recent research literature describes inner-city orphans and HIV-affected children as at highest risk based on their histories of parental drug abuse, inner-city poverty, and HIV illness and death. However, despite numerous emotional and social risks, our participants do not conform to the standard description of this population in the areas of sexual and drug use behavior.

Our young participants attributed their successful avoidance of high-risk behavior to their parents' membership in the Women's Center program. This process of instruction in which parents are educated by staff and peers and, in turn, educate their children is the foundation of an intergenerational model of prevention. This model defines the direction of communication from program to parent to child, and it identifies parental concern and community collaboration as elements in a causal chain that results in informed children who practice safer sex. The children's own activity sustains and reinforces the educational content as they, in turn, extend the message of safer sex to their peers. Although depressed and at highest risk for a plethora of undesirable behaviors, our young participants were not abusing substances. They were committed to the practice of safer sex, and they have remained connected to the Women's Center community, the locus of activities that empowered and educated their parents.

Male responses to female authority are telling expressions of gendered power relations. Over the course of the 12 years of the Women's Center program, male social workers and case managers have been employed. For some of these men, clinical supervision is the activity through which power relations are most energetically expressed. One male social worker, after having withheld critically important information from his clinical supervisor about a breach of confidentiality, was asked for an explanation for his omission. He had none to offer. He reported that he did not know why he did not communicate important matters to the clinical director. He "just chose to keep some things to himself."

Other men, however, have abandoned struggles based on gendered power relations and have become solid members of the Women's Center community. These men engage in the therapeutic services, renounce violence as a means of conflict resolution, and coexist with women in authority without rancor or divisive maneuvering. Such men engage in a process of acculturation in which they accept and integrate the feminist values that are the foundation of the Women's Center.

In retrospect, the Women's Center has held up well as a project designed by women and for women. We remain committed to family treatment and comprehensive, integrated services. Multigenerational education for HIV prevention has proved an important contribution in an inner-city community with few activities aimed at prevention. Family therapy is particularly effective in a setting in which children's academic and social needs are directly addressed. Because funding for comprehensive services is difficult to sustain in an atmosphere of fiscal constraint, the additional effort required to provide food, emergency funds, and after-school services can be daunting. However, the success of the Women's Center speaks to the desirability of collaborations premised on women's cultural values and to the power of communities created by principles of nurturance and inclusion.

REFERENCES

Anastos, K., & Marte, C. (1989, Winter). Women—the missing persons in the AIDS epidemic. *Health/PAC Bulletin*, 6–13.

Arras, J. D. (1990). AIDS and reproductive decisions: Having children in fear and trembling. *The Milbank Quarterly, 68,* 353–382.

Levine, C., & Dubler, N. (1990). Uncertain risks and bitter realities: The reproductive choices of HIV-infected women. *The Milbank Quarterly, 68,* 321–352.

Liebow, E. (1967). *Tally's corner.* Boston: Little, Brown.

Minuchin, S. (1967). *Families of the slums.* New York: Basic Books.

Mitchell, J. (1988). Women, AIDS, and public policy. *AIDS and Public Policy, 3,* 50–53.

Moreno, J. L. (1946). *Psychodrama* (Vol. 1). New York: Beacon House.

Moreno, J. L. (1953). *Who shall survive? Foundations of sociometry, group psychotherapy and sociodrama.* New York: Beacon House.

The most tragic victims of AIDS: Thousands of children. (1989). *The New York Times,* p. B4.

Piven, F. F., & Cloward, R. (1971). *Regulating the poor: The functions of public welfare.* New York: Vintage Books.

Pivnick, A. (1996). Kinchart-sociograms as a method for describing the social networks of drug using persons. In E. Rahdert, (Ed.), *Treatment for drug-exposed women and their children: Advances in research methodology* (NIDA Research Monograph No. 165). Washington, DC: U.S. Department of Health and Human Services, National Institutes of Health.

Pivnick, A., Jacobson, A., Eric, K., Mulvihill, M., & Drucker, E. (1991). Reproductive decisions among HIV-infected, drug using women: The importance of mother–child coresidence. *Medical Anthropology Quarterly, 5,* 153–169.

Pivnick, A., & Villegas, N. (2000). Resilience and risk: Childhood and uncertainty in the AIDS epidemic. *Culture, Medicine and Psychiatry, 24,* 101–136.

Stack, C. (1970). *All our kin: Strategies for survival in a Black community.* New York: Harper & Row.

U.S. Department of Health and Human Services, Centers for Disease Control. (1985). Recommendations for assisting in the prevention of perinatal transmission of human T lymphotrophic virus Type III/lymphadenopathy associated virus and acquired immunodeficiency syndrome. *Morbidity and Mortality Weekly Report, 34,* 721–731.

Villegas, N. (2000). *Family therapy and a therapeutic afterschool program: The value and meanings of co-located services.* Unpublished manuscript.

Wofsy, C. (1987). Human immunodeficiency virus infection in women. *Journal of the American Medical Association, 257,* 2074–2076.

VI

ADDRESSING SOCIOPOLITICAL FORCES

22

CREATING COLLECTIVES OF LIBERATION

RHEA V. ALMEIDA

The *cultural context model* (CCM) is an expanded family paradigm. It offers a clear analysis of the social patterns that contribute to the dislocation of family and community life. This paradigm offers solutions to families through the creation of a community that supports a *collective* consciousness of liberation. This collective knowledge is necessary to dismantle linkages of power, privilege, and oppression. The model has seven components: orientation, sponsorship, socioeducation, culture circles, family process, graduation, and community advocacy. In this chapter, three components are emphasized: socioeducation, culture circles, and family process. Clinical vignettes are used to explicate this approach. For a more extensive description of the model, see Almeida, Woods, Messineo, and Font (1998).

The major objective of the CCM is to create a collective experience that moves systems and individuals within those systems. A guiding premise is that the liberation of women is intrinsically tied to the accountability of men, and likewise the liberation of oppressed peoples is linked to the accountability of those in power. Therefore, dismantling the power imbalances and restructuring the power that exists between men and women from diverse social locations is a critical aspect of therapeutic change.

In contrast to the CCM, the structure of individual, couples, or even family therapy limits the experience of change to the interior boundary of family life. This type of structural change maintains the status quo around the notion of change as a force driven by individual action. The CCM provides the individual woman with a coalition of women, thereby increasing her power. Simultaneously, we provide the individual man with a coalition of men who will challenge male privilege and also support him as he struggles to change. These coalitions alter the very boundaries and power distribution of family life.

CULTURE CIRCLES

The term *culture circles*, borrowed from Freire (1972), describes a heterogeneous helping community that includes families who come for treatment, a team of therapists, and sponsors from the community. Prior to beginning to work in this model, therapists must first train four to six adults (e.g., graduate students, church or civic leaders). The training consists of 12 weeks of "critical conscience" training in the broad social forces that constrain people's lives, for example, institutionalized racism, male dominance, homophobia, and class discrimination. After their training, these individuals serve as sponsors for the families who come for treatment. As sponsors, they serve three important purposes, outlined below.

1. Sponsors function as partners with therapists. The roles that sponsors serve are multiple, but all contribute to a context of accountability and support within and outside of the therapeutic encounter. The specifics of a sponsorship program are described elsewhere (Almeida & Bograd, 1990). However, several fundamental concepts deserve mention here. Sponsors are men from the community who support nonviolence and equity and form partnerships with men who engage in violence and patterns of domination. Their goal is to mentor these men into a life of liberation through equity and justice.

2. Sponsors serve to break down the barriers of privacy that maintain male domination by expanding conversations with men about family life to a community process. Through help, men view the impact of their behavior on their partners, children, and extended family members.

3. Sponsors model an expanded notion of masculinity that includes vulnerability, nurturing, gentleness, and empathy for others. They also model respect for women, children, people of color, sexual minorities, and others who are different from themselves. The notion of accountability as it relates to power is a central theme for sponsors. Male sponsors are crucial links to expanding notions of gender within family and community life. The goal of the smaller culture circles is to help families understand how their personal problems relate to the oppressive forces within their broader social context. After the sponsors are in place, families can be accepted into treatment.

At the point of intake, each family is introduced to two therapists: one who will be behind the one-way mirror, and the other who will be in the room with the family. After a basic genogram is constructed with the entire family present, all family members join small, ongoing culture circles. These small culture circles are same-sex groups made up of members of multiple families. Within these small culture circles, clients are oriented to our model of therapy.

We create our small culture circles by separating families by gender after the first interview. If children or adolescents are present, they are connected with others of their age. Families within the same culture circle might happen to share different life problems. For example, some might experience difficulty at work, whereas others may not have work; some might experience violence, whereas others may struggle with single parenthood.

The families are not consciously joined by diagnostic category or presenting problem. It is our belief that this type of segregation around presented problem, although intended to create community through shared experience, in fact further compartmentalizes one's sense of being. It reforms the identity of a family/individual around "pathology" and punctuates time around "the problem" rather than around alternate life stories and themes of liberation.

When the family members are assigned to the small culture circles, each member is assigned a same-sex mentor. The point of this mentorship is to help each family member develop a critical consciousness through the process of socioeducation. Socioeducation helps clients increase their awareness of the ways in which cultural ideas about gender, power, class, and race construct relationships. Families remain in these small culture circles for a period of 8 weeks.

Following the socioeducational process, family members are invited into the larger culture circles. Most of the work of therapy within the CCM occurs in larger same-sex culture circles. Intermittent family or couple sessions are done with the entire community consisting of both men's and women's culture circles.

Very generally speaking, women's culture circles empower members by helping them prioritize their needs, dreams, and desires at a level they have been taught to reserve only for others. They are further encouraged to experience the full range of emotions, especially anger, in healthy ways. Empowerment also includes different types of social action that mobilize women in families. This would include women helping women in court action, advocating for improved work conditions, sharing in the daily dilemmas of raising children, accessing a high level of medical care, learning to celebrate their lives, and working as a community to better the lives of women and children.

These types of social endeavors entail learning many new skills within the context of a continuously expanding critical conscience. Expecting and ensuring that men as partners, fathers, brothers, or sons are part of this alliance is a necessary element of this liberation process. The larger circles include one or two sponsors, a few newly entering families, and many more members who have been working in the model for a longer time. The goal of the larger culture circles is to help the families find solutions that liberate them through both empowerment and accountability.

In the larger culture circle, the role of therapist behind the mirror is to assist the therapist in the room toward achieving a sense of balance between the process of accountability and empowerment. This process is achieved through the discussion of liberation-based stories, letters of accountability, intergenerational legacies, rituals, and concrete interventions designed to assist clients in moving beyond traditional family/gender/race-based loyalties.

With each client, the therapist in the room is attending to the way in which the client interacts with a wide range of people: her or his family, other members of the culture circles, and sponsors. In addition, the therapist is monitoring how willing the client is to expand her or his gendered, racial, and sexual preference norms (Font, Dolan-Del Vecchio, & Almeida, 1998). Throughout the process of therapy there are at least one or more therapists (some who are students in training) behind the mirror helping to attain balance around these complex experiences of diversity.

This process of separating the family into larger gatherings of men and women who create a community together emphasizes the notion of a family as an open unit. It also rapidly shifts expectations for change away from the psychology of individual autonomy to that of a collective consciousness: the collective of social origin within which all families are located (Crenshaw, 1994). Change within this context is community driven. We believe that it is especially important to work with families in this broader context because it is at this point of social location that many experiences of oppression and of power and privilege are generated (Almeida, 1993; Almeida et al., 1998).

SOCIOEDUCATION

Socioeducation is the presentation of didactic materials to clients in an effort to raise consciousness around issues of gender, race, culture, and sexual orientation. This process begins in the smaller culture circles in which these issues are dealt with in a general way. It continues in the large culture circles that tailor the discussions to the specific life problems of the families in the circle.

Freire (1972) said that critical consciousness is exemplified by an experience of living within which historical/cultural prescriptions for making choices are not blindly followed as though they are "the natural order of things." For example, a blind belief in the idea that men are aggressive by nature is the antithesis of critical consciousness. Critical consciousness requires an inquiry into this "cultural myth" and a recognition that adherence to this notion is an act of choice and not simply fate or nature.

Freire tied critical consciousness to economic and political systems, noting that domination and oppression essentially rely on a social order within which critical consciousness is replaced by a "paternalism" of the oppressing class. Within this kind of system, learning/education is synonymous with indoctrination. Education for critical consciousness, in contrast, dismantles indoctrination and oppression, supporting inquiry and dialogues instead, and is therefore the foundation for liberation and democracy.

In preparation for this process, we ask clients numerous questions regarding the continuum of male and female norms that helped shape their family over time. For example, how did the women and men in their family respond similarly/differently to loss, adolescent sexuality, adult sexuality, success, life-cycle transitions, migration, intermarriage, work, loss/lack of employment, and racial sameness/difference?

A combination of video clips, books, articles, and musical lyrics expands the therapeutic conversation. These socioeducational materials particularize a number of issues relating to the dismantling of gender, race, culture, and sexual orientation proscriptions. Socioeducation begins to shift clients' awareness toward a balancing of the personal and the political, the intrapsychic and the social, and from interior experience to exterior experience.

Consider a vignette from the movie *The Great Santini*. In this movie male domination and female subordination are normalized within family life. The Great Santini's wife implores the children to attend to their father's needs and desires. They salute him upon his arrival from duty at the airstrip. They eat their family dinner with all of the focus, service, and conversation centered on the "The Great Santini." He then challenges his 17-year-old son to a game of basketball and loses. In order to regain his sense of masculinity, he assaults his son and wife.

What ensues is a typical family drama. The son is outraged and dares to confront his father. At first, the mother challenges the father, who threatens to hit her if she does not respect him, and he does kick her. She makes an unsuccessful effort to challenge the morality of his behavior. Then the mother tries to get her fallen son to forgive his father, because his father "loves him but is simply not accustomed to losing." The son counters her position by expressing a lack of respect for his father and questions the meaning of a father's love in this context.

Sons in this position are at great risk to continue the male legacy of violence. The role of the mother is pivotal to the continued legacy of male domination—the sanctioned role as *culture bearer* (Almeida & Durkin,

1999). In the movie, the wife attempts to absorb the family anxiety through reframing the traditional masculine norms into a more palatable legacy for her son, that is, "he's not accustomed to losing." This strategy is commonly used by women who have little or no power. When women begin to counter this position, they are often ostracized and restricted from access to the privileges offered within the constraints of heterosexual partnering.

This is a critical juncture for change in families. The context of the culture circles, with its support of women by women, changes a woman's power position vis-à-vis the men in her family and her community. From this new power position, she has the opportunity to challenge male dominance without being totally isolated.

Within the men's culture circle, similar change is occurring. Men who support these traditional norms are challenged by a community of men and are required to be accountable to a different set of norms. These norms represent gender equity within diverse cultures and prescribe an ethic of caring that is relational. This is the point at which the traditional norms of patriarchy can be challenged and transformed into expanded ways of being men (Dolan-Del Vecchio, 1997). This is crucial to the liberation of women in all spheres of their lives, and to greater spiritual embodiment for men as well.

These conversations between the members of the culture circle and the team of therapists in response to a video (or other stimulus) are extremely useful to the dismantling of traditional norms of family life for women, men, girls, and boys. The discussions differ on the basis of the different types of cultures represented in the circle. For example, a Chinese woman, ensconced in tradition, might say that in her culture, norms concerning hierarchy and respect based on gender and age are essential to family life (Almeida, 1990). Therefore, her role as a good wife/mother is to respect her husband and explain the husband's behavior in a positive manner to their older son, in order for the younger children to understand the importance of respect and hierarchy.

To address this cultural dilemma, we carefully select video clips and writings by Chinese feminists. These clips depict powerful Chinese women who challenge tradition and maintain cultural legacies that do *not* support male domination and female subordination. Films such as *The Joy Luck Club*, *The Wedding Banquet*, and the *Slayed Dragon* are some examples. Members of the culture circle can then draw from this knowledge to challenge the traditional proscriptions for women while simultaneously creating a strong context of support for cultural diversity.

Socioeducation also serves to educate the White members of the circle about commonly held myths relating to people of color: for example, the idea that all Chinese women are comfortable with subordination, or that heterosexuality is the only type of partnering within Chinese culture. Similarly, an African American might say that the history of slavery requires that women honor the status of men to counter the racism experienced in the public domain of men's lives. The circle might present films such as *Warrior Marks*, *Straight Out of Brooklyn*, and *Celebration of Our Lives*, in which a number of African American women challenge the entire way in which even the civil rights movement obscured their visibility as freedom fighters.

Another commonly presented dilemma is the culture of religion. For example, many women and men of the Islamic faith will argue in favor of the spiritual necessity to veil their adolescent daughters or ascribe the concept of female enslavement to the Koran. We use videotapes of some of our Muslim sponsors and notable Arab feminists who accurately challenge patriarchal interpretations of the Koran that neglect the simple fact that Mohammed had only daughters and honored every single one of them. Similarly, a movie titled *Morning Voices* depicts the clashes that confront young women of the Muslim faith who need all the strength they can gather to survive in a Western anti-Muslim culture while simultaneously battling with their own family and community to carve an identity across new frontiers.

Members of the culture circle, steeped in this new knowledge, can begin respectfully to have conversations regarding the intersection of gender and culture. We include a particular knowledge base surrounding each culture. It is not sufficient to read articles on ethnicity or ask clients to explain their culture, because often their reference point will echo the lack of a critical consciousness.

We also encourage participants to question each other about gendered norms within family life. For example, "In your culture, who is expected to educate children regarding the rules of relationships?" "How are children taught to respect elders, fathers, mothers, uncles, and aunts?" "Are children taught to respect all elders regardless of class and society?" "Who gets blamed when children do not follow these expected rules of society?" It becomes apparent through such dialogue that in most cultures, wives/mothers are expected to socialize children according to patriarchal standards that excuse abuse/misuse of power behaviors of the man in the house. Women who challenge that role are seen as less than perfect mothers, wives, or daughters.

Articulating the norms that maintain patterns of domination and subordination in families is crucial to experiences of liberation. The therapeutic alliance for such change can be between the mother and her son, the mother and other women, or the mother and other men who support more flexible ideas about gender. At times, the discussion might illustrate how culture shapes certain responses. Culture is often used as a boundary marker for male domination. Cultural legacies that engender community for both men and women can be separated from those that authorize male control over women and children.

The possibilities within the context of socioeducation are limitless. The film and video catalogue from Women Make Movies[1] has a rich array of diverse productions on women from numerous cultures. This, together with popular films and documentaries, can be used as a critical resource for therapists interested in using the medium of film to expand the context of therapy (Almeida, 1998).

FAMILY THERAPY PROCESS

Family therapy in the CCM is typically done with one or more members of the family. Whereas larger systems, such as work, church, or school, may be considered in understanding the family's or individual's problem and eliciting solutions, the boundary that defines the therapeutic circle is most often the family itself. Whereas family therapy in theory views the family as an open system, the very closure of this system within the therapeutic encounter preserves, certainly in heterosexual families, the quintessential fabric of male hierarchy and dominance.

Because the CCM addresses family issues in the presence of a larger community of clients and sponsors, people just learning about the model often raise questions about confidentiality. From our perspective, confidentiality is often a euphemism for the rules of patriarchal privacy. This highly regarded ethical/legal value evolved out of mental health systems defined by men for men. We are careful to share information judiciously to ensure safety for all clients. Clients feel safe working in the context of a larger community setting because they developed relationships with community members during the socioeducational phase of treatment.

Dismantling the system of male dominance depends on opening up the boundary of the patriarchal family. With this in mind, we conduct family/couple sessions in the culture circles. Intervention with mothers, fathers, uncles, brothers, sisters, grandparents, partners, and children is all done as subsystem work, thereby defining the family system not as autonomous but as connected—a boundary within a boundary. Knowledge gained from these therapeutic experiences is knowledge that is held within the

---

[1]Established in 1972 to address the underrepresentation and misrepresentation of women in the media industry, Women Make Movies (www.wmm.com) is a multicultural, multiracial, nonprofit media arts organization that facilitates the production, promotion, distribution, and exhibition of independent films and videotapes by and about women. The film and video catalog, a great resource on women's film, is available on request online or from Women Make Movies, 462 Broadway Suite 500WS, New York, New York 10013.

family as well as the community. A circle of liberation ensues that embraces both empowerment and accountability within family and community life.

THE MOTHER WHO CHOSE LOVE AND HOPE FOR HER SONS OVER SPORTS: AN IRISH CATHOLIC FAMILY

The mother, Angela, is 41 years old. She had been married for 13 years to Michael but is now divorced. She is a social worker and he is a police officer. They have two sons. Although Michael entered therapy briefly, he did not see it as benefiting his life in any way. Shortly before the divorce, he chose to discontinue. This occurred after the socioeducation phase and a few sessions in the culture circles. Although he was able to articulate problems associated with hierarchy and domination, he was unable to think of accountability with respect to his personal life. The reasons for their divorce centered on issues of his abuse of power in the marriage.

For example, Angela was back at work when their second son was 5 years old. Thus, she needed Michael's support with the second-shift responsibilities, especially knowledge of his work schedule so that she could arrange for child care. She also suggested that he request a permanent shift, which would enable her to plan her work around child care. Note that she was not even asking that he be responsible for arranging child care. When we suggested that he might share that responsibility, he was furious that we would expect him to take care of such things because it was agreed between them that this was Angela's responsibility.

The sponsors commented that refusing to share second-shift responsibilities was an abuse of male privilege. He complained that asking him to make these additional changes did not acknowledge his status as the primary breadwinner who needed to have his schedule at work protected. He was a high-ranking officer, so there was no threat of losing his position. However, even if there had been a threat of his losing work, we would still have encouraged him to brainstorm with his culture circle about how to hold on to his work while simultaneously supporting his partner to carry out her dreams as well. The notion of only one partner being fulfilled is a heterosexual model that we encourage men and women to rethink.

Michael refused to negotiate Angela's work schedule while privileging his work as a police officer. His refusal to get a stable shift made it difficult for Angela to obtain and maintain employment. Thus, they became financially dependent on his work, another measure of his domination. Michael also denied her emotional and sexual affection. Finally, he saw nothing wrong with leaving the children with his parents who were both active alcoholics. His father often abused the children physically and emotionally. The grandfather also encouraged rigid male behavior as a sign of healthy boyhood and chastised them if they showed any signs of vulnerability.

This difficult process of unmasking power is made easier with the use of culture circles and sponsors. Although clients such as Michael may choose to leave therapy, the therapeutic context still has an ethical responsibility to define the power imbalances and subsequent assault to a woman's integrity and selfhood. Critical to empowering Angela (women) is the creation of a social structure that will support her mothering while encouraging her to develop different aspects of her self, for example, work, recreation, and spirituality. The therapeutic problem highlighted in this narrative is the violence absorbed by both boys and the process of change that followed.

This legacy of rigid male norms accelerated following the divorce. Ian, age 7, beat up a boy of color on the bus and smashed the head of a squirrel. He came to his culture circle with drawings of violent record covers and magazines that he had gathered at his friend's home. He described the violence on television and glorified images of the swastika without a sense of its history. Tommy, age 11, spoke of wrestling as life-giving to him. At 11 he was already on the high school team, which carried considerable status. Over the past several years, he had used his physical prowess and technical skill to bully his brother and other boys weaker than he.

Angela struggled to take a position against the wrestling, going up against his father, the coaches, the principal, and all of the other parents on the team. Although Tommy had lost 26 days from the previous school year because of fatigue, the pediatrician claimed it was "normal" for young male athletes engaging in this type of vigorous sport. The coaches and principal gave Tommy passing grades despite his excessive absences.

This mother and her sons have been through their respective socioeducational experiences. In her circle Angela vacillated between relief over being out of her assaultive marriage and anger about being dumped with the entire responsibility of raising two sons who were engulfed in the sea of rigid male socialization. She wondered if she were to blame: for not spending enough time with the boys, for too much time at work, for leaving her marriage. She feared losing her sons if she set too many limits.

The women in her culture circle helped her understand the limited power of mothers within the larger social context and the paradox of still being able to raise good sons. One African American woman talked about raising three sons in the face of numerous sources of adversity. She set a standard and stuck to it, getting a lot of support for herself and the boys from places where she knew they would get the right message. This testimony from another mother was greatly reassuring to Angela, who began to internalize the notion that she did not have to give up work to be a competent mother, a message with which her husband continually barraged her. It also gave her permission to seek support for her parenting from the members of her culture circle, and support for accountability from her sons within the men's culture circle.

Numerous conversations were held with Angela and her sons within the men's culture circle. Tommy described, with a sense of glory, the masculine rites of passage that accompanied his abuse of power with other boys including his brother. His brother, Ian, joined in the moment of glory through descriptions of how his father was an undercover drug agent and "just made a big bust." Ian ended his story reporting that some of his friends act "gay" and he does not like it!

The male sponsors and participants began gently to dismantle the multiple expressions of rigid masculinity, always suggesting new and different forms of male courage. There were several gay men in the culture circle. They, together with the heterosexual men, asked questions about what it meant to be gay. They asked if the boys knew the origin of the word. Ian was not aware, but Tommy knew that it was a disparaging comment, intended to harm boys who seemed feminine or relational in any way. However, he did not actually know anyone who was gay.

We shared the video, *This Boy's Life,* which offered the men the opportunity to disclose their sexual orientation, leaving the boys shocked, especially because they were quite connected to one of the men who happened to be gay. During the car ride home, they apparently had an open discussion with their mother about who in their life was gay or lesbian and what it would mean to them if they had a gay friend or if their mother had a gay friend.

Patiently, over many months, the conversation continued within an ethic of caring, asking that the boys be accountable for their behavior and accept new ways of being boys. Respect for their mother, her ideals, for women in general, and for men requires this type of care. At times the boys held back tears and then cried in the car when they were alone with their mother, saying it was too shameful to cry in a room full of men.

This process was brought back into the culture circle. The men exchanged stories of how they too were raised with the same harmful ideals of emotional armor. They reported that now they can cry, and some of them chose that occasion to do so.

Almost a year later, 2 years after the family started therapy, the boys have finally incorporated this circle of men as their models of masculinity. Angela realized that her work as a mother was not finished, but her life is considerably more liberated. She was empowered with the knowledge of having sources of support that actively countered negative gender role norms. The boys felt a sense of relief that they could be loyal to their father's legacy through connections with other men.

CONCLUSION

This chapter presented the cultural context model, an approach that essentializes the importance of the social location of individuals and families in psychotherapy. Family members participate in a process of socioeducation about the sources of societal power, privilege, and oppression. The knowledge of social location is critical to advancing experiences of liberation. The process of socioeducation occurs in same-sex cultural circles that include other families, sponsors, and therapists. These culture circles represent supportive communities of men and women that help each family member develop a critical conscience that challenges cultural norms that preserve oppression, male dominance, White superiority, and homophobia. The chapter provided numerous examples of the ways in which popular culture in the form of books or movies can be used by the circles to challenge traditional norms. This process simultaneously offers expanded norms for those in power and empowering strategies for those who are oppressed. A clinical example illustrated how one family built a new collective conscience, one that upholds liberation through both accountability and empowerment for men and women.

REFERENCES

Almeida, R. (1990). Asian Indian mothers. *Journal of Feminist Family Therapy*, 2, 33–39.

Almeida, R. (1993). Unexamined assumptions and service delivery systems: Feminist theory and racial exclusions. *Journal of Feminist Family Therapy*, 5, 3–23.

Almeida, R. (1998). Expanded reference guide to feminism for family therapists. In R. Almeida (Ed.), *Transformations in gender and race* (pp. 20–22). New York: Haworth.

Almeida, R., & Bograd, M. (1990). Sponsorship: Men holding men accountable for domestic violence. *Journal of Feminist Family Therapy*, 2, 243–256.

Almeida, R., & Durkin, T. (1999). The cultural context model: Therapy for couples with domestic violence. *Journal of Marital and Family Therapy*, 25, 169–176.

Almeida, R., Woods, R., Messineo, T., & Font, R. (1998). Cultural context model. In M. McGoldrick (Ed.), *Re-visioning family therapy: Race, culture, gender in clinical practice* (pp. 414–431). New York: Guilford Press.

Crenshaw, K. W. (1994). Mapping the margins: Intersectionality, identity, politics, and violence against women of color. In M. A. Fineman & R. Mykitiuk (Eds.), *The public nature of private violence* (pp. 39–51). New York: Routledge.

Dolan-Del Vecchio, K. (1997). The foundation of accountability: A linking of many different voices. *American Family Therapy Academy Newsletter, 64*, 2–23.

Font, R., Dolan-Del Vecchio, K., & Almeida, R. (1998). Finding the words: Instruments for a therapy of liberation. In R. Almeida (Ed.), *Transformations of gender and race: Family and developmental perspectives* (pp. 85–98). New York: Haworth.

Freire, P. (1972). *Pedagogy of the oppressed.* New York: Herder & Herder.

23

BIRACIAL LESBIAN-LED ADOPTIVE FAMILIES

NATALIE S. ELDRIDGE AND SUSAN E. BARRETT

The biracial lesbian-led adoptive family is a growing subset of American families. What contextual and systemic dimensions of these families do therapists need to understand to work with them effectively? In most aspects of family functioning, biracial lesbian-led adoptive families are more similar to other subsets of families than different. Concerns for their children's health, safety, education, and future are embedded in the everyday activities and choices of the parents. Yet the multiple group identities that these families reflect simultaneously position them in both dominant and nondominant groups within society. It is the dynamic interaction of these group identities that we wish to highlight here, providing guidance to therapists in approaching these families from a feminist perspective that affirms both the challenges and the strengths these families demonstrate.

Feminist therapy, in highlighting the gendered and racial power hierarchies in the larger society, has explored the impact of group identity on individual experience, whether the individual is aware or unaware of this identity. Barrett (1998) asserted the importance of integrating "group identity, from both a minority and majority position, into a personal understanding of oneself and one's connections" (p. 52). For example, we (the authors) benefit from understanding the sexism or misogyny we often encounter as women. At the same time, as White women we benefit from understanding the significant, and sometimes unnoticed (by us), privilege we consistently are awarded because of our White group identity. Other group identities emerge in our relational contexts with our clients, such as professional status, age, physical ability, sexual orientation, or parental status. The relevance of each group identity shifts from one relational context to another. As we practice holding the complex and shifting dimensions of our own many identities in awareness, we become better able to perceive our clients with similar flexibility.

Four specific contextual identities that are relevant for the biracial lesbian-led adoptive family involve adoption issues, racial dimensions, heterosexism, and gender issues. These are explored next, followed by a case example that illustrates how these various dimensions might be considered in treating a particular family.

ADOPTION ISSUES

Smith, Surrey, and Watkins (1998) asserted that in mainstream Western culture, "there is a legacy of cultural hesitation and apprehension about adoptive motherhood, based on dominant European American beliefs about the primacy of blood ties, ethnocentricity, and traditional patriarchal inheritance systems" (p. 195). The cultural beliefs that adoptive families are less legitimate or "natural" than their genetically related counterparts are often accompanied by assumptions that children in these families face inevitable identity disturbance or psychopathology.

In the mental health field, the biological nuclear family has been viewed as both normative and optimal, underlying all of psychology's assumptions about family dynamics and child development (Martin, 1998). Other constellations and structures have been viewed as deficient by mainstream psychology. These embedded cultural beliefs echo those that stigmatize lesbian-led families as "unnatural," "immoral," or "unfair to the children." Lesbian adoptive mothers experience this cultural stigma through overt statements or actions by others and within themselves in the form of doubts about their viability as mothers. Coming to understand how these cultural ideologies about adoption affect them can move these mothers to resist the biases more effectively and promote optimal functioning for their unique families.

Like all adoptive families, the biracial lesbian-led adoptive family must come to terms with how to handle the facts of adoption with the children, extended family, and the larger world outside the family (neighbors, schools, etc.). What actual or metaphorical role will the birthparents have in the family's history, definition, and rituals? How will each family member come to terms with the losses inherent in adoption, particularly the loss of specific information and memories about the first days, months, or years of the child's life?

RACIAL DIMENSIONS

When the adoption is cross-racial, additional dilemmas emerge concerning how to acknowledge the larger cultural groups with which the child may identify or in which she or he is assigned membership by others. Will the family develop new connections with these larger groups, will they provide opportunities for the child to develop his or her own connections, or will the parental culture(s) alone determine the family cultural identity? Barrett and Aubin (1990) described the emotional debate at the core of many international and cross-racial adoptions: the relative importance of culture versus family for the welfare of individual children and for society as a whole. Reviewing a family's mediation of this debate in their stories of how the children came to be adopted may be an essential aspect of therapy. Broad issues such as economic and political forces (war, poverty, or overpopulation) and social stigmatization (the devaluation of women and girls, of unwed mothers, or of racially mixed children) need to be considered.

The distribution of power and privilege in the United States results in the majority of cross-racial adoptions being initiated by White, middle-class adults adopting children of color, either through a domestic or an international adoption. Most children available for adoption are children of color, with healthy White infants in high demand by prospective White parents. This context sets the stage for an amplification of the generational power hierarchy within a family, in which the parents have power by virtue of age and position in the family. At the same time it may affect the way racist bias is absorbed into the family culture.

A biracial family may also be created through a biracial parental relationship, with the adopted child being identified as a member of the same racial group as one of the parents, or as a racial mixture of the races each parent represents. This creates a different set of dilemmas for the family in terms of how race is used to differentiate people within the family. Another scenario might be that a biracial couple adopts a child of a race different from either parent, creating a multiracial family. Our example in this chapter involves the more typical scenario of White adults adopting children of color.

We believe that the cultural context that created the conditions for a particular child to become adopted by middle-class, mostly White Westerners needs to be an aspect of the systemic perspective that a feminist family therapist brings to her work with these families. The current cultural context in which the family is raising children is another essential dimension to include.

SAME-SEX PARENTING IN A HETEROSEXIST WORLD

The incidence of adoption by lesbian or gay adults has been difficult to document because the disclosure of sexual orientation can often result in the prospective parents being disqualified or denied access to adoption.

For this reason, lesbians or gays have frequently adopted as a "single parent," no matter what their relationship status might be. Unlike heterosexual couples, when a same-sex couple decides to adopt, they must decide who is going to be the adoptive parent and who is going to be relegated to the margins of the official process of preparing for, participating in, and finalizing the adoption. Sometimes this forced imbalance in family roles is temporary, as when the nonrecognized parent can later coadopt the child. This is not a legal option in most places in the United States, however. Where this is not possible, the differing status of the two parents will be consistently brought up by everyday events in the life of the child, such as registering for school, providing health insurance, and so on. Although the family can do much to deemphasize the legal versus nonlegal status in the eyes of the family and the world beyond, the fact that both parents are not legally permitted to have parental status is a constant reinforcement of the hetero-sexism of the larger culture (Scrivner & Eldridge, 1995).

Another way the heterosexist environment can threaten the lesbian-led or gay-led family integrity is through the assertion of the heterosexual nuclear family assumption. Children get asked who their Dad is, or which is their "real" Mom. That there has never been a "Dad" in the family structure is often not comprehensible to peers inoculated in the heterosexist myths. "You have 2 moms, that's cool. But where is your dad?"

The concept of family is more elastic in lesbian families, allowing for parenting responsibilities to be distributed over several adults (Clunis & Green, 1995). Not only does the female-only parenting context challenge the sexism embedded in the cultural understanding of mother and father, but many lesbian-led families reach out to a wider network of adults that the child may include in his or her family constellation.

GENDER ISSUES

One of the few ways that the gender dynamics of the culture provide advantages to women is in the realm of single-parent adoption. Of course, many adoption sources are closed to anyone but married heterosexual couples. However, when single-parent adoption is an option, women have historically been provided a more direct route than men have. The gender mythology of women being "natural caregivers" gave single women some advantage over single men in the world of adoption. Until recently, it was difficult for a single man to adopt a child, which eliminated this parenting option for many gay men. However, as the perception of the male role has expanded to include a nurturing element, and as the men's parenting has become more visible in positive ways, the prohibitions against single men adopting have been relaxed. Still, lesbians are parenting in greater numbers than gay men are.

Another perspective on gender and adoption has to do with the ways that birth mothers and adoptive mothers are disconnected or pitted against one another in the legal and logistical system of adoption. This competition between women is reminiscent of the larger dynamic of patriarchy in separating and isolating women from one another. The feminist movement has long been engaged in empowering women through connection with one another, building alliances against oppression, and learning how to recognize and address the power imbalances among women so that we can understand one another and engage in dialogue.

The feminist family therapist, while working to solidify the family integrity and boundaries of the family she is serving, can also introduce the systemic connections between adoptive mothers and birthmothers. Establishing such a context for the parental connection to the birthmother and the conditions in which she was forced to relinquish her parental role can pave the way for the psychological integration of both families that the child will later be required to do.

One of the bases for the polarized positions of birthmother and adoptive mother is the legal precedent, based on deep-seated patriarchal Western beliefs, that a child can have only one "real mother." It is the same legal precedent that has denied so many lesbian couples the right to have joint status as parents of their children. Typically, the biological mother is required to relinquish her parental rights in order for her female partner, a nonbiologically related mother, to adopt the child. Perhaps it is in working with lesbian couples, in which parents and therapist alike are challenged to expand their views of motherhood to include more than one mother, that the foundation can be laid for a more global, systemic view of family and roles. This might ultimately challenge the capitalistic and patriarchal conditions that create the foundation for many cross-racial and international adoptions that are increasing on such a growing scale.

In summary, we have highlighted four contextual arenas that often influence the identity development of members of biracial lesbian-led adoptive families. Feminist approaches to therapy have established the benefits of understanding the larger cultural contexts that can shape, trigger, and mediate both our intrapsychic and our interpersonal perceptions and experiences. Systemic approaches have illustrated the mutual influence that individuals (as within a family) and systems have on one another. The concept of contextual identities, then, provides a tool for identifying, naming, and integrating various influences that are shaping our day-to-day experiences. Therapists can use this concept to help their clients gain new perspectives on family conflicts and impasses, finding creative and compassionate solutions that move family members toward greater integration of their multiple identities.

CASE STUDY

Becky, Linda, Joseph, and Maria are a family of four coming into therapy because of tension that keeps erupting between Becky and Joseph and reverberating throughout the whole family. Becky and Linda are White, professional women in their 40s. Joseph is Mexican-born, adopted when he was 2. He is now 12 years old and in the seventh grade. Maria is 8 years old and in the third grade. She was adopted from Honduras when she was about 1 year old.

Becky and Linda have been partners for 15 years. They decided together to adopt, with Linda being the adoptive parent, as a way of creating a family with children. Linda's family of origin accepts them and functions as an extended family for them. Becky's family does not accept her partnership with Linda or the children. Historically, Linda and Joseph have had a primary affective connection and Becky and Maria have had one. Both children, however, have also been strongly connected to the other adult. Linda called Janet, a family therapist, to set an appointment. Janet is an experienced therapist who is also an adoptive parent of two grown children. Her children were born in the United States. Janet, her husband, and their children are all White.

As Janet listened to Linda describe her family and the tension between Becky and Joseph, she realized the many issues that could be converging at this time for this family. Issues of race, ethnicity, gender, sexual orientation, family structure, and genetic identity all could be influencing the developmental pushes and pulls of the family as a whole, especially of Joseph at prepuberty. She knew she would have to continually keep all these contextual factors in mind to understand the particular issues of these four people.

For the first session, Janet decided to meet with Becky and Linda without the children to get a family history. Becky and Linda told the story of their relationship, their adoption of the children, and their current struggles. They both described a change in Joseph when he moved from elementary into middle school in the sixth grade. The academic expectations in middle school were a stretch for him, although he worked hard and was doing satisfactory work. Socially, he was finding his place, primarily through sports. At age 12, he was beginning to have some physical changes related to puberty.

A particularly bad fight erupted between Becky and Joseph after Becky decided to take a trip alone to the neighboring state to visit her parents, something she does two to three times a year. The fight started, as usual, around household chores. However, at one point Joseph said, "Sam and Louise (Becky's parents) are not my grandparents and you are not my mother. As a matter of fact, you all are not my real family." This outburst stunned them all, including Maria who was present and burst into tears.

Joseph's arrow hit home for Becky and Linda, arousing fear, sadness, and anger. Becky responded first with anger, but Linda stopped her and asked Joseph what he meant. All he would say was that "they were not his grandparents." Linda and Becky said, "Yes, they are, and we are your parents." Joseph went to his room and that was the end of the discussion.

Janet was interested in why this remark from Joseph was so painful for Becky and Linda. To her, it seemed like a barb by an adopted preadolescent who was using whatever weapons available to fight with his parents. Painful as that was, the statement echoed other adopted children pushing against their parents. Despite this similarity to other adopted families, Janet knew the context for these issues was different from her own experience of adoption and from most of the experiences of the heterosexual families she sees in therapy. Tempting as it was to intervene with a discussion of the confluence of puberty and adoption for Joseph, she held back to enlarge the context rather than narrow the focus at this point. She kept probing, encouraging Becky and Linda to elaborate on the meaning of the argument and the barb from Joseph.

As she did so, several other relevant pieces of information emerged. Linda is the legal parent for both children. Second-parent adoption, which would give Becky equal legal status as a parent, is not possible in their state. Becky and Linda, however, have always seen themselves as equal parents and present themselves to the world as a family of four (Barrett, 2000). Most people, including teachers, friends, and neighbors, never question the mothers' legal status. Becky and Linda have decided not to disclose their differing status to keep others from perceiving Linda as more the "real" mother. Joseph and Maria have been told about the absence of legal papers linking them to Becky as part of their adoption story and as part of understanding all the news stories about lesbian and gay parenting. However, emotionally, it had appeared to have no real meaning for them until now.

When Janet asked more about the timing of Joseph's outburst regarding Becky's trip to visit her parents, she learned yet more information. Becky has always had a push/pull, love/hate relationship with her parents. On the one hand, she is deeply attached to them, particularly to her father. As their only child, she also feels a tremendous sense of responsibility for them as they age. This particular trip was one of duty to check on her mother's health. On the other hand, she hates being around her parents because they completely ignore Linda and the children. They see Becky as single, but with these appendages of three other people with whom she lives. Her parents are both openly racist and homophobic. These attitudes are part of the reason why Linda is the legal parent. They both knew that if Becky were the legal parent and she died, her parents would not see Linda as a parent to the children and would take them away from her. One way that Becky protects her children and Linda is by visiting her parents by herself.

When Janet asked how Joseph and Maria understand the situation with Becky's parents, both Becky and Linda admit they underplay it, not wanting Joseph and Maria to feel rejected. Instead, they mostly visit Linda's family and simply do not discuss Becky's parents much. When Becky's parents do not acknowledge the children's birthdays or Christmas, Becky has told Joseph and Maria that she and her parents are not close and that is just how they operate. They have not told the children directly that a major reason why they are not close is the racist and homophobic beliefs of Becky's parents.

Janet also asked about how Becky and Linda handle the fact that their family is biracial. She learned that Becky and Linda have, over the years, talked openly about Mexico, Honduras, and Latin America in general. They integrate the children's birth cultures through cultural events, books, and other ways. They have also cultivated friendships with other families who have adopted children from other countries.

By the end of the first session, Janet had gathered much information. After Becky and Linda left, she felt a bit overwhelmed with all the various pieces of data. She understood this family well, because they were similar to many other families she has seen. She was experienced personally and professionally with adoption. She has also seen several families with White parents and children of color. However, this is the first time that she has seen a lesbian-led family in therapy. Janet had a positive experience in getting consultation from an African American colleague concerning racial issues and decided to look for similar consultation from a lesbian therapist concerning issues related to sexual orientation. That consultation led her to literature that she read in preparation for the next session.

Janet, Becky, and Linda had decided that the second session would include the children with the primary focus being on listening to Joseph and Maria. Janet began the session by telling Joseph and Maria that she had met with their parents the week before and heard some of the history of their family and some of their concerns about the stresses of their family. She emphasized that it was important to understand everyone's concerns to see how their family functions well and what could change. She explained to the children that she sees families as patterns of connections and also tries to understand factors outside the family, such as school or work, and how these affect the family as well.

Maria started by saying that she was really upset with the fighting between Becky and Joseph and wished they would both stop. When asked why she thought they fought so much, she said she thought they were both alike and got on each other's nerves. Joseph seemed conflicted about talking in front of a therapist. Both Becky and Linda encouraged him to say whatever he wanted, telling him that they needed his viewpoint to be able to change what was going on. They said that they were willing to make adjustments that Janet might suggest, but if he did not contribute, the adjustments would be one-sided and probably would not work.

Once he began talking, Joseph had a lot to say. He said he did not want to hurt his parents' feelings, but they just did not understand what it was like to be him. With probing from Janet, he talked about being in junior high and being different from most of the other children. His school is predominantly White, with about a quarter of the students being African American and a small number of children of other racial/ethnic backgrounds. He reported that he felt very secure in the arena of sports but very insecure when his classmates began talking about girls. He is short, looks different, and has brown skin. Who is going to want to date him?

Linda brought up the statement about them not being his real parents. Again, he hemmed and hawed a bit, and kept glancing at Maria. She told him that she did not know what he was going to say or why he kept looking at her, but to "please, just spit it out." He finally said that Becky's parents did not want him and Maria as grandchildren because they were not White. He also knew that they did not like the fact that Linda and Becky are lesbians. He was also aware that the fact that Becky did not have legal adoption papers for them was another reason her parents did not consider him and Maria their grandchildren. He thought they were mean, racist, and homophobic and he wished Linda and Becky would "quit saying that they were his grandparents, because they aren't." A stunned silence followed Joseph's remarks, and then Maria burst into tears.

In the aftermath of Joseph's comments and in the sessions that followed, Janet helped the family understand some of the underlying patterns that had come forth with Joseph as spokesperson. These were not secrets in the traditional sense, but nuances and shadings of the truth that needed to be sharpened (Imber-Black, 1998). The issues that needed to be addressed included the following: Becky does not have full legal standing as a parent; her parents are racist, homophobic, and have never claimed Joseph and Maria as their grandchildren; Joseph and Maria have brown skin and their parents do not; and Joseph and Maria have genetic ties different from their familial ones. All of this information had been conveyed either directly or indirectly to the children all their lives. However, the meaning of it had radically shifted for Joseph as he entered puberty, high school, dating, and a new level of independence.

Attending to both the integrity of the family unit and the integrity of the child is critical in biracial lesbian-led adoptive families. The integrity of the family unit for these families is constantly challenged by society (Barrett, 1997; Martin, 1998). In this family's case, the challenge comes from within the extended family as well, that is, Becky's parents. This kind of intrafamily rejection is extremely painful. In this case, one part of Joseph's reaction is a response to being rejected by his nominal grandparents. If they are rejecting him, he is going to reject them.

Linda and Becky had been attending to the integrity of their family by focusing on the ways they *are* one unit rather than on the ways they are not. For example, they think, act, and present themselves as a two-parent family (Barrett, 2000). Linda is called Momma and Becky is Mom. Most people have no idea that only one of them is a legal parent. They have used this presumption of equal parenting as a basis for saying that any relative of either of the adults is also a relative of the children. Therefore, they have chosen to say that Becky's parents are poor grandparents rather than saying they are not grandparents because they do not claim the children as grandchildren.

With regard to the racial/ethnic differences between the children and adults, Becky and Linda have overtly acknowledged the cultural background of the children. However, their family as a whole more or less lives a middle-class, White existence. Becky and Linda's extended families are totally Euro-American, middle-class families. Being embedded in this context has been helpful for Joseph and Maria to feel part of their family. However, at this time, Joseph is pushing for something different.

He is pushing, indeed, for acknowledgment of his integrity as an individual. Part of this push involved seeing how he is different from other members of his family. He has brown skin, which puts him in a minority, devalued status in society. Becky and Linda, with their White skin, are in a majority, valued position in society. This creates a difference between parents and children that cannot be totally bridged on the experiential level. With regard to skin color and all that brings with it, these parents and children will forever live in different worlds. They can "travel" back and forth between worlds, as the children already do. However, they do not, minute by minute, live the same experiences (Lugones, 1990). Becky and Linda understood this at an intellectual level, but Joseph's naming of this difference brought it home to them emotionally as well. Because of the love they have for their children, it is painful for them to hear.

Adopted children and all children of out lesbians not parented by their genetic birth father have birth parents who are not their social parents. Joseph is responding to this fact as well as he strives for his personal integrity. His statement about Becky and Linda not being his parents was, in part, a statement about his origins. The adults have always talked openly about the lack of knowledge of the birth parents for both children. However, it is still emotionally hard for both Joseph and his parents to acknowledge the painfulness of this loss.

Another possible context for Joseph's statement about his parents is that he has no father but has two mothers instead. He has, over the years, said he wished he had a father as many children of lesbian parents do. However, that has meant many things from wanting shaving cream to fight with (as he did at a friend's house with the other child's father's shaving cream) to not wanting to be different from his friends. This time, however, it may have more to do with the male role in dating. Joseph admitted as much when his parents subsequently arranged for him to have more time with his godfather, cueing the godfather ahead of time that this topic might come up. Janet recognized that a common heterosexist assumption might have prompted her to focus on Joseph's gender identity development as the son of lesbian parents. However, she is aware that research does not support the idea that children of same-sex parents are more likely to have gender identity problems (Patterson, 1995), and thus resists a digression in this direction.

Janet, using her knowledge and experience of adoption issues, was able to help Becky and Linda see that this focus on his personal integrity as a Hispanic boy, adopted by two White lesbians, is essential for Joseph. She was also able to frame it as part of the larger picture regarding the integrity of their family unit. In other words, their family has to stretch large enough to encompass the differences of the members, even when this stretch is painful. For Joseph, this means acknowledging the meaning for him of being Hispanic, adopted, and raised by lesbian parents. None of these particular characteristics applies to either Becky or Linda, yet they must expand the family identity to address Joseph's needs.

Janet, as therapist, modeled the stretch for Becky and Linda. She was experienced in family therapy and adoption issues. She was aware that ethnicity, race, and sexual orientation could be relevant issues but was not experienced enough in these areas to be able to see ahead for the family. She acknowledged this to Becky and Linda, told them about her consultant, and gave them some of the written resources she had found. On the meta-level, this communicated to Becky and Linda that their family is complex and that there is always room to learn more. In this way, she communicated that asking for help and expanding one's thinking and practice is not a negative evaluation on what one already does well.

SUMMARY

An integrated contextual identity for a family as a group and for each member of a family is an important feminist goal. Members of traditional families usually share common group identities, for example, ethnicity, race, and sexual orientation. However, for biracial lesbian-led adoptive families, parents and children have different group identities. The family circle has to be large enough to encompass the individual identity of each member, while still allowing for the development of a family identity that is congruent with all members, parents and children.

REFERENCES

Barrett, S. E. (1997). Children of lesbian parents: The what, when and how of talking about donor identity. *Women and Therapy, 20,* 43–55.

Barrett, S. E. (1998). Contextual identity: A model for therapy and social change. *Women and Therapy, 21,* 51–64.

Barrett, S. E. (2000). *Intent (and love) makes a family.* Unpublished manuscript.

Barrett, S. E., & Aubin, C. (1990). Feminist considerations of inter-country adoptions. In J. Knowles & E. Cole (Eds.), *Woman-defined motherhood* (pp. 127–138). New York: Harrington Park Press.

Clunis, D. M., & Green, G. D. (1995). *The lesbian parenting book: A guide to creating families and raising children.* Seattle, WA: Seal Press.

Imber-Black, E. (1998). *The secret life of families.* New York: Bantam Books.

Lugones, M. (1990). Playfulness, "world"-travelling, and loving perception. In G. Anzaldua (Ed.), *Making face, making soul* (pp. 390–402). San Francisco: Aunt Lute Books.

Martin, A. (1998). Clinical issues in psychotherapy with lesbian-, gay-, and bisexual-parented families. In C. J. Patterson & A. R. D'Augelli (Eds.), *Lesbian, gay, and bisexual identities in families* (pp. 270–291). New York: Oxford University Press.

Patterson, C. J. (1995). *Lesbian and gay parenting.* Retrieved January 22, 2002, from http://www.apa.org/pi/parent.html

Scrivner, R., & Eldridge, N. S. (1995). Lesbian and gay family psychology. In R. H. Mikesell, D. D. Lusterman, & S. H. McDaniel (Eds.), *Integrating family therapy: Handbook of family psychology and systems therapy* (pp. 327–345). Washington, DC: American Psychological Association.

Smith, B., Surrey, J. L., & Watkins, M. (1998). "Real" mothers: Adoptive mothers resisting marginalization and re-creating motherhood. In C. G. Coll, J. L. Surrey, & K. Weingarten (Eds.), *Mothering against the odds: Diverse voices of contemporary mothers* (pp. 194–214). New York: Guilford Press.

24

ASSESSMENT OF DOMESTIC VIOLENCE

MICHELE HARWAY

As we enter the new millennium with 20 years or more of generalized awareness of the problem of domestic violence, we would expect mental health practitioners to be well versed in how best to intervene with affected families. Unfortunately, this is not the case. Thus, we have a responsibility to continue to train clinicians so that all can be more effective in stopping violence in the home. In this chapter, I describe feminist and systemic understandings about domestic violence. I then argue for the routine assessment of domestic violence and provide an assessment model. Space limitations preclude a detailed discussion of treatment issues, so they are addressed only briefly. After a critique of common approaches for the treatment of domestic violence, a discussion of issues related to diversity concludes the chapter.

THEORETICAL UNDERSTANDINGS ABOUT BATTERING

Feminist perspectives about domestic violence describe battering as an act of control by one intimate partner over another. It may involve physical violence, that is, using one's physical strength or presence to control another, or it may involve verbal and emotional abuse, that is, using one's words or voice to control another. Men who use verbal or emotional abuse often graduate to using physical violence to control their partner. Even

Portions of this chapter are modified from Harway (2000), Harway and Evans (1996), and Hansen and Harway (1993).

when verbal abuse does not eventuate in physical abuse, the psychological mechanisms that stimulate and maintain these two forms of control are the same.

Battering may include a variety of behaviors ranging from those appearing moderate (e.g., holding down, unplugging the phone) to those appearing more extreme (e.g., trying to run over with a car, using guns and knives). To recognize that batterers use a spectrum of violent behaviors is to recognize battering not as a response to anger but as a strategy to maintain power in the relationship. Such power is seen as the man's entitlement. It is this faulty belief and the maintenance of the sense of entitlement through self-pity, denial, rationalization, manipulation, and general disregard for the partner that need to be challenged in treatment.

By contrast, systemic perspectives describe any relational issue, including battering, as the result of dysfunction created by the couple. As a result of this view, each member of the couple is regarded as contributing equally to the violence, as being equally responsible for it, and as gaining equally from it.

Many believe that feminist and systemic approaches to working with domestic violence are incompatible. Early feminist critiques of family systems approaches to battering pointed to the inappropriate use of couples therapy with couples who experienced domestic violence (Pressman, Cameron, & Rothery, 1989; Yllo & Bograd, 1988). Systemic perspectives and couples therapy were criticized for inherently blaming the victim and attributing coresponsibility for the battering to her. Even when the victim is not overtly blamed for the battering, the focus on identifying characteristics of the victim or her behavior supports a conceptualization of the violence as a response provoked by the victim (Hansen, 1993).

Moreover, diagnosing victims on the basis of preexisting psychological characteristics leads to the development of interventions based on these diagnoses (Bograd, 1984; Hansen, Harway, & Cervantes, 1991; Harway & Hansen, 1990; Weitzman & Dreen, 1982). Women who experience this process in therapy are likely to continue to regard themselves as responsible for the battering. Because this perception is at least in part responsible for the couple's entering therapy, changes in the pattern of interaction as a result of therapy is unlikely. No matter how well-informed the therapist is about the dynamics of battering or how well-meaning she is about her approach to working conjointly with a battered woman and her batterer, couples therapy implies that the problem is systemic when it is not. In spite of these early perspectives, feminists who espouse systemic approaches to therapy generally agree that once the violence is under control, there remain many relational issues that will benefit from couples' interventions (Hansen & Goldenberg, 1993).

THE CASE OF SAMANTHA AND CARL

> Samantha and Carl have been married for 6 years and have two young daughters: Katie, 5, and Carol, 2. Samantha calls, stating that she and Carl have been having communication problems recently and that she wants to come for marital counseling with Carl.

A systems perspective would suggest that marital counseling with Samantha and Carl might eventually lead to family counseling, bringing into the therapy the two young daughters and perhaps even extended family members. Systemic thinking suggests that the communication problems Samantha mentions in her initial call must be something the system (Samantha and Carl) has created. Perhaps the problems represent multigenerationally transmitted patterns. Perhaps they are an effort to defuse anxiety in the system. Perhaps there are structural problems in the family.

What the reader cannot know from the description (but the psychotherapist should assess) is that Samantha's stated reasons for seeking therapy are a cover for the existence of domestic violence. The dilemma that most systemic thinkers have is that the most effective interventions for treating couples experiencing violence in the early phase do not emerge from a systems perspective. Given the high prevalence of domestic violence in all walks of life, the clinician must approach the intake from a counterintuitive perspective—one that is not systemic.

Assessment for Domestic Violence

It is rare for an abusive individual to present for therapy on his or her own. It is much more common that a couple or a survivor of domestic violence will present for psychotherapy. Occasionally, a symptomatic child will be the client.

Because clients seldom volunteer information about the battering, assessing for the existence of violence is critical. O'Leary, Vivian, and Malone (1992) indicated that fewer than 5% of couples seeking marital therapy spontaneously report violence as a problem during the intake, yet as many as two thirds of these couples admit to some form of violence on self-report measures. (This finding is consistent with those of Cascardi, Langhinrichsen, & Vivian, 1992.)

In exploring why couples do not report violence at intake, Ehrensaft and Vivian (1996) noted that these couples do not consider the violence itself the problem because it is unstable and infrequent. Thus, the violence appears to be secondary to other problems. Moreover, the shame that both parties in domestic violence feel serves to keep them from volunteering the information at intake. Some survivors may already have experienced the misguided reactions of family members, friends, clergy, and medical personnel who have encouraged them to modify their behavior to achieve a change in the relationship. Consequently, they think that they will not be believed or that no one is interested in their predicament. Goodstein and Page (1981) reported that battered women who presented at emergency rooms for treatment following a violent episode had often sought out psychotherapy but had not returned after their first session because the therapist failed to ask them about the battering. Finally, survivors of domestic violence experience the very real fear of increased danger if they tell. All of the above factors make it clear that mental health professionals must ask about the existence of violence, even (especially) when clients do not mention it.

Let us return to Samantha and Carl and turn the clock back to see how I would have handled this case from the outset.

> When Samantha calls with her request for marital counseling with Carl because of communication problems, I tell her that I am happy to see them for an evaluation, but that I want to be clear up front about how such a session will proceed. I tell her that I will see them together for a few minutes at the beginning of the session, that I will next spend about 15 minutes with each partner alone, and that in the final minutes of the evaluation, we will come together briefly to discuss treatment options. I caution her not to expect that the issues that bring them into marital counseling will be addressed or resolved in this first session.

My intake session is organized in this way so as to allow me to find out about the existence of violence without endangering the person who is experiencing it.

> When Samantha and Carl arrive, I spend a few minutes taking a history of their relationship. I remind them of the plan for the session. I interview Samantha first and then Carl.
>
> My questions to Samantha eventually lead to this one: "All couples have disagreements. Tell me about your last disagreement (or your worst disagreement). What happened? What did you say? What did he say? What did you do? What did he do? And what did you do/say next? What did he do/say next? And then . . . ?"

The questions ask the woman to recount the disagreement step by step, one freeze-frame at a time. It is important to slow the questioning down to this speed because otherwise there is (on the part of both) a tendency to gloss over the violence. It would be easy to overlook the push or the slap and get to the end of the discussion without ever recognizing that a violent interaction had taken place. I also look for any evidence of fear in the wife. Once she has acknowledged the violence to me, then I have to use this information to get the husband to tell me that he has been violent. However, I have two responsibilities to her—both related to keeping her safe. First, I must let her know that no matter what he says to me, I will not acknowledge that she has given me information about the violence. My second responsibility to her is to give her information about how to stay safe during the next violent episode.

> During my interview with Samantha, I learn that during their latest disagreement, Carl became violent and slapped her. She also tells me that this is not a first time occurrence. Once, things got so out of hand that she ended up at the emergency room for five stitches to her chin. I assure her that Carl will not learn from me that I know about the violence. I also encourage her to steadfastly deny that she has told me anything about it. Then, I bring Carl into my office.
>
> Getting Carl to acknowledge the violence is far more difficult. However, armed with the information that Samantha has given me, I know to be infinitely persistent with my questioning. Eventually, I accomplish my goal of getting Carl himself to tell me about the violent episode.

It is particularly important during the individual questioning that I speak first with the potential victim, because she is most likely to acknowledge the violence. Batterers are typically in denial about the violence, and even when they do acknowledge it, they minimize a great deal. In addition, many batterers are extremely charming. It may be difficult to believe that such a charming individual can be violent with someone he loves. Batterers are also likely to try to control the therapist and the therapy session. Without direct evidence about violence, it is easy for a therapist to fail to be persistent enough to uncover it. Questions about possible violent interactions need to be consistent and specific. Batterers will seldom acknowledge that they have been "violent" or "abusive" when asked with those words. However, they may acknowledge that they "may have pushed her—a little" or "slapped her—but only to get her attention."

When Carl comes into the room for his individual interview, I have a bigger challenge. I know about the violence, but I must somehow help him to tell me about it. It is crucial that the information come from him. My questions to him are along the same line as they were to her, except that I am likely to prolong the questioning and ask for more details if he fails to reveal the violence the first time around. I look for patterns of control in their relationship. I assess whether I feel controlled by this client. I listen to see whether he blames everything on his partner and whether he seems willing to hurt her in order to win. I assess his ability to be empathic to his partner and also whether he speaks as if he knows *the* right way or answer.

Usually through persistent questioning, especially where I have been forewarned that violence did in fact occur, I can get the batterer to acknowledge that there was some violence.

I bring Samantha and Carl back together in my office. I begin by telling them that while they indeed have a number of issues as a couple that will need marital counseling, it would be premature to work on these prior to resolving some of the individual issues that get in the way first. At that point, I would recommend that Carl attend a men's group with men who have similar relational issues and that Samantha work on her individual issues that may affect their relationship.

Note that I never use the words *violence, abuse, anger, control,* or any other trigger words in making my referral to Carl. I refer him to a group that will work not just on the anger and the violence but on the underlying issues that the violence represents. I refer Samantha to an individual therapist, not because she has a myriad of individual issues that need resolving but because she needs support in dealing with the battering. I cannot suggest a battered women's group at this point or I risk scaring them away from treatment.

Other Aspects of Assessment

Once it has been ascertained that domestic violence is indeed a part of the presenting picture, I assess the level of danger. Gelles (1998) asserted that assessing the severity of risk along with the stage of change (Prochaska & DiClemente, 1982) can help determine whether incarceration or psychotherapy would be most effective. Others, such as Sonkin (1998), indicated that knowing the comorbidity, if any, of the batterer will give important information about treatment options. Finally, assessing for the possibility of lethality is crucial to keeping the client safe. Key factors in determining whether a batterer has the potential to kill include the following: threats of homicide or suicide; acute depression and hopelessness; possession of weapons; obsessive feelings about the partner and family, accompanied by beliefs that he cannot live without them or that they are the center of his universe; drug and alcohol consumption combined with despair; history of pet abuse; and easy access to the battered woman and/or family members (Harway & Hansen, 1994).

KEY TREATMENT ISSUES

Intervening with the perpetrator of family violence is the most important goal in working with domestic violence. Although the recipients or witnesses of violence will need to be treated, nothing will change in the family unless the violence is stopped. Domestic violence does not remit on its own. Rather, battering usually escalates in severity and frequency. While most battered women who leave an abusive relationship go on to form healthy relationships, the same is not true for a batterer who is not treated. Men who batter, unless they are treated for partner abuse, are likely to go on to additional battering relationships (U.S. Commission on Civil Rights, 1982). When a battered woman leaves her partner, the batterer simply cycles women: He finds another woman whom he can control. This situation occurs because battering is not the result of a dysfunctional relationship but rather the result of an individual man's dysfunctional relational style (Harway & Hansen, 1993). Unless a batterer is court-mandated to treatment, he will rarely seek it out on his own. The sole exceptions are men who are "wife-mandated" to treatment, that is, whose spouses give them a choice of seeking treatment or losing the relationship.

It is important in working with batterers to be clear about what the presenting problem is. Equally critical is the need to educate the batterer's partner about the issues of violence. Although batterers have been described in the literature in a variety of ways, it is currently believed that no single profile of batterers exists, but rather that there are subtypes of batterers (Holtzworth-Munroe & Stuart, 1994; Sonkin, 1998) and that somewhat different forms of treatment are most appropriate for different types of batterers.

Approaches to Treating Batterers

Although it is increasingly believed that one-size-fits-all approaches to treating batterers are ineffective, there are certain points of agreement about what is likely to be most useful. First, although data are somewhat equivocal, several studies indicate that treated men fare better than untreated men (Dutton, 1986; Dutton, Bodnarchuk, Kropp, Hart, & Ogloff, 1995; Edleson & Syers, 1990; Rosenfeld, 1992; Tolman & Bennett, 1990). Treatment must be comprehensive, going beyond anger management to bringing about durable personality change.

Most experts on the treatment of batterers agree that group work should be the primary modality (Gondolf, 1993). One rationale for group treatment is that men are socialized into the culture of women-blaming and violence and can best be resocialized in groups. In addition, the more experienced men in the group can confront the denial and beliefs of the newer group members more effectively than a therapist can and also reinforce their own changes at the same time.

The best reason for groups may be that they facilitate working with men in the area of interpersonal functioning. Some men are so filled with shame that it takes hearing that other men have the same problems, and have found a way to be different, for them to find the courage to examine themselves. For example, clients who espouse feminist convictions and a conscious commitment to nonviolence may actually be controlling and hostile in their interactions with others. This behavior in the group provides the focus for change.

Limitations of Anger Management, Skill-Building, and Confrontational Approaches

The three major approaches to group treatment of batterers include programs that focus on anger management, build skills in a psychoeducational setting, or confront men's tendency toward power and control (often referred to as the feminist approach). Some treatment programs include several of these components.

Anger management programs are based on the belief that battering is caused by a man's inability to control his temper. Intervention consists of teaching the batterer to avoid outbursts by identifying the cues that precede them and the behaviors of the partner that provoke them. Anger control programs by themselves are ineffective in part because they give the batterer, whose problem is control, yet one more thing to control (Gondolf, 1993). Gondolf suggested that anger management programs do not properly identify men's sense of entitlement and privilege as causes of battering. Consequently, modifications in batterers' behaviors seem to be relatively superficial.

Similarly, skill-building programs do not lead to permanent change. Rather than attempting to modify underlying psychological processes, skill-building programs focus on communication skills, stress reduction, gender roles, conflict management, and the like. Some also include attention to cognitive restructuring. Skill-building programs by themselves often yield batterers who become more effective at controlling others through psychological abuse.

Other interventions confront men's tendency toward power and control and teach batterers to take responsibility for the abuse. However, this type of intervention tends to produce shame and guilt, which in turn produces a high dropout rate. Nonetheless, when properly incorporated into a broader program of intervention, confrontation is a critical component of treatment.

Effective Batterer Treatment

The intervention that is most effective with batterers combines therapy and education, a blend of cognitive–behavioral techniques, traumatology, feminist analysis, and psychodynamic approaches. As in therapy with other resistant clients, behavior change remains the most important goal with batterers.

The batterer's experience, as captured by the *cycle of feeling avoidance* developed by Evans (and described in Harway & Evans, 1996), focuses on the phenomenology of the man's experience: his feelings, his behavior, and the consequences of his behavior. These dimensions are examined simultaneously in the context of his history, his culture, his current situation, his relationships in general, and the violent relationship in particular.

In the cycle of feeling avoidance, the partner's behavior is irrelevant: whether she is passive or placating does not matter. This cycle is the individual abuser's cycle. Moreover, although an abuser may be violent only in intimate relationships, he is usually controlling in most of his relationships. Often we do not label his behavior as abusive because it is within the ordinary range of what is expected of men. Nevertheless, men's controlling behavior, and the coercion they use to enforce the control, is the core of partner abuse from the survivor's perspective. Men's avoidance of their central psychological and emotional issues by being abusive is the core issue for batterers themselves. If this pattern is not changed, abuse will continue.

This model is consistent with the work being done with alcohol and other addictions, as well as in the treatment of sex offenders, especially in relapse prevention. This parallel is no accident. Alcohol and drug abuse are related to domestic violence, as many correlational studies have shown (Dutton, 1988; Edleson & Tolman, 1992). However, the relations between the factors remains elusive unless one assumes that alcohol and drug abuse are related to domestic violence by being part of the cycle of defense against feelings.

Treating Battered Women

The previous section has focused on treating batterers rather than working with those who are the recipients of violence. This focus is deliberate. This should not be interpreted to mean that it is unimportant to provide support and the possibility of therapeutic change to those who experience violence. From a feminist perspective, the best outcome would be the eradication of domestic violence as a social problem, rather than just concentrating on "fixing" people who have already been negatively affected by it. Yet the overwhelming evidence is that leaving batterers untreated leads to the perpetuation of the problem. Nonetheless, helping those who are affected by domestic violence (primarily women and children) remains a high priority.

Issues of Diversity

Domestic violence is color-blind. Violence in the family crosses color, class, and ethnicity lines, occurs across all age groups, and affects married couples as well as those in dating relationships. It affects people in heterosexual as well as in homosexual relationships. Generally speaking, assessment and treatment remain the same across all types of relationships affected by domestic violence. However, there are subtleties in understanding violence across diverse groups that merit comment here.

First, as Sanchez-Hucles and Dutton (1999) indicated, understanding the racial and cultural dynamics that mediate men's violence toward women of color has not been a priority for experts in domestic violence. Thus, we do not readily understand what factors contribute differentially to violence across different ethnic groups. Second, prevalence statistics are incomplete because national survey data and crime statistics do not routinely include data on racial groups. Consequently, we do not know to what extent overall prevalence statistics explain the prevalence of violence in families of color. Third, people of color have turned inward and learned to rely on each other and their religions for survival. To the extent that these strategies prevent affected persons from asking for help, survivors remain largely invisible to helping professionals. Finally, we do know that families of color are expected to fulfill the gender roles of the majority culture as well as those of their own ethnic group. The disparity between these two standards may put them at greater risk for violence in the home.

Burns's (1986) thesis is that the most impermissible violence in the United States is against European American men, followed by European American women when violence is perpetrated by men of color. Further, the thesis holds that violence against people of color, particularly women of color, is permissible because they have the lowest status in society. Consequently, people of color are least likely to receive sympathetic treatment when they report the violence. Thus, mental health professionals have great responsibility in making an accurate assessment and providing competent treatment for families of color. Clinicians must go beyond their own prejudices and ensure that competent assessment is achieved.

When families are recent immigrants with low English proficiency, linguistically appropriate treatment must be provided. When a man's violence against his spouse is within normal parameters for his culture, the clinician must be particularly sensitive to honor the family's culture while making it clear that violence is not permissible in this society. This delicate balancing act may not be within the repertoire of every therapist.

Gay and lesbian domestic violence is a similarly delicate issue. The greatest problem is the lack of a treatment infrastructure. For example, there are few shelters for male victims of domestic violence (whether they are gay or straight). Women's shelters often face a dilemma when both parties in a lesbian relationship present for treatment and shelter.

A second problem concerns societal myths about violence. One is that only straight women get battered. Another is that a fight between two men is a fair fight between equals. Assessment in same-sex relationships is complicated by the clinician's inability to "use the odds" in deciding who is the likely perpetrator and the likely victim. With heterosexual couples, batterers are almost always men. During an assessment, the woman is usually interviewed alone before her male partner. But how should a clinician decide which of two gay men (or two lesbians) is the likely perpetrator? Some of the markers of violence described earlier may help, for example, looking at which partner blames the other, who is trying to control the session, and who has a win/lose mentality. However, there are sometimes surprises.

Battering issues across age groups brings ethics and mandatory reporting into the picture. The parameters for reportable child abuse when youngsters are in violent dating relationships varies by geographical location. Similarly, requirements concerning elder abuse (when the victim is over 65) vary. The wise clinician will consult his or her state's legal and ethical codes.

SOME FINAL THOUGHTS

Working with couples involved in domestic violence is hard work and change is slow. Nevertheless, working with this population is extremely important given how common and how devastating violence can be to families. Although this chapter has been critical of systems approaches because they serve to disempower individuals whose control over their day-to-day life is usually already severely curtailed by a violent partner, repairing damaged relationships once violence has ceased is an important goal of treatment. Systemic modalities are important strategies for working with postviolence couples. A key to understanding domestic violence is the core issue of power and control. Feminist-informed psychotherapy, particularly when applied in a group format and delivered in a nonshaming way, can be useful in helping violent clients change.

REFERENCES

Bograd, M. (1984). Family systems approaches to wife battering: A feminist critique. *American Journal of Orthopsychiatry, 54*, 558–568.

Burns, M. C. (Ed.). (1986). *The speaking profits us: Violence in the cries of women of color*. Seattle, WA: Center for the Prevention of Sexual and Domestic Violence.

Cascardi, M., Langhinrichsen, J., & Vivian, D. (1992). Marital aggression, impact, injury, and health correlates for husbands and wives. *Archives of Internal Medicine, 152*, 1178–1184.

Dutton, D. G. (1986). Wife assaulters explanations for assault: The neutralization of self-punishment. *Canadian Journal of Behavioral Science, 18*, 381–390.

Dutton, D. G. (1988). *The domestic assault of women*. Boston: Allyn & Bacon.

Dutton, D. G., Bodnarchuk, M., Kropp, R., Hart, S., & Ogloff, J. (1995). *A ten year follow-up of treated and untreated wife assaulters: Psychological and criminal justice perspectives*. Vancouver, British Columbia, Canada: Institute on Family Violence.

Edleson, J. L., & Syers, M. (1990). The relative effectiveness of group treatments for men who batter. *Social Work Research and Abstracts, 26*, 10–17.

Edleson, J. L., & Tolman, R. M. (1992). *Intervention for men who batter*. Newbury Park, CA: Sage.

Ehrensaft, M. K., & Vivian, D. (1996). Spouses' reasons for not reporting existing marital aggression as a marital problem. *Journal of Family Psychology, 10*, 443–453.

Gelles, R. J. (1998, October). *Lethality and risk assessment for family violence cases*. Paper presented at the Fourth International Conference on Children Exposed to Domestic Violence, San Diego, CA.

Gondolf, E. W. (1993). Treating the batterer. In M. Hansen & M. Harway (Eds.), *Battering and family therapy: A feminist perspective* (pp. 105–118). Newbury Park, CA: Sage.

Goodstein, R. K., & Page, A. W. (1981). Battered wife syndrome: Overview of dynamics and treatment. *American Journal of Psychiatry, 138*, 1036–1044.

Hansen, M. (1993). Feminism and family therapy: A review of feminist critiques of approaches to family violence. In M. Hansen & M. Harway (Eds.), *Battering and family therapy: A feminist perspective* (pp. 69–81). Newbury Park, CA: Sage.

Hansen, M., & Goldenberg, I. (1993). Conjoint therapy with violent couples: Some valid considerations. In M. Hansen & M. Harway (Eds.), *Battering and family therapy: A feminist perspective* (pp. 82–92). Newbury Park, CA: Sage.

Hansen, M., & Harway, M. (1993). *Battering and family therapy: A feminist perspective*. Newbury Park, CA: Sage.

Hansen, M., Harway, M., & Cervantes, N. N. (1991). Therapists' perceptions of severity in cases of family violence. *Violence and Victims, 4*, 275–286.

Harway, M. (2000). Families experiencing violence. In W. C. Nichols, M. A. Pace-Nichols, D. S. Becvar, & A. Y. Napier (Eds.) *Handbook of family development and intervention* (pp. 391–414). New York: John Wiley & Sons.

Harway, M., & Evans, K. (1996). Working in groups with men who batter. In M. Andronico (Ed.), *Men in groups* (pp. 357–375). Washington, DC: American Psychological Association.

Harway, M., & Hansen, M. (1990). Therapists' recognition of wife battering: Some empirical evidence. *Family Violence Bulletin, 6*, 16–18.

Harway, M., & Hansen, M. (1993). Therapist perceptions of family violence. In M. Hansen & M. Harway (Eds.), *Battering and family therapy: A feminist perspective* (pp. 42–53). Newbury Park, CA: Sage.

Harway, M., & Hansen, M. (1994). *Spouse abuse: Treating battered women, batterers and their children*. Sarasota, FL: Professional Resource Press.

Holtzworth-Munroe, A., & Stuart, G. L. (1994). Typologies of male batterers: Three subtypes and the differences among them. *Psychological Bulletin, 116,* 476–497.

O'Leary, K. D., Vivian, D., & Malone, J. (1992). Assessment of physical aggression against women in marriage. The need for multimodal assessment. *Behavioral Assessment, 14,* 5–14.

Pressman, B., Cameron, G., & Rothery, M. (Eds.). (1989). *Intervening with assaulted women: Current theory, research, and practice.* Hillsdale, NJ: Erlbaum.

Prochaska, J. O., & DiClemente, C. C. (1982). Transtheoretical therapy: Toward a more integrative model of change. *Psychotherapy: Theory, Research and Practice, 19,* 276–288.

Rosenfeld, B. D. (1992). Court-ordered treatment of spouse abuse. *Clinical Psychology Review, 12,* 205–226.

Sanchez-Hucles, J., & Dutton, M. A. (1999). The interaction between societal violence and domestic violence: Racial and cultural factors. In M. Harway & J. M. O'Neil (Eds.), *What causes men's violence against women?* (pp. 183–204). Thousand Oaks, CA: Sage.

Sonkin, D. (1998, October). *Assessment based treatment: The risk assessment.* Paper presented at the Fourth International Conference on Children Exposed to Domestic Violence, San Diego, CA.

Tolman, R. M., & Bennett, L. W. (1990). A review of quantitative research on men who batter. *Journal of Interpersonal Violence, 5,* 87–118.

U.S. Commission on Civil Rights. (1982). *Under the rule of thumb: Battered women and the administration of justice.* Washington, DC: U.S. Government Printing Office.

Weitzman, J., & Dreen, K. (1982). Wife beating: A view of the marital dyad. *Social Casework, 63,* 259–265.

Yllo, K., & Bograd, M. (Eds.). (1988). *Feminist perspectives on wife abuse.* Newbury Park, CA: Sage.

25

CLASS, CULTURE, AND GENDER IN IMMIGRANT FAMILIES

JAIME INCLÁN

Over the last 15 years, family therapists have devoted much effort to understanding family and couple therapy in a social context. Feminists have effectively conceptualized couple dynamics in terms of the social and political history of gender relationships (e.g., Almeida, 1994). Similarly, McGoldrick (1998; McGoldrick & Giordano, 1996) and others (Falicov, 1998; Moore-Hines, Garcia-Preto, McGoldrick, Almeida, & Weltman, 1999) have alerted the field to the value of understanding couples and families in their cultural context. Understanding families in a cultural context then opened the way for a consideration of the particular experience of immigrant families (Hernandez & McGoldrick, 1999; Inclán & Hernandez, 1992; Inclán & Herron, 1989).

The contextualization of family therapy to gender and culture started as fields of study independent of each other. They shared an orientation to social class, namely, benign neglect. However, research and clinical experience indicate that social class differences account for the greatest variability in social behavior (Kliman, 1998; Sennett & Cobb, 1972). Nevertheless, social class does not yet sit at the family therapy table in the way that gender and culture do. It is especially important for family therapists to address social class at this historical moment when the integration into society of a new generation of immigrants will redefine the future of the United States.

In this chapter, I treat social class as the primary variable necessary for understanding gender relationships in immigrant couples. This approach supplements a cultural and gender analysis. Because cultural adaptation is a process that evolves over time, a developmental perspective that is specific to social class informs this initial attempt at outlining treatment issues in feminist family therapy with immigrant couples.

OVERVIEW OF SOCIAL CLASS THEORY

Marx (Marx & Engels, 1967/1848) made a significant breakthrough in our current understanding of social class. He was the first to propose that the most common psychology (culture) of groups is constructed by material well-being, that is, size of income, living conditions, and ability to manipulate resources for personal gain. Each class experiences reality from within the limits (context) of its position in society. Class differences manifest themselves in syndromes of behaviors, beliefs, and attributions that we call *culture*. Thus, culture does not exist independent of social class.

Marx delineated two main social class cultures: the bourgeoisie and the working class. There are also further subgroups within each of the two main class groupings. For example, both large and small business owners belong to the bourgeoisie, yet their life experiences differ significantly. Workers from an industrial background and workers with peasant backgrounds are both part of the working class, yet they differ dramatically from each other. Finally, the intelligentsia is a group with a broad class composition that includes members close to both the working class and the bourgeoisie.

Within-class variability also results from the degree of consonance between class position and class consciousness. *Class consciousness* refers to one's awareness of the privileges and burdens that accompany each class position. Many members of the bourgeoisie are critical of class differences in society and of their privileged access to sources of power. Their class consciousness generates values that differ fundamentally from the values of other members of the bourgeoisie that affirm the legitimacy of a class-stratified system.

Immigrants in the United States show significant variation in class position and in class consciousness. Most identify with their class roots and work hard either to maintain or change their class status. Others, who are focused on simply surviving, see improving their class status as a more distant task. Differences due to social class consciousness are important markers because class consciousness implies a highly developed capacity for meta-thinking. Each class position represents a significant context for interpreting and promoting behavior, including transactions related to gender. Thus, familiarity with differences in social class contexts can be helpful to therapists.

IMMIGRATION AND ADAPTATION FOR THE BOURGEOISIE

Bourgeois immigrants come with many instruments necessary for participation in mainstream American society: language, education, economic resources, and class ideology. However, the immigrant bourgeoisie also have difficulties. These are largely related to rejections they experience within the host society. These can be structural: for example, difficulties in achieving a residence status that allows for work participation, or the devaluation of training and credentials from their country of origin that limits access to professional positions. Other rejections result from the insecurity that established immigrants feel when they are faced with competent and able "others" who can favorably compete for seemingly limited opportunities. The arenas in which this discrimination plays out include schools for children, the real estate market, and employment and promotion contexts.

The ways in which rejection and discrimination are understood and processed vary. On the one hand, most bourgeois immigrants understand the rejection process because, in their countries of origin, they were members of the same social class and therefore played by the same rules. They are neither shocked by the system, nor do they attempt to play outside the system. Generally, they are greatly impressed by it and quite ready to attempt to make it work for them.

On the other hand, members of the bourgeoisie who have developed class consciousness are able to critique class rules in addition to using them to their advantage. This critical ability seems to serve an acculturation function. They are able both to stand apart (from the White majority and from other more established members of the bourgeoisie) while at the same time standing within their class group. Standing *entre dos mundos*—between two worlds—affords them comfort and a sense of identity.

Bourgeois immigrants with a class consciousness (usually from the intelligentsia) accept the dual-earner family structure, understand the need for gender role change, place less distance between themselves and their poor and working-class countrymen, and come with an interest in remaining different from the American mainstream. They affirm their ethnic identity and uphold the critique of a class-stratified system. Usually they are affiliated with liberal political positions and view themselves as having immigrated because of discontent with the class culture, including gender role norms and attitudes, in their country of origin. They are much more ready to embrace a resocialization process.

For many couples in this group, their relationship problems have to do with the implementation of changes that they have, in principle, embraced. They tend to define their problems as couple problems and come in for consultation as a couple; therapy with them can proceed conjointly. The husband and wife share enough understanding and belief systems to make meaningful discourse possible between the partners.

A large number of bourgeois immigrants, however, are small- or medium-level business people. Generally, they lack a developed sense of class consciousness. Their interests are more operational. This limits their outlook and perspective. They operate as if economic advancement could proceed without renegotiations of cultural identity and gender relationships. For people in this group, access to material goods increases the possibility of the family adopting (or maintaining) a single-parent (father) working model. The sole provider model then results in differential access to economic resources for the husband and wife. This differential economic reality then exacerbates a division between the personal and social worlds and generates power issues in the couple relationship.

Separate spheres develop between the family/personal and the business/social lives of small- and medium-level bourgeois immigrants. Formal work relationships are developed (typically by men) with people from different ethnic, racial, and social class groups. These contacts bring exposure to a range of power and gender role models. The husband's response is frequently a defensive one. He will attempt to maintain family life in isolation from perceived external pressure to change. The socialization process for women and children in these types of families emphasizes contact within one's ethnic group and sometimes almost exclusively within the extended family. Within-group socialization generally means an emphasis on a more traditional model of gender relationships.

However, women in these immigrant families will not remain completely insulated within a traditional cultural belief system. An awareness of more fair and equal relationship models develops sooner rather than later. When women begin to raise questions about their marital relationship, it is common for the husband to ignore the communication or to disqualify the message. If the wife persists, her husband may attempt to make her feel ungrateful toward him as the breadwinner.

During this initial questioning phase, the cultural blanket provides complicity with the husband's point of view. Women have internalized cultural values that limit their ability to confront men; and men have the idea that their views are correct and should be obeyed by their partners. Women further develop their aspirations in private thought and in the company of other women. Solidarity and support from other women most often precede confrontation.

Men, in contrast, defend against the new possibilities and attempt to preserve the old relationship. They often attempt to retain control. Socially, they can critique and even prohibit the woman's new friendships. Within the marital relationship, they emphasize the positive things in the relationship and try to impose a good-health cognitive affirmation onto the relationship. Acting within the traditional provider role, men may seek to provide additional material goods. A quiet, tragic, and potent marital schism grows. Little opportunity for friction and coevolution is tolerated. These couples are not ready for conjoint therapy. It is necessary to work with the husbands alone in an initial phase of therapy that prepares the men to be more open to renegotiation with their wives.

IMMIGRATION AND ADAPTATION FOR THE POOR

The poor immigrants arrive with a more fundamental challenge: earning enough money to survive and to adapt in a foreign country. Driven from their countries primarily by economic need, their initial orientation is to improve their family's living conditions. To do this, they are willing to occupy jobs at the lower end of the socioeconomic ladder and to assume the posture of deference that is expected. In short, they occupy a social position that renders them vulnerable to open abuse.

For the poor, immigration is not a strategy for personal improvement. It is an operation sanctioned and launched by the family of origin to meet the fundamental economic needs of the whole family. The poor come without prior socialization into the bourgeois values of individualism. The family, linear and lateral, is the usual initial framework of reference. Moneys earned provide for basic needs here and contribute to the sustenance of their families in their country of origin. For some, the midrange goal is to return to their country of origin. For others, the goal is to facilitate family reunification in the United States. In either condition, the new immigrants' goal is to earn money to provide sustenance and perhaps even advance their family's welfare.

Poor immigrants train for the voyage to the United States. Mental preparation is especially important. Training for immigration is based on the idea that life in the new country will be full of contradictions. Multigenerational stories about the experiences of kin with discrimination, racism, abuse, and oppression make up the first chapter of the study text. The second one narrates the opportunities for success that are available in a society in which class mobility can be achieved.

To meet the challenges ahead, the immigrant learns to develop a thick emotional skin. This survival tool will subsequently become a hindrance to mobility into the mainstream because it postpones openness to acculturation. Toughness of character is advocated for the insulation it provides from dangers and temptations (from within as well as from without) and as a deterrent against losing focus from the main economic goal.

The training for survival and adaptation of poor immigrants emphasizes several interconnected principles: do not think about your feelings; do not doubt or question yourself; do not react to taunting and temptation; hold onto the belief that things will improve. This frame of mind enables poor immigrants to work long and hard. Endurance is lauded as a key virtue. The purpose is to stay focused on the goal: to advance economically to help the family. To achieve their goal, poor immigrants endure much adversity, sacrifice, and social injustice.

For poor immigrants, work is low paying and hard to come by. At the same time, needs are great. In contrast to the bourgeoisie, they do not have a prior class status that needs to be preserved. Poor women may have had experience working outside the home (although generally in nonindustrial sectors). Thus poor immigrants, both men and women, are open to the first work opportunity they encounter. They play the game as if there were little clock time left. Sometimes women find work before the men do, sometimes the other way around. Sooner or later, both are contributing to the family economically.

Thus their material reality is frequently structurally different from that of the bourgeoisie. A shared practice of work precedes any ideological transformation of roles and relationships. Working long and hard, the initial focus of attention is on the availability of work (Is there work for tomorrow? Is there a second job available?). The second priority is remaining connected to their family of origin (communicating with extended family, getting goods transported back, preparing for the migration of others).

However, the most difficult struggles will ultimately take place within the couple relationship. For the poor, to a greater extent than for the middle class, immigration is a catalyst for the renegotiation of gender relationships and the reformulation of cultural identities. Immigrants are generally unprepared to meet these challenges. Prepared or not, however, poor immigrants will need to reformulate gender relationships and ultimately gender role ideology.

Contradictions between economic and personal adaptation needs, between the values of their culture of origin and those of the new culture, and between old and new gender ideologies are always present and mature at different points along the adaptation time line. For example, the first stage of immigration adaptation emphasizes self-sacrifice and emotional suppression. It is biased in favor of traditional male values and supposes (at best) the postponement of the woman's fair participation. Economic goals are privileged over relationships. The suppression of feelings and the development of a "tough skin" are considered necessary. In general, traditional roles are upheld. "Success" at this stage reinforces values and interpersonal patterns that will subsequently turn into excess weight for social class mobility and for the evolution of new roles in the relationship.

The road to a new cultural identity is at best bumpy. It involves intense overt or covert struggle between the partners. Therapists are sometimes asked for help in this transformation. Familiarity with the conflicts that immigration catalyzes helps the therapist understand the dynamics of immigrant couples and contextualizes their therapy to the class, cultural, and gender struggles that are inherent to the process.

Couple therapists framing the dilemmas of the couple narrowly in terms of the power distribution in the relationship will clearly observe inequality and be moved to challenge it. Will the couple accept this formulation of their dilemmas at this time? Culturally oriented therapists may overlook the power imbalance in the relationship and assume that cultural values determine the framework for meaning in the relationship. However, culture is changing—always and particularly for new immigrants who need not only to preserve their original identity but also to forge a new one that is consistent with their current social experience. Given this dual identification process, it is helpful to conceptualize immigration as a developmental process.

IMMIGRATION AS A DEVELOPMENTAL PROCESS: IMPLICATIONS FOR THERAPY

Adjustment to immigration occurs in phases. These take place over time, often over generations. Adjustment challenges are specific to the social class group of the immigrant. This section presents a developmental orientation for understanding these challenges in both poor and bourgeois families and argues that effective therapy must take into account both the social class and the developmental stage that a couple is in.

Poor Families

Contrary to the classical immigrant of prior historical periods, many new immigrants do not come with the idea of "burning their bridges" behind them. Many poor immigrants are what Shorris (1992) has called *transporters* [of their culture] and *sojourners* longing to return home. Others fit the classic immigrant picture. Most fall in between the two. Thus many poor immigrants live with multiple contradictions: between old and new learning, and between the more rigid and inflexible class society where men and women had a determined place and the possibilities of class mobility within the new society.

Immigrants live through these experiences with varying degrees of awareness of the concomitant changes in family relationships that are required. Adjustment to immigration has a social and a personal dimension. The pace of social and economic integration of the family, including attempts to move across class divides, may be more rapid than the pace of relationship reorganization. Working out personal solutions to these complex dynamics is the challenge of newcomers. The process, however, follows somewhat predictable developmental sequences.

Poor immigrants do not have an easy voyage or a comfortable landing. The first phase of the developmental process, getting settled, is akin to the military process of establishing a beachhead. It assumes a hostile environment and prioritizes securing a perimeter from which operations can be organized and launched. Initially, operations (family and social transactions) within the beachhead are oriented by a "command center" in the motherland, which is also the source for food, supplies, entertainment, and other aspects of life. The general purpose is to achieve a specific objective and return home. The objective is usually defined as economic advancement to achieve a better quality of life for their families. Preservation of the familiar is emphasized. Commingling with the new is strictly conceived as an operational necessity. The bodies arrive much earlier than their spirits.

Although names of beachheads vary (Little Italy, Chinatown, Odessa, Lower East Side, El Barrio, Little India), the neighborhoods established by recently arrived poor immigrants share a fundamentally similar class culture. That is, although food condiments, dress fashion, music and dance, and even religions may be distinct among the groups, the social patterns are similar. The assignment of tasks within the family—for example, who buys and prepares the food, takes care of the children, participates in family and social decision making—is more similar across ethnic groups of the poor than it is different. The fundamental similarity is due to the class background of the immigrants; the differences derive from the particular expression of class values in different historical and social contexts.

New immigrants know that they must work, and their children must attend school. More than in any other group, one hears "All I do is work" and "All we do is for our children." For the poor, arrival, survival, and settlement are the primary goals of the first phase of the immigration process. All other considerations, including the observance of traditions common to their ethnic group (religious participation, Sunday as a family day, etc.), are dependent on the pursuit of economic survival.

Consequently, gender role ideology as well as the interpersonal negotiation of ideas needed to achieve it is not an open subject of discussion for early immigrants who are poor. This does not mean, however, that change in gender relationships is not occurring. The lack of directness in this early phase of change is sometimes frustrating for therapists who, because of their social class background and stage of personal relationship, favor transactions that are verbal and cognitive. Therapists unaware of the distinct nature of gender role change in poor immigrant couples may precipitate a discussion of gender ideology that may be appropriate for a bourgeois couple but that is likely to result in resistance or even premature termination in a poor immigrant family.

Women and men from working-class and poor socioeconomic backgrounds move away from traditional gender *practices* prior to their acceptance of an alternative (more equal) gender ideology. Women usually become wage earners and participants in important family decision making before they and their partners acknowledge a shift in gender role ideology. Often, although the man is exalted as "in charge" in the home, the actual management of the resources of the family (power) is more equally shared. Likewise, because of the demands of double shift work, husbands are often left at home alone with the children during the wife's work shift. Thus men in working-class and poor couples are more likely to engage in traditional women's activities, such as cooking, cleaning, and doing laundry, before they accept (usually even forcefully combating) their male identity as encompassing gender role crossovers.

The picture of the poor immigrant couple in negotiation of relationship change, however, is not an ideal one by any means. Practice precedes ideology in part, but not solely, on account of the power differential and potential for male violence that can protect that power. This presents a decision point in the therapy between evolutionary or revolutionary approaches to relationship change. Therapists may perpetuate injustice by not challenging male privilege enough. Conversely, therapists may catalyze injustice by challenging too forcefully.

Therapists, like other people in power positions, tend to be ready to order "others" to fight the revolutionary ideological fight. However, it is important for therapists to hear what the women and men consider to be appropriate for themselves at this point in their relationship. More often than not, what emerges is an appreciation of the wisdom of incremental change in the context of the power of the very traditional multigenerational gender role background of poor immigrants and the firm values held about preserving the family. A developmental understanding of class differences in the process of gender role change can provide therapeutic guidance.

The couple, at this early stage of the acculturation process, presents with concrete relational (gender or cross-generational) problems or defines the problems as child focused. Usually, the woman approaches the clinic for services. At this time, the couple may not have a full awareness of the ideological differences and challenges inherent in the problems that may surface later. Gender skirmishes are common, but gender war is usually avoided by a "policy agreement" between the partners. On the one hand, the couple implicitly agrees to modify power in the relationship in terms of decision making about family matters, housework, and money. On the other hand, they simultaneously agree to maintain an explicit ideology of traditional gender roles.

This initial help-seeking contact can be critically important in the life of the couple's relationship. At this point, I have found it useful to observe the following therapy guidelines:

1. Reach out to the man and make every effort to establish a couple and/or family approach to the treatment.
2. Avoid resistance associated with a premature challenge of traditional gender role ideology in the relationship. One way to do this is to postpone direct discussion of power issues and

focus on actual power sharing as a practical problem-solving tool. That is, focus first on modifying traditional gender role practice as a means of addressing the couple's issues.

3. Inform your therapy model with a broad ecological and developmental (pre–early–later immigration) perspective about adaptive values, expectations, and behaviors.

4. Develop a "primary care" and "political" orientation to treatment. That is, do what is possible now, as a primary physician would, and establish alliances with both members of the couple for further therapy later.

5. Review your own feelings regarding the fact that for some couples, the "policy agreement" described above serves as a lifetime relationship framework. The couple's insistence on maintaining a traditional gender ideology, even though their behavior has become more egalitarian, is sometimes offensive to U.S. therapists. Therapists must guard against imposing their cultural biases if this position is culturally consonant with both members of the couple.

The importance of techniques that foster early involvement and retention of poor immigrant couples in therapy cannot be overemphasized. In my experience, when therapists do not heed early warnings of conflict in the adaptation to the immigration process, opportunities for systemic intervention are missed and many relationships dissolve. The woman subsequently seeks individual therapy to address her underlying feelings of anger and loss. These typically surface when "her" children are negotiating leaving home. Families in this stage of the adjustment process make up a very significant number of cases at public mental health centers.

Poor immigrant couples often seek treatment at a second point in the developmental sequence, namely, when open ideological struggles (conflict about traditional roles) emerge. This presentation of relationship problems almost by itself denotes a more advanced stage in the acculturation process of immigrants. This phase usually follows years in which both members of the couple have participated in both gender traditional work (double shift work for men, single shift plus the second shift of child care and housework for women) and gender crossover responsibilities (experience in doing nontraditional gender role functions).

Some common treatment issues in this phase can de anticipated. Usually the woman plays the gender card. She attempts to get the therapist to collude with her and confront her partner with his "machismo." The man, in turn, sets up the cultural defense: "You have changed; you have become too Americanized." Therapists must help the couple face gender contradictions between ideology and social practice. The therapist can help by reviewing the dynamics of immigration/acculturation and specifically emphasizing how adaptation is necessarily connected to social ecology, how changes in social ecology (i.e., from the culture of origin to the United States) necessitate changes in relationship patterns, and how developmental changes are necessary and inevitable. When the therapist is able to help the couple arrive at a broader understanding of how immigration and acculturation inevitably affect relationships, they are able to feel less personally attacked, their positions will become less polarized, and dialogue becomes more possible.

Bourgeois Families

Bourgeois couples present patterns according to their level of class consciousness. Many small entrepreneurs present an adjustment model that poses significant difficulty for their wives. These men are driven by a deep belief in the "American way": Democracy means opportunity for all, and hard work will enable one to climb the social class ladder. However, their understanding of the current American family model is dated. They uphold the traditional model of work and power distribution in relationships. With this internalized value system, men assume responsibility for economic progress and expect, in turn, acceptance of the traditional gender hierarchy. They believe that if they are able to provide the amenities of a developed consumer society, their wives and family will be or should be happy.

Women in these couples often are less well educated than the men and certainly have emigrated from societies that are more traditional than the United States. During the early phase of their adaptation to migration, they do not have either the material or ideological conditions with which to claim a more participatory voice. In the early stages of the adjustment to immigration, they frequently respond with silence and tolerance. This may well be a developmentally and contextually appropriate position. However, this position has the potential to become burdensome because power inequities in the relationship can become extreme and frequently include abuse.

Men tend to dismiss their partner's protests as insensitive and as a failure to be supportive of them. One client described his wife as a "good but ignorant wife" who did not know how to take care of him as a husband. Having economic hegemony, the men often attempt to maintain control by denying that there is any problem. Usually it is the wife who suggests that they seek counseling. A client described her husband's response: "You have no problems and no reason to have problems." When a husband does initiate therapy, it is usually around anxiety that negatively affects his work or around his somatic expressions of distress.

Unfortunately, immigrants do not have available to them the equivalent of marriage enrichment programs to assist them in understanding the inevitable stresses and transitions that are part of the process of adaptation to immigration. As a result, in this initial phase of therapy, I review, from a psychoeducational perspective, the developmental challenges that immigration presents and the changes that may be considered adaptive in the new environment. I have found that reviewing these challenges with the men *individually* prepares them for the relationship renegotiations that will continue to take place in the couple whether or not they enter therapy.

This phase of therapy has three goals:

1. Listen empathically to the husband's experience of "unrecognized" effort on behalf of the relationship. This recognition helps to attenuate the initial blaming posture of the husband and expands the possibilities of establishing a respectful attitude for the experiences of his partner. One or more individual sessions are also scheduled with the wife to facilitate her understanding of the precouple therapy goals.

2. Encourage a curiosity to understand couple dynamics and the evolution of problems from a historical perspective. The therapist crosses the bridge of time and place to join the client in understanding the social ecology that endorsed the traditional values akin to those of the recent immigrant. From that position, the couple relationship is examined developmentally in relation to the parameters of its changing social ecology.

3. Review the important role of emotions in psychotherapy. Immigrant men generally present with an exclusive valuation of cognition over emotions. They come, as one client said, "to understand if what they think is appropriate, and to correct their thinking if necessary." Opening the door to the world of feelings and to their importance in relationships can create an opportunity for "novel" questions such as, how happy is he? The role of feelings in happiness and the relationship of material success to happiness are also addressed.

There is great suffering in these couples, and work with them is difficult. The men have a deep belief in traditional values that are nonadaptive in their current environment, and they are very forceful in their insistence of these values. The women have neither the income nor the ideology that allows them to question the runaway patterns that tend to develop. It usually takes either a "crash" of economic fortunes and development of psychosomatic symptoms on the part of the husbands, or the realization of their oppression and commencement of work outside the home on the part of the wives, to start a relationship questioning process.

For the intelligentsia sector of the bourgeoisie, ideological changes away from traditional gender roles tend to precede changes in the practice of relational transactions. Men and women in this subgroup have often questioned the traditional gender role structures that govern relationships in their countries and may have initiated a personal change process before their immigration. They express a commonality of ideological position. Thus they are amenable to treatment as a couple from the beginning of therapy.

The therapy process with these couples focuses on clarifying interpersonal resistance to change and confronting the differences between perception of self and self as experienced by the other. In my clinical experience, it is mostly the immigrant men in this group who raise the reverse discrimination argument: "It is I, and men in general, who are at a disadvantage, and women who have the greater privilege and power." They often generate elaborate intellectual reframing of traditional practices as new, gender-sensitive ideological positions. Sometimes their argument produces short-term partner mystification and acceptance. However, acceptance quickly turns to its opposite and expresses itself in hopelessness: "He doesn't get it."

Class-conscious bourgeois women often demand privileges that are consistent with a less traditional role. This claim can precede their willingness to participate in the concomitant gender crossover tasks, such as working outside the home. In response, men sometimes complain of a double standard and confront their partners with gender contradictions in the relationship, for example, the fact that the wife wants more power over how to spend money without accepting more responsibility for earning it.

However, more often, the opportunity for further evolution is thwarted by the husband's response to his wife's request for privileges with the refrain: "That is within the traditional male role." In this case, the man points to the double standard only as a complaint, not as something that he wants to change. Rather, he insists on maintaining the "burden" (and power that goes with it). For example, in one couple, the wife began to work part time and kept her earnings in her own bank account rather than using them to repay a credit card debt. Her husband responded: "It's unfair, you should also pay into that account (the family account), but, OK, I'll pay it also."

These couples exemplify the social issues of the time and are negotiating at a personal level what society is negotiating more broadly. That is, they have internalized the progressive ideology of the women's movement and are attempting to establish relationship roles and responsibilities that are consistent with a more egalitarian relationship. This means, in practice, clash and struggle over the allocation of wage work, housework, and childcare responsibilities. Avoiding these clashes does not advance the therapy process with these couples. Rather it represents a pseudo-accommodation that usually leads to resentment, rebellion, and emotional distancing.

SUMMARY

This chapter presented the position that immigration is a catalyst for cultural change, including gender role and gender ideology transformations. The acculturation process of immigrants takes place over time. The beginning point, pace, and outcome of the acculturation transformation greatly depend on the social class of the immigrant. There is also great variation within social class groups. Level of class consciousness accounts for a significant amount of this variability. Therapists working with immigrant couples may be better able to help their clients when they are able to contextualize the relationship struggle to the couple's social class and developmental stage in the immigration process.

REFERENCES

Almeida, R. (Ed.). (1994). *Expansions of feminist family theory through diversity.* Binghamton, NY: Haworth Press.

Falicov, C. (1998). *Latino families in therapy: A guide to multicultural practice.* New York: Guilford Press.

Hernandez, M., & McGoldrick, M. (1999). Migration and the family life cycle. In B. Carter & M. McGoldrick (Eds.), *The expanded family life cycle: Individuals, family and social perspectives* (3rd ed., pp. 169–183). Boston: Allyn & Bacon.

Inclán, J., & Hernandez, M. (1992). Cross-cultural perspectives and codependence: The case of poor Hispanics. *American Journal of Orthopsychiatry, 62,* 245–255.

Inclán, J., & Herron, G. (1989). Puerto Rican adolescents. In J. T. Gibbs & L. N. Huang (Eds.), *Children of color* (pp. 251–277). New York: Jossey-Bass.

Kliman, J. (1998). Social class as a relationship: Implications for family therapy. In M. McGoldrick (Ed.), *Revisioning family therapy: Race, culture and gender in clinical procedure* (pp. 50–62). New York: Guilford Press.

Marx, K., & Engels, F. (1967). *Communist manifesto.* New York: Penguin Books. (Original work published 1848)

McGoldrick, M. (1998). Revisioning family therapy through a cultural lens. In M. McGoldrick (Ed.), *Revisioning family therapy: Race, culture and gender in clinical practice* (pp. 3–20). New York: Guilford Press.

McGoldrick, M., & Giordano, J. (1996). Overview of ethnicity and family therapy. In M. McGoldrick, J. Giordano, & J. K. Pearce (Eds.), *Ethnicity and family therapy* (2nd ed., pp. 1–31). New York: Guilford Press.

Moore-Hines, P., Garcia-Preto, N., McGoldrick, M., Almeida, R., & Weltman, S. (1999). Culture and the family life cycle. In B. Carter & M. McGoldrick

(Eds.), *The expanded family life cycle: Individual, family and social perspectives* (3rd ed., pp. 69–83). Boston: Allyn & Bacon.

Sennett, R., & Cobb, J. (1972). *The hidden injuries of class*. New York: Vintage Books.

Shorris, E. (1992). *Latinos: A biography of the people*. New York: Norton.

VII

EXAMINING SUPERVISION
IN FEMINIST
FAMILY THERAPY

26

THE GENDER METAFRAMEWORK

BETTY MAC KUNE-KARRER AND CATHERINE WEIGEL FOY

This recent discussion took place between Joanna and her supervisor:

> *Joanna:* I just held a first session with the couple. I like them. They're newly married and seem to be struggling with some tasks typical in early marriage: regulating contact with each partner's family and establishing an understanding about how much time is spent with friends. They are really at odds about how to resolve these issues. As far as I can tell, they attempt to solve their differences through a pattern of avoidance, confrontation, and then withdrawal. They're pretty frustrated at this point.
>
> *Supervisor:* (Asking about the contextual data that are missing) What's the couple's racial, ethnic, and socioeconomic background? And how does this contribute to their conflict?
>
> *Joanna:* The couple is White, but I am not sure about their ethnic background. I think I can tell their socioeconomic status by the fee that the clinic set.

Although discussions about development and conflict frequently occur in marital and family therapy supervision, cultural topics such as gender, race, ethnicity, socioeconomic status, religion, and sexual orientation—called the *contextual variables*—often receive less attention. If supervision is to influence the supervisee-therapist to include contextual variables in her or his practice, we as supervisors have to be willing to "walk the walk, and talk the talk" by examining our personal and professional beliefs about the diverse sociocultural contexts that influence our beliefs.

We thank Kathy Stathos, Stan Starkman, Cassandra Ma, and Victor Dye of the Chicago Center for Gender Studies for their participation in the development of this chapter, as well as Linda Rubinowitz of the Family Institute for her helpful comments.

The objective of supervision is to transform the supervisee-therapist's thinking and behavior in therapy. Although the transmission of ideas and shaping of skills is often the content of supervision, the process is the medium through which the therapist changes. This chapter describes an approach that develops a therapist's awareness of gender issues by focusing on contextual variables. The aim is to help a therapist move to a more complex way of conceptualizing human interactions at three levels of analysis: the intrapsychic, the interactional, and the sociocultural.

The theoretical framework that guides our supervision is the *gender metaframework* (Breunlin, Schwartz, & Mac Kune-Karrer, 1997). In comparison with other feminist family therapy approaches to supervision (e.g., Ault-Riché, 1988; Libow, 1986; Wheeler, Avis, Miller, & Chaney, 1989), the gender metaframework adds a unique developmental dimension to the training of therapists. This added dimension has proved to be an invaluable tool in supervisory tasks.

THEORETICAL FRAMEWORK

We (the authors) have worked together as teachers and supervisors for over 10 years. We have been part of a work group known as the Chicago Center for Gender Studies (CCGS). Along with three other women and two men, we have struggled with how to address gender in our lives, in the lives of our clients, and in training and supervision. The main focus of the CCGS is on applying the gender metaframework to training and supervision.

The gender metaframework assumes a multidimensional continuum of beliefs, affect, and behaviors that evolve from simple to complex. Five positions along this continuum were initially hypothesized: traditional, gender-aware, polarized, in-transition, and in-balance. The gender metaframework includes suggestions for assessing and intervening with families to facilitate progression along the continuum. Treatment begins by considering where the members of the family are positioned in the process of gender evolution and then develops objectives aimed at a gradual progression toward the in-balance position.

The initial project for the CCGS was to investigate whether the notion of a gradual evolution along the continuum could be substantiated. Through focus groups, we gathered information about the types of events that are likely to trigger transformations from simpler to more complex ways of conceptualizing the role of gender in our lives. Our research corroborated the theoretical assumptions in the gender metaframework. It also significantly differentiated students in each of four categories (traditional, gender-aware, polarized, and in-balance) but did not discriminate between the in-transition and in-balance positions. We therefore collapsed these two categories and adopted only the four positions that consistently discriminated between students.

A corollary focus of our group was to examine whether supervision could facilitate a paradigmatic shift regarding gender. Our research showed that indeed supervisors could facilitate such a shift (Mac Kune-Karrer, Weigel Foy, Stathos, & Starkman, 2002). Because a full discussion of the gender metaframework is not feasible here, we summarize its key points and refer readers to the book *Metaframeworks* (Breunlin et al., 1997) for added depth. We begin by briefly describing each position.

The *traditional* position on the continuum reflects a belief that men are biopsychosocially superior to women. This belief informs both behaviors and expectations. It further prescribes complementary roles in which men are problem-solvers and task-oriented, and women are relational and nurturing. Expected behavior for both sexes is narrowly defined. Men are expected to protect women and children from the external context and to provide economic support. Women are expected to protect the family from within and take care of everyone's needs in the family.

A therapist who believes that this traditional view does not accurately reflect men and women is in the *gender-aware position*. The traditional division of power between men and women is unsettling to this therapist, although the therapist may not know how it should be different. Because a lack of clarity in beliefs defines this position, the therapist may often feel confused about what to do or what to expect from men and women.

The *polarized position* is marked by a clear belief that the traditional roles and expectations are not acceptable. This firm belief fuels an openly challenging stance that often polarizes interactions and relationships. In contrast, a therapist in the *in-balance position* believes that egalitarianism provides the context for optimal development of men and women and of relationships. Although convinced that all are capable of achieving equal status in relationships, this therapist nevertheless recognizes gender constraints. The in-balance therapist is able to intervene in a manner that takes into account the context of the relationship, including the positions on the continuum of all people in the therapeutic system and the effect of these positions on the relationship.

The Metaframework advocates that the therapist's stance in treatment be collaborative. We prefer to use the language of collaboration rather than that of power, although we do not deny that power differences exist between women and men, between adults and children, between minorities and members of a dominant society, as well as between supervisors and supervisees. Further, at the political level, we distrust power because historically it has been used to dominate others and foster competition. We believe that through the balancing of opportunities and the establishment of egalitarian roles and expectations, we can go beyond power imbalance.

Treatment begins by taking into consideration where the members of the family are positioned in their process of gender evolution, and then moves on to develop objectives aimed at an in-balance position. At first glance, developing awareness of gender inequalities might appear to progress neatly from stage to stage. However, unlike other aspects of human development that develop gradually, achieving a feminist perspective seems to occur more in fits and starts. For example, one might behave from a gender-aware position in one's personal life while holding an in-balance position in one's professional life.

DILEMMAS IN CHANGING PERSPECTIVES

Over the years, we have learned that a "don't ask, don't tell" ethic prevails when it comes to discussing contextual variables. To change this pattern, we begin the academic year by addressing these with our supervisees, asking the following two questions:

- How do your clients identify gender imbalance in their relationship?
- How comfortable do you feel in raising the issue of gender imbalance with your clients?

In answer to the first question, supervisees tell us that many of their clients complain about the distribution of family duties. Other clients express dissatisfaction with the way money is handled in their family. A few are unhappy with how decisions are reached in their family.

The most common response to the second question suggests that most of our supervisees are at the gender-aware level. They feel unsure about addressing gender with their clients and therefore do not discuss gender unless the clients raise the issue. They do not know how to introduce issues related to gender inequality in an unobtrusive way.

Other responses from supervisees break down into two opposing themes. Some challenge the assumption that gender concerns need to be brought forth. Their rationale is that they want to respect the beliefs of the families. This group would be considered to be at the traditional level of evolution. The other group responds as though they expect us to support an overzealous approach and frequently give us examples of how they would confront the family to face its gender imbalance. This group responds by anticipating what they believe we want to hear and is likely stuck at the polarized level of evolution.

The following conversations with three supervisees illustrate the typical dilemmas they experience. In each case, we provide our assessment of their position on the evolutionary continuum from traditional to in-balance.

Ellen, a 23-year-old, married, White female of German descent reported:

> I don't bring it [gender in-balance] up because of the way I was raised. I didn't feel gender was an issue in my difficulties. In couples therapy, I just see it as an interpersonal problem. She is this way, and he is that way. Not because society has made them that way because of their gender, or their family has made them that way because of their gender. As I think more about it, however, it might be more helpful for the couple to look at it as a gender issue rather than an internal character flaw.

For this supervisee, gender was of questionable relevance to the couple's therapy. She is at a traditional level of evolution in which trainees are not likely to raise gender concerns because they agree with the traditional view. The goal with Ellen was to help her move to a gender-aware position and help her consider gender as a more comprehensive explanation of the couple's behavior. Discussing gender prescriptions as a way to make the partner's behavior more acceptable to each member of the couple may be the first step. However, the overall goal is to expand the couple's understanding of their gender constraints and increase their choices.

A second supervisee, Inez, a 28-year-old, married, White woman of Puerto Rican descent, reported:

> Sometimes I feel uncomfortable [about raising gender] but I think, "OK, how do I solve this? How is this going to get balanced out?" This is up to the couple. I do feel it's a sensitive issue. It's very hard as a woman to make a man see some of his privilege.

Inez shows more confidence in naming the contribution that gender prescriptions make to her clients' dilemma. She is at the higher gender-aware level of conceptualization. The question for this supervisee is how to best intervene with the couple, not whether to intervene. Expanding her command of language about gender imbalance will give her more confidence in raising gender issues in her sessions and help her move toward the in-balance position. Also, becoming more aware of her own gender prescriptions will open the door for "self of the therapist" work.

A third student, Donna, a 33-year-old, White woman of Jewish descent, married with two children, reported,

> I take every opportunity I have to challenge gender roles in my clients. I believe that I should not condone statements that are denigrating to the women in the family. I usually use these opportunities to teach them about how their expectations can stunt the growth of their daughters or decrease the wife's self-esteem.

Donna is clearly identifying dilemmas related to societal gender arrangements and recognizing the costs that these attitudes and behaviors have for all the members of the families she sees. What seems polarized is the overzealous way she has of approaching these concerns. She seems to be intervening to "right a wrong" rather than to expand the family's beliefs and behaviors along a continuum. She is at the stage where certainty about her beliefs clouds her appreciation of her clients' context and their evolution regarding gender-related issues. This outlook is typical of a person who has discovered oppressive themes in society and is ready to make them right.

There is an appealing part to Donna's behavior for us. It is always nostalgic to go back to the time when we discovered these wrongs ourselves and experienced the same degree of certainty about our vision. At the same time, we can see how interventions stemming from this "righteous" place are likely to shame and alienate families. Her interventions risk being disrespectful of the clients' position in their own evolution.

Each supervisee wrestles with different constraints in adopting an approach more relevant to gender inequities. Ellen struggles with her own beliefs about gender. For Inez, there is no question that the politics of gender affects all relationships. She seems to feel secure in her beliefs, but she is uncertain about how to intervene effectively. Donna has a need "to right wrongs" and is dedicated to her "truth." All of these young women need to expand their own positions gradually to an in-balance position. This movement will take time and frequent conversations in supervision that examine the constraints and opportunities of each position on the evolutionary continuum.

THE PROCESS OF SUPERVISION

The art of supervision lies in guiding supervisees to discover what they need to know to be effective therapists. It involves freeing the supervisees to use their talents. This liberation can be in the form of expanding their beliefs, informing their affect, and/or shaping their behavior. For some supervisees, we may only need to "polish" their gifts. For others, we need to promote a paradigmatic shift in thinking. Whatever the work, it requires an accepting, collaborative supervisory context that facilitates the development of specific learning skills.

Collaboration

On the surface, collaboration seems like a straightforward process whereby we cooperate with each other. A more archaic definition of the term might be a more apt description of the process. In earlier times, a "collaborationist" was a citizen whose country was invaded or occupied by foreign troops and who chose to cooperate with the enemy. For some supervisees, the paradigmatic shift might mean consorting with the enemy.

No wonder supervisees sometimes jump to using polarized language! So, when we invite supervisees to collaborate with us, we might call to mind the revolutionary leap we are asking them to take.

Although it seems self-evident that a collaborative context allows ideas to emerge and develop, it is not always clear how to identify the ingredients of collaboration in a supervisory relationship. One cannot assume that collaboration will evolve in a safe, supportive context with mutual respect and clear goals and expectations. We believe that collaboration requires vigilance on the part of the supervisor about how differences in leadership between herself and her supervisees unfold over time. It is also important to be mindful of the constraints that these differences place on both the supervisee and supervisor. Careful monitoring of this relational context will keep both supervisor and supervisee accountable to each other.

We have learned how ambiguous expectations may prompt therapists to act prematurely. Thus, after we assess the supervisees for their initial position on the continuum of responsiveness to gender issues, we focus on their expectations, asking them about their fears, insecurities, and "worst possible scenarios." We assume that social conditioning has been primary in the development of everyone's constraints. Therefore, we emphasize examining cultural themes connected with our families of origin and social backgrounds. We then proceed to set goals for the supervision—goals that make explicit the differences in evolution between our supervisees and ourselves. The last stage is to invite them to explore how language can expand meaning, connecting ideas and behavior to a variety of situations as well as connecting gendered behavior in each stage of the evolutionary process in our model.

Baselining

In order to assess the supervisees' position on the continuum, we ask the two questions mentioned earlier—about how their clients bring up gender concerns and about their own comfort level in raising the topic of gender imbalance in therapy. Once we have established their place on this continuum, as well the cultural and family legacies that have influenced their evolution, we are ready to set up objectives for the supervision. This is often a difficult process because it uncovers the affect connected to the assumptions that we all make about gender. Frequently, the affect proves to be stronger than we had imagined.

Expectations

We want to know the supervisees' expectations concerning learning a feminist approach to therapy, as well as what they think our expectations are for them. They invariably think that we want them to challenge the gender imbalance of their clients, immediately, firmly, and irrespective of context. They express insecurity about their ability to raise gender concerns with clients without doing so in an invasive way

Our expectations as supervisors rest on the belief that a paradigmatic shift can occur through the supervisory process. We believe that therapists need to be agents of social change, and therefore that cultural beliefs, when oppressive, need to be examined. Mutual goals about changing oppressive scripts need to be formulated with clients. We expect supervisees to challenge sexism, racism, classism, ethnocentrism, and homophobia because these discriminatory beliefs constrain the development of family members and impede their relationship to their community. We take particular care in helping supervisees with how (the language) and when (the timing) to help clients expand their beliefs and behaviors.

Setting Goals

Once expectations are clarified, we begin to develop mutual learning objectives with the supervisees. This is a gradual process, and much care is needed to respect different learning styles. We discuss their position on the evolutionary scale and their ideas about how to develop a more complex perspective regarding gender issues. We also discuss our primary objective: to help them make a paradigmatic shift toward conceptualizing gender as a primary context in all interactions.

Throughout the supervisory experience, we validate supervisees' experiences by examining how a particular belief served an adaptive purpose at a particular time and in a specific context. Focusing on the adaptive aspect of traditional ideas and identifying the types of contexts that promote these adaptations simultaneously sensitize us to the limitations of these ideas in different contexts. This perspective strengthens our ability to seek out and create new contexts that are likely to provide opportunities for expansion in individuals, families, or organizations. Finally, we examine how supervision can be a context that supports the supervisees' own growth and evolution in all learning areas, and consequently that of their clients.

Expanding Language

Change can take place through the exploration of both meaning and action in the therapy session. Both of these changes are expressed through language (description). Narrative therapists underscore the significance of meaning in therapy and use narrative as the primary process for therapeutic change. They deconstruct the various meanings that inform beliefs and guide behavior. However, expanding behaviors and emotions directly gives us additional paths toward change.

We introduce the language of change by examining descriptions and explanations, specifically focusing on the contextual variables of the supervisees. We ask them to discuss their family's legacies regarding gender (in both their families of origin and of procreation). In addition, we explore the power of language, both in constraining and expanding change. This exercise illustrates how gender is ever present in our lives and increases the supervisees' ability to identify gender scripts embedded in the descriptions and explanations given by their clients.

However, to become agents of change with clients, supervisees need to develop the skill to connect gender scripts with the therapeutic themes presented by their clients. In other words, we help them to use the language and themes their clients present, and to expand these by connecting them at the intrapsychic, interactional, and sociocultural level.

We pay careful attention to the supervisees' descriptions of their clients. These descriptions provide us with the language the supervisees' use in their therapy. Using language toward change is a common denominator in all therapies, and every supervisor has developed her or his own favorite way of expanding the development of supervisees through language. We find that a language that sanctions a "both/and" option will facilitate the process of expansion.

The next step is to connect therapeutic themes developed by the client and therapist at the intrapsychic, interactional, and sociocultural levels. For example, clients may describe their experiences in terms of their immediate interactions. The therapists can then expand these descriptions to encompass their clients' family of origin and sociocultural background. We prompt supervisees to connect descriptions that their clients make with larger sociocultural themes to contextualize these descriptions.

For example, a supervisee, Dan, reported that a female client stated, "My husband has always been aggressive. His family was a bickering family." This description focuses on the husband's family, ignoring both the wife's family and the sociocultural context. We suggested asking questions about how men are socialized into believing that aggression is a necessary way to respond, and how aggression may trigger themes for the wife from her own family. For supervisees, the goal is to clarify how to connect the personal/intrapsychic level of description with the interactional and sociocultural levels for both spouses. In other words, therapy connects language to various levels of context.

A CASE IN POINT

Before we discuss the following case, we wish to emphasize that we always discuss all contextual variables (i.e., race, class, ethnicity, and gender) in our supervision. However, space makes it impossible to address all of these variables for all of the case examples in this chapter. We decided to return to Joanna, the supervisee introduced at the beginning of the chapter, in this section because she explicitly asked for help in expanding her own struggles with gender issues. We believe that contextual variables affect everyone's behavior, not only people of African American or Latin American or Asian American descent. Therefore, if we had described our discussion of these variables only for Joanna, who is an African American therapist, and not for the other case examples, we would have confounded ethnicity and race with minority status.

We oppose the notion that contextual variables only refer to minorities and not to the dominant group. To consider contextual variables only applicable to minorities maintains two of the most insidious sources of unexamined privilege: the dominant group's role in defining what is relevant information and the maintenance of splits such as "us" and "others." This case represents all of the complex, diverse contextual variables that exist in the couple who are White and upper middle class, the therapist who is African American, and the supervisor who is Latino American.

Joanna is a young, African American woman who has been married for 5 years. She does not have children and works for a mental health agency serving a predominantly African American community in Chicago. She is a very good therapist in the second year of a postgraduate training program. She is familiar with the gender metaframework from a theoretical point of view because all students are taught this perspective in their first year of training. She is receptive to supervision and has shown great openness to considering new ways to converse with families. However, she was insecure about my (Betty Mac Kune-Karrer) expectations as supervisor regarding gender issues. Joanna's description of the couple revealed her knowledge of the developmental tasks in marriage as well as her ability to identify and track conflictual patterns in relationships. The glaring omission of sociocultural data made me wonder how completely this information was out of her awareness. Was the fact that Joanna is African American contributing to her reluctance to focus on contextual variables? Was she avoiding contextual variables because she experienced herself at a disadvantage in a program that consisted of mostly students and faculty from the dominant group? The fact that Joanna did not focus on any of these variables prompted a series of questions that clarified and expanded all of these levels of complexity. Many of these discussions served to highlight the gender inequality among the couple, the therapist, and me as the supervisor and facilitated understanding of how contextual variables affect meaning, emotion, and behavior.

The discussions covered the racial, ethnic, majority/minority, educational, and religious differences and similarities between the therapeutic and supervisory systems and pointed out the interconnections of belief systems in the couple, the therapist, and the supervisor. This exploration allowed the supervision group to engage in a rich exploration of the meaning of contextual variables in therapy and in supervision. It also allowed differences among members of the supervision group to be discussed.

Joanna commented that the husband's avoidance and the wife's pursuit of conflict seemed to be a familiar pattern in couples she treated. I wondered what was behind the husband's avoidance of conflict. I speculated that the wife's pursuit of conflict might represent her way of maintaining engagement—a task she saw as her "job" in the family. Joanna grasped this interpretation at an intellectual level, but when the discussion turned toward exploring the couple's gender scripts in therapy, she was clearly uncomfortable and said so. She voiced her fear that the couple would react by leaving therapy.

Joanna revealed her own struggles in dealing with gender scripts in her family of origin, with her husband, and at work in a mental health agency that had predominantly male administrators who favored male therapists. Joanna's traditional upbringing had taught her to support men in authority. However, she was becoming increasingly more aware of the unfairness of this practice at times.

These discussions placed Joanna's developmental level as gender-aware. Although Joanna's family of origin and marriage prepared her to be traditional, her chosen profession had opened up other options for her. I was very aware of Joanna's personal and professional struggles regarding gender imbalance and did not want to dislocate these areas of her life by pushing her into action prematurely. We spent several sessions in supervision discussing the difficulties we all experience in changing gender roles and expectations in our families and with our colleagues. We talked about the consequences that too rapid change could have for her marriage and her work.

Joanna stated that she had been thinking about her husband's patriarchal position before she began talking about the couple in supervision. She said that she felt her relationship with her husband was strong enough to withstand continued conversations about her dissatisfaction. She was confident that he would be responsive to her needs. This discussion introduced the importance of focusing on small steps and gradual change. The members of the supervision group helped Joanna with the language to use with her husband. The group consisted of four women, all struggling with various levels of gender awareness with their partners, husbands, or significant others. The obvious parallels in their personal lives and their therapeutic work became a theme in supervision.

At this time I introduced a discussion of our mutual expectations, asking Joanna how she thought I wanted her to intervene with this couple. She stated that she thought she was expected to find out more about how the couple's ethnic, religious, and socioeconomic background contributed to their difficulties. I agreed, but wondered how she might comfortably do so. We then role-played several scenarios. Giving Joanna both the language and an opportunity to practice her questions seemed to increase her comfort level.

When I asked her what she thought my expectations were in terms of intervening with the gender scripts, she replied that she thought I expected her to change them. To counter thoughts she might have about the speed and size of change, I described various small steps the couple might take in expanding their thinking and behavior beyond their traditional stance. Joanna focused on both the similarities and differences in her own personal experiences and those of the couple. Identifying their commonalities and differences enabled her to formulate several feasible objectives to begin her work with this couple. This discussion seemed enough for Joanna at this time.

Two weeks later, Joanna and I met to set her learning contract. I began by asking what she thought I expected from her regarding her own development in understanding gender issues. She replied that she thought I wanted her to become more astute at seeing and changing gender scripts. I asked her how she might do that. Joanna stated that she wanted to increase her understanding of the subtle and not-so-subtle ways gender informs interactions. She wanted to practice various interventions in supervision to increase her comfort in using them with clients

I supported Joanna's very appropriate goals and added that I hoped she remembered the "small steps" conversation. I acknowledged that years of practice had taught me to be both vigilant about learning new ways that gender informed relationships and also patient with myself. I assured her that I would extend this patience to her, helping her take small steps in her ability to observe and intervene with gender scripts. I wanted her to know that I did not expect her to reach an in-balance position overnight.

Our discussion then moved to clarify some specific small steps in expanding her thinking. Joanna thought it would be useful to examine every behavioral sequence she uncovered for possible gender scripts. I supported her idea, especially because observing interactional patterns is one of her strengths. I suggested we explore the ways previous clients had discussed gender.

Joanna wanted to tackle interventions next. We discussed sharpening her skills at being attuned to her clients' language and using it in working with gender imbalance in sessions. I pointed out that in some cases, she might not use the word *gender*, even while dealing with gender issues. Joanna was curious about this work and eager to begin. What else could a supervisor ask for? We were off to a good start. We have found that making the discussion of cultural variables an expectation in supervision from the beginning has been invaluable in interrupting the "don't ask, don't tell" pattern that has plagued supervision in the mental health fields for so long.

REFERENCES

Ault-Riché, M. (1988). Teaching an integrated model of family therapy: Women as students, women as supervisors. *Journal of Psychotherapy and the Family, 3,* 175–192.

Breunlin, D. C., Schwartz, R. C., & Mac Kune-Karrer, B. M. (1997). *Metaframeworks: Transcending the models of family therapy.* San Francisco: Jossey Bass.

Libow, J. (1986). Training family therapists as feminists. In M. Ault-Riché (Ed.), *Women and family therapy.* Rockville, MD: Aspen Systems.

Mac Kune-Karrer, B. M., Weigel Foy, C., Stathos, K., & Starkman, S. (2002). *Evidence of a fixed sequence of gender sensitivity within the human systems metaframework theory.* Manuscript submitted for publication.

Wheeler, D., Avis, J. M., Miller, L., & Chaney, S. (1989). Rethinking family therapy education and supervision: A feminist model. In M. McGoldrick, C. Anderson, & F. Walsh (Eds.), *Women in families: A framework for family therapy* (pp. 135–151). New York: Norton.

27

NAMING INJUSTICE, ENGENDERING HOPE: TENSIONS IN FEMINIST FAMILY THERAPY TRAINING

JEAN TURNER AND JUDITH MYERS AVIS

Initially, feminist family therapy training focused on consciousness-raising among trainees, intensifying their awareness of gender-related power dynamics in the lives and relationships of female clients and in therapy itself (e.g., Avis, 1988, 1989; Caust, Libow, & Raskin, 1981). In the past decade, this training has expanded to examine the intersection of other oppressions with those related to gender (e.g., Akamatsu, Basham, & Olson, 1996; Hall & Greene, 1994; Sirles, 1994; Turner & Fine, 1997). It has also expanded to explore the impact of gender relations—and the cultural discourses that support them—on men as well as on women (e.g., Nutt, 1991).

We have found that in our conversations with trainees about oppression, they recognize more fully how they have been affected by injustices in their own lives. They also come to the painful acknowledgment that they have often unwittingly participated in the reinvention and perpetuation of oppressive conditions. These realizations are emotionally evocative. One of the greatest challenges we have faced as teachers is how to navigate the river of emotions that begins to flood when we explore issues of violence, abuse, and subjugation. There are inherent tensions in honoring the rage and shame associated with injustice while simultaneously maintaining hope in the possibility of change.

In this chapter, we explore the tensions between naming injustice and engendering hope from a feminist, social constructionist perspective and discuss implications for training. Most of our exploration describes a class created for family therapy trainees. However, the principles and exercises used there can be used as well in a supervision group, a supervisor–supervisee relationship, a continuing education seminar, or, in some instances, alone in self-reflection. We believe that addressing issues related to oppression is key to becoming an effective therapist, and we offer our experience and suggestions in the hope that they are useful to others regardless of the stage of their professional development.

OUR CONTEXT AND FEMINIST STANDPOINT

The ideas we present here have emerged from our work as faculty members in a university master's-level couple and family therapy training program. Although we bring different backgrounds to our work, we both seek to create learning environments that reflect a critical feminist standpoint. For us, this standpoint entails analyzing power relations and privilege, including the linkages of multiple oppressions related to gender, class, race, sexual identity, age, and ability. We also attend to the ways in which historical context, structural factors, and politics lead to oppression and support its continuation. We engage in collaborative ventures in which a diversity of views is valued and contradictions are welcomed. Finally, we commit ourselves to reflexivity such that we analyze and critique our own practices with the same rigor as we critique those of others. We thus consider our teaching, itself, a kind of anti-oppressive action.

Our critical feminist standpoint is concerned with power relations, both those inherent in course material and those that are part of classroom interaction. In teaching about diversity, Jean Turner includes an analysis of gender oppression as a core power relation that cuts across the range of other oppressions. In training students how to work with issues of abuse and violence in families, Judith Myers Avis highlights gender power relations while at the same time exploring their intersection with other dimensions of inequality related to class, race, ability, and so on.

CONCEPTUALIZING THE LEARNING CONTEXT:
THE TEXT METAPHOR

Texts and Their Authors

In thinking about working with tensions and contradictions in feminist family therapy training, we have found it helpful to adopt a literary metaphor (White, 1993). We consider any content presented in a course as *texts*. This term refers not only to written materials (articles, chapters, legal documents, interview transcripts) but also to content that is packaged in verbal or visual format (lectures, dialogues, videos, dramatizations). Extending the term *text* to cover all these formats reminds us that, whether we are showing a video or lecturing on a particular course topic, the content is always "authored" by some person or group of persons who are located in a larger sociopolitical context. As such, all texts represent constructed realities. They invariably are partial accounts and portray the particular perspective of their author(s), who also occupies a particular social location that has meaning for the reader. Thinking about the course content as a set of texts raises the following questions about power and inequality:

- What is highlighted and what is obscured in this text?
- Whose voice is heard and whose is silenced? Who is free to act and who is not?
- Who are the authors? What are their social locations and experience with oppression?
- Who benefits most from the construction of reality presented by this author?
- Does the text support the status quo or challenge it?

These questions are part of a critical analysis in which texts are considered as political, that is, as constructions of reality that have implications for power relations. As such, texts will differ in the emotions they evoke depending on how each reader answers these questions.

Interpreters

In the text metaphor, all classroom participants (teachers and students) are thought of as *interpreters*. As they read, listen, view, and observe, each person in the class will attach her or his own unique meaning to the course content based on their prior personal experience and their social locations. Their emotional responses, especially if intense, may not be revealed immediately or in the classroom setting. Through fear about others' reactions to their feelings, or because they cannot find the words, students may silence themselves at the time but speak later, or use indirect strategies to communicate their experience.

THE CLASSROOM AS INTERPRETIVE CONTEXT: RELATIONS OF POWER

The group of interpreters (in this case teachers and students) are part of an *interpretive context* in which they coconstruct new ideas and perspectives in dialogue with each other. Within this context, as in any other, there are relations of difference in social location (such as gender, class, race, and sexual identity). There are also dominant discourses about what these social location differences imply in terms of expectations for particular behavior and attitudes. Power is attributed to class members by other class members on the basis of perceived group membership and depends on the privilege assigned to that group in the larger sociopolitical context outside the classroom. Intersections of differences and multiple inequalities create added complexity and sometimes confusion in the attribution of power. For example, in our local context a heterosexual Black woman who is a middle-aged professional may be perceived as having more power than a younger gay White man who is in the early stages of training.

In an interpretive context in which the joint goal of the participants is to learn about oppression and abuse, the relations of power that are always present between the participants cannot help but come more clearly into view. For example, to discuss ideologies of racism and acts of racial discrimination in a mixed-race group of students brings to the foreground the racial differences among the people in the class, including those between instructor and students. The increased awareness creates the potential for heightened emotional interactions between class participants. Similarly, when a female instructor shows a mixed-gender class a video about spousal abuse, the gender differences in the class are highlighted. There is an increased sensitivity to what the men and women say about the video with the potential for angry responses from the women and defensive ones from the men.

Relations of power are also formally structured into most learning through the practice of assigning grades. This act of evaluation constructs in a concrete way the unequal power between teacher and student, in addition to the power and status already attributed to teachers because of their greater experience and higher level of training. We are also aware that as instructors we exercise power by selecting most of the texts and that our choices may well reflect the biases of our own social locations. We address these concerns by examining our choices for what might be missing, leaving room for student input, and by sometimes using "cultural" interpreters or consultants to increase our consciousness of embedded messages in the texts. We also acknowledge that what we say about any particular text may have a greater weight than what another class member says, because of our position of greater power.

WORKING WITH THE TENSION BETWEEN RAGE AND HOPE

The process of naming and documenting various forms of violence and oppression, and examining their effects, invariably evokes strong emotions among class members. Feelings of anger, sadness, and shame tend to surface quickly: anger on the part of those students who identify with the oppressed, shame and guilt on the part of those who recognize themselves as having a connection to the oppressor. These emotions are usually not cleanly felt but are often accompanied by confusion, with rapid and unexpected shifts from one emotion to another. If this emotional flow is left unchecked, rageful currents, along with eddies of shame and depression, may build and eventually overflow in ways that threaten everyone's learning. The space available for dialogue and exchange of ideas may then close down. As some students become angrier, others may respond with increased guilt and shame. Eventually, those who are angry may take up more and more room, whereas others feel silenced.

We believe that it is essential for family therapy trainees to experience the pain and the accompanying sense of helplessness, hopelessness, and anger that ensue from truly hearing the experiences of those oppressed by violence, sexism, racism, and homophobia. We believe that it is this hearing that enables trainees to identify and empathize with the oppressed while also confronting their own vulnerability to engage in oppressive acts.

One of our purposes in teaching these topics is, in fact, to disrupt people's usual ways of thinking about power and abuse. However, we have found that in feeling unmitigated pain, there is a danger that students may become overwhelmed and paralyzed by hopelessness or rage and lose sight of possibilities for change. Our goal is for students to experience the intensity of the pain of violation and oppression while not getting so stuck in it that it blocks either their creativity and ability to act or their capacity to see possibilities and potential for both themselves and their clients. We also recognize that anger itself can provide energy for action as long as it is not so intense that it is immobilizing.

Using the text metaphor, we have found at least three significant factors in the learning context that affect the amount of space open for generative dialogue. These are the relationships between each person in the classroom (including the instructor), the selection of materials (texts) and their presentation format, and the relationship between each interpreter and any particular text.

THE RELATIONSHIP BETWEEN INTERPRETERS: ATTENDING TO ISSUES OF POWER, VOICE, AND SAFETY

Generativity of the classroom dialogue depends on participation of interpreters. Issues of "voice" (who feels free to speak, whose comments will be given the greatest attention) are intimately connected to power. In addition, the degree of safety in the learning context will depend on the predictability of the consequences for taking risks and whether or not there are mechanisms to redress any violations of trust that might take place. In this section we outline several practices that we have developed to take into account the problems of power, voice, and safety that can constrain the dialogue between class members.

Safety and Trust Among Interpreters in the Learning Context

We have found that directly addressing the issue of safety in the interpretive context is an important way of acknowledging power differences within the class and the unique background of each person. Obviously, there is no way to ensure that all class members will feel safe all the time. What we can do is to set some parameters that might secure a "safe as possible" context for discussion. Judith Myers Avis approaches the issue of safety by making time in the first class of a course on violence to create a joint "contract" among class members. This contract comprises a set of agreements generated through class discussion that guides the journey through the course. Some examples include making "I" statements, asking for clarification before expressing a different point of view, avoiding generalizations such as "Women are . . ." or "Men do . . . ," and announcing the subject matter of videos a week in advance so class members can make an informed choice about whether they wish to view them or not. Both trainees and instructor monitor class activities and process to ensure that they comply with the safety agreement.

At the very beginning of a course on diversity, Jean Turner engages the class in a discussion of the trade-offs between constraints imposed by political correctness and the potential dangers of unedited spontaneity. Conflicts and misunderstandings are predicted as inevitable in a course on oppression. By the end of this discussion, the class puts together some guidelines for what to do when anyone in the class (including the instructor) makes a comment that offends another person, as will surely happen. Usually the guideline agreed on is that the offended person will state her or his feelings and whatever is planned for the rest of the class will be suspended until the issue has been dealt with.

This usually involves "unpacking" the meaning of the comment for the offended class colleague, for the person who said it, and then for the rest of the class. In the unpacking process, there is respect for different meanings and acknowledgment of the power dynamics. Knowing that this process is available frees most class members to participate in class dialogue with a sense of sufficient safety. They own their ideas and put them in a tentative format. They withhold judgment. As one student put it, we present ideas as though they are "draft text"—they are not to be considered as "final copies."

Adding to Minority Numbers

One way in which the power relations that are usually present in any classroom can become more apparent, and therefore available for everyone to reflect on, is to invite guests whose social location shifts the usual power balance in the class. For example, a speaker was asked to present his experiences of being both a survivor of childhood sexual abuse and a therapist for clients who have experienced similar kinds of abuse. He talked about serving gay clients and being a member of the gay community. In the discussion that followed, a class member who identified as bisexual commented that she had noticed that she and the one other colleague in the room who was gay had been freer to contribute than at any other point in the semester. She posed the question: "What would it be like if there were always more than two queer people in the class?" This reflection was echoed when the entire class went to a campus center for students of color to view the video *Color of Fear*, which provided an in-depth look at racism. The three students of color in our class were much more active than usual in the discussion following the video. Later, we all talked about this change, exploring the reasons for the shift and how it might be prolonged even when the color balance returned to what it had been.

ASPECTS OF TEXTS THAT EVOKE PARTICULAR EMOTIONAL REACTIONS

Ultimately, how a text is responded to depends on how it is "read" (interpreted) by each individual. However, there are several aspects of texts themselves that we have found predictive of particular emotional reactions.

Naming Oppression and Naming Resistance

Language is significant. The act of naming a behavior as "oppressive" or "abusive" by an author of a text tends to evoke reactions of rage, shame, or guilt in the interpreter. To focus on the negative effects of oppression and abuse for victims, without also exploring survivorship and coping strategies, tends to further deepen the emotional response. In contrast, naming and providing information on acts of resistance by the person who has been victimized invites a consideration of human resilience and strength. We have therefore found it essential in this training to include a focus on the *acts of resistance* of those who have been subjugated physically, sexually, economically, culturally, racially, or emotionally (Wade, 1997). Acts of resistance are those personal responses, including both behaviors and mental stances, that enable those who have been victimized to ward off the effects of violation or oppression. These acts range from physical protection of oneself or others, through small verbal protests, to purposeful passivity and silence in the face of coercion. When we bring into view the small acts of personal agency that oppressed people manage, students experience hope. When we fail to acknowledge resistance, rage and despair can dominate.

As part of a course on violence, a speaker presented an ongoing therapy situation in which there was not only very serious spousal abuse but also multiple dimensions of oppression that had affected all family members. The situation involved a Central American family who had arrived in Canada as refugees. They had all suffered directly or indirectly the effects of widespread political violence and atrocities in their country of origin. They had also lost their home, their employment status, and contact with family members who had stayed behind. They had arrived in Canada during a period of recession when jobs were scarce, attitudes toward immigrants were generally negative, and racism was high. This was the background for the therapist's attempts to help the wife and children deal with the effects of violence perpetrated by the husband/father who had pursued them from city to city across North America.

As the presenter recounted the story of pain and desperation, the class became more and more silent. It was as if we, too, had become caught into a web of suffering from which there appeared to be no escape. Looking back, we now realize that the presenter's account was missing a perspective on the resilience of these family members who had miraculously managed to survive in the face of multiple oppressions. Because it was ongoing therapy, there was not yet an ending or resolution. The future looked bleak. To avoid repeating this situation, in the future we would ask class members to identify the ways in which family members had made choices to resist oppression. We would also look for family members' strengths and resources, and how these might be used in helping them deal with their current situation.

Denying Versus Taking Responsibility

A key factor in how most readers are affected by a text seems to be the degree to which a person who has acted abusively takes responsibility for the effects of their actions on others. For example, in an interview in the late 1980s, Sean Connery strongly asserted his belief that it was right and appropriate for a man to hit a woman across the face with his open hand if she "won't let something alone" or "if her behavior warrants it." He denied any responsibility for how this behavior might affect a woman, even suggesting that if she were to hit back it might be a sign that she liked it. This clip invariably elicits anger and shock in observers. On the other hand, in the film *To Have and To Hold,* men who had previously abused their partners express their new understanding of their responsibility for their violent behavior and its impact on their partners. They also acknowledge how the abuse served their own needs for power and control in their relationships. This film usually elicits hope in possibilities for change.

Blaming Versus Contextualizing

Anger is a likely response when oppressors are simply blamed personally without contextual explanation for how they might have come to act abusively. Rage may be further fueled when they are described as "abusers" or "perpetrators" rather than "persons who have abused." This kind of labeling has the effect of reducing their personhood to a category. In contrast, when information is included about their personal history and the factors that may have constrained their ability to take different action, the interpreter's emotional reaction may be attenuated by their recognition that the person is also human. Although contextual information never absolves a person who has abused from responsibility, it may allow trainees a fuller understanding and enable them to feel the compassion necessary for working in therapy with those who have misused their power.

The effects of this latter kind of text were very evident when, through happenstance, a therapist who worked with violent men visited our program. Her compassionate portraits of these men, and her stories about their traumatic histories and the changes they had managed to make in therapy, created a different beginning to the course. As the term progressed, that initial encounter with the humanity of these men provided a touchstone from which to draw hope and to balance the rage felt later in the course as we explored the impact of male abuse on women and children.

Although we draw deliberate attention to acts of resistance, responsibility-taking, and contextualizing, we are aware that such a focus risks underestimating the ongoing struggle of the abused/oppressed person or group. Concentration on individual stories of survival and transformation can also blind us to the sociopolitical and contextual aspects of oppressive relations. These risks are at least partially reduced when the victim's suffering and the oppressor's self-serving attitude are juxtaposed with the courage of victims to protest and endure, and the capacity of those who have acted oppressively to change. We have found that coming as close as possible to a simultaneous consideration of oppression, resistance, and responsibility-taking fosters the most generative learning context.

FACTORS THAT AFFECT THE INTENSITY OF INTERPRETERS' RESPONSES TO A TEXT

Individuals in the class will each have a unique interpretation of any text depending on their own life experiences, their values and personal ideologies, and their particular state of being at the time that they come in contact with the text. These variables affect the strength of the student's emotional response to material presented in training. For example, a student who has experienced childhood sexual abuse will likely have a more intense reaction to the readings, videos, or other texts on this topic than a student who has not experienced such abuse. A student who has faced discrimination as a member of a minority religious denomination will react with more emotion to material on religious oppression than a student who identifies as agnostic. In addition to these individual level variables, several factors related to the relationship between text and interpreter appear to be important predictors of the depth and intensity of emotional response.

First-Person Accounts

Texts that are first-person accounts are likely to evoke a stronger emotional response than those written in the third person, partly because most readers connect more closely with the author of an autobiographical account. This does not mean that they will agree with the author, only that they will likely experience the person, and therefore the person's story, as more engaging (either positively or negatively). For this reason, listening to a presentation by a formerly battered woman or by an individual who has experienced racism is likely to have more impact than reading a research study summarizing the findings. In general, actual interviews, transcripts of testimony, or autobiographies evoke more emotional intensity than do more removed formats such as biographies and academic lectures.

"Truth"-Saying and Social Location

We have noticed that texts are often more emotionally compelling when they are presented as true and delivered with a high degree of certainty and personal passion. In these types of "truth" situations students tend to become more emotionally involved, taking positions that are either for or against the author's perspective. One way we have tried to be proactive in anticipating such polarizing discussions is to set up formally structured debates on contentious topics. This allows students to argue enthusiastically for strongly opposing positions having already carried out some research and reflection. The polarization process can then be deliberately used to help clarify different points of view and the assumptions behind them.

Alternatively, we sometimes choose to deescalate or avoid polarization by locating the author of a text within the context of the author's personal life experience and within her or his broader historical and sociopolitical context. An author's text begins to be viewed as a partial account rather than as a representation of reality or truth. The reasons an author presents a particular truth and has an investment in arguing for it begin to make sense, based on the meanings that are most congruent with her or his personal experiences and selected from those discourses most available in her or his local context.

Action on the Part of the Interpreter

We have noted that the relation between the interpreter and the text shifts when some avenue is opened up for the interpreter to take action. For example, students' intense reaction of rage, shame, or guilt regarding a situation of racial oppression or violence may be attenuated when they are able to see some way to address the effects of the abuse/oppression personally (Porter & Yahne, 1994). Just considering a possible action is often sufficient to change students' emotional response, for example, imagining what they might do if they were a therapist (advocate, friend, consultant, etc.) for this person. We are particularly focused on how therapists can practice in ways that mitigate the effects of abuse and oppression on clients' lives.

Opportunity for Reflection

We have noted that the intensity of the emotional response to material about abuse or oppression tends to increase if there is no opportunity for the interpreters to reflect on the reasons for their reaction to the text. Intensity is decreased when interpreters have the opportunity to step back and analyze what evoked their response. A particularly powerful vehicle for reflection is the ongoing journal that students write as part of the course on working with violence in families. In this journal they comment on what stands out as important for them, as well as their personal thoughts and feelings in reaction to texts presented in class and encountered in daily life. This is a particularly significant avenue of expression for those students who tend to be silent during class discussions. Students pass the journal to the instructor at various points in the semester for review, affording the instructor the opportunity to dialogue with them in writing.

Another format for encouraging a reflective stance is to ask students to respond to a set of questions such as those in Exhibit 27.1. These questions may be used for students to interview each other, either in class or outside, about their reaction to a text (reading, client account, video, etc.). Alternatively, they can be used as a written exercise.

EXHIBIT 27.1
Questions for "Interpreters" to Clarify Their Emotional Responses

1. *Emotions.* What am I feeling most strongly as I read (listen to) this "text"? What am I not feeling?
2. *Identification and Social Locations.* With which person(s) in the text do I feel most connected? Along what dimension do I feel connected to them? With whom do I feel least connected? What role would I be likely to take if I were a participant in the story?
3. *Power.* In this text, who directly benefited by what happened? Who benefited indirectly? Who did not benefit? Whose "voice" was heard? Whose was not heard?
4. *Responsibility.* Who is portrayed as responsible for the oppression/abuse in this text? Who else might be implicated indirectly? How?
5. *Personhood.* What do I not know about the lives and characters of the people portrayed, beyond their connection to the oppression/abuse?
6. *Context.* In what historical period and local culture does the abuse/oppression take place? What are the ideological and structural constraints faced by each person in the text?
7. *Resistance.* What small acts of protest can be identified during the abuse and after the abuse? If these are not part of the text, what do I imagine they might have been?
8. *Partialness.* Am I leaving enough space for the not-yet-told parts of the story that is presented? What might these parts be?

SUGGESTIONS FOR TRAINING

In summary, we would like to present the following guidelines that we have found helpful in working with the tension between rage and compassion in feminist family therapy training:

1. Acknowledge the power hierarchy between teacher and students, and between the students in the class. Seek ways to reduce power inequalities while acknowledging openly that power will never be equalized. Clarify differing roles and responsibilities.
2. Take into account the effects of the texts about abuse/oppression on everyone. Give information about the possible impact of the material before presenting it. Expect vicarious traumatization and predict it for class members. Expect shame or guilt-by-association and predict it. Give opportunity for personal and joint reflection about emotional reactions.
3. Select texts that provide narratives of resistance to oppression as well as of victimization, and of the taking as well as the denying of responsibility.
4. Present less material in more depth to give time for focused intensity, broadening of abuse/oppression accounts, and personal reflection.

5. Look for ways to contextualize material with respect to historical period and local culture in order to expand on narrow blaming that might be written into the texts used.
6. Evoke agency and self-empowerment in class members by discussion of what actions they could take, either individually in their professional practice or as members of an advocacy group.
7. Expect tensions and emotional interchanges between class members. Codevelop guidelines for how to deal with these situations when they emerge.
8. Ensure that the intersections between gender and other social locations are explored both in the course content and in the classroom context.
9. For each text, analyze each "author's" ideological position and intentions. Note the possible impact of this position on the listener/reader/viewer and on the range of actions conceived possible. Look for what is said and what is not said. Invite this kind of critical analysis for all texts, including (especially) those presented by the instructor.

THIS CHAPTER AS TEXT

This chapter itself is a "text" that, because it focuses on teaching about oppression and abuse, might be emotionally evocative for the reader and might raise questions of credibility, partiality, and power. We are involved in a lifelong process of informing ourselves about inequalities. Our own social locations and feminist standpoint expand our vision in some directions and, at the same time, limit our ability to "read" and write texts as a differently located person might. Our observations and suggestions for training are also influenced by the kind of interpretations circulating in our particular local context. We therefore recommend that, in applying these ideas to other training contexts, readers make revisions to take into account their own local educational "culture."

REFERENCES

Akamatsu, N. N., Basham, K., & Olson, M. (1996). Teaching a feminist family therapy. *Journal of Feminist Family Therapy*, 8, 21–36.

Avis, J. M. (1988). Deepening awareness: A private study guide to feminism and family therapy. *Journal of Psychotherapy and the Family*, 3, 15–46.

Avis, J. M. (1989). Integrating gender into the family therapy curriculum. *Journal of Feminist Family Therapy, 1,* 3–26.

Caust, B., Libow, J., & Raskin, P. (1981). Challenges and promises of training women as family systems therapists. *Family Process, 20,* 439–447.

Hall, R. L., & Greene, B. (1994). Cultural competence in feminist family therapy: An ethical mandate. *Journal of Feminist Family Therapy, 6,* 5–28.

Nutt, R. (1991). Family therapy training issues of male students in a gender-sensitive doctoral program. In M. Bograd (Ed.), *Feminist approaches for men in family therapy* (pp. 261–266). New York: Haworth Press.

Porter, N., & Yahne, C. (1994). Feminist ethics and advocacy in the training of family therapists. *Journal of Feminist Family Therapy, 6,* 29–48.

Sirles, E. (1994). Teaching feminist family therapy: Practicing what we preach. *Journal of Feminist Family Therapy, 6,* 1–26.

Turner, J., & Fine, M. (1997). Gender and supervision: Evolving debates. In T. C. Todd & C. L. Storm (Eds.), *The complete systemic supervisor: Context, philosophy, and pragmatics* (pp. 72–82). Boston: Allyn & Bacon.

Wade, A. (1997). Small acts of living: Everyday resistance to violence and other forms of oppression. *Contemporary Family Therapy, 19*(1), 23–39.

White, M. (1993). Deconstruction and therapy. In S. Gilligan & R. Price (Eds.), *Therapeutic conversations* (pp. 62–80). New York: Norton.

AUTHOR INDEX

Numbers in italics refer to listings in the reference section.

Abadio-Clottey, A., 154, *158*
Ackerman, N., 18, 21, *34*
Adelmann, P. K., 81, *87*
Akamatsu, N. N., 365, *377*
Allen, K. R., 10, *14*, 51, *62*
Alliger, G. M., 81, *89*
Almeida, R., 24, *34*, 228, 237, *237*, 293, 294, 296–298, 300, *304*, *305*, 333, *346*
Anastos, K., 282, *289*
Anderson, C., 19, 20, *33*, *35*, 88
Anderson, D., 56, *63*
Anderson, H., 26, *34*
Androcino, M., 168, *175*
Annenberg Public Policy Center, 4, *14*
Anyan, W., 148, *159*
Arras, J. D., 282, *290*
Aubin, C., 309, *318*
Ault-Riché, M., 21, *32*, 352, *363*
Avis, J. M., 26, *32*, 80, *87*, 89, 168, *175*, 352, *363*, 365, *377*, *378*

Baber, K. M., 10, *14*, 51, *62*
Bahr, M., 254, *264*
Bakan, D., 270, *279*
Bales, R. F., 17, *35*
Barrett, S. E., 307, 309, 313, 316, *318*
Basham, K., 365, *377*
Bass, E., 115, *119*
Bateson, G., 21, *34*, 66, *76*, 135, *144*
Beach, S. R. H., 211, *222*, *223*
Begg, E., 148, 149, 156, 158, *158*
Benjamin, J., 204, *210*
Bennett, L. W., 325, *331*
Bennett-Goleman, T., 154, *159*
Bepko, C. S., 26, *33*
Bergman, S., 203, *210*
Bernstein, A. C., 92, *103*
Berry, W., 14, *14*
Bettinger, M., 227, *237*
Bianchi, S. M., 81, *87*
Billson, J. M., 186, *188*
Binda, W., 276, *279*
Blair, S., 226, *237*

Blau, M., 56, *63*
Blehar, M. D., 211, *223*
Blos, P., 66, *76*
Blumstein, P., 7, *14*
Bly, R., 170, *175*
Bodnarchuk, M., 325, *330*
Bograd, M., 19, 23, 24, *32*, *34*, 168, *175*, 256, *264*, 294, *304*, 320, *329*, *331*
Bond, M., 137, *144*
Bourne, E. J., 109, *120*
Bowen, M., 22, 28, *34*, 53, *63*, 80, *87*
Boyd-Franklin, N., 28, 29, *33*, *34*, 41, 50, 109, 111, *119*, 131, *132*, 155, *159*
Boyer, M. F., 153, *159*
Bradbury, T. N., 211, *223*
Braverman, L., 20, *32*, *34*, 80, *87*
Breunlin, D. 199, *210*, 352, *363*
Brooks, G. R., 81, 88, 165, 168, 169, *175*, *176*
Brown, L. S., 75, *76*
Browne, A., 259, *264*
Bruner, J., 74, *76*
Bruns, C. M., 246, *251*
Buchler, C., 92, *103*
Burns, M. C., 328, *329*

Cameron, G., 320, *331*
Campbell, T. L., 255, *265*, 268, *279*
Candib, L. M., 253, 254, 256, 258, *264*, 272, *279*
Canino, G., 148, *159*
Canino, I., 148, *159*
Carmichael, L. P., 255, *264*
Carter, B., 19, 23, *34*
Carter, C., *33*
Cascardi, M., 321, *329*
Castillo, A., 150, 153, 154, *159*
Catalyst, 4, *14*
Caust, B., 365, *378*
Cazenave, N. A., 187, *187*
Cervantes, N. N., 320, *330*
Chaney, S., 80, *89*, 352, *363*

Chartrand, S., 191, *197*
Cherlin, A., 91n, *103*
Cherlin, A. J., 92, *103*
Chesney-Lind, M., 242, *251*
Cienfuegos, A. J., 153, *159*
Cigoli, V., 276, *279*
Clottey, K., 154, *158*
Cloward, R., 283, *290*
Clunis, D. M., 310, *318*
Cobb, J., 333, *347*
Cohen, F., 241, *252*
Coleman, S. B., 26, *34*
Comas-Díaz, L., 29, *33*, 148, 151, 157,
    159
Combs, G., 66, *76*, 122, 123, *132*
Commonwealth Fund, 268, *279*
Coontz, S., 62, *63*
Cotroneo, M., 20, *34*
Crenshaw, K. W., 296, *304*
Cromwell, P., 148, *159*
Crosby, F. J., 81, *87*
Crossette, B., 3, *14*
Crowley-Jack, D. C., 213, *223*

Davies, P., 241, *251*
Davis, J. E., 187, *187*
Davis, L., 115, *119*
Deaton, A. V., 271, *279*
deGruy, F. V., III, 256, 258, *264*
Dempsey, K. C., 81, *88*
Dickerson, V. C., 66, *76*
Dickinson, L. M., 256, 258, *264*
Dickinson, W. P., 256, 258, *264*
DiClemente, C. C., 324, *331*
Diedrick, P., 57, *63*
DiLapi, E. M., 11, *14*, 58, *63*
Doherty, W. J., 23, *34*, 254, 255, *264*,
    265, 269, *280*
Dolan-Del Vecchio, K., 296–298, *305*
Donigan, J., 247, *251*
Dovidio, J. F., 186, *187*
Dreen, K., 320, *331*
Drucker, E., 283, *290*
Dubler, N., 282, *290*
Durkin, T., 298, *304*
Dutton, D. G., 325, 327, 329, *330*
Dutton, M. A., 328, *331*

Edleson, J., 325, 327, *330*
Ehrensaft, M. K., *330*

Eldridge, N. S., 310, *318*
Elliot, P., 230, *237*
Ellman, B., 20, *32*, 80, 88, 199, *210*
Engels, F., 334, *346*
Epp, L. R., 174, *176*
Epston, D., 122, 123, *133*
Eric, K., 283, *290*
Eshleman, S., *223*
Evans, K., 326, *330*

Falicov, C., 27, *34*, 333, *346*
Farmer, D., 154, *159*
Fine, M., 365, *378*
Finkelhor, D., 259, *264*
Fishman, C. H., 243, *252*
Fishman, H. C., 19, 21, *35*
Font, R., 228, *237*, 293, 296, *304, 305*
Foucault, M., 66, *76*
Frankel, R. M., 258, *265*
Franklin, A. J., 111, *119*
Fraser, N., 122, *132*
Freedman, J., 66, *76*, 122, 123, *132*
Freire, P., 294, 296, *305*
French, M., 5, *14*
Fritz, H. L., 212, *223*
Furstenberg, F. F., Jr., 92, *103*

Galland, C., 149, *159*
Ganley, A., 24, *34*
Garcia-Preto, N., 27, 29, *33, 34*, 153,
    159, 333, *346*
Gelles, R. J., 324, *330*
Gerson, R., 80, *88*, 155, *160*
Gibson, J. M., 247, *251*
Gilbert, L. A., 169, *175*
Giles-Sims, J., 93, 94, *103*
Giordano, J., 27, *33*, 333, *346*
Gladding, S. T., 241, *251*
Glass, S., 96, *103*
Glenn, M., 254, *264*
Goldenberg, I., 320, *330*
Goldner, V., 22–24, *32*, 212, *223*, 256,
    264, 268, *279*
Gollan, J. K., 211, *223*
Gondolf, E. W., 325, 326, *330*
Good, G. E., 169, *175*
Goode, W. J., 10, 13, *14*
Goodrich, T. J., 20, 23, *32, 34*, 80, *88*,
    199, *210*, 227, 235, *237, 238*

Goodstein, R. K., 322, *330*
Goolishian, H. A., 26, *34*
Gordon, S. L., 7, *15*
Gortner, E. T., 211, *223*
Gotlib, I. H., 211, *223*
Gottman, J., 85, 88, 180, *187*
Green, G. D., 310, *318*
Green, R.-J., 227, *237*
Greene, B., 30, *33*, 41, 45, *50*, 107–111,
    117, *119*, *120*, 130, 131, *132*,
    365, *378*
Grossman, L., 241, *252*
Guisso, R., 137, *145*
Gurman, A., 18, *34*, 139, *145*

Halevy, J., 232, *238*
Hall, R. L., 30, *33*, 107, 108, 111, 115,
    120, 365, *378*
Halstead, K., 20, *32*, 80, 88, 199, *210*
Hammen, C., 212, *223*
Hammond, C., 202, *210*
Hansen, M., 320, 324, 325, *330*
Hardiman, R., 174, *175*
Hardy, K., 28, *35*, 232, *238*
Hare-Mustin, R. T., 18, 20, *32*, *33*, 80,
    88
Harper, J., 202, *210*
Harris Associates, 6, *14*
Hart, S., 325, *330*
Hartman, A., 25, *33*
Harway, M., 320, 324–326, *330*
Hawley, J. S., 152, *159*
Hayes, C., 56, 57, *63*
Heer, C., 228, *237*
Helgeson, V. S., 212, *223*, 270, *279*
Helms, J. E., 17, *34*, *120*, 174, *175*
Hepworth, J., 255, *265*, 269, 271, *280*
Hernandez, M., 333, *346*
Herron, G., 333, *346*
Hershatter, G., 141, *145*
Higgenbotham, E., 108, *120*
Higginbotham, H. N., 154, *160*
Hill, R., 118, *120*
Hines, P. M., 153, *159*
Ho, M. H., 148, 157, *159*
Hochschild, A., 8, *14*, 85, 88, 226, *238*
Holtzworth-Munroe, A., 325, *331*
Honig, E., 141, *145*
hooks, b., 17, *34*, 123, 128–129, *133*
Hovestadt, A. J., 26, *35*

Hughes, N., *223*
Hunter, A. G., 187, *187*
Hwang, K. K., 137, *144*

Ihinger-Tallman, M., 93, *104*
Imber-Black, E., 192, *198*, 315, *318*
Inclán, J., 333, *346*

Jackson, L. C., 41, 45, *50*
Jacobson, A., 283, *290*
Jacobson, N. S., 211, 212, *223*
Jansen, M. A., 157, *159*
Johnson, N. G., 80, *89*
Jones, A. C., 174, *175*

Karney, B. R., 211, *223*
Karrer, B. M., 28, *35*
Keita, G. P., 211, *223*
Kelly, J., 177, *187*
Kerr, M., 54, *63*
Keshet, J. K., 100, *104*
Kessler, R. C., 85, 88, 211, *223*
Kiecolt-Glaser, J. K., 267, *279*
King, K., 123, *133*
Kliman, J., 333, *346*
Klonoff, E. A., 6, *14*
Kluckhohn, F. R., 135, *145*
Kniskern, D., 18, *34*, 139, *145*
Knudson-Martin, C., 206, *210*
Koerner, K., 212, *223*
Komter, A., 8, *14*
Kopecky, G., 177, *187*
Krestan, J. A., 20, 26, *33*, *35*
Kropp, R., 325, *330*
Krystal, H., 177, *187*

Laird, J., 25, *33*
Landrine, H., 6, *14*
Langhinrichsen, J., 321, *329*
Larson, J., 202, *210*
Laszloffy, T. A., 232, *238*
Lawson, E. J., 259, *264*
Learner, S. M., 81, *89*
Lee, E., 153, *159*
Leon, N., 151, *159*
Lerner, H., 22, *33*
Lerner, J. V., 85, 88

Lesko, T. M., 246, *251*
Levant, R. F., 168, *176*, 177, 179–182, 186, 187, *187*, *188*
Levine, C., 282, *290*
Libow, J., 352, *363*, 365, *378*
Lichter, D., 226, *237*
Liebow, E., 283, *290*
Lipschitz, D. S., 148, *159*
Lorber, J., 7, *14*
Lorde, A., 107, *120*
Lott, B., 206, *210*
Luepnitz, D., 17, 18, 21, *33*
Lugones, M., 316, *318*
Lundberg, U., 81, *88*
Lusterman, D.-D., 81, 88, 169, *176*

Machung, A., *14*, 85, *88*
Mac Kune-Karrer, B., 199, *210*, 352, 353, *363*
Madsen, W. C., 67, *76*
Magaña, H., 258, *265*
Mahoney, A., 206, *210*
Majors, R. G., 186, *188*
Malone, J., 321, *331*
Mann, S., 138, 144, *145*
Mannis, V. J., 52, *63*
Marta, E., 276, *279*
Marte, C., 282, *289*
Martin, A., 308, 316, *318*
Marx, K., 334, *346*
Masters, R., 81, 85, *88*
Mato, T., 149, *159*
Mazure, C. M., 211, 213, *223*
McDaniel, S. H., 255, 256, *265*, 268, 269, 271, 277, *279*, *280*
McDermott, R. F., 152, *159*
McGoldrick, M., 19, 20, 27, *33*, *35*, 80, 88, 153, 155, *159*, *160*, 333, *346*
McGonagle, K. A., *223*
McKegney, C. P., 261, *265*
McLean, C., 170, *175*
Meile, H., 152, *160*
Messineo, T., 228, *237*, 293, *304*
Metzner, J., 241, *252*
Michelin Green Guide, 153, *160*
Milkie, M. A., 81, *87*
Miller, J. B., 255, *265*, 352, *363*
Miller, L. A., 80, *89*
Minuchin, S., 19, 21, *35*, 243, *252*, 283, *290*

Mirkin, M. P., 24, *33*
Mitchell, A. G., 152, *160*
Mitchell, J., 282, *290*
Monelli, C., 153, *159*
Montague, J., 174, *175*
Moore-Hines, P., 333, *346*
Moreno, J. L., 285, 286, *290*
Morse, D. S., 258, *265*
Mulvihill, M., 283, *290*
Myss, C., 154, *160*

Narayan, U., 123, *133*
National Coalition for Domestic Violence, 229, *238*
National Museum of American Art, 157, *160*
Nelson, C. B., *223*
Nelson, M. K., 5, *14*
Newton, T. L., 267, *279*
Nichols, M. P., 138, 139, 142, 144, *145*
Nicholson, L., 122, *132*
Niolon, R., 43, *50*
Nobles, W. W., 108, 118, *120*
Nolen-Hoeksema, S., 212, *223*
Nonini, D. M., 138, *145*
Nutt, R. L., 80, 81, 88, 169, *176*, 365, *378*

Ogloff, J., 325, *330*
Okazawa-Rey, M., 257, *265*
Okin, S. M., 229, *238*
Olbrisch, M. E., 271, *279*
O'Leary, K. D., 321, *331*
Olkin, R., 187, *188*
Olson, M., 365, *377*
Ong, A., 138, *145*
O'Reilly, A., 11, *15*
Orenstein, P., 191, *198*

Page, A. W., 322, *330*
Paniagua, F. A., 174, *175*
Papp, P., 19, *33*
Parker, L., 226n, 231, 233, 234n, 236, *238*
Parsons, T., 17, *35*
Pasley, K., 93, *104*
Patterson, C. J., 317, *318*
Patterson, W., 56, *63*
Paz, O., 151, *160*

Pearce, J. K., 27, *33*
Pearson, V., 141, *145*
Penn, P., 24, *32*
Peplau, L., 7, *15*
Phelps, T. M., 190, *198*
Philpot, C. L., 81, 82, 85, 88, 169, *176*
Piercy, F. P., 26, *35*
Pinderhughes, E., 27, *33*
Pinsof, W., 199, *210*
Pipher, M. B., 74, *76*
Pittman, F., 85, 88, 165, *176*
Piven, F. F., 283, *290*
Pivnick, A., 283, 284, 288, *290*
Pleck, J. H., 169, *176*
Pollack, W. S., 168, *176*
Porter, N., 375, *378*
Press, J. E., 81, 88
Pressman, B., 320, *331*
Prince, S., 212, *223*
Prochaska, J. O., 324, *331*

Quispel, G., 149, *160*

Rampage, C., 20, *32*, 80, 88, 199, *210*,
    235, *238*
Randall, M., 150, *160*
Raskin, P., 365, *378*
Rasmusson, A. M., 148, *159*
Real, T., 203, *210*
Remer, P., 80, 89
Rhode, D. L., 6, *15*
Rice, D. G., 51, 53, 56, *63*
Rice, J. K., 51–53, 56, 61, *63*
Roberts, P. W., 152, *160*
Robinson, J. P., 81, 87
Robinson, T., 74, 75, *76*
Rodriguez, C., 151, *160*
Rodriguez, J., 149, 150, 158, *160*
Rolland, J. S., 272, *280*
Rollins, J., 5, *15*
Roper Center, 5, *15*
Roschelle, A. R., 11, *15*
Rosen, E. J., 86, 88
Rosenfeld, B. D., 325, *331*
Rosewater, L. B., 80, 88
Roth, S. A., 27, *33*
Rothery, M., 320, *331*
Ruddy, N., 261, *265*
Ryan, C., 92, *103*

Saba, G. W., 28, *35*
Sanchez-Hucles, J., 328, *331*
Sayer, L. C., 81, 87
Schaefer, R. T., 109, *120*
Scher, M., 168, 169, *175, 176*
Schulhofer, S., 205, *210*
Schwartz, P., 7, 9, *14, 15*, 227–229, *238*
Schwartz, R. C., 138, 139, 142, 144, *145*,
    199, *210*, 352, *363*
Scrivner, R., 310, *318*
Seaburn, D., 255, *265*, 268, *279*
Sennett, R., 333, *347*
Shandler, S., 74, *76*
Sheinberg, M., 24, *32*
Shorris, E., 339, *347*
Shweder, R. A., 109, *120*
Sifneos, P. E., 177, *188*
Silver, N., 85, 88
Silverstein, L. B., 19, *33*, 168, *175*, 179,
    188
Sirles, E., 365, *378*
Smith, B., 308, *318*
Solomon, K., 169, *176*
Sonkin, D., 324, 325, *331*
Southwick, S. M., 148, *159*
Spiegel, J. P., 135, *145*
Stacey, J., 10, *15*, 51, *63*
Stack, C., 283, *290*
Starkman, S., 353, *363*
Stathos, K., 353, *363*
Stephens, G. G., 256, *265*
Stohs, J. H., 85, 88
Strassfield, M., 65, *76*
Strassfield, S., 65, *76*
Stuart, G. L., 325, *331*
Stuart, R., 207, *210*, 236, *238*
Suchman, A. L., 258, *265*
Sue, D. W., 174, *176*
Suls, J., 81, 89
Surrey, J. L., 108, *120*, 233, *238*, 308,
    318
Syers, M., 325, *330*

Taffel, R., 81, 85, 88
Tanaka-Matsumi, J., 154, *160*
Teish, L., 149, 150, 153, *160*
Thompson, C. L., 111, 115, 118, *120*
Tolman, R. M., 325, 327, *330, 331*
Townsley, E., 81, 88
Trobe, K., 152, *160*

Turin, M., 26, *34*
Turner, J., 365, *378*

U.S. Census Bureau, 4, *15*
U.S. Commission on Civil Rights, 325, *331*
U.S. Department of Commerce, 110, *120*
U.S. Department of Health and Human Services, Centers for Disease Control, 282, *290*
U.S. House of Representatives, 60, *63*

Valian, V., *15*
Villegas, N., 288, *290*
Vivian, D., 321, *329–331*
Vontress, C. E., 174, *176*

Wade, A., 371, *378*
Waitzkin, H., 258, *265*
Walker, G., 24, *32*
Walker, L. E. A., 80, *88*
Walsh, F., 19, 20, *33, 35, 88*
Walters, M., 19, *33*, 53, *63*
Wan, C. K., 81, *89*
Ward, J. V., 74, 75, *76*
Warshaw, C., 256, *265*
Watkins, M., 308, *318*
Wear, D., 253, 256, *265*
Webster's Third New International Dictionary of the English Language Unabridged, 121, *133*

Weigel Foy, C., 353, *363*
Weingarten, K., 26, *33*, 66, 74, *76, 77,* 123, *133*, 208, *210*
Weitzman, J., 320, *331*
Weltman, S., 86, *88*, 333, *346*
West, C., 118, *120*, 130, *133*
Weston, K., 57, *63*
Wethington, E., 85, *88*
Wettstein, R., 241, *252*
Wheeler, D., 80, *89*, 352, *363*
White, M., 66, *77*, 122, 123, *133*, 366, *378*
White House Project, 4, *15*
Williams, K. J., 81, *89*
Winkle, W. C., 26, *35*
Winternitz, H., 190, *198*
Wofsy, C., 282, *290*
Woods, R., 228, *237*, 293, *304*
Worell, J., 80, *89*
Wulff, D. M., 152, *159*
Wyche, K. F., 110, *120*
Wynne, A., 208, *210*
Wynne, L., 208, *210*

Yahne, C., 375, *378*
Yllo, K., 320, *331*
Young, C., 111, *120*

Zacks, E., 227, *237*
Zhao, S., *223*
Zimmerman, J., 66, *76*

SUBJECT INDEX

Abuse
  and family medical care, 259–261
  reciprocity in, 53
  secrecy about, 190
Acceptance
  of lesbian relationships, 47
  as stage of coming out, 44
Ackerman Project, 212, 214–215
Adoption, 195–197. *See also* Biracial
    lesbian-led adoptive families
African American family(-ies), 107–119
  balance of power in, 117
  case studies of therapy with, 112–
    119, 124–130
  cultural context of therapy with,
    108–109, 111, 118
  family constellations in, 109
  gender roles in, 110–111
  socioeconomic status of, 110
African American lesbians, 41
African American men, male alexithymia
    in, 186–187
African American women, 299
  in family therapy, 28–30
  incarcerated, 241–251
Agency, communion vs., 270, 271,
    277–279
AIDS, 281–286, 288. *See also* The Wom-
    en's Center
Alexithymia, 177. *See also* Male alexi-
    thymia
Alpha bias, 20, 21
Anger
  and blaming, 373
  female, as obstacle to couples' inti-
    macy, 203–204
  in Latinas, 151–154
  and male alexithymia, 178, 179
Anger management programs, 326
Anorexia, 24–25, 193–194
Artificial insemination, 191
Asian American families, 135–144
  boundaries in, 139–140
  and Confucianism, 135
  feminist family therapy with, 141–144

gender roles in, 141–142
migration patterns of, 136
patriarchy in, 137–138
structure of, 140–141
therapeutic interventions with,
    142–144
Ault-Riché, Marianne, 21

Baird, Macaran, 254
Balance of power, in African American
    families, 117
Baselining (in gender metaframework),
    357
Battering. *See* Domestic violence
Behavioral saliency, 207
"Being heard," 215–216
Belief systems, and depression, 217–222
Bepko, Claudia, 26–27
Beta bias, 20–21
Biopsychosocial systems theory, 270
Blaming, 373
Bograd, M., 24
Bograd, Michele, 19
Book of Rites (Confucianism), 137, 138,
    142
Both/and perspective, 31
Boundaries, 54
  in Confucianism, 139–140
  as feminist therapy principle, 49
Bourgeoisie, 334–336, 343–345
Bowen, Murray, 28
Bowenian family therapy, 247–249
Boyd-Franklin, Nancy, 29
Brown, Laura S., 75–76
Bulimia, 24
Bullying, 8

Campbell, Tom, 254
Candelario, Nora, 285
Caregiving, 227, 276–277
"Caring Days" exercise, 207–208
Carmichael, Lynn, 255
Carter, Betty, 9

Catastrophic expectations, 203
CCCS (Chicago Center for Gender Studies), 352
CCM. *See* Cultural context model
CDSs (controlled dangerous substances), 242
Centers for Disease Control, 283
Chabon, Brenda, 284
Chicago Center for Gender Studies (CCGS), 352
Children
    desire of lesbian couples for, 46–47
    parentified, 109
Child support, 60–61
Chinese American families, 136
Chinese women, 298–299
Chivalry (as term), 121
Circularity, 31
Class
    and role of mothering, 11
    and wife's role, 8
Class consciousness, 334, 335
Cognitive restructuring, 154
Collaboration
    in gender metaframework, 356–357
    in medical family therapy, 270, 271
    in narrative therapy, 26
Collaborative Family Healthcare Coalition, 255
Color, as issue in family therapy, 27–30
Color of Fear (video), 371
Coming out, lesbian families and stages of, 43–45
Commitment ceremonies, 40–42, 44
Communication
    power issues in, 227–228
    as problem for couples, 179–180
    during serious illness, 278
Communion, agency vs., 270, 271, 277–279
Confucianism, 135–144
Connectedness, 109
Consciousness-raising, 231–233
Contextual relevance, 108–109
Contextual variables, 351
Controlling behaviors, 233
"Cool pose," 186
Covert/overt hierarchy, 31
Covert power, 8

Critical consciousness, 296–297
Cross-cultural training, 108–109
Crowley-Jack, D. C., 213
Cultural context model (CCM), 293–304
Cultural legacies, 299–300
Cultural norms, 54
"Cultural transformer," therapist as, 138
Cultural transitional map, 148, 156
Culture
    and assignment of roles with illness, 272–273
    as feminist therapy principle, 49
    of immigrant families, 336
    and social class, 334
Culture bearers, 297–298
Culture circles, 294–296, 298

Denial, 6, 41–42
Depression, 211–222
    and sexual relationship, 275
Depression Project (Ackerman Institute for the Family), 212
Devi, 152
Diego, Juan, 149, 150
"Different Standards," 229
Disclosure, as stage of coming out, 43, 44
Discrimination against women, 4–6
Distance, emotional, 179–180
Diversity
    and domestic violence, 327–329
    as feminist therapy principle, 49
Division of labor, 6, 79, 85, 226–227
Divorce, 51–62
    and daughter—father relationships in stepfamilies, 91–103
Doherty, William, 254
Doing things, 203
Domestic violence, 319–329
    assessment for, 320–324
    case study involving, 320–324
    feminist approaches to, 319–320
    responsibility for, 24
    treatment issues with, 324–329
    vulnerability to, 228–229
Domination, 12–13
    Black Madonna and resistance to, 149
    in partnerships, 8
    "power-over" behaviors, 233
"Don't ask, don't tell" ethic, 354, 363

"Don't Worry Your Pretty Little Head,"
228–229
Drug abuse, 242, 327
Dual-income households, African American, 110

Eating disorders, 24–25, 193–194
Emotional distance, 179–180
Emotional Response Log, 183, 184
Emotional talk, 203
Emotions. *See also* Male alexithymia
    reading others', 183
    vocabulary for, 182
Empathy
    of heterosexual couples, 206–207
    therapist's transmission of, 170,
        183–184
Employment, 4, 216–217
    of African American women, 110
    and motherhood, 11
    and vulnerability to domestic
        violence, 228–229
Enmeshment, 109
Equality, gender, 9–10
Equilibrium, 53
Erectile dysfunction, 275
Eric, Kathleen, 284–288
Ethnicity
    and domestic violence, 327–328
    and intimacy between heterosexual
        couples, 204
    as issue in family therapy, 27–30
    as issue in MASTERY model,
        173–174
Ethnorace, 31
Eurocentrism, 111
Expectations, catastrophic, 203
Extended family, 112

Falk, Marcia, 147
Families, Systems & Health, 254
Family(-ies), 7–12. *See also specific headings, e.g.:* African American
    family(-ies)
    changing forms of, 52
    contemporary definition of, 51
    as emotional unit, 22
    gay, 40
    "normal," 17

relationships between women in,
    121–132
socialcultural factors affecting,
    22–23
source of conflict in, 40
as term, 7, 39
traditional beliefs about, 39
traditional definitions of, 51
Family Institute, 199
Family life cycle, 61–62, 272, 283
Family medicine, 253–256. *See also* Medical family therapy
Family practice movement, 255
Family roles, analysis of, 85–86
Family Systems Medicine, 254
Family systems theory, 22, 241, 243, 320
Family therapy, 17–30, 253–258. *See also*
    Feminist family therapy; Medical
    family therapy
    appearance of gender issues in,
        17–26
    and cultural context model, 300–301
    emergence of, 17
    ethnicity and color as issues in,
        27–30
    and family medicine, 253–255
    and feminism, 255–256
    for lesbian couples, 26–27
    multigenerational work in, 60
    and physicians, 256–258
    power as emerging issue in, 21–24
Fathers
    in Confucianism, 141–142
    child care responsibilities of, 10–11
    daughter's relationship with, in
        stepfamily, 91–103
    and failure to pay child support, 60
Feeling avoidance, cycle of, 326–327
Feinberg, Paul, 215
Female anger, 203–204
Female-headed households, African American, 109
Feminism, 4–6, 200, 253
    African American community's perception of, 108
    and concept of family, 39
    and family medicine, 255–258
    and narrative therapy, 123–124
    and traditional family therapy,
        18–26
Feminist couple therapy, 200–201

Feminist family therapy, 12–14. *See also* Tensions in feminist family therapy training
   case study involving, 65–76
   emphasis on female-centered spiritual development in, 148
   and family medicine, 253, 255–258
   gender inquiry in, 81–82
   individual in, 139
   social constructivist stance of, 60
   with stepfamilies, 93–103
   for traditional men, 168–174
Figueroa, Ruth, 285
Four Attributes (Confucianism), 137–138, 143, 144
Freire, Paolo, 296–297

Gay families, 40
Gay partnerships
   and domestic violence, 328, 329
   power relationships in, 227
   "wife" position in, 7
Gender
   and African American families, 107
   and daughter—father relationships in stepfamilies, 91–103
   and depression, 212–214
   as emerging issue in family therapy, 17–26
Gender and Violence Project, 24
Gender bias, 20–21, 207
Gendered power relations, 31
Gendered secrets, 189–194
Gender inquiry, 81–82
Gender metaframework, 351–363
Gender role psychotherapy, 169
Gender roles, 54
   in African American families, 110–111
   among poor immigrants, 340–341
   and caregiving, 276–277
   during chronic/terminal illness, 278
   and closeness/distance, 179–180
   and division of labor, 226–227
   and male socialization, 177–178
   and power, 9
   teaching, 11–12
Gender role stereotyping, 80–81, 118
Gender-sensitive (term), 31
Gender socialization, 21, 268–269, 272

Genograms, 80, 83–84, 155–156, 232
Glenn, Michael, 254

Handbook of Family Therapy, 18
Hare-Mustin, Rachel, 18
Harmony, 137
Heterosexism
   as feminist therapy principle, 49
   and same-sex parenting, 309–310
Heterosexist bias, 46
Heterosexual couples
   intimacy in, 201–210
   power issues with. *See* Power
Heterosexual marriage, 7–10
Heterosexual privilege, 40
Hidalgo, Father, 150
Hierarchy, in Confucianism, 140
Hill, Anita, 190
Hinduism, 152
Holism, 108
Homeostasis, 140
Homophobia, 49

I-Ching, 140
Identified patient (IP), 79–80
Identity, reconstruction of, 157
Illness
   and gender socialization, 268–269
   and sexuality, 273–276
Immigrant families, 333–346
Indigenous psychology, 158
Individuality
   in Confucianism, 138–139
   as family force, 53–54
Inequality
   gender, 9–10
   as reason for divorce, 56
Integration, as stage of coming out, 44
Intelligentsia, 334, 335, 345
Interpretive context (of classroom), 367–368
Intimacy in heterosexual couples, 201–210
Isis, 149
Islam, 299

Jacobson, Cecil, 191
Japanese American families, 136

Jewish families, 86–87
Johnson, Norine, xi
Journal of Feminist Family Therapy, 20

Klein, Gloria, 215
Klonoff, E. A., 6
Korean American families, 136

Laird, Joan, 25
Latin American families, 147–158
Latinas
    in family therapy, 30, 31
    incarcerated, 241–242
Lesbian family(-ies), 39–50
Lesbian mothers, struggle for legitimacy
        by, 11
Lesbian partnerships
    and divorce, 57
    and domestic violence, 328
    family therapy for, 26–27
    power relationships in, 227
    sharing of responsibilities by, 7
Li, 139–140
Life cycle, family, 61–62

Machismo, 30
Male alexithymia, 177–187
Male modes of being, 170
Male privilege, 227–228
Male role models
    in African American families,
        109
    for children of lesbian parents, 11
Marianismo, 30
Marriage, 6
    balance of power in, 117
    changes in, 52
    equilibrium in, 53
    and feminist couple therapy,
        200–201
    heterosexual, 7–10
Married couples
    depression in, 211–222
    secrecy between, 190–191
Marx, Karl, 334
Masculinity, 9
    of client, and therapist reactivity,
        166–167

"dark side of," 168–169
and gender role psychotherapy, 169
as pathogen, 24
"Master therapists," 21
MASTERY model, 168–174
Media, women in, 4
Medical family therapy, 267–279
Men
    African American, 111, 118–119
    alexithymia in, 177–187
    benefits of feminist family therapy
        for, 13
    as consumers of feminist family ther-
        apy, 23–24
    depression in, 211–214, 216–217
    feminist family therapy for tradi-
        tional, 168–174
    MASTERY model with traditional,
        171–174
Mikulski, Barbara, 190
Minuchin, Salvador, 21
Misogyny, 5, 21
Money, as power issue, 228–229
Morality
    of drug-using and HIV-positive preg-
        nant women, 282, 283
    of lesbian couples having children,
        47
Moral masochism, 111
Morenas, Las, 148–157
Mother blaming, 32
Motherhood, 10–12
Mothers, value of traditional vs. nontradi-
        tional, 58
Multigenerational issues, 60, 85
Muteness, and alexithymia, 178–179

Narrative therapy, 26, 66, 122–124, 358
Natural systems theory, 22
Nodal point, 31
Noncompliance to medical treatment,
        271–272
Nontraditional mothers, 58
"Normal" families, 39–40
Normative male alexithymia, 177
Norms, and depression, 213

Oneself, keeping secrets from, 192–194
Oppression of African American men,
        186–187

Oppression of women, 4–7, 20
Our Lady of Guadalupe, 149–150, 153, 157
Our Lady of Monserrat, 156–157
Overfunctioning, 22
Overfunctioning/underfunctioning dyad, 31
Oya, 153

Palmer, Verna, 285
Parenthood, and marriage, 52
Parentified children, 109
Parenting, in lesbian families, 46–47
Patriarchy, 5, 21
    in Confucianism, 137–138
    definition of, 31
    divorce as resistance to, 52
    gender socialization within, 21
    mothering in, 11–12
    relational patterns deriving from, 12–13
    resistance to, 57
Peer relationships, 9
Personal agency, 286–287
Physical abuse, secrecy about, 190
Physicians, 253–258, 261–263, 271
Poor families
    immigrant, 337–343
    man as Provider in, 7
Postmodernism, 31
Postmodern narrative therapy, 66, 122–124
Posttraumatic stress disorder, 148
Poverty, 4, 242
Power, 13, 225–237
    in African American families, 117
    in alexithymic men, 180
    and battering, 326
    case example of therapy involving issues of, 234–237
    in classroom context, 368
    Different Standards as misuse of, 229
    in doctor—patient relationship, 270
    Don't Worry Your Pretty Little Head as misuse of, 228–229
    and economic responsibility, 228–229
    as emerging issues in family therapy, 21–24

    as feminist therapy principle, 49
    in heterosexual marriage, 7–9
    King of the Castle as misuse of, 227–228
    and privacy, 192
    raising consciousness about, 231–233
    and response to female authority, 289
    and social location, 229–230
    therapeutic strategies for dealing with issues of, 230–234
    Unfair Bargain as misuse of, 226–227
"Power-over" behaviors, 233
Prison, women in. See Incarcerated African American women
Privacy, and secrecy, 191–192
Privilege
    gender-based, 205
    heterosexual, 40
    in heterosexual marriages, 9
    male, 227–228
    and social location, 229–230
    unawareness of, 228
Psychodrama, 285
Purification, 153–154

Race
    and African American families, 107
    and role of mothering, 11
    and wife's role, 8
Racial healing, 154–158
Racism
    and employment of African Americans, 110
    family discussions about, 13
    as feminist therapy principle, 49
    internalization and projection of, 148
    and Latinas, 148
Rage, tension between hope and, 368–369
Rainbow flag, 40
Ransom, Don, 254
Reactivity (of therapist), 165–167
Rebalancing, 32
Reciprocity, 22, 32, 53
Reframing, 126
Relational dread, 203

Relationship validity, 42–43
Respect, gender differences in, 8
Responsibility(-ies), 80–81
    in child raising, 10
    for domestic violence, 24
    for family life, 12
    of mothers, in Confucian families,
        141–142
Rituals, 25, 153–154
Rolovich, Sandra, 215
Rotger, Carmen, 285

Samantha and Carl (case study),
        320–324
Sandy (case study), 124–131
Sara (case study), 193–194
Sarah and James (case study), 112–119
Sara-la-Kali, 152–153
Satir, Virginia, 17–18
Secrets, 189
    in braided social context, 194–197
    gendered, 189–194
Seibel, Jeffrey, 215
Self-abuse (among incarcerated women),
        242–243
Self-awareness, emotional, 183–184
Self-destructiveness, 74
Self-differentiation, 54
Self-esteem, gender differences in, 8
Self-identification, as stage of coming
        out, 44
Self-in-relation theory, 255
Self-recognition, as stage of coming out,
        43, 44
Sex, and power within marriage, 23
Sexism, 6
    and African American women, 110
    family discussions about, 13
    as feminist therapy principle, 49
    internalization and projection of,
        148
    and Latinas, 148
    in traditional family therapy, 21
Sexual abuse
    and family medical care, 259–261
    secrecy about, 190
Sexual harassment, 190
Sexuality, illness and, 273–276
Single fathers, as heroes, 7
Single mothers

anxiety and guilt of, 58–60
    as handicapped, 7
    increase in number of, 52
    struggle for legitimacy by, 11
Single parents
    adoption by, 310–311
    therapy with, 60
Skill-building programs (for batterers),
        326
Slayed Dragon (film), 298
Social class, 333–339
Socialization
    male gender role, 177–178
    as stage of coming out, 43–44
Social justice, ix
Social location, 32, 229–230
Society of Teachers of Family Medicine,
        255
Sociocultural factors, 22–23
Sociodrama, 286
Socioeconomic status, of African Ameri-
        can families, 110
Socioeducation, 296–300
Sojourners, 339
Spirituality, 148–149, 157
Stepfamilies, daughter–father relation-
        ships in, 91–103
Stephens, G. Gayle, 256
Straight Out of Brooklyn (film), 299
Stress, of daughters in stepfamilies,
        92–93
Superiority, feelings of, 202–203
Supervision, gender metaframework for.
        See Gender metaframework
Systems theory
    and Confucianism, 140
    divorce in, 53–54
    and impact of relationships on indi-
        vidual behavior, 179
    and medical family therapy, 270

Talk, emotional, 203
Tamil Indians, 153
Tensions in feminist family therapy train-
        ing, 365–377
    factors affecting intensity of,
        374–376
    guidelines for dealing with, 376–377
    between interpreters, 369–371

Tensions, *continued*
    and interpretive context of class-
        room, 367–368
    between rage and hope, 368–369
    from texts that evoke emotional reac-
        tions, 371–373
Therapist(s)
    alliance between client and, 200
    cross-cultural training for, 108–109
    "cultural transformer" role of, 138
    empathy and understanding transmit-
        ted by, 170
    "master," 21
    neutrality of, ix
    reactivity of, 165–167
Therapy, ix. *See also specific headings*
Thomas, Clarence, 190
Three Obediences (Confucianism), 137,
    142–144
Tikkun olam, 65, 75
Togetherness, as family force, 54
To Have and to Hold (film), 373
Tonantzin, 149–150, 157
Traditions, in lesbian families, 45–46
Training. *See also* Tensions in feminist
        family therapy training
    cross-cultural, 108–109
    feminist theory in, 26
Transporters, 339
Trauma
    in Latin American families, 148
    from medical testing/procedures,
        258–261
Tyler family (case study), 94–96

Unbalancing, 18–19, 32
Understanding, therapist's transmission
    of, 170
"Unfair Bargain," 226–227

Valian, Virginia, 5
Validity, relationship, 42–43

Value(s)
    Afrocentric, 108
    harmony as, 140
Venn diagrams, 253
Viagra, 275
Vietnamese American families, 136
Virgen de la Guadalupe, 149–150, 153,
    157
Virgin of Monserrat, 156–157

Wages, 4
Warrior Marks (film), 299
Warshaw, Carole, 256
The Wedding Banquet (film), 298
Whiteness, 123, 127
Wives, in heterosexual marriages, 7–10
Women
    in Confucianism, 137–138
    depression in, 212–218
    discrimination against, 4–6
    in family therapy, 19, 27
    incarcerated, 241–242
    psychological gains following divorce
        of, 57
    relationships between, within fami-
        lies, 121–132
The Women's Center, 281–289
    children's inclusion in, 288–289
    establishment of, 283
    evolution of group process in,
        286–288
    gender as unifying force in, 285
    gendered power relations at, 289
    and HIV-positive women's responsi-
        bility for AIDS babies, 282–283
    men's participation in, 286
    psychodrama in, 285
    research by, 283–284
    service orientation of, 284–289
    sociodrama in, 286
Women's Project, 19–20
Work. *See* Employment
Working class, 334
World War II, 17
Worth, Dooley, 284

ABOUT THE EDITORS

Louise B. Silverstein, PhD, is an associate professor at the Ferkauf Graduate School of Psychology at Yeshiva University, Bronx, New York, where she has taught courses in family therapy and the social construction of gender since 1992. Dr. Silverstein is a past president of the American Psychological Association's (APA's) Division 43 (Family Psychology).

Dr. Silverstein is cofounder, with Dr. Carl Auerbach, of the Yeshiva University Fatherhood Project, a qualitative research study of fathering from a multicultural perspective. In 2001, Dr. Silverstein and Dr. Auerbach received the Distinguished Research Award for this project from APA Division 51, the Society for the Study of Men and Masculinity.

Dr. Silverstein's publications focus on fathering, feminist theory, and the social construction of gender. She also has a book forthcoming entitled *An Introduction to Coding and Analyzing Data in Qualitative Research*, coauthored with Carl Auerbach. In 2000, the Association of Women in Psychology awarded Dr. Silverstein and Dr. Auerbach the Distinguished Publication Award for coauthoring the article "Deconstructing the Essential Father," which was published in APA's flagship journal, the *American Psychologist*.

Dr. Silverstein is also a family therapist in private practice in Brooklyn, New York.

Thelma Jean Goodrich, PhD, is the associate director of the Family Medicine Residency Program and the director of Behavioral Science at the University of Texas Medical School at Houston after 3 years at Columbia University in New York and 15 years with Baylor College of Medicine in Houston. She is the coauthor of *Feminist Family Therapy: A Casebook* (T. J. Goodrich, C. Rampage, B. Ellman, & K. Halstead, 1988) and editor of *Women and Power: Perspectives for Family Therapy* (1991).